The Chinese Macroeco
Financial System

The Chinese Macroeconomy and Financial System

A U.S. Perspective

Ronald M. Schramm

Routledge
Taylor & Francis Group

NEW YORK AND LONDON

First published 2015
by Routledge
711 Third Avenue, New York, NY 10017
and by Routledge

2 Park Square, Milton Park, Abingdon, Oxon, OX14 4RN

Routledge is an imprint of the Taylor & Francis Group, an informa business

© 2015 Taylor & Francis

Library of Congress Cataloging-in-Publication Data

A catalog record for this book has been requested.

ISBN: 978-0-7656-4390-2 (hbk)
ISBN: 978-0-7656-4391-9 (pbk)
ISBN: 978-1-315-71808-8 (ebk)

Typeset in Times
by Apex CoVantage, LLC

Printed and bound in the United States of America
by Edwards Brothers Malloy on sustainably sourced paper

China My Muse, America My Home

Brief Contents

Contents

Preface and Acknowledgments

I began to write this textbook on China in 2003, but gave up on the project after writing one chapter. At that time it seemed there was neither enough good research being done to synthesize, nor enough good data available to say something meaningful. What is more, China was transforming and mutating in incomprehensible ways. *What a difference a decade makes.* There has been an explosion of economic and financial research by both Western and Chinese scholars and the data are more than adequate to provide good insights. The country, however, continues to change and grow at a dizzying pace.

Necessity truly is the mother of invention—the absence of a textbook with a modern approach to China's macroeconomy was one compelling motivation for writing this book. Another was the question so many MBA and Master's students have asked me over the years after completing the intermediate macroeconomics course I taught: "Is there an advanced macro course that follows this one that I can take?" My answer was: "No—the PhD macro course is quite technical with limited practical application and that is the only course available—someday, I will write one though." A final interest in writing this book was that I wanted to bring macroeconomics a bit back to its finance, accounting, and microeconomic roots; there are so many worthwhile frameworks in those fields that I had already incorporated into my teaching. I wanted an opportunity to explore where that would take me (and the student) in the China context.

This book is intended for anyone interested in understanding the Chinese macroeconomy and financial structure. It should be of good use to faculty teaching a general course on the Chinese economy from a macroeconomics perspective. This textbook is self-contained in that it provides the theory, data, and institutional detail needed to understand China's economic performance. It is suitable for students in economics departments and business schools, international studies programs, and Master's programs in public policy. In the same context, students who are seeking an advanced course in applied macroeconomics where they learn the practical skills needed to work as an economist would find this book extremely useful. Given China's success as a large emerging market, this textbook could also be used in a course on emerging markets. Certainly, business practitioners seeking a deeper understanding of China and its institutions would find many parts of this book necessary knowledge.

That the United States and China are now the world's two largest economies makes a textbook like this both inevitable and necessary. To write about China or the United States in isolation would be to write without context. I believe that this truly is a case where "the whole is greater than the sum of the parts." The reader gains a deeper understanding of each economy by way of comparison.

Organization of the Text

Every chapter contains a number of Case Studies and Macro Finance Insights. Case Studies provide an in-depth look at what makes China's economy unique: everything ranging from China's Five-Year Plans or One Child Policy, to the use of the *fapiao*. Macro Finance Insights borrow and explain critical concepts from finance, microeconomics, and management in order to elucidate financial and economic phenomena in China. For example, how can we assess the financial situation of China as we would a company, or the role of the International Monetary Fund, or why Chinese companies would prefer one capital structure over another. Included in these Case Studies and Macro Finance Insights are the many topics we read about daily with regard to China, for example, the environment, urbanization, the depletion of the labor force in the agricultural sector and, of course, bubbles in real estate. Wherever useful, we provide the U.S. experience as a counterpoint.

Chapter 1 presents the four key drivers for the Chinese economy—what makes China different and why those drivers matter. Furthermore, we review some basic ideas from macroeconomics that we will need to know as we read the rest of the book. In Chapter 2 we discuss the different ways that China measures GDP compared to the United States, the quality of Chinese economic data, and how alternate measures of GDP are relevant when discussing China. This also gives us the opportunity to discuss China's environment in a Case Study. Chapter 3 presents the very important topic of the Balance of Payments—how it is defined, measured, and determined. Here we examine how China accumulated over US$3 trillion in foreign exchange reserves, especially as it relates to its trading and financing relationship with the United States. In Chapter 4 we examine the critical question of economic growth: Are growth rates of 7–10 percent sustainable in China and what are the fundamental factors which cause growth in the United States to be so much lower?

While the earlier chapters give us a broad perspective in terms of measurement and long-run growth in China and the United States, the remaining chapters provide great detail regarding institutions and policies in China that are fundamentally different from their U.S. counterparts. Chapter 5 examines China's famously high savings rate (or alternatively, low levels of consumption). Here we have an opportunity to provide historical context, myths surrounding the data, and where savings and consumption are likely to trend in the coming years. We also look in detail at a key element in Chinese savings—corporate profits. Chapter 6 discusses the companion element to China's high savings—its high rate of investment. In a Macro Finance Insight, we look at a key player in China's investment activity, the China Development Bank, applying some simple concepts from finance.

Chapter 7 on monetary institutions and policy allows us to look very deeply at the complex set of tools used by the People's Bank of China and why such complexity is necessary. Both Chapters 7 and 8 discuss how China holds its wealth and how that profile almost certainly will change in the coming years. We compare Chinese monetary policy to that of the United States in recent years, especially during times of financial crisis. Chapter 9 presents the basic Keynesian framework plus more sophisticated extensions to that model that will matter to China in the coming years. The basic model gives us a chance to understand the significance of some unique features of the Chinese economy, ranging from the *hukou* system to the high degree of adaptability of the labor force. Chapter 10 shows how recent policies in times of crisis have been decidedly Keynesian. Furthermore, we make a detailed comparison of the differing profile of public finance, ranging from taxation to expenditures and fiscal transfers, between China and the United States.

The Case Studies should be required reading for all purchasers of the textbook. Those users with a deep interest in understanding Chinese data would benefit from Chapters 1–4. Those readers with a deep interest in government institutions and policy will benefit most from Chapters 1 and 7–10. Those readers with a keen interest in China's key drivers would most benefit from Chapters 1 and 4–10. Reading all of Chapters 1–10 will move the student to the "China Scholar" level!

The reader needs only a good macroeconomic principles course that covers demand-side economics and long-term growth. For the Macro Finance Insights, some familiarity with finance would be helpful, but in most cases the explanations of concepts are self-contained. Part II of Chapter 4 and the last half of Chapter 5 on corporate savings have a heavy dose of financial analysis. I intentionally did not relegate these chapters to appendices, since one of my goals in writing this book was to incorporate finance into our macroeconomic understanding of China and the United States to the fullest extent possible. Students without any background in finance may find these sections challenging but mind-expanding.

Acknowledgments

There are so many people to thank. Of course, the thousands of Master's students I have taught over the years at Columbia University in New York, the University of International Business and Economics (UIBE) in Beijing, Shanghai Jiao Tong University, Chinese European International Business School (CEIBS) in Shanghai, Hong Kong University of Science and Technology, IESE, and now Xian Jiao Tong Liverpool University's IBSS in Suzhou. At the other end, are the 老百姓 (*lao bai xing*, or the common man in China) who have taught me so much about their daily lives, full of aspirations and challenges.

My editor at M.E. Sharpe, would certainly come out at the top of any academic's list. When I explained this project to him, he immediately "got it" and has been an unflinching supporter ever since—a real intellect. Irene Bunnell, also of M.E. Sharpe, has shown enormous patience untangling all the charts, tables, and text that become a textbook. Laurie Underwood came in to skillfully edit and improve my writing, and push me over the top in the penultimate stage of this project. The extraordinary Angela Piliouras, the final editor at M.E. Sharpe, caught a number of mistakes in everything ranging from style to economic fundamentals. It is hard to imagine anyone with a sharper eye and greater interest in Asian studies. I would be remiss not to thank Emily Kindlysides, Economics Editor, and Mhairi Bennett at Routledge; they held my hand and guided me with incredible skill and encouragement in the transition from M.E. Sharpe to Routledge. I utilized one final pair of keen eyes on the text—Eva Schramm caught the errors in grammar and style that we all missed. I give particular praise to the very excellent research assistance of Jiale (Javelin) Dong (董佳乐), a Master's student at IBSS. Able assistance has also been provided by Pan Wang, Pinpin Jiang (蒋频频), and Qi Ji (齐迹). The uniquely beautiful cover design concept was created by Qiu Haiyan (仇海艳).

And then there are the scholars and professionals who provided their gentle advice and encouragement. Dean Sarah Dixon has created a wonderful and supportive atmosphere for research at IBSS, making this task all the more satisfying. Professors Lin Guijun (林桂军), Jin Wei, Lydia Price, KC Chan, Don Sexton, Yang Chen, and Sun Liu have all helped in their own way. A lifetime of thanks to Professors Guillermo Calvo, John Donaldson, Maurice Obstfeld, and Nachum Sicherman for their scholarship and humanity. Tom Easton, former China editor at the *Economist* and my former student at Columbia, has taught me much regarding China. Thanks to David Adams of the Fulbright Scholars program who pushed for my great year in Beijing as a Fulbrighter at UIBE. Many parts of this book were presented to the China Group (which I founded) at the Harvard Club of New York. Participants' comments have been incorporated, especially those of G.A. Donovan of HBS. Insights were also gained through participation in the China Investment Group, the China Forum, the China Institute of New York, and the Hong Kong Economic and Trade Organization in New York. I wish to thank Harvard College and a Harvard College scholarship—which is where all of this actually started.

Finally, I truly thank my loving family, Connie Chung-Schramm, Mark, Eva, and David, who put up with my long absences while in China. I would be lost (literally) without Connie—her support has helped me see this through. I dedicate this book to the memory of my parents, Sophia and Russell.

Ron Schramm

1 Introduction

书山有路勤为径
Diligence is the Royal Path to Learning

China and the United States are married. Whether it is a good marriage or a bad marriage will only be determined in the coming decades. In the chapters that follow, we explore their economic relationship—an important factor in all marriages.[1] It is remarkable that along almost any economic dimension, we find China and the United States as complementary partners who often operate in starkly opposing ways. This makes for a truly fascinating study. In most of this text, the primary focus is on China. Comparisons are made with the United States as a counterpoint; a way to highlight similarities and differences.

China's economic reforms toward a market-based economy began in 1978 (two years after the death of Chairman Mao Zedong) and have continued since then without halt. Throughout the following chapters, we must keep that date in mind since most of the discussion, data, and analysis we use really applies to the modern Chinese economy—and the process of moving to a market-based economy which started in earnest in 1978. Although China is one of the oldest civilizations on earth (dating back to at least 221 BCE), it is, in another sense, one of the world's youngest large modern economies. We could say that China is historically and culturally older but economically younger than the United States. Many scholars have written about the significant steps in China's development process since 1978. Wu Jinglian (2005) and Barry Naughton (2007), for example, provide excellent step-by-step descriptions of China's remarkable path of economic progress from both before and after that critical year. Naughton describes how the post-1978 period represents both an abrupt departure from and a continuation of historical economic patterns. We will not attempt to cover the same ground in this book.

Instead, this textbook combines macroeconomic analysis and data for China and the United States, and incorporates a novel approach to macroeconomics using tools and frameworks from finance, microeconomics, and management. This approach is particularly useful when thinking about China, a country that is often managed like a company. China is an incredibly dynamic economy, and its significance in the world arena is ever increasing. In tandem with China's development into an economic powerhouse, there has been an explosion of academic research and news coverage related to the Chinese economy. In writing this textbook, we owe much to other academic scholars in China and around the world, as well as the excellent China research being done by the International Monetary Fund (IMF), the World Bank, the Organisation for Economic Co-operation and Development (OECD), the Bank for International Settlements (BIS), the Chinese Academy for Social Sciences (CASS), China's National Bureau of Statistics (NBS), the Federal Reserve System (FED), a number of other international organizations and of course, the *Economist* magazine. This is the first textbook to tap into much of that new knowledge, synthesize it, and present it in a modern macroeconomic framework.

Four Key Drivers for the Chinese Economy

At least four key drivers of the Chinese economy today distinguish it from the United States and other large countries around the world. These key drivers help to explain many of the aspects we find puzzling about China—both in terms of macroeconomics and in daily life.

A Large Population

China has the world's largest population; at 1.35 billion people, it is larger than its nearest competitor (India) by roughly 100 million citizens. This large population resides on a substantially smaller plot of arable land than is found in the United States, and must be fed, clothed, housed, and kept healthy. Accomplishing this is still a daily struggle for a good portion of China's population. This vast labor pool, which is available to a cohesive political system, deeply influences which industries thrive in China and which products are traded with the rest of the world. Furthermore, economic growth relies heavily on labor growth, a key factor of production. Chapters 1, 4, 5, and 9 discuss China's economic growth, savings, and consumption, demographic shifts, and employment—all of which deal with this key factor from different angles.

A Very High Savings Rate

Among the world's large economies, China has the highest savings rate in the world—at close to 50 percent of GDP. To put this in perspective, the highest national savings rate achieved in the United States since World War II was 25 percent (in the mid-1960s). That rate has steadily declined to today's rate of around 18 percent. This large savings pool has important implications for investment, future growth, and China's current account imbalance with (and capital account lending to) the United States. In Chapter 5, we examine why China's savings rate is so high (or why its consumption is so low) and try to gauge what future Chinese savings will look like. Chapters 3, 4, and 6 look deeply into the implications of China's high savings rate both domestically and globally.

The Government's Role

The role of government in economic management is significantly greater in China than in the United States. China establishes and implements Five-Year Plans, which provide direction from the top down for China's key economic institutions—all the way from China's central bank to provinces, townships, and academic institutions. While, at a microeconomic level, Chinese individuals and companies can be ferociously competitive and independent, they operate in an arena managed from the top. Paradoxically, the fierce competition at the microeconomic level is partially a result of the **absence of a government role**. Rule of (commercial) law and regulatory enforcement are still at an inchoate stage in much of China—particularly at the local level.

The directives in China's Five-Year Plans are not mere blandishments; rather, they are targets which anyone operating in China must understand and respond to. In many of the coming chapters, we ask how a Chief Financial Officer (CFO) or Chief Executive Officer (CEO) might look at a particular macroeconomic problem. This approach is intended to help us understand how top-down management works in an economy such as China's. Chapters 7–10 discuss both the institutional arrangements and structures for making macroeconomic policy in China, and the actual policies undertaken in recent years.

Labor: The Great Economic Shock Absorber

China's workforce is extraordinarily flexible and adaptable. The willingness of the 老百姓 (pronounced *lao bai xing,* the common man) to relocate and be relocated, work assiduously for low

Table 1.1 Wages in China remain low, but in recent years have begun to rise substantially.

Position	Monthly RMB Compensation	Monthly USD Compensation**
Business student (just graduated college)	¥4,000	$656
Business student with Masters (just graduated)	¥7,000	$1,157
Computer science Masters (just graduated)	¥11,000	$1,818
Taxi driver	¥4,000	$661
Restaurant worker (did not finish high school)*	¥1,500	$248
Street hawker (did not finish high school)*	¥1,500	$248
Construction worker (estimated)*	¥2,500–5,500	$413–909
Factory worker (estimated)*	¥2,500–5,500	$413–909

Source: Author created.

* May also receive housing and meals.
**Assumes exchange rate of 6.05 Yuan per U.S. Dollar.

wages under difficult circumstances, hold savings with negative real returns for prolonged periods (all in the hope of a better future) is arguably unmatched anywhere else in the world. At the core of China's great economic development is its great **economic shock absorber**. No other economy in the world boasts this extra degree of freedom. This unique characteristic allows Chinese policymakers greater freedom as they experiment with new reforms and major shifts in economic policies. Labor force malleability is, in part, a necessary response in an economy with a large population, scarce resources, and a Confucian tradition of obedience to authority (see Case Study 1.1 below). Table 1.1 presents recent monthly wages for workers in Shanghai, with differing skill sets. Government officials in China are constantly trying to strike the right balance between economic progress and the pressures placed on the average Chinese citizen. In Chapter 5, 7, and 9 we gain greater insight into how this flexibility plays out in China.

Macroeconomics Review and Overview

Macroeconomics is the study of a nation's economy in the aggregate. Analyzing how the national economy performs, how to enhance its performance, and how its performance impacts global linkages are all key macroeconomic questions. As such, macroeconomics deals with questions of recession and recovery, unemployment, inflation, interest rates, savings, current accounts, investment, and long-run economic growth. Meanwhile, microeconomics deals with individual and firm (company) behavior, and how distinct markets operate. In theory, we should be able to aggregate individual agent behavior in the microeconomy up to the macroeconomy and achieve meaningful results—after all, the macroeconomy should equal the sum of its parts. But this has, so far, proven difficult, especially since the individual agents are not identical (heterogeneous) and can interact in ways that seem irrational. Another approach attempts to take some of the results from microeconomics and finance, and assume that the macroeconomy behaves like one large firm. We often use that approach in this textbook (see the "Macro Finance Insights"), and find that this indeed does provide useful insights into both the Chinese and United States economies.

The Macroeconomic Tradition

Here, we briefly review some important paradigms for macroeconomic analysis that have developed to the present. Before the expression "recessions and recoveries" came into use in the twentieth century, Europe and America experienced "panics." For example, the Panic of 1819 was America's first true economic crisis involving high unemployment, bankruptcy, and declines in agriculture and manufacturing production fueled by unchecked bank expansion, credit, and a building boom, all following on the heels of the war of 1812 (this has a certain modern familiarity) (Rothbard, 1962). The fact that economies could fluctuate from boom to bust formed the basis for **business cycle analysis**, an early attempt at classifying these crises. Early business cycle theorists tried to find regular patterns to economic declines and recoveries (e.g., Kuznet Waves, Juglar Cycles, Schumpeterian Waves), but statistical work has failed to find a regular predictable pattern. Later business cycle scholars made significant contributions in dating historical peaks and troughs in economic activity (Wesley Mitchell and Geoffrey Moore) and in specifying leading, lagging, and coinciding economic series (e.g., stock prices, unemployment, or retail sales). This work still finds great use today, continuing, for example, with the dating committee of the National Bureau of Economic Research (NBER).

While business cycle theory had an empirical bent, economic theory developed simultaneously during the latter half of the nineteenth and early twentieth century. Say's Law posited that all goods produced and supplied would one way or another be demanded (i.e., that markets would clear based on prices that would always serve to equilibrate demand and supply). Incomes generated in the production process would always be sufficient to demand the goods and services that had been produced. Monetary theory centered around the work of political economists such as David Hume, David Ricardo, John Stuart Mill, and, later, Irving Fisher.

The quantity theory of money linked the amount of money in the economy, M, the average circulation of money or velocity, V, with the price level, P, and real output or real Gross Domestic Product, Q. In this framework, velocity and quantity were determined by institutional or fundamental factors such that the only real role for money was to determine either the level of prices or inflation.

A simple equation provides a snapshot of that relationship:

Money × Velocity = Prices × Real GDP

Both business cycle theory and the quantity theory of money held, as a matter of faith, the inevitability of economic outcomes. In other words, economies will settle at an equilibrium level of output and prices, and little can or need be done about it. A panic or crisis is a temporary aberration, and an economy would (on its own) gravitate to where it "ought" to be. In the wake of the Great Depression in 1929, John Maynard Keynes in the *General Theory of Employment, Interest and Money* (1936) demurred unconditionally. Prolonged deviations from an economy's true potential could occur and these deviations, in fact, stabilize at a sub-optimum equilibrium. Keynes demonstrated the significant role of money and tight credit as a potential drag on economic performance while emphasizing that the **decision not to demand** goods and services by consumers, investors, the government, or foreign importers could all push an economy into a recession. Rather than serving as an equilibrating flexible force, prices were sticky or fixed and their inability to adjust to **declines in demand** was a sufficient condition for a recession or depression.

The activist approach of Keynesianism—which argues that there could be a role for the government to increase demand and output in times of economic crisis—was rejected by monetarists. The monetarists built on the earlier quantity theory of money and even Keynes and concluded that policy attempts to restore the economy to full employment were futile. In fact, monetarists such as Milton Friedman and Anna Schwarz in *A Monetary History of the United States* (1963) argued that monetary policy intended to stabilize the economy was actually counterproductive because such efforts only lead to greater economic fluctuations. Rather, monetarists saw a need for stable and predictable monetary growth that does not react to economic fluctuations. In this way, economic fluctuations can largely be avoided.

While monetarists posited a stable and predictable demand for money, empirical evidence showing a good deal of volatility in the velocity of money suggested otherwise. New classical macroeconomics was (and is) an attempt to provide an internally consistent, more "scientific" approach to macroeconomics. Research in this area has contributed enormously, both technically and conceptually, to the analytical rigor of macroeconomics (e.g., Robert Lucas and Thomas Sargent). Micro-foundations using the behavior of firms and individuals are first modeled, then explicit or implicit aggregations of these individual units are built up to the macroeconomy. In this way, the role of expectations is more consistently modeled, because the expectations of firms and individuals must be consistent with the economic model in use.[2] A real contribution from this line of research is the explicit formulation of budget constraints for various sectors in an economy: government, business, consumers, and external (foreign). Any realistic economic model must acknowledge the fundamental fact that an economy has scarce resources across time.

Lucas argued that the current class of Keynesian models was unstable in the sense that too much of the structure was static, and did not incorporate the response of individual agents to government policies. Once these responses were endogenized (defined below) into new classical equilibrium frameworks, the effectiveness of stabilization policies was questioned. Lucas's further work emphasized the role of supply shocks (e.g., technology shocks) in real business cycle theory. Economic fluctuations caused by supply shocks such as a crop failure or oil embargo had taken a back seat to the demand side economics found in the Keynesian framework. Real business cycle models of macroeconomies allowed for simulation and parameterization of economies and, in turn, a more scientific approach in model validation.

The rapid ascendancy of Asian economies inspired other economists to develop new theories of economic growth (Romer, 2011). Neoclassical models of the 1970s (Solow and Swan—henceforth, the "Solow Model") provided an accounting framework for decomposing growth, and identifying exogenous drivers for growth (such as population growth and technological progress). New growth theory was an attempt to endogenize factors which could help explain the extraordinary growth in Asia. Factors including increasing returns-to-scale and spillover effects, innovation, and human capital were now identified as internal, and explained by these models (rather than assumed to be external factors).

Implicit in the variety of approaches to macroeconomics described above are a set of challenges which each paradigm either chooses to confront, for the sake of rigor, or ignore, for the sake of simplicity and tractability:

- Aggregation: How important is it to model and then aggregate individual economic units (firms and consumers) in order to usefully describe macroeconomic performance? A tradeoff exists between a scientific approach to modeling and aggregate models which are closer to reality. Greater refinement of micro-foundations can diminish tractability and validity in the aggregation. Karl Popper's critical rationalism provides a basis for testing aggregation in economics; a simple counter-example to an aggregate theory allows for falsification.
- Disequilibrium vs. Equilibrium: Are well-defined markets found in the macroeconomy generally in equilibrium or are there imbalances? Do equilibrium models provide a better notion of macroeconomic performance as opposed to models that allow for disequilibrium? In practical terms, is unemployment better thought of as a rational and optimal choice by all involved, or is it a form of market failure?
- Fixed or Floating Prices: Directly related to the notion of equilibrium vs. disequilibrium models is the question of whether certain institutional factors prevent prices (for goods, labor, or assets) from moving the economy toward equilibrium. Will there be shortages or surpluses if prices cannot adjust to shifts in supply and demand in individual or aggregated markets?

- Expectations: Can economic agents reliably predict outcomes based on expectations that are internally consistent with the economic model at hand? If not, then on what basis do economic agents form their expectations? Individuals may look at past performance or may form no expectations at all. If expectations are often wrong or ill-formed, then what arbitrage opportunities might this present—and do such opportunities actually exist?

Different approaches to the above challenges present a unique set of valuable insights into the macroeconomy. Importantly, some are more useful for the long run and others more useful for the short run.

Case Study 1.1: Confucius, Adam Smith, and Family Values

"What is prudence in the conduct of every private family can scarce be folly in that of a great kingdom."

—Adam Smith. *The Wealth of Nations* (1776).

"It is not possible for one to teach others while he cannot teach his own family. Therefore, the ruler, without going beyond his family, completes the lessons for the state."

—Confucius. *The Great Learning* (500 BCE).

Both the great Scottish economist Adam Smith (of the early Industrial Revolution) and the great Chinese philosopher Confucius (from the fifth century BCE) tell us that the activities of individual units—such as the family—provide the basis for a strong nation (or a nation's economy). Smith argued that the state can learn how to manage its finances from the family unit, especially in terms of frugality or savings. He suggested that the behavior of individuals and individual units acting in their own self-interest lead to a greater good for society. Confucius stated that a well-run family is the starting point and training ground for running the state. It is at the base of the pyramid that has at its pinnacle, national governance.

Without doubt, the family unit continues to serve as a critical component woven into the fabric of society. Given the modern industrialized and industrializing economies of the United States and China, we ask in this textbook if national macroeconomic management can also be enhanced with lessons from a more recent basic unit in society—the corporation.

Nevertheless, the models and approaches described above rely heavily on the experience of Western industrializing or industrialized economies. Are these experiences relevant for emerging economies such as China? Consider the question of aggregation. Do economists need to invest as much intellectual capital in this question in the presence of a Five-Year Plan, a tool China has put forth twelve times over the past sixty years? Is aggregation already accomplished via the plan, and can we more usefully adjust our macroeconomic questions to assess the rationale for aggregation rather than concern ourselves with technical questions on how to aggregate economic activity? In this text, we look to the theory of the corporation for guidance. Rarely are questions asked about aggregation when it comes to the theory of the firm or in corporate finance. Rather, it is assumed that workers work toward a goal (a strategy, a plan) and that management devises and implements that strategy.

Rather than struggling with questions of equilibrium or disequilibrium, perhaps a better question for emerging economies is management decisions and incentives that yield the desired results of the plan or strategic mission. Instead of price flexibility or fixity, we suggest developing a pricing strategy and analyzing where the firm has market power. In this context, we assess the competitive advantages of a nation and how to exploit them. If governments have some degree of monopsony power in labor or credit markets, how will this impact the operation of markets?

Instead of making static assumptions about how expectations are formed, it may be more relevant for us to think of how management can shape expectations in order to achieve desired outcomes. Specifically, can expectations be shaped by management or the government so as to build confidence? Furthermore, just as with a firm, some information is privy only to insiders while other information is publicly known. Can expectations be controlled through the flow of information? In emerging markets, perhaps it is more fruitful to examine asymmetry of information between insiders and outsiders than to attempt to model the expectations of individuals and firms.

Back to Supply and Demand

"All of economics is either just supply or demand," or so said a sage MBA student after listening to a lecture chock full of technical detail. Figure 1.1 illustrates how simple macroeconomics is at this basic level. The level of output, employment, and price will be determined by the intersection of supply and demand. As discussed above, Western macroeconomics has wavered back and forth between emphasizing the role of demand (the basis for Keynesian economics) and the role of supply (real business cycle theory and growth theory). This difference can also be found in the Chinese and Western approach to macroeconomic policy and as we shall see is of great importance

In China, the traditional macroeconomic focus has been on what to supply, where to supply output, and how it should be supplied. In Western macroeconomics, the traditional focus has been on the question of demand—is it adequate to absorb all of what is produced? Even when Western

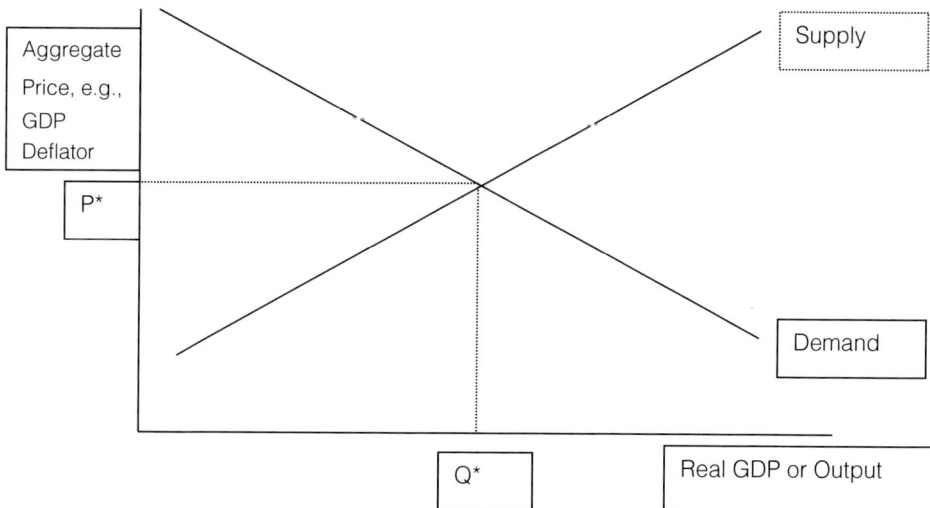

Figure 1.1 We can summarize the macroeconomy with a simple demand and supply curve. Where they intersect will determine the level of real output for an economy and the aggregate price level.

Source: Author created.

economists analyze supply, it is an abstraction rather than a careful sectoral look at who needs to produce what in order to satisfy the demands of society. Western economists are mostly concerned with how to manipulate aggregate demand so as to ensure full employment of resources. The Chinese emphasis has traditionally focused on promoting output industry by industry—so that demand is more or less assumed.

These differences are seen clearly in the way economic activity is described in national statistics. Western economists begin the measure of GDP with retail sales, corporate investment, government spending, and exports—all of which are components of demand. In fact, as we discuss later, these are part of consumption (C), investment (I), government spending (G), and net exports (XGS-MGS)—the traditional demand-side decomposition of GDP used in Western economies. In China, GDP has traditionally been presented in terms of Primary Sector Output (agriculture, mining, and forestry), Secondary Sector Output (manufacturing and construction), then Tertiary Sector Output (services including the government's contribution to output). Further statistical breakdowns of output cover sectors within manufacturing, construction, or services. All the while, the statistical breakdown focuses on supply and output—including which provinces and important cities are producing which output.[3]

For example, we could compare the emphasis in China's twelfth Five-Year Plan with the U.S. Economic Report of the President. In the latest Five-Year Plan, we see the following targets:

- GDP to grow by 7 percent annually on average
- More than 45 million jobs to be created in urban areas
- Rise in domestic consumption
- Service sector value-added output to account for 47 percent of GDP, up 4 percentage points
- Annual grain production capacity to be no less than 540 million tons
- Construction and renovation of 36 million apartments for low-income families
- Expenditure on R&D to account for 2.2 percent of GDP

In contrast, in Chapter 2 of the *Economic Report of the President 2011*, we see the following sections:

- Consumption and Saving
- Developments in Housing Markets
- Business Fixed Investment
- Business Inventories
- Government Outlays, Consumption, and Investment
- State and Local Government
- Real Exports and Imports

Despite the obvious differences in emphasis between supply and demand, we also see some convergence in the approaches. China's twelfth Five-Year Plan discusses at length the need for greater consumption in China, while the *Economic Report of the President* examines issues related to innovation, infrastructure, education, healthcare, and clean energy. Comparing the contents of each document against the ability of the respective governments to actually implement these goals shows very different outcomes. In China, as we shall see, the tools for controlling the supply side of output are generally more sophisticated than are those of the United States; however, the United States' tools for managing demand are relatively more refined than China's.

The existence of these differences clearly reflects the differing economic histories of the two nations. In China, we see a tradition inherited from the Soviet planning model, including Five-Year Plans. We could trace events back through twenty centuries of Chinese history to consider great public works projects including the Great Wall and China's canals and water management efforts. Clearly, China has a very long history of viewing demand—particularly consumer demand—as an afterthought. Since the Chinese government was fully Communist before 1978, it could and did control the means of production.[4] While government ownership of the means of production in China is shrinking, the notion that output can and should be controlled has not.

In the United States, the laissez-faire tradition combined with perhaps the world's most vibrant marketing, advertising, and branding infrastructure has established demand as a pillar of the U.S. economy—particularly consumer demand, in which 70 percent of national output is used. The U.S. production mix (supply) is primarily affected by how much the government demands, as well as tax policy (to some extent). The latter can also impact consumption. In the United States, production at the industrial level is determined by individual firms; in China, production at the industrial level often is still influenced by the government taking the lead, and firms from within the industry following. In the United States, tax policy and government spending can impact consumption, investment, and (of course) government demand. In China, the tools available for influencing demand fall more heavily on investment, exports, and the government.

Key Analytic Distinctions in Macroeconomics

In this book, we will introduce a number of data-related measures. It is important to keep in mind a few basic distinctions when we are looking at macroeconomic data.

Business Cycles vs. Growth Cycles

Business cycles, in Western economies, correspond to absolute declines in economic activity broadly defined to include specific indicators such as GDP, industrial production, retail sales, personal income less transfer payments, and the number of employees on non-agricultural payrolls.[5] Rapidly growing economies such as China's rarely experience absolute declines in economic output, but rather a slowing of growth. In fact, China in its post-reform period has only had one period of absolute decline in output, 1988–89, a period of political turmoil. In the business cycle case, a recession would be represented by a prolonged period of negative growth in key indicators, while in the growth cycle case, growth would still be positive—just not as positive as before.[6]

Figure 1.2 shows the U.S. GDP in the post-World War II era. The shaded columns indicate business cycle recessions, periods in which there was an absolute decline in economic activity. For every shaded area, we see outright declines in GDP levels. Figure 1.3 shows the coincident index for China along with a leading index as calculated by the Conference Board, a United States-based business organization. But the coincident index in this case depicts economic growth in China, not the level of economic activity, while the leading index is a forecasting tool used to suggest future economic growth. Components in the coincident index for China are manufacturing employment, value-added of industrial production, retail sales of consumer goods, electricity production, and volume of passenger traffic. In Figure 1.4, we see continuous positive growth typical of a rapidly emerging economy such as China. We do, however, also observe the correspondence between the shaded columns in Figure 1.3 and periods of relatively slow growth in 2000–01, 2004, and 2008–09.

Nominal and Real Variables

Another distinction is the difference between nominal variables and real variables. Nominal variables and numbers are variables and numbers that we can actually observe in our day-to-day life. For example, the price we actually pay for an apple or a bowl of rice at a store or restaurant is a nominal price.

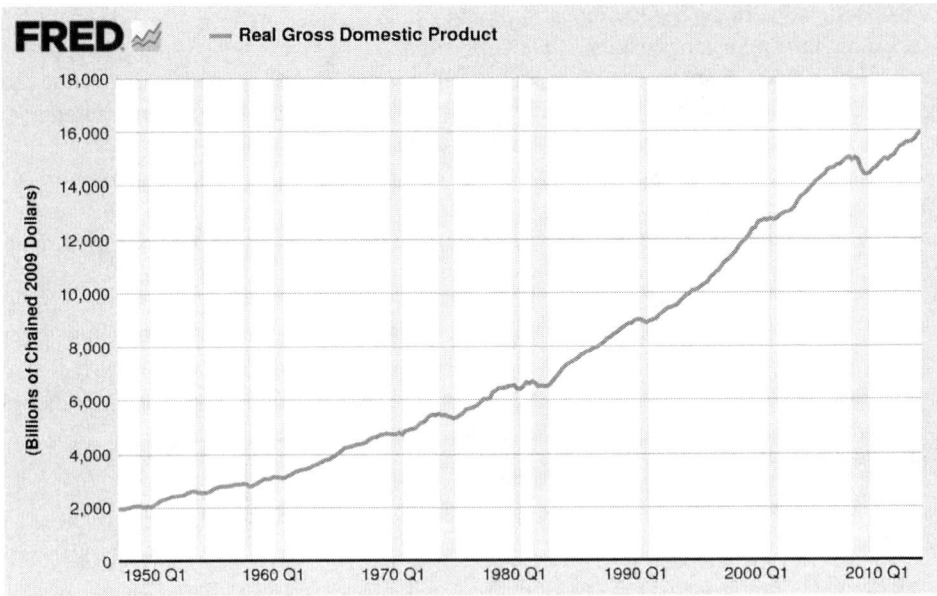

Figure 1.2 The United States, being a mature economy, experiences outright declines or recessions (shaded areas) and recoveries. This is known as the business cycle.

Source: FRED, Federal Reserve Economic Data, Federal Reserve Bank of St. Louis: Real Gross Domestic Product; U.S. Department of Commerce: Bureau of Economic Analysis.2014 research. stlouisfed.org

Note: Shaded areas indicate U.S. recessions

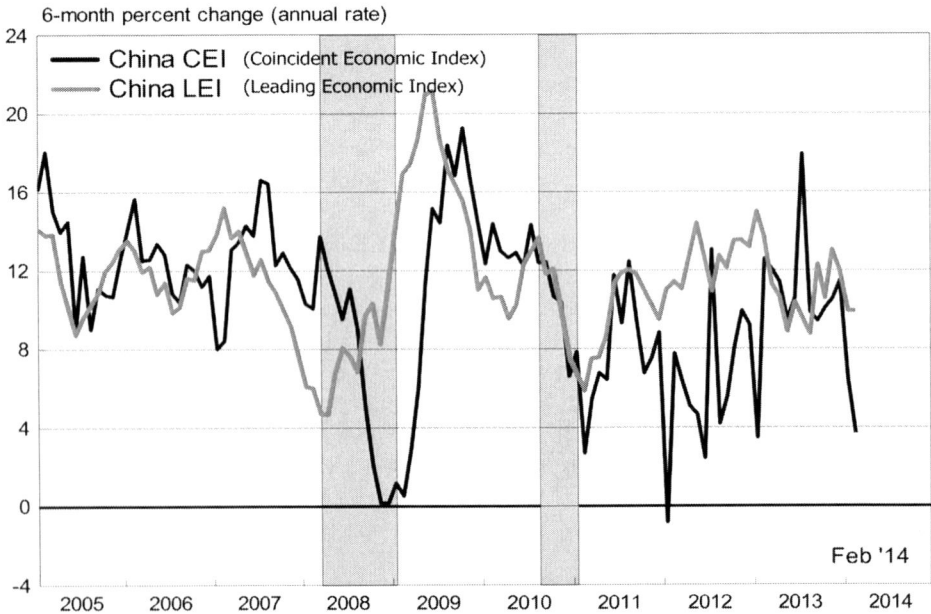

Figure 1.3 China tends to experience only growth cycles (slower positive growth) as indicated by the shaded areas.

Source: Conference Board.

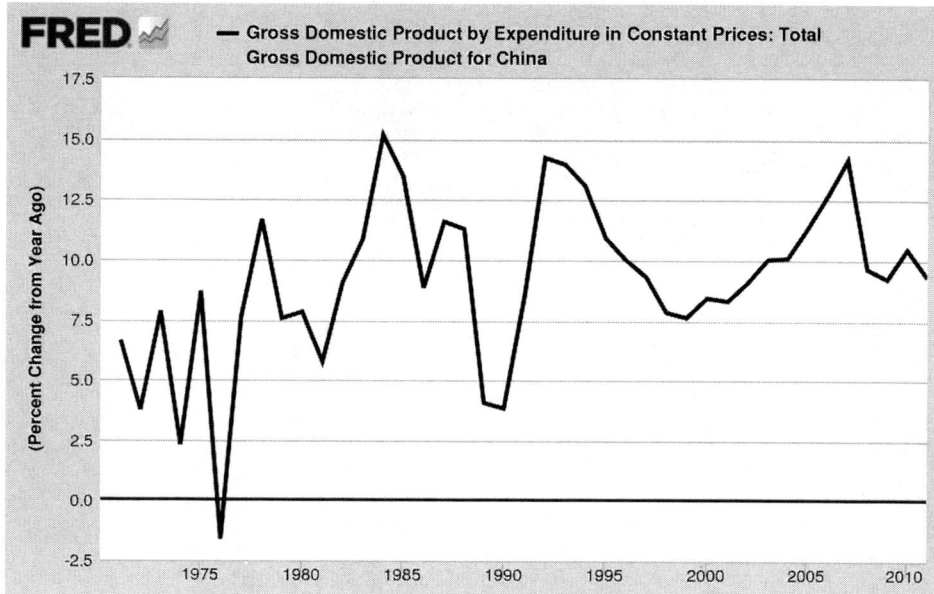

Figure 1.4 China's real GDP growth has been positive over the past two and a half decades but has fluctuated considerably—sometimes as a result of political turmoil.

Source: FRED, Federal Reserve Economic Data, Federal Reserve Bank of St. Louis: Gross Domestic Product by Expenditure in Constant Prices: Total Gross Domestical Product for China; Organisation for Economic Co-operation and Development. 2014 research.stlouisfed.org

In contrast, real variables are an attempt to measure physical volumes—or at least a measure that removes the effects of price changes over time. The goal here is to examine fundamental activity rather than allowing price changes to confound what is happening in a real sense. For example, between one year and the next, the nominal price of a bowl of rice may increase by 50 percent. It would be wrong, in a real sense, to say that our consumption of rice went up year over year by 50 percent if in fact we are just consuming the same single bowl each year. We might describe our real consumption as one bowl of rice each year, or US$1 "in constant US$" each year (assuming that was the initial price).

We can remove the price effect from nominal variables, converting them to real variables, through price indexes. Price indexes are numerical measures of average prices for goods and services, and are used to compare average price changes over time. If we know how prices change, we can then subtract their effect to derive the real value of an item.

We must ask two central questions regarding indexes: "Which is the typical market basket that should be used to estimate inflation?" and "Should that basket be allowed to vary over time?" Table 1.2 presents differing measures of inflation depending on how we answer those questions. In the table we are considering a basket containing only two goods that are relevant—apples and pears—and are assumed substitutes for one another. We assume the prices of apples rise faster than pears and we note that consumption of apples drops accordingly while pears rise in some reasonable way. The fixed basket Laspeyres Index assumes that consumers keep consuming the same basket of apples and pears found in 2012 and measures how much that same basket would cost year after year. This tends to overestimate inflation since it ignores the fact that apple consumption actually drops—a phenomenon that is ignored if the same old market basket is used.

The fixed basket Paasche Index, in contrast, assumes that the 2016 market basket is consumed throughout the entire period. But this turns out to be unreasonable since it assumes that consumers

Table 1.2 Price indexes are used to both measure inflation but also to gauge the "real" changes in variables as opposed to their nominal changes.

Year	2012	2013	2014	2015	2016
Apple Price	$1	$1	$ 1.05	$ 1.08	$1.15
Quantity of apples purchased	100	100	98	97	95
Pear Price	$1	$1	$1.03	$1.06	$1.09
Quantity of pears purchased	100	100	102	103	107
Fixed Market Basket Indexes					
Laspeyres Index		$200	$208	$214	$224
Laspeyres Inflation			**4.000%**	**2.928%**	**4.756%**
Paasche Index		$202	$210	$216	$226
Paasche Inflation			**3.941%**	**2.932%**	**4.653%**
Fisher Ideal Inflation			**3.970%**	**2.930%**	**4.705%**

Source: Author created.

have always consumed more of the less expensive pears. This index underestimates inflation. The Fisher (Ideal) Index is the simple square root (geometric mean) of the Laspeyres and Paasche Indexes, and theory suggests this is a good compromise in correcting the flaws of these two indexes used in isolation. Finally, the chained Laspeyres Index uses last year's basket to weight the index. It asks how much more expensive is last year's basket if we labeled it using today's price tags. It updates the basket each year. It is a "chained index" in the sense that, in order to calculate price changes over a span of years, we must multiply the three corresponding years of inflation by each other. Constant updating of the basket keeps the index up to date but at the cost of greater confusion with respect to exactly which base year market basket is in use.

There are many price indexes employed in the United States. The Consumer Price Index (CPI) measures how much a typical market basket of goods and services consumed by an urban consumer changes over time.[7] Another index—the Personal Consumption Index (PCI)—is very similar in that it measures the cost of consumption items. Some key differences relate to coverage: the CPI measures out-of-pocket expenses for urban consumers while the PCI measures the total cost of a good or service if the consumer had to pay the entire cost of that item. For example, consumers pay only a fraction of healthcare costs due to private insurance or government programs such as Medicare. Thus healthcare would have a low weight in the CPI but a relatively high weight in the PCI (U.S. Bureau of Labor Statistics). Another major difference is of a technical nature. The CPI uses a representative market basket of goods from an earlier year—a convenient solution to the inability of statisticians to know what is being consumed in real time (today). The PCI is a chained Fisher Index, using current and last year's consumption baskets as a base. This provides more reality by allowing for consumers substituting one good or service for another as prices fall or rise, and represents an updated consumption pattern.

Another important U.S. price index is the Gross Domestic Product (GDP) Deflator, which is a broad measure of prices for all goods and services produced. Another is the Producer's Price Index, a measure of prices at the wholesale or industrial level for goods and services absent taxes and distribution costs. The PPI measures prices from the perspective of the seller; the CPI from the perspective of the urban consumer. The GDP Deflator uses the chained approach mentioned above, while the PPI uses a market basket from a prior period.

China produces a similar set of indexes, including fixed and chained consumer price indexes but with an emphasis geared toward China's own economic structure. For example, not only is a Consumer Price Index produced for urban consumers, but a separate CPI is calculated for rural residents—close to half of China's population lives in the countryside. A producer price index with a focus on manufactured goods highlights China's role as the "factory to the world." Another index, the purchasing price index for raw materials, fuel, and power highlights China's heavy reliance on imports for these key inputs. Finally, a price index for investment in fixed assets highlights the critical role in GDP (over 50 percent in recent years) that residential construction, infrastructure, and property and equipment play. Both the United States and China provide some of these indexes on a national and a regional basis.

Flow Variables vs. Stock Variables

In macroeconomics, we see a number of economic variables being presented. Some variables are flow variables and some variables are stock variables. Flow variables represent economic phenomenon that appear during a period of time. For example, a person's gain or loss of weight would be a flow variable. Stock variables are levels of economic phenomenon that represent the accumulation of flows (e.g., one's total weight—the **sum** of the flows of weight gains and losses per year that occurred over a lifetime). At the company level, the income statement and cash flow statement contain many of the company's key flow variables; the balance sheet accumulates many of those flows into stocks. Table 1.3 provides a sampling of flow and stock variables that we will see in some of the following chapters.

Exogenous vs. Endogenous Variables

In economics, we explain how the economy works—specifically, what causes certain key economic variables such as unemployment or economic growth or inflation to occur. We use economic models in our attempt to explain the behavior of these key variables. We call these types of variables *endogenous,* because they are the output of our economic models. Other variables are inputs into our economic models; they have a critical role (typically as a driver toward an outcome), but we accept them as a given and do not attempt to explain them. We call these kinds of variables *exogenous.* For example, the weather in most economic models would be exogenous; economists are not meteorologists; they have neither the ability nor an interest in explaining the weather. But clearly weather is an important factor. For example, bad weather may cause a crop failure and inflation (an endogenous

Table 1.3 One way to better understand an economic model is to understand the difference between flow and stock variables.

Types of Economic Variables	
Flow	*Stock*
Inflation	Price level
Savings	Wealth
Balance of payments	Foreign exchange reserves
Birth rate	Labor force
Open market operations	Money supply
Investment	Capital stock
Budget deficit	Public debt
Current account deficit	External debt

Source: Author created.

variable). Economists accept the weather as an input and a driver but do not attempt to explain or predict it. We say it is exogenous to the model.

Ten Basic Macro Facts Most Economists Could Agree Upon: A Chance to Review

We have reviewed some of the main ideas and challenges in the study of macroeconomics and have highlighted how China fits into that analysis. Below are some central ideas in macroeconomics that the reader should review before progressing to the chapters that follow.

1. Demand is important. A large drop in aggregate demand can cause a recession.
2. Supply is important. A large drop in aggregate supply can cause a recession.
3. The money supply is important. High persistent inflation is caused by an overly rapid increase in the money supply relative to output over a long period of time.
4. Increased government spending when the economy is at full employment can crowd out other economic sectors: Private Investment, Exports, and Consumption.
5. Monetary policy works through several channels. A key one is known as the "transmissions mechanism," in which (1) the central bank open market operations impact short-term interest rates; (2) short-term interest rates impact longer-term interest rates; (3) both short- and long-term rates impact investment demand and consumer demand; (4) the change in investment and consumer demand impacts economic output and employment.
6. Lack of flexibility in wages and prices opens up the possibility of prolonged periods in which the economy is either in recession or operating above full employment.
7. There is no long-run tradeoff between inflation and the unemployment rate.
8. Fiscal policy is relatively more effective under fixed exchange rate regimes; monetary policy is relatively more effective under floating exchange rate regimes.
9. The presence of rational expectations (in which economic agents form expectations accurately and consistently with a true economic model) tends to reduce the effectiveness of activist fiscal and monetary policies.
10. Recessions triggered by financial crises have greater depth and length than recessions triggered by conventional demand and supply shocks.

Challenging Questions for China (and the Student): Chapter 1

1. Go to FRED (Federal Reserve Economic Database) OECD Based Recession Indicators (http://research.stlouisfed.org/fred2/series/CHNRECM) and compare this to Gross Domestic Product by Expenditure in Constant Prices: Total Gross Domestic Product for China: (http://research.stlouisfed.org/fred2/series/NAEXKP01CNA652S).
   a.   Are the OECD recession indicators for growth cycles or business cycles?
   b.   Identify the years of any outright business cycle recessions for China since 1980.
2. Schramm identifies the adaptability and flexibility of the labor force as one of the key drivers for the Chinese economy. Pick one of the Ten Macro Facts at the end of the chapter that plays a similar role (a shock absorber) in a traditional Keynesian framework. Explain.
3. Identify some key economic drivers (important economic/institutional/demographic factors that are fundamental and fundamentally different) that make the United States exceptional. Contrast with China.
4. Decompose the three constituent components of Investment flows into the types of stocks that they accumulate into.
5. If certain institutional structures in society, such as the family or the company, are important, compare and contrast their broader role in the Chinese and American economies.

Notes

1. As an old Egyptian saying goes "When poverty comes in the door, love goes out the window!" But one wonders what happens when riches comes in the door . . .
2. The Phillips Curve, an artifact from the Keynesian world, assumed adaptive expectations in which future expectations represented a weighting of past or lagged information. The modeling of inflationary expectations highlights key differences between traditional Keynesian models and the new classical economics.
3. In recent years, China has begun to present GDP using the Western, demand-side approach of C, I, G, and NX, but the supply-side approach is still very much paramount in China's statistical reporting (see Chapter 2).
4. The method employed was one of input/output tables and the primary methodology was linear programming (Leontief, 1986).
5. The Conference Board and the National Bureau of Economic Research track similar, but not identical, sets of coincident indicators. In the United States, the NBER set of indicators provides the basis for determining when recessions start or recoveries end.
6. In calculus terms, we state that business cycles have a negative first derivative while growth cycles have a negative second derivative.
7. The CPI is presented both as a fixed Laspeyres Index and a chain-weighted Fisher Index, the former being more frequently referred to as the CPI.

References

Chair of the Council of Economic Advisers. 2011. *Economic Report of the President Transmitted to the Congress, February 2011, Together with the Annual Report of the Council of Economic Advisers.* Washington, DC: U.S. Government Printing Office.

Confucius. "The Great Learning" (500 BCE). *The Internet Classics Archive.* http://classics.mit.edu/Confucius/learning.html

Friedman, Milton, and Anna Schwarz. 1963. *A Monetary History of the United States, 1867–1960.* Princeton: Princeton University Press.

Leontief, Wassily W. 1986. *Input-Output Economics.* 2nd edn. New York: Oxford University Press.

Lucas, Robert. 1976. "Econometric Policy Evaluation: A Critique." In *The Phillips Curve and Labor Markets,* eds. K. Brunner and A. Meltzer, 19–46. New York: American Elsevier.

Naughton, Barry. 2007. *The Chinese Economy: Transitions and Growth.* Cambridge: MIT Press.

Romer, David. 2011. "Endogenous Growth." In *Advanced Macroeconomics.* 4th edn. New York: McGraw-Hill.

Rothbard, Murray. 1962. *The Panic of 1819.* New York: Columbia University Press.

Sargent, Thomas. 1996. "Expectations and the Nonneutrality of Lucas." *Journal of Monetary Economics* 37 (3): 535–48.

Shasha, Deng,. ed. 2011. "Key Targets of China's 12th Five-Year Plan." Xinhua News Service (2013 Xinhua, english.news.cn), March 5.

U.S. Bureau of Labor Statistics. 2011. "Current Price Topics: Differences between the Consumer Price Index and the Personal Consumption Expenditures Price Index." *Focus on Prices and Spending—Consumer Price Index: First Quarter 2011,* 2 (3).

Wu Jinglian. 2005. *Understanding and Interpreting Chinese Economic Reform.* Mason, OH: Thomson/South-Western.

2 Measuring and Accounting for the Output of a Nation: GDP

人比人，气死人

Comparisons Can Be Difficult If the Other Man's Grass is Always Greener

In 2013, China's Gross Domestic Product (GDP) was an estimated RMB 58.7 trillion. In the past decade, it has grown at rates near 10 percent while more recent growth rates have edged closer to 7.7 percent. In this chapter, we explore what exactly these numbers mean and how they are derived. GDP is the gross value of final goods and services produced within the geographic borders of a country over a period of time (normally, one calendar year). As we see in the paragraph below, each term used in defining GDP is of significance. We need a solid understanding of GDP and Gross National Product (GNP) because there are fundamental differences in the definition, measurement, composition, and (of course) size of GDP between China and the United States. Figures 2.1 and 2.2 show GDP since 1960 for both countries. We immediately notice a sharp convexity in China's profile after 1978 as compared to that of the United States. This is a normal contrast for an emerging economy with increasing returns-to-scale compared to a mature economy experiencing diminishing returns.

The term *gross* refers to the stage before netting out (or subtracting) depreciation and the depletion of resources involved in the production of GDP. By *value*, we mean the monetary value (a function of the price of products and services, as well as their quantity). By *final goods and services,* we mean products and services which reach their end use (e.g., consumption; investment in plant and equipment, inventory accumulation, or government goods and services; or exports abroad). *Within* a country's *geographic borders* means that this particular measure (GDP) is calculating output occurring domestically (as opposed to the output from domestic firms or local citizens working abroad). The latter kind of production is included in an alternative measure to be discussed later and is referred to as Gross National Product (GNP). GDP is a flow rather than a stock, and is dependent upon the time period of that flow. By *time period*, we mean the amount produced in the current period, for example, the fiscal or calendar year. For example, a used auto that was sold this year would not be included in this year's GDP since it was not produced this year. The services of the car dealership in refurbishing and marketing the car, however, are currently produced and would be included in this year's GDP.

Different Approaches to Measuring GDP

There are four basic approaches to measuring GDP: The Value of Final Goods and Sales approach; the Expenditure (Uses) approach; the Value-Added approach, and the Income approach. All four approaches are used because they enable us to (a) cross-check our measurement of GDP, and (b) allow additional insights into the basis for the creation of GDP. The Sales approach starts, for example, with retail sales, and then makes appropriate adjustments. The Expenditure approach

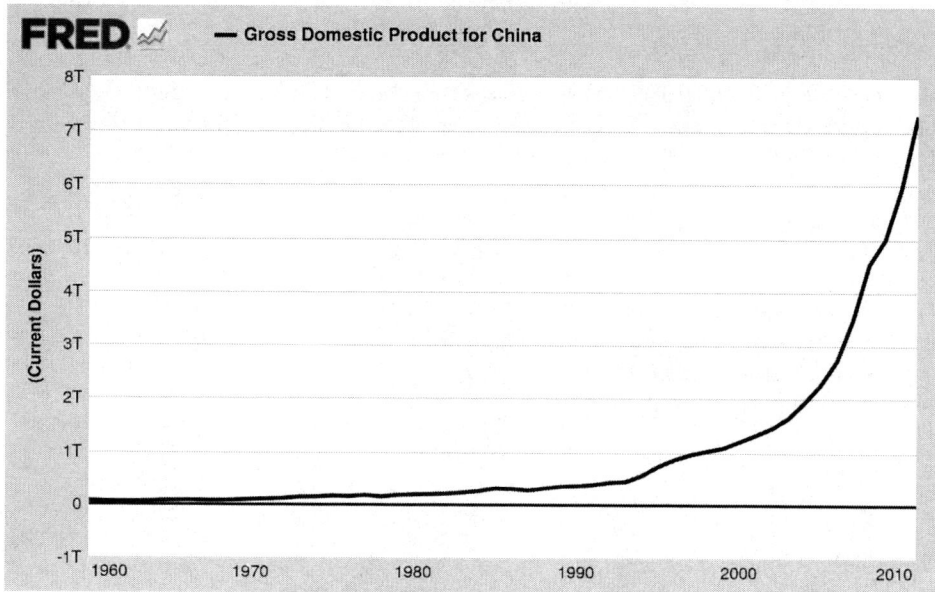

Figure 2.1 China's economic output as measured by GDP has surged since economic reforms began in 1978.

Source: FRED, Federal Reserve Economic Data, Federal Reserve Bank of St. Louis: Gross Domestic Product for China; World Bank. 2014 research.stlouisfed.org

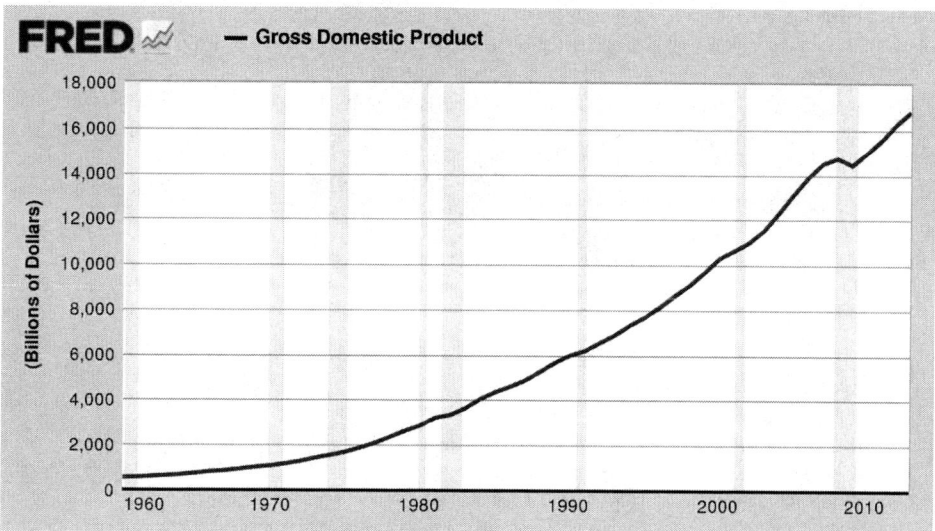

Figure 2.2 United States economic growth as measured by GDP has stabilized at rates consistent with a mature economy.

Source: FRED, Federal Reserve Economic Data, Federal Reserve Bank of St. Louis: Gross Domestic Product; U.S. Department of Commerce: Bureau of Economic Analysis. 2014 research.stlouisfed.org

Note: Shaded areas indicate U.S. recessions.

breaks GDP into its final uses. The Value-Added approach breaks GDP down into inter-firm stages of production. The Income approach breaks down GDP into recipients of the income generated in the process of creating GDP. If (although not usually the case in such a complex statistical effort) all four measures were taken without error, they would provide an equivalent measure of GDP.

Case Study 2.1: China's Basic Numbering System

Perhaps one of the most difficult tasks for a translator from Chinese to English (or vice versa) would be a negotiation regarding buying or selling an apartment. The simplest part of the task might actually be just translating (converting) the words. But consider the following necessary conversion factors:

- The Chinese would measure the size of an apartment in terms of square meters not square feet. **(Conversion Factor: 1 square meter is 10.763 square feet)**
- The quoted price would be in RMB not U.S. dollars. **(Conversion Factor: an exchange rate of .15 US$ per RMB)**
- The price per square meter would be in a numbering system different from that used in the West. **(Conversion Factor: For large numbers, Chinese use a basic unit of 10,000 [10^4] while Westerners use a basic unit of 1,000 [10^3]).**

Thus, a Chinese apartment quoted at 五万 (5 times 10,000 or 50,000) RMB 一米 (per meter) would come out to be about US$740 per square foot (or an overall conversion of about 50000/740 = 68)—a comfortable home by Chinese standards.

Because using both language skills and arithmetic skills simultaneously employs different sides of the brain, any negotiation involving numbers becomes an extremely challenging task. No wonder a wrong number is usually the outcome! The message here: Be very careful when converting Chinese numbers—it is extremely easy to make a mistake. In conversation, it is probably best to write the number down as a power, for example, "10^7." The following are the basic units in which Chinese (and Western) economic and financial data are typically displayed. After 1,000 the basic unit diverges—the Chinese start to use powers of 10,000 while the Western numbering system progresses through powers of 1,000. For example, in the West, the next major step after 1,000 is 1,000,000; in China, it is 10,000 (and from 10,000 to 100 million). This difference is highlighted in Table 2.1. Throughout the text in this chapter, whenever possible, we preserve each country's basic numbering system and currency—if you are working with Chinese data, you will need to get used to the differences!

Table 2.1 The Chinese numbering system starts to use powers of 10,000 for large numbers instead of 1,000 as seen in the Western numbering system. After 1,000 the **bold** highlighted numbers represent the different basic units that the Chinese numbering system would employ.

Chinese Number	Spoken/Written	Western Equivalent
1	yi 一	One
10	Shi 十	Ten
100	Bai 百	Hundred
1,000	Qian 千	Thousand
10,000	**Wan** 万	**Ten thousand**
100,000,000	**Yi** 亿	**Hundred million**
1,000,000,000,000	**Zhao** 兆	**Trillion**

Source: Author created.

Value of Final Goods and Sales Approach

This is the simplest and most fundamental approach to measuring GDP, which simply measures the total quantity sold during the year—whether it be at the retail consumer level (i.e., to new homebuyers), to other firms or the government, or as exports abroad. By *final sales*, we mean that the product or service has reached its final end user (rather, than say, an intermediary user such as another firm or wholesaler). We then adjust our final sales number for inventory that was added during the year but not sold to a final user (this would add to our GDP estimate) as well as inventory produced in a prior year but sold this year (this would subtract from our final estimate of GDP).

MACRO FINANCE INSIGHT 2.1: ONE FIRM'S CONTRIBUTION TO GDP

Let's consider GDP creation from the perspective of a single firm. Our company, CMM, is a 50/50 joint venture with one partner based in the United States, the other in China, and with operations in China (represented by the income statement in Table MF2.1a). CMM produces computerized measuring machines that are sold to automotive and other industrial companies to measure accuracies below the width of a hair. During the income statement period found in the table, inventories fell by US$0.14 billion. Costs of production and interest are all paid to Chinese entities; half of the profits, however, are claimed by the U.S. joint venture partner. Since we are measuring Gross Domestic Product not net product, we can ignore CMM's depreciation estimate of US$0.20 billion throughout.

Table MF2.1a We can view the different ways of calculating GDP from the perspective of a single company's income statement such as CMM.

Revenues	US$2.98 (billions)
Domestic Sales	$2.94
Export Sales	$0.04
Costs of Production	US$2.27(billions)
Materials	$1.4
Wages, Salaries	$0.87
Depreciation	$0.20
Operating Income	$0.509
Interest to Bondholders	$0.09
Taxes	$0 (On "tax holiday")
After Tax Profits	$0.42

Source: Author created.

Value-of-Output Approach

Since all output is produced in China, CMM's contribution to Chinese GDP would be US$2.98—0.14 billion or US$2.84 billion. We subtract the US$0.14 billion because this inventory decumulation represents output produced in an earlier year (and was accounted for in that year's GDP). CMM's contribution to U.S. GDP would be 0, since no output was physically produced in the United States. When looking at GNP for China, however, we would need to subtract out (1/2) of US$0.42 + 0.20 = 0.62 or US$0.31 (billions) since half of the pre-depreciation profits are paid in dividends to the U.S. partner. Thus, Chinese GNP from CMM's operations would be US$2.84 − 0.31 or US$2.53 billion. U.S. GNP from CMM's operations is US$.31 billion. We note that the sum of GDPs for the two countries must always equal the sum of GNPs (2.84 = 2.53 + 0.31).

Expenditure Approach

Using this approach, we assume that this product is used neither by consumers nor the government, but by firms as an addition to their plant, property, and equipment. We then base our estimate of GDP on the following uses: investment and exports. We must subtract US$0.14 billion of inventory decumulation from domestic sales (*I*) of US$ 2.94 billion or US$2.8 billion and identify exports as US$ 0.04. We then have GDP for China as US$2.84 billion, which is consistent with our Value-Added approach.

Income Approach

Income generated from CMM's sales is accrued to the following recipients: CMM's employees, CMM itself (as a corporate entity), CMM's bondholders, and to a similar (but unknown to us) set of stakeholders in the entities providing "materials" to CMM.

Beginning with US$2.84 billion, we see that US$0.87 billion goes to CMM's workers and managers. Gross income to CMM after adjusting for depreciation (+) and inventory decumulation (−) is:

$$US\$0.42 + 0.20 - 0.14 = US\$0.48$$

US$0.09 billions goes to CMM's bondholders and US$1.4 billions to CMM's material suppliers (who would distribute income to their own stakeholders). Thus gross GDP from the Income approach equals US$2.84 billion for China and US$2.53 billion in GNP for China.

Value-Added Approach

Value-Added comprises the contribution to GDP from CMM (its entire set of stakeholders—workers, investors, and lenders) plus the value added from its suppliers. Since material inputs (from outside suppliers) add up to US$1.4 billion, the remainder of the US$2.84 billion of GDP (which equals US$1.44) must come from CMM itself. We can check this by noting that US$1.44 adds up to US$0.87 in wages, US$0.09 to lenders and 0.62 − 0.14 = 0.48 billion to CMM shareholders.

Expenditure Approach

The Expenditure (or Uses) approach identifies four major classes of users of final output or GDP. They are: consumption (*C*), investment (*I*), government (*G*), and net exports (*NX*). This approach focuses on determining the actual end user, rather than analyzing the intrinsic property of the good or service itself. Thus, a pencil sold to a consumer would be classified as *C*, to the government as *G*, if exported, as *NX*, and if it is added to a company's inventory, as a component of *I*. Consumption includes products and services that consumers buy via retail sales, as well as the flow of services provided by the housing stock (i.e., the economic benefit provided by an individual's place of dwelling during a given year, whether rented or owned[1]).

Government includes all goods and services produced during the year and used by the government. Some of these items are provided by the private sector (such as office supplies or food served within government cafeterias). Other items are produced by the government itself (i.e., the services of police and fire departments, the military, and the administrative services of government entities under income transfer programs, including veterans' benefits or social security[2]). As suggested, *G* includes government purchases at the local, provincial, and national level.

Investment is a very broad measure that includes new residential housing, increases in the capital stock by companies or firms, and finally increases in inventories resulting from current production.

When inventories increase, one possibility is that the firm has chosen to use current output to build up inventory (planned inventory accumulation). Another possibility, however, is that the firm had hoped to, but was unable to, sell all of its production (unplanned inventory accumulation). Either way, the currently produced output is included in GDP (as part of inventory, and more specifically, as "inventory accumulation"). Thus inventory serves as a "plug," a catch-all, for goods that were currently produced but did not find their way into *C*, *G*, or *NX*.

Within the three uses covered so far—*C*, *I*, and *G*—some purchases will also include goods and services produced abroad but sold domestically, i.e., imports (*MGS*). In addition, some of the goods produced domestically will be exported. Since, in our measure of GDP, we are only interested in goods produced domestically, we somehow need to eliminate imports as a use (since these goods should not be included in GDP). We also want to identify exports (*XGS*) as a use of GDP since these goods were part of domestic output. Thus, we must subtract out imports (which are not a use of our GDP, but that of another nation's) and add in *XGS*. We do this by defining net exports (*NX*) as

$$NX \equiv XGS - MGS^3$$

where, again, *XGS* and *MGS* include both goods and services. We can summarize the relationship between GDP (using Y_{GDP} to represent GDP) and expenditure (using the Expenditure approach) as follows:

$$Y_{GDP} = C + I + G + NX$$

Again, this relationship must always hold true because any good or service that is not consumed (*C*), acquired by companies for investment (*I*), bought by the government (*G*), net exported (*NX*), or otherwise "used" can always be categorized under (*I*) as inventory accumulation.

In Table 2.2, we compare uses of GDP between China and the United States.[4] The most dramatic difference is in consumption. In the United States, most output is used by consumers (69 percent).

Table 2.2 The Uses approach to GDP shows that consumption accounts for much more GDP in the United States as compared to China. China uses much more of its GDP for net exports and investment.

	China (2012) (100 Mill. ¥)	Percent of GDP Exp.	USA (2011) (US$ Bill)	Percent of GDP
Gross Domestic Product Expenditure Approach	**465731**		**16244**	
Personal consumption	164945	35%	11150	69%
Gross capital formation or investment	213043	46%	2409	15%
Change in inventories	11964	3%	66	0%
Net exports of goods and services	12163	3%	−547	−3%
Government consumption	63616	14%	2548	16%
Government investment	NA	NA	619	4%
Statistical discrepancy	−7151	−2%	NA	NA
Gross Domestic Product Value-Added	**472882**	102%	**16244**	100%
Net factor payments	−767	0%	253	2%
Gross National Product	**472115**	101%	**16497**	102%
Minus depreciation	67388	14%	2543	16%
Net National Product	**404727**	87%	**13954**	86%

Source: CSA Tables 2.16 and 2.18 and Bureau of Economic Analysis.

Expressed alternatively, the product mix in the United States is geared toward consumer goods. By contrast, Chinese consumers only consume about 35 percent of the Gross Domestic Product pie. The mirror image of this difference can be found in private investment, in which about 49 percent of China's output (including inventories) is used for investment versus about 15 percent in the United States. We will explore the basis for these differences in later chapters; they are in part explained by savings patterns as well as development stages for each country. One final, related comparison: China runs a relatively large, positive net export surplus (around 3 percent of GDP) while the United States runs a large net export deficit (around −3 percent of GDP). Netting out trade with global partners shows that, on balance, China's surplus has as its counterpart the U.S. deficit.

Value-Added Approach

As suggested by the name, *value-added* recognizes that most firms in an economy utilize not only their own inputs (mainly capital and labor) to produce products and services but also rely on the inputs of other firms. The Value-Added approach integrates the contribution that each firm alone makes to GDP across all firms, excluding the contribution from other firms (suppliers) along the value chain. China's National Bureau of Statistics (NBS) provides exceptional detail utilizing this approach. As a gross look at this method, we could disaggregate any economy into primary, secondary, and tertiary activities: primary being principally agriculture, fisheries, forestry, and mining; secondary being manufacturing and construction; and tertiary being services such as retailing and the government. We could initially think of the first stage of GDP as goods and services created by the primary sector, then passed to the secondary, then the tertiary, and finally turned over to the end user. At each stage, the receiving sector adds value and passes a further refined part of GDP onto the next. The reality, of course, is much more complex. For example, the primary sector (agriculture) will likely purchase inputs from other sectors (e.g., accounting services from the tertiary sector). In other words, value-added is not a simple linear process running from primary to tertiary, but is a much more integrated process.

In any economy, however, it is interesting to ask where value is being added. In this way, we can determine why one nation's productivity (output per worker) is higher than another's, or which sectors could achieve greater efficiencies. Formally, we can describe the Value-Added approach to GDP for an economy with N producing firms (or entities) as:

$$Y_{GDP} = \sum_{i-Firm1}^{i=FirmN} (Value\ of\ Output - Value\ of\ Input)_i$$

It would be a mistake to simply add each sector's output into total GDP without subtracting the value added by other sectors as this would create a double counting of output.[5] In fact, this was a serious problem under the system of Net Material Product employed in China up until 1995 (see below).

Figures 2.3 through 2.5 portray how value is added to create GDP in China and the United States. The largest share of output in China comes from the secondary sector, while in the United States most output is now produced in the tertiary sector. The largest share of employment in China is in the primary sector, but the tertiary sector (services) has been growing rapidly in recent years. The United States sees most employment in the tertiary sector. Chapter 5 covers how this difference helps to explain the share of national income that workers, as distinct from companies, capture. Based on the data from Figures 2.3 and 2.4, we can see in Figure 2.5 that, in China, output per worker (productivity) is highest in the secondary sector, while in the United States, it is highest in

Employment Share By Sector

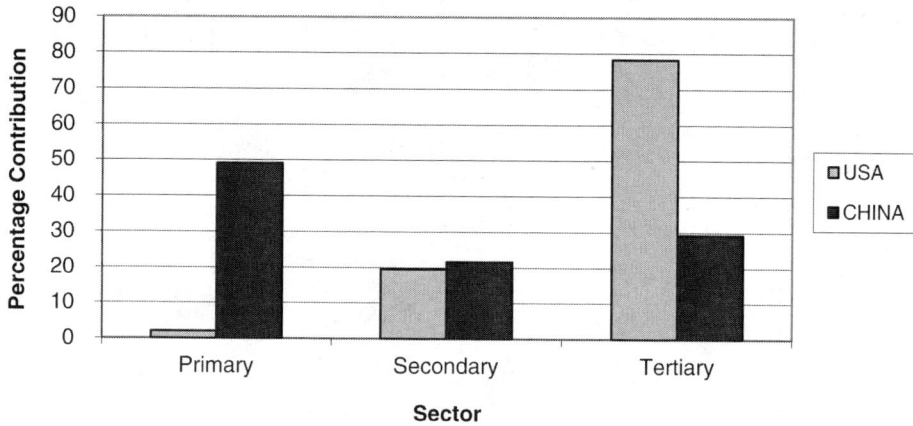

Figure 2.3 China still employs relatively more people in the primary sector than in the United States. The United States employs relatively more in the tertiary (services) sector.

Source: Author created.

Contribution To Output By Sector

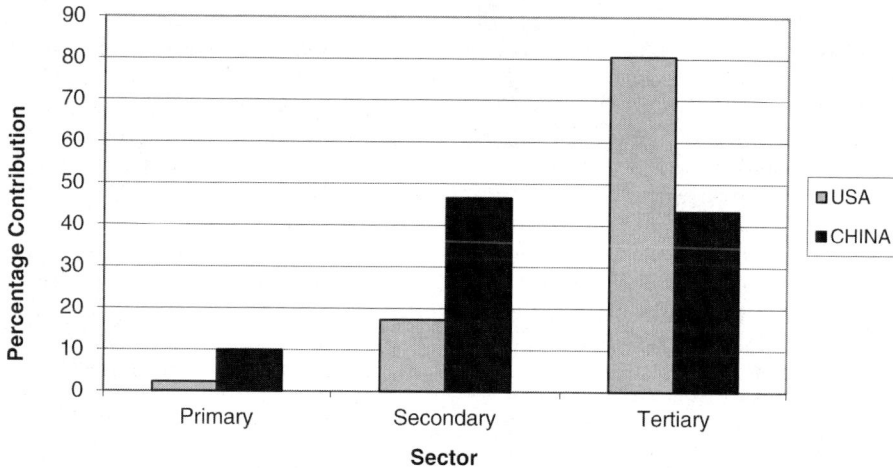

Figure 2.4 The secondary sector (manufacturing) is now the largest sector in China; the tertiary sector (services) the largest in the United States.

Source: Author created.

the primary sector. Across all three sectors, U.S. workers are more productive than Chinese workers; this explains the higher average standard of living found in the United States. Needless to say, these numbers reflect national differences in relative abundances of physical capital, labor, and the use of technology, issues to be explored in later chapters.[6]

Value of Output Per Worker By Sector

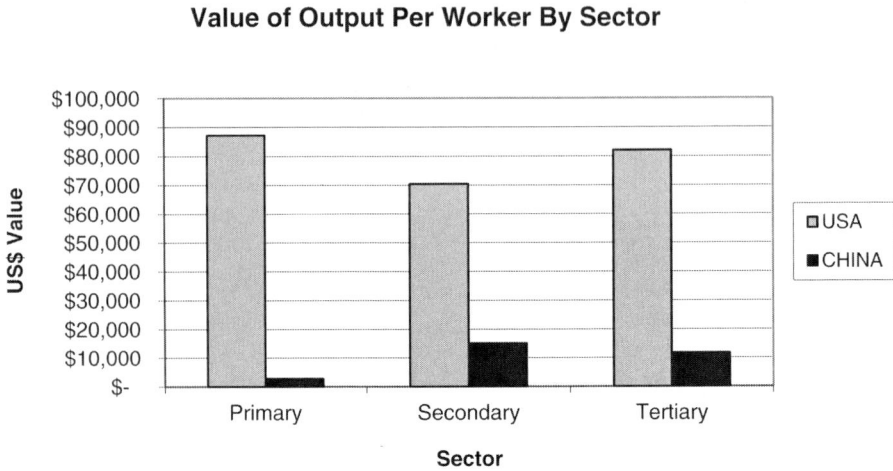

Figure 2.5 The United States is still far more productive than China across all sectors, especially the primary sector (agricultural and mining etc.). China has a relative advantage in the secondary sector (manufacturing).

Source: Author created.

Case Study 2.2: Goldilocks Data—Who Inflated and Shrunk China's GDP?

Accuracy of Data

Given that China only began using the United Nation's System of National Accounts (SNA) for GDP measurement in 1995 (abandoning the old Soviet system of National Material Product), the Chinese National Bureau of Statistics has made enormous progress in measuring prices and output. If we consider the economic size of the economy (by any dimension) and the movement from a planned to a market economy that overlapped the new measurement efforts, we can appreciate the enormity and difficulty of the task. On virtually every economic statistic produced by China, scholars have at least two views—the number is too small or too big. This uncertainty probably reflects both a lack of understanding of the data and systems of collection, and a lack of transparency on the part of officials regarding methodology.

In fact, China has developed a clear regulatory and legal framework for the collection and presentation of statistics, including serious penalties "on the books" for fraudulent reporting. Furthermore, governments at all levels base their decision making (including those expressed in the Five-Year Plans and the job promotion of government officials) on the data that are published. Much of the data collection effort is managed locally, however, which creates problems of consistency across regions and, in some cases, reporting biases. Some of the features and problems of the GDP and price statistics include:

Value of Output Issues

1. Industrial output is likely overestimated. About 40 percent of China's GDP can be attributed to this sector.
2. Productivity growth in the service sector is likely overestimated (thus, the size of the service sector is also likely overstated). The tertiary sector represents about 43 percent of GDP.
3. Estimates of agricultural output growth appear to be realistic but the value (level) of this sector's output may be too low.
4. Estimates of GDP based on regional estimates are too large—they generally exceed those of nationally based production estimates.
5. Output of services is underestimated (especially government and real estate services, including imputed rents).

Expenditure and Income Issues

1. Quarterly based measures of GDP on the expenditure side are still not reported (seasonal adjustment of production-based GDP began in 2011).
2. In most years since 1978, GDP measurements based on the Expenditure approach exceed those based on the Production approach, sometimes by a wide margin.
3. For some years in which growth has slowed considerably, official estimates do not seem to show as large a decline—some income smoothing appears to have taken place (see Macro Finance Insight 2.2: GDP Smoothing and Earnings Management).
4. Value-added measures of GDP are substantially stronger than expenditure-based measures, given that the former have longer roots in the old Soviet methodology.
5. Measures of personal income are underestimated.
6. Measures of consumption are underestimated (especially for services). The size of the consumer sector is likely underestimated due to underreporting of government consumption and imputed costs of housing. Consumption makes up about 49 percent of China's GDP on an expenditure basis (including government consumption).
7. Measures of retail sales are underestimated (especially for services).

Index and Other Issues

1. Services and imputed rents are still seriously lacking in China's CPI indexes.
2. Revisions of GDP deflators have created serious discrepancies in how real GDP is measured.
3. A shortage of census-based surveys in estimating national statistics (China's first economic census was undertaken in 2004).
4. Discrepancies among series that should track each other reasonably closely (e.g., GDP deflator and CPI price index, provincial GDP and national GDP, expenditure-based GDP, and production-based GDP).

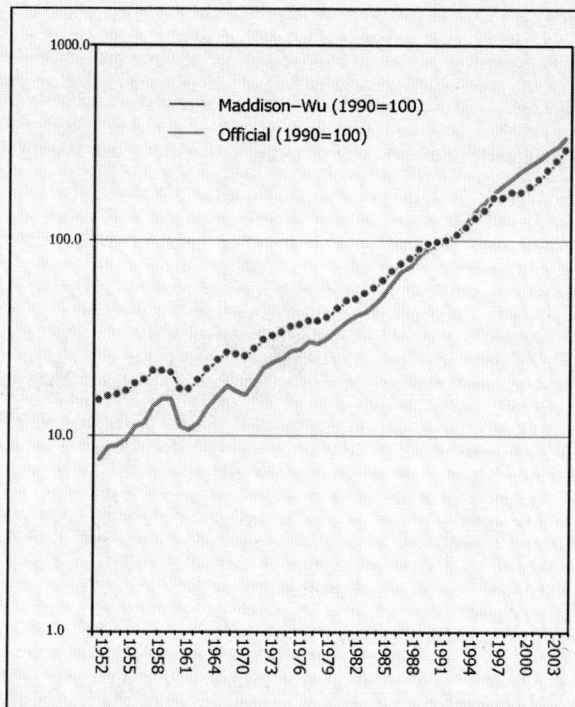

(Continued)

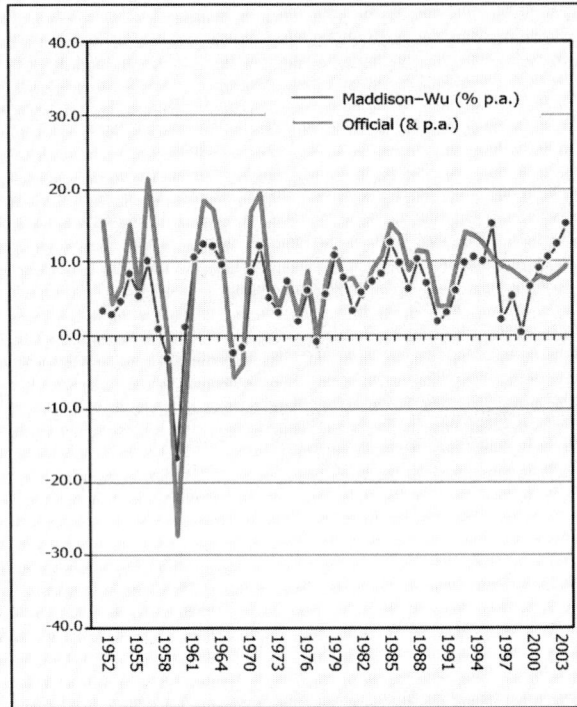

Figure CS2.2a Maddison and Wu (2008) contend that China's official measurement of GDP has two offsetting errors (on growth rates and initial levels of GDP) making current estimated of China's GDP essentially correct.

Source: Maddison and Wu, 2008.

Considering the above biases, authors such as Maddison and Wu estimate that during the 1978–2003 period, for example, actual growth in real GDP was 7.9 percent compared to the official estimate of 9.6 percent. To put this in perspective, that gap suggests a real value of output of one-third lower than the official 2004 estimates. However, they also believe the level of real output was seriously underestimated before SNA was adopted, creating a difference that almost fully offsets the growth effects. In other words, on balance, current estimates of the size of China's economy are essentially correct! Figure CS2.2a shows the year-by-year Maddison and Wu differences.

Figure CS2.2b depicts both the official estimate of GDP (using the Value-Added approach) and compares it to an average of other estimates which use other methodologies (such as the Expenditure (Uses) approach or, in the case of Klein and Ozmucur, a broad set of other indicators.) For the period between 1978 and 2000, the official estimate is about .8 percent higher on average than the average estimate of outside academics. The most notable difference occurs during the 1987–89 period, in which average estimated GDP growth was considerably lower than that of the official estimate. A similar gap occurs again in 1999. Fernald et al. (2013) make a similar comparison and come up with a similar conclusion. (See Macro Finance Insight 2.2, which highlights potential causes for biases in measuring GDP both for China and the United States.)

Outside analysts have looked at a number of other measures beyond GDP real growth to gauge the accuracy of China's official numbers; these include iron ore output, electricity use, coal output, and rail transport, to name a few. As we noted earlier, these measures do track GDP fairly well—except at the critical juncture of the 2008 financial crisis when reported GDP growth at the trough was substantially higher than the level suggested by other indicators.

China: Real GDP Growth: 1979–2003

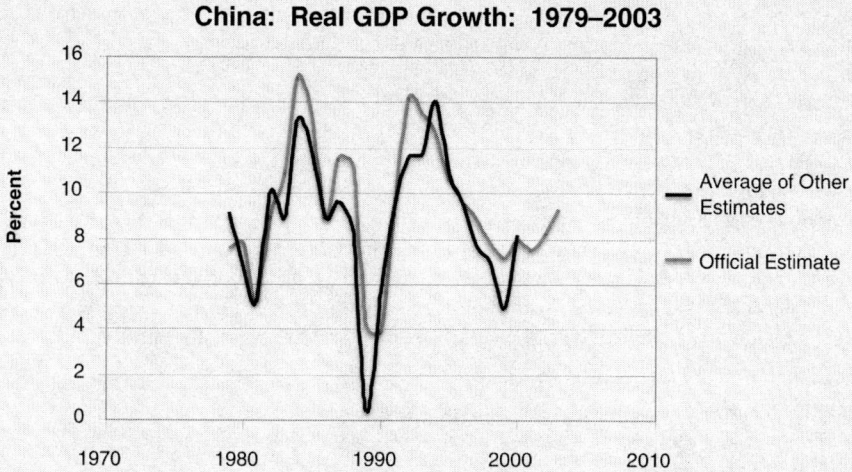

Figure CS2.2b Comparing China's official GDP growth estimates with an average of outside estimates are consistent except when growth is either at a peak or a trough.

Source: Author created based on NBS, 2012; Klein and Ozmucur, 2003 (for years 1981–2000); Keidel, 2001 (for years 1979–2000); and Wang and Meng, 2001 (for years 1979–1997).

It appears, however, that the NBS is not the only organization which struggles to come up with reasonably good measures. The World Bank seems to face similar difficulties. Feenstra et al. (2012) estimate that a World Bank revision of GDP per capita output for 2005 was 50 percent too low! On that basis, working backward several decades from the World Bank estimate using reasonable growth rates would lead to a negative GDP for China (theoretically possible but nearly impossible). They base their findings on more theoretically sound deflators of nominal consumption—including rural (not just urban) price measures and using a command GDP concept (discussed later in this chapter).

MACRO FINANCE INSIGHT 2.2: GDP SMOOTHING AND EARNINGS MANAGEMENT

Estimates for real GDP and growth are just that, estimates. There is a fair amount of leeway in exactly determining any nation's actual output. The United States, for example, revises its quarterly GDP data twice in the quarter following the target quarter. In the G7 economies, the revisions can be substantial— as much as a full percentage point. But these revisions are largely unpredictable (unbiased). On the other hand, some have suggested that China's National Bureau of Statistics (NBS) has engaged in "smoothing" (i.e., exaggerating) growth rates in times of economic slowdowns. Figure CS2.2a and Figure CS2.2b suggest that China's estimates of growth do diverge from other estimates, notably during 1990–91 (the U.S. recession) and 1997–98 (the Asian Financial Crisis). Some economists suggest that, for example, the growth rate estimate for 1998, (of 7.8 percent), while close to the planned target of 8 percent set by the government, is unrealistically low (see Rawski 2001). The GDP growth targets set in the Five-Year Plan may pressure localities within China to adjust their own production data so that targets are met. Provinces and localities compete with one another to impress the central government. Behavioral finance suggests the important role that any major benchmark plays in setting expectations and even results, and in this context, the opportunity to rationalize a more favorable growth rate is clear. We should remember that there are two opposing forces at play when reporting income and sales: On one hand, strong results boost the reputation of local officials; on the other hand, they invite great interest from the tax collectors at all levels of government. It is not obvious which effect is more important.

In fact, income smoothing occurs in the United States as well, but in the form of "earnings management" at the corporate level rather than the national statistical level. A large body of evidence suggests that firms try to smooth earnings using accepted accounting methods such as accruals rather than recognizing income or profits. For example, standard accounting principles allow leeway regarding when a non-cash sale is recognized in earnings. A variety of explanations are offered for such smoothing, including investors' preferences for a stable pattern of earnings. Thus firms work to make their reported earnings appear smoother in order to reduce their cost of capital. In an insightful paper, Lin and Shih (2002) suggest that U.S. firms may underestimate income in times of downturn—just the opposite of the suspected pattern in China. By underestimating income in downturns and accruing that income for a later recovery period, the authors highlight a pro-cyclical type of income smoothing. The rationale for this is twofold:

1. Since profits are down economy-wide, firms' losses in a down period are discounted by investors, but the earnings that are later booked will be rewarded.
2. Bonuses in down periods are unlikely, but the corresponding earnings accrued for a later recovery period will be rewarded.

To the extent that earnings management involves accruing (deferring revenues or sales), the impact on measured GDP is direct. It is unknown to what extent pro-cyclical earnings are exaggerated by management during downturns in the United States. It is interesting, however, that China and the United States— because of the peculiarities of their respective economic systems—appear to be biased in opposite directions in their GDP reporting. Particularly during downturns, China may overestimate real growth while the United States may underestimate it.

Income Approach

The Income approach recognizes that the products and services produced and used in any given year generate income attributed to the various factors of production (e.g., labor, land, and owners of capital). This income can be earned in a variety of forms: pre-tax wages and salaries, pre-tax profits, net interest payments (to bondholders, for example), and rental payments for the use of productive capital.[7] For example, a firm's revenues (sales) will be distributed to various stakeholders in the company (employees, owners, lenders, and possibly landowners). Under this approach, China's presentation of GDP data using the income approach remains weak.

In Table 2.3, we see an estimated decomposition of output by GDP, GNP, and Net National Product (NNP) for China and the United States for 2011–12.[8] GDP and GNP do not subtract out

Table 2.3 Here we see that labor receives a significantly smaller share of income than owners of capital (companies or shareholders) and property than in the United States. The income approach remains a weak spot in China's GDP estimation.

	China (100 Mill. ¥)	Percent of GDP	USA (US$ Bill.)	Percent of GDP
Gross Domestic Product	472,882	100%	16,244.0	100%
Labor income	212,488	45%	8,611.6	53%
Capital, land and renter income	260,393	55%	7,632	47%
Net factor payments abroad	−767	0%	253	2%
Gross National Product	472,115	100%	16,497	102%
Depreciation	67,388	14%	2,543	16%
Net National Product NNP	404,727	86%	13,954	86%

Source: CSA Table 2–16 and author's pro-rata estimates and Bureau of Economic Analysis.

depreciation (capital consumption) occurring during that year for businesses, private residences, or the government. Also, remember that the difference between "domestic" measures (such as GDP) and "national" measures (such as GNP) are net factor payments abroad (NFP). That is:

GNP = GDP – Net Factor Payments

These factor payments represent interest payments, dividends, and employee compensation that are earned by either foreign entities or individuals located in the home country, or home entities and individuals operating abroad. Since GDP represents goods and services geographically produced within the home country's borders, factor payments to foreigners must be subtracted in order to arrive at GNP.

We see significant differences in the composition of income between China and the United States. In the United States, over half (53 percent) of GDP accrues to labor. In China, the worker's share is reported at 45 percent; personal income data for China remains weak, however. Many economists believe the gap between China and the United States in terms of personal income as a share of GDP to be more dramatic. (In Chapter 5, we discuss these estimates in greater detail.)

In part, these differences reflect the relative abundance of labor to capital in China. From a neo-classical microeconomic perspective, the marginal product of labor is low and that of capital is high, with the marginal wage and return on capital at corresponding levels.[9] But there are other fundamental causes for this difference, relating to the size of the service sector and the market power of workers compared to firms' owners.

China, on balance, makes net factor payments abroad, thus creating a wedge between GDP and GNP (the former being larger). The United States finds itself in the reverse position. Further examination of the underlying data show another contrast: while China makes dividend payments on net sales to the rest of the world (representing the substantial foreign direct investment (FDI) into China), on balance the nation also receives interest payments from the rest of the world (representing its substantial holdings of foreign exchange reserves). The United States, by contrast, finds itself in exactly the complementary position—receiving dividends but paying interest to the rest of the world.[10] As we discuss elsewhere, this difference creates an odd result, given that China is a net creditor to the United States: the high-yield investments (FDI) of the United States into China compared to the low-yielding investments of China in U.S. assets (mainly U.S. Treasury instruments) result in a net factor payment outflow from China to the United States. Over time, as China shifts its portfolio from U.S. government securities to FDI, the flow will likely turn favorably toward China.

Finally, we note the lower depreciation rate found in China (14 percent) compared to the United States (16 percent), as a share of GDP. China's ratio of GDP to capital is significantly higher than in the United States, meaning that the depreciation rate on capital is actually higher in China. This likely reflects several factors: (1) the newer (on average) vintage of capital stock found in China (recently installed capital depreciates at a higher rate than older vintages); and (2) the need to write off substantial investments as reflected in the substantial non-performing loan (NPL) problem of the banking system (to be discussed in a later chapter).

China's Presentation of GDP Data

It is useful to understand the recent historical context of China's data collection efforts in order to gain insight into the methodological and presentational issues in China's GDP accounts. The earliest modern estimates of China's output were for the period before World War II by Pao-San Ou (1946). In the pre-reform period (1950–78), China's GDP methodology closely mirrored that of the Soviet Union. This approach had two major underpinnings: (1) an emphasis on the production of physical volumes (as opposed to intangible production such as services), and (2) a reliance on the input–output approach consistent with that of a planned economy.[11] The latter element, in effect, allowed a central planner (rather than the "invisible hand" of a capitalist economy) to ask what outputs were desired and what combination of inputs should be produced and allocated across different sectors in order to achieve the desired output targets. The metric used in the pre-reform period was Net Material Product (NMP). This measure excluded most services and "netted" out depreciation of capital stock. Net exports (relatively small during this period) were not independently estimated, but treated as a residual. China published its first GNP measure of output consistent with the System of National Accounts (SNA) and discontinued reporting NMP in 1995.

A vestige of the old system remains, however, in that the emphasis has been on measuring output as all that was produced rather than all that was used. During pre-reform China, in the absence of a market-based economy, the principal users (consumers) were deemphasized relative to the perceived more important user (the government's investment in plant, property, equipment, and infrastructure). Without a true consumer market, effectively measuring retail sales, for example, was difficult. In other words, China's GDP measurement relied more heavily on the Value-Added and Incomes approaches (especially the former) as opposed to the Expenditure (Uses) approach.[12]

In fact, China's official GDP estimate continues to be presented primarily in terms of value added and secondarily in terms of uses. For example, in 2011 the official GDP estimate based on the value-added approach was RMB 47.3 trillion while the uses/expenditure estimate was RMB 46.6 trillion—a difference of 1.5 percent. As of 2011, the presentation of output using an income measure was quite limited. The presentation is provided at a provincial level by the authorities but is not readily available at the national level. Furthermore, while estimates for GDP on a quarterly basis (as opposed to an annual basis) have been available using the Value-Added approach since 1992, they are still not calculated using the Expenditure (Uses) approach.

In contrast, the official estimate for United States GDP is based on the Expenditure (Uses) approach. In 2012, for example, estimated GDP using the Expenditure (Uses) method came to US$16.2 trillion, but rose less than 1 percent to US$16.3 trillion when calculated under the Income approach (also defined as Gross Domestic Income). Given each country's belief that it will achieve a more accurate measure of output using its preferred approach, the residual approaches (e.g., Expenditure (Uses) approach for the Chinese, and Income approach for the United States) tend to be adjusted in the direction of the official measurement.

As we will see in later chapters, these differences go beyond mere statistics. Western economists emphasize the ultimate goal of an economic system as consumption—normally the only argument found in the utility function in neoclassical economics. Traditionally, Chinese economists have emphasized the role of production and growth (the size and progress of GDP). Needless to say, both are important and both countries are converging toward similar economic goals and ways of measuring output.

Issues in Measuring GDP

To better understand exactly what we are measuring when calculating a nation's GDP, we must look more deeply at some of the assumptions, definitions, and methodologies employed in its measurement.

Does GDP Correspond to Well-Being?

Economics is defined as the study of "how best to match individual's unlimited wants with society's scarce resources." Thus, the basic assumption in the field of economics is that individuals seek to maximize their consumption of goods and services over some relevant timeframe. It is natural, then, to focus on the production of those goods and services (GDP) as a measure of well-being in any given economy. Economists and philosophers agree that meeting basic needs such as shelter, nutrition, and health is a desirable goal. It also seems probable that the more a country produces, the more

Table 2.4 The United Nations Human Development Index presents at a broader measure of well-being within a country than per capita GDP.

	China	*USA*
Life expectancy at birth 2002 (years)	70.9	77
Adult literacy rate 2002 (% ages 15 and above)	90.9	N/A
Combined gross enrollment ratio for primary, secondary, and tertiary schools 2001/2002 (%)	68	92
GDP per capita 2002 (PPP US$)	4,580	35,750
Life expectancy index	.76	.87
Education index	.83	.97
GDP index	.64	.98
Human Development Index (HDI) value 2002	.699	.937

Source: Human Development Report of the UNDP.

likely it is that such a goal will be met. But at what point does the production of material goods (and services) cease to correlate with improved well-being and even happiness? There is no clear answer to this question, particularly when we consider that the production of "goods" may also involve the production of certain "bads" such as pollution, congestion, resource depletion, and even unhappiness. None of these latter outcomes, referred to sometimes as "negative externalities," is taken into account when measuring GDP. Similarly, GDP does not measure how much leisure time is available to individuals in an economy, nor how income is distributed among its individual members.[13]

The United Nations Development Program (UNDP) provides an alternative measure to GDP: the Human Development Index (HDI). This measure includes life expectancy, educational attainment, other social factors, and the more traditional measure of per capita income. We see that China does well in comparison with its "medium human development" peers both in terms of life expectancy and education. Its per capita income, however, is still relatively low. By UN measures, China ranks 101st in the HDI (out of 187 countries), with a score of .699 (the range is from 0 to 1). The United States is third in HDI, with a score of .937 (Table 2.4). In terms of income distribution, estimates of Gini coefficients for the United States and China are at .41 and .47, respectively.[14] Keeping in mind the above caveats regarding well-being and per capita GDP, but also remembering the likely high correlation between per capita GDP and economic well-being, we will focus on GDP as our main target in the body of this book.

Case Study 2.3: The Environment and Trade with the United States

That China's economic growth is coming at a tremendous environmental cost has been well-documented. The degradation of air and water quality across the country has been enormous. It is estimated that more than half of the water sources near urban areas are unfit for drinking. About one-third of China's famous and economically significant Yellow River is too polluted even for agricultural use. And this is in a country in which water for agriculture and personal use has always been in extremely scarce supply. In many parts of China, PMI indexes (a measure of the concentration of tiny but harmful particles in the air) regularly exceed ten and sometimes forty times the levels that the World Health Organization considers safe. In December 2013, Shanghai had a PMI reading of 580, exceeding "hazardous." Air quality is part of the daily conversation in local newscasts. It is not unusual to see citizens wearing face masks with air filters when walking outside. Some international schools in major cities have created air-filtered sanctuaries within school buildings since students are regularly not permitted outdoors due to the poor air quality.

China now burns over half the world's coal, and evidence of that is particularly acute in major cities across the country—especially Beijing and Shanghai. China surpassed the United States in terms of carbon dioxide emissions several years ago. The *Economist* reports that China's cumulative emissions of carbon dioxide in the coming years will exceed the entire world's CO_2 output from the start of the Industrial Revolution to 1970.

A fascinating article published in the proceedings of the *National Academy of Sciences* (Lin et al., 2014) links China's exports (most of which are directed to the United States) to pollution not just in China but also to the U.S. West Coast. Approximately one-third of some critical pollutant levels in China can be attributed to its manufacture or reprocessing and export of products to other countries. Conversely, the authors find that if these same products were produced in the target countries rather than being imported, pollution levels would be substantially higher there; countries such as the United States are not unscathed by China's pollution. The authors find a significant impact from China's export-related air pollution on the western United States (where sulfur levels, for example, are 12 to 24 percent higher due to China's pollution spillover). In terms of improved air quality, the primary beneficiaries are those living along the U.S. East Coast where manufacturing that would have otherwise harmed the environment is now located in China. Another factor to consider are the massive landfills being created across the United States to ultimately dispose of these imported goods.

Quality of Growth

Macro Finance Insight 2.3 examines the important question of quality of growth vs. the quantity of growth. That the above effect is important in a country such as China (in which investment use represents close to 50 percent of GDP), can be shown as:

$$\text{GDP Growth} = \acute{\alpha} \times \text{Investment Growth} + (1 - \acute{\alpha}) \text{ Non-Investment Growth}$$

Here, $\acute{\alpha}$ represents the share of GDP use going to investment and $(1 - \acute{\alpha})$ represents the share going to non-investment uses, meaning consumption, government, and net exports. Rearranging, we have:

$$1 = \frac{\acute{\alpha} \times \text{Investment Growth}}{\text{GDP Growth}} + \frac{(1 - \acute{\alpha}) \times \text{Non-Investment Growth}}{\text{GDP Growth}}$$

The equation above shows how much of GDP growth can be attributed to investment growth and non-investment growth. We note that China's investment is now about 50 percent of GDP, or $\acute{\alpha} = .5$. Furthermore, it has been growing at a faster rate than GDP. The first term on the right-hand side of the last equation then suggests that over half of China's growth is due to investment. Meanwhile, at most one-fourth of U.S. growth can be explained by the investment component. Both the share of investment in GDP and its growth combine to create this result.

In a pure accounting sense, more investment leads to higher output (by definition). Here, we are not referring to the role of investment as an input into the production function (we will discuss that later). Rather, we are making the simple accounting observation that if growth in the capital stock is large (and this is a large fraction of GDP), then GDP growth as a quantity concept will be large as well. For example, a company such as General Motors increased assets in the United States (the capital stock) by a factor of thirty-nine between 1965 and 2003, while increasing sales by a factor of nine. With poor financial performance it ultimately fell into bankruptcy in the 2008 global financial crisis. Both the investment of GM and its sales were included in measured GDP over those four decades. If enough companies in any economy followed this pattern, we would see high GDP growth rates (based on asset and sales growth) but eventual value destruction and economic collapse.

The fact that so much of China's growth is the result of measured investment (as a use of GDP) does raise certain "red flags." When consumption is considered as a use, we feel more comfortable with its direct link between its pricing and economic value; after all, consumers willingly made purchases at prices determined by supply and demand. When investment goods are a primary use, the link between economic well-being and production is less clear. It may be a decade or more before we can understand whether an investment actually created value or not. This concern becomes elevated in the presence of state-directed loans and significant distortions (such as controlled interest rates) in the financial system. We will present this distinction between quantity and quality, value creation, and value destruction in a dynamic setting in Chapter 4 within a Solow framework.

MACRO FINANCE INSIGHT 2.3: QUANTITY OF GDP VS. QUALITY OF GDP

As mentioned above, because GDP is measured using market prices, it is reasonably assumed that what is being measured reflects the true value of output. While for consumer goods and services this is an acceptable assumption, it is not necessarily so for investment goods. Measuring the latter is particularly problematic in economies in which investment by the "private sector" may be made at the behest of government policymakers and/or with the support of a state-dominated financial sector (meaning that the cost of capital is either artificially set or even irrelevant to the investment decision). This situation may be an appropriate description of investments in China's past. Although we can measure the investment component of GDP by examining its selling price, this method may not truly reflect the "value" of that investment from a sound GDP measurement perspective. Thus, we are now focusing on the quality of GDP rather than the raw quantity measure of GDP with respect to the investment component of GDP.

When an investment is undertaken in which its cost (the quantity measure of its GDP contribution) is greater than the present value of the profit stream it generates (its quality measure), we refer to this as value destruction rather than value creation—the latter being what GDP is intended to measure. At the GDP accounting level, we note that the investment would be measured at its purchase price (i.e., the value of its final sale in the year it was purchased). The profit stream would be measured in GDP for later years, year by year, as profits are generated. We immediately see two problems that create a gap between the value or quality of what is produced and the GDP measure. The first problem is that GDP is a gross measure, meaning that we never subtract out from the profit stream the depreciation of the initial investment. Thus, even if, on an undiscounted basis, the stream of profits after depreciation is less than the initial investment, we would not see it reflected in the GDP numbers themselves. The second problem is that GDP accounting, by its very nature, does not provide a present value of the stream of benefits from an investment. Thus, this is a second way in which a value-destroying project would never come to light. In summary, both an investment and its aftermath of profits will boost the raw quantity of GDP over several years without telling us directly whether that investment was in fact creating or destroying value.

These points are not intended to diminish the importance or usefulness of the GDP measure, but simply to point out that the main focus of this measure is on economic activity and employment, not necessarily value creation (or the quality) of GDP.

Figure MF2.3a demonstrates the difference between value maximization and quantity maximization at the single-firm level. A level of investment consistent with point A, in which the return on invested capital just equals its opportunity cost, yields value maximization. Points below A (such as B) may yield higher quantities of GDP but at the cost of value destruction. Value-destroying points below A (such as B) can occur if the cost of capital line is artificially set below its location in Figure MF2.3a, or because credit is directed by government fiat for excessive capital accumulation. As discussed above, GDP accounting implicitly pushes the return on capital line artificially high (above its location in Figure MF2.3a) because it neither depreciates the capital over time nor uses present value methodology.

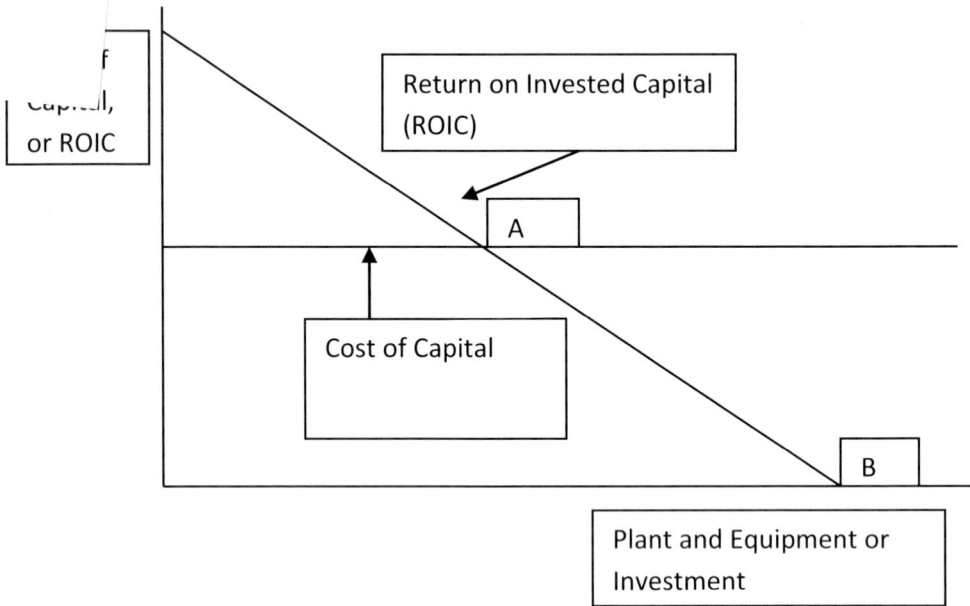

Figure MF2.3a If companies in an economy are investing up to point A, they are creating value (as measured in the triangle in the upper left of the graph. Investing beyond A destroys value since the cost is greater than the return.

Source: Author created.

Prices and GDP Measurement

Several key issues must be discussed within this broad area. First, GDP is ideally measured at market prices (prices we would actually pay for the good or service in a competitive market). Second, we often are interested in real or constant dollar GDP as opposed to nominal GDP. Real GDP attempts to measure output in physical volumes rather than in current dollars, as is the case with "nominal GDP." The latter creates the illusion of increased output when, in fact, only nominal prices have changed (when inflation is present, for example). Third, we may be interested in measuring output using international prices rather than domestic prices. We would describe this as a measure of purchasing power parity (PPP) GDP. Finally, we are interested in measuring GDP through factoring in changes in the price/cost of goods and services that a country exports and imports. For example, if the cost of oil rises in world markets, and our economy is a major importer of oil, our own exports may not command as much in real purchasing power in world markets. We refer to this latter concept as "command GDP."

Price Distortions

Since GDP measures the value of final output, the extent to which prices reflect true value of output is of critical concern. If, for example, an apple is twice the price of a lemon, then the production of one apple should add twice as much to the value of GDP as would one lemon. Implicit in such a calculation is the idea that relative prices (i.e., 2:1) reflect relative values. But this will only be true in markets that operate under competitive conditions. China's entry into the World Trade Organization (WTO) in 2001 accelerated the process of price liberalization that had begun in 1978. Before that, most prices had been set by the state and were thus not market determined. By 2004, Chinese officials estimated that 96 percent of all prices were market determined, but these were mainly consumer prices and did not include the many investment goods that were still subsidized. In addition, prices for certain critical products were still controlled by local price bureaus; these included electricity, transportation, fertilizer, medicine, and fuel.

Government subsidies for the production of goods and services can also distort prices since the resulting prices that consumers or investors finally pay will generally be lower than their market value. This issue, however, has less impact if the government records the subsidy as expenditure and the value is captured under "government uses."[15] Indirect taxes (such as sales taxes) are included in measures of GDP since, if consumers are willing to pay the full price for something (inclusive of taxes), we can assume that the price paid reflects the value. Sales tax, in recent years, including value-added taxes, represents about 7 percent of GDP in China.

Consider another issue in determining GDP accurately: how to factor in the wide range of products and services that are not sold in a market, but are provided by the state—that is, public goods. These goods and services are normally valued at cost, since no market prices are available. In the case of China, this issue is both important and complex. Prior to 1979, all output was produced by the government (central and local) either directly or through state-owned enterprises (SOEs). After 1979, locally owned SOEs and private enterprises tended to move into the production of private sector goods while the central government and other SOEs produced output more closely aligned with public goods (those goods traditionally provided by the public sector).

Furthermore, a significant portion of China's substantial investment occurred as a result of government directives. Accordingly, China tends to have a substantially higher proportion of output which is not resulting from an explicit market-based force, but rather from government decision making (especially policy-directed investments). Therefore, the value assigned to a large fraction of China's GDP may be estimated without reference to any market-determined mechanism. It would be worthwhile to estimate the potential size of this part of GDP. In 2011, China's government spending reached RMB 109,248 (100 million) or about 23 percent of GDP—a share only slightly higher than that of the United States. Two other facts to consider: (1) state-owned units produced approximately 30 percent of China's GDP and, (2) investment in China composed about half of GDP. Even if we assume only a small fraction of both of these outputs (which substantially overlap), it would still be possible to attribute one-third of total output to the public sector. This would compare with the United States, in which about 20 percent of GDP is attributed to the government.[16] In summary, a relatively large part of China's GDP may not reflect value based on conditions of supply and demand, but instead is based upon government purchasing decisions and cost.[17]

Converting Nominal GDP into Real GDP: The Use of Price Indexes

Nominal GDP represents the current dollar (or RMB) value of output. For example, if we only produce ten apples this year and each apple sells for $1, then nominal GDP for this simple economy would be $10. Similarly, if in Year 1 we produce ten apples and in Year 2 we produce ten apples while the price of apples rises from $1 to $1.25, our nominal GDP has risen from $10.00 to $12.50. But has there been any real change in output? No, real output has remained at ten apples. The latter real amount, of course, is of great interest since it is the amount that corresponds to our productivity, our consumption possibilities, and so forth. In one sense, the increase from $10 to $12.50 in earnings is not a very relevant measurement since it simply reflects inflation. We must find a way to remove from nominal GDP the effect of price changes so as to arrive at real GDP. The tool for this is a price index. Price indexes attempt to measure price changes. As such, they not only help measure real GDP, but also help determine intrinsic interest, by allowing us to measure inflation and deflation.

Creating a price index generally involves picking a representative basket of goods and services for a particular year (the "base year"), then measuring how the price of that same basket, that is, containing the same output in the same amounts, evolves over time. If the year 2009 is our base year, and we measure the cost of a basket then at $100, and we find that prices are rising by 3 percent every year, we would then have the price index valued at $109.3 for 2013. It is as if we took a particular basket of goods for the selected base year, removed the price tags from the base year, and reattached new price tags from other years. This method clearly shows the changing cost of the same goods in different years. Typically, we assign an index value of 100 to the base year. Of course, the selection of the base year is very important in determining how the index changes. There are three main choices: (1) a market basket from a past year, (2) a market basket from the current year, or (3) a composite average basket containing a past and a current year.

Let's examine how to use price index numbers P^{2009} and P^{Base} to determine real output Q_{real}^{2013} for 2013. If we let P^{2013} represent the price level for 2013, as measured by a price index, and P^{Base} represent the price index for the base year, then the equation below gives us a definition of nominal GDP in 2013:

$$GDP_{nominal}^{2013} = Q_{real}^{2013} \times P^{2013}$$

By multiplying the ratio P^{Base} / P^{2013} times the equation shown below, we arrive at real GDP for 2013, but expressed in "base year dollars," as seen in the second equation (below). This is how we apply price indexes to interpret real GDP. We would refer to a price index that is used to convert nominal GDP to real GDP as a "GDP price deflator."

$$GDP_{real}^{2013} = Q_{real}^{2013} \times P^{2013} \times \left(\frac{P^{Base}}{P^{2013}} \right)$$

Table 2.5 below provides an example of how the choice of market basket can affect the value of the price index and in turn our measure of inflation.

Table 2.5 The table below shows how we might calculate inflation for a consumer who consumes a market basket of candy and beer. Depending on whether we use an old basket, a new basket, or a mixed (chained) basket for our base year basket, we will come up with higher or lower estimates of inflation.

	Comparison of Different Price Indexes			
Year	*Price of Candy (RMB)*	*Candy Consumed/ Output*	*Price of Beer (RMB)*	*Beer Consumed/ Output*
2009	1.00	70.00	1.00	30.00
2010	1.03	72.80	1.02	31.50
2011	1.06	75.71	1.04	33.08
2012	1.09	78.74	1.06	34.73
2013	1.13	81.89	1.08	36.47
Year	*Base Year: 2000*	*Base Year: 2004*	*Chained Index*	*Simple Square Root*
2009				
2010	2.7000%	2.6919%	2.6990%	2.6960%
2011	2.7020%	2.6940%	2.6990%	2.6980%
2012	2.7041%	2.6960%	2.6991%	2.7001%
2013	2.7061%	2.6981%	2.6991%	2.7021%
Cumulative Growth Rate	11.2586%	11.2237%	11.2412%	11.2411%

Source: Author created.

To see shows how inflation would be measured using price indexes, if Index$_{2013}$ represents one of our price indexes in year 2013, then we could define inflation (Π) between 2012 and 2013 as:

$$\Pi_{2013} = [\text{Index}_{2013} / \text{Index}_{2012}] - 1$$

In Table 2.5, we assume that consumption and output are the same for two goods, candy and beer, which are the only products produced and consumed in this simple economy. Prices grow (inflation) for candy faster than for beer (3 percent per annum versus 2 percent per annum). As a result, demand and consumption grow faster for beer than for candy (5 percent compared to 4 percent). We refer to this phenomenon as a "substitution effect," which impacts how different price indexes perform over time. If we use a 2009 market basket as our base, measured inflation tends to be higher (cumulatively 11.3 percent) than if we had used a 2013 market basket, for which measured inflation is cumulatively 11.2237 percent. If the 2009 basket is used, then we are implicitly assuming that consumers do not adjust their buying patterns (and output correspondingly is a constant). In particular, they continue to consume candy as if relative prices had never changed. Similarly, if we use the 2013 market basket, we are implicitly assuming that consumers had anticipated the price change and, in 2009, shifted their consumption basket toward beer. Of course, neither is an accurate representation, and we infer that the use of the old basket will actually overstate inflation as experienced by the consumer, while the newer market basket will understate it.

To correct for these biases inherent in using a fixed market basket, a "chain price" index can be employed. This index uses a combination of the current period's market basket and the last period's market basket. It is a geometric average of old and new baskets which, in theory, gives an accurate measure of inflation. The third column of the bottom half of Table 2.5 shows how a chain price index measures inflation. The cumulative estimate of 11.2 percent falls between the other two estimates. The last column shows the simple geometric average of the first and second columns. Cumulatively, it provides a good approximation for the "chain index," though for any single year the differences may be larger. Meanwhile, in Table 2.5, we use quantity weights to derive a price index. Note that we could have solved a symmetric problem of determining real GDP by using price weights and allowing output to change. An overestimate of real GDP growth would have occurred if we had used an older market basket.

While the above differences in estimates may seem small, they can, over time, accumulate into large differences. In the United States, many programs, contracts, and benefit schemes are based on measures of inflation—including the U.S. public pension scheme and the social security system. Thus, small differences in the measured inflation rate can make billions of dollars of difference in terms of expenditures or incomes over time. In fact, use of an outdated market-basket price index (such as is used in the U.S. Consumer Price Index) has resulted in estimated overpayments to U.S. social security recipients of US$1 trillion (Boskin, 1996). As a result, efforts to change the price index can be quite politically charged—suggesting that price indexes are not as dry a topic as one might think.

China's Price Indexes

China produces several kinds of price indexes, all of which are compiled by the NBS. Specifically, a Consumer Price Index (CPI) with urban and rural sub-indexes, a Retail Price Index, Industrial Products Price Index, Agricultural Price Index, Raw Materials Price Index, Fixed Asset Price Index, a Real Estate Price Index, and a broad-based GDP Deflator Price Index (based on production) also began in 1985. As of yet, there is not an expenditure-based GDP deflator.

Consumer Price Index (CPI)

The CPI attempts to measure how typical baskets of goods and services, purchased by average consumers, change in price over time. Since consumers are the most significant users of output, this price index is the most commonly used. In contrast to the United States, China's CPI measures price changes not just for urban households but also for rural households. This, of course, reflects China's substantial rural population.[18] China provides both an old-style market-basket index for the CPI (base year 1985) and a chain-weighted index. It does this by conducting monthly surveys across 226 counties and cities, using 1,000 workers to survey 110,000 households (of which about 65 percent are rural, 35 percent are urban). Efforts are made to survey purchases made at active marketplaces and department stores, and to conduct surveys consistently from month to month in terms of location, time of day, and market participants. Prices of domestic goods and services, as well as imported goods, are also included in the CPI. The inclusion of imports highlights that the CPI focuses on what consumers actually buy, regardless of the source. Figure 2.6 shows the CPI inflation in China from 1986 to the present, and suggests substantial variation in the measured inflation rate with a peak inflation of over 28 percent in February 1989.

An appropriate market basket for the CPI should include a balanced representation of how urban consumers actually spend their income. Figure 2.7 compares what Chinese consumers buy as a share of expenditure compared to Americans. Key differences emerge; Chinese spend a disproportionate amount of their income on food and beverages compared to Americans, while Americans spend a disproportionate amount on rent (actual or imputed) for housing, and fuel. Americans also devote a good deal of their budget to transportation (both automobiles and gasoline).

The GDP Deflator

Unlike the CPI, the GDP deflator is a price index which measures price changes on all output produced by a country. While the CPI focuses on the consumer, the GDP deflator represents price movements for all classes of output: consumption, investment, exports, and government. It excludes

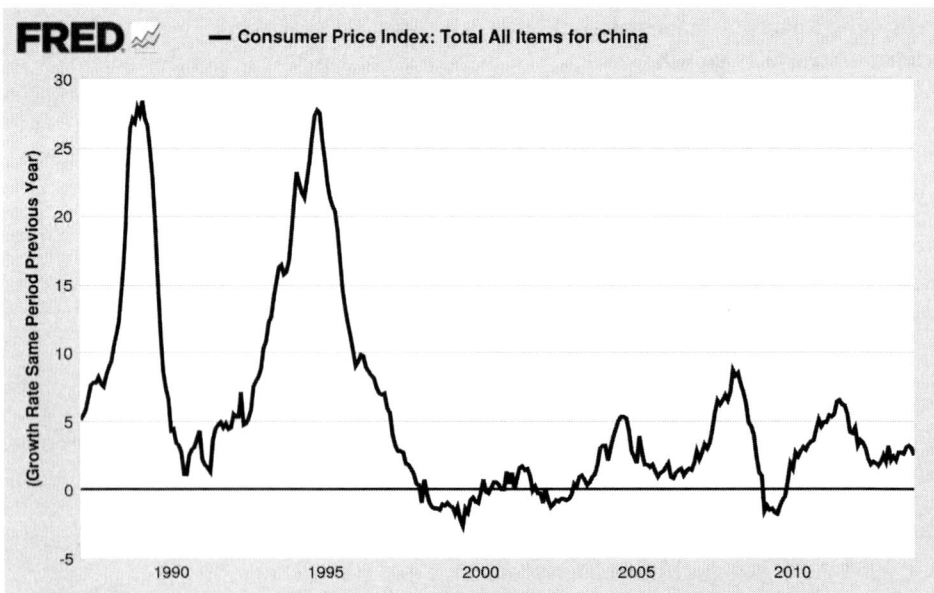

Figure 2.6 China's inflation rate has come down substantially from double-digit growth rates in the 1980s and 1990s.

Source: FRED, Federal Reserve Economic Data, Federal Reserve Bank of St. Louis: Consumer Price Index: Total All Items for China; Organisation for Economic Co-operation and Development. 2014 research.stlouisfed.org

Expenditure Shares as a Basis for the CPI market basket

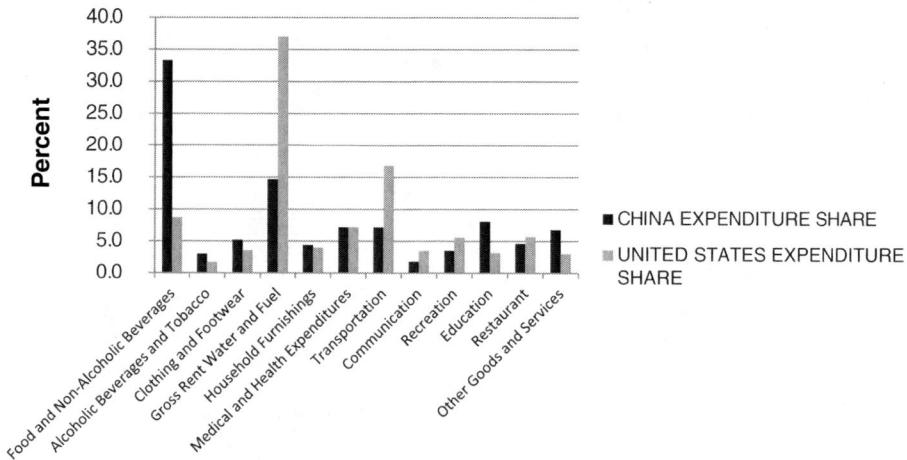

Figure 2.7 Here we see expenditure shares for Chinese and U.S. citizens. Some key differences emerge. Chinese spend a disproportionate amount of their income on food and beverages compared to Americans, while Americans spend a disproportionate amount on rent (actual or imputed) on housing and fuel. Americans also devote a good deal of their budget to transportation (automobiles and gasoline).

Source: United States Bureau of Labor Services; Feenstra et al., 2012.

imports since these are not produced domestically. In this sense, the GDP deflator is the broadest measure of a country's inflation or deflation. China established base years every five years beginning in 1952, then switched to every ten years beginning in 1970, with the most recent base year being 2005. In 2005, the NBS launched its first national economic survey in order to create base year data. Determining the GDP deflator has been a complex and difficult process. It has combined outright measures of volume increases as well as use of available price deflators to apply to particular sectors (e.g., agricultural price indexes to be applied to the agricultural sector). The 2005 base year generally does not attempt to establish base year quantities, but rather uses separate price indexes (such as the CPI) to deflate nominal output for specific sectors. Though a GDP deflator is not published per se, it is implicit in official estimates of nominal GDP and real GDP. It is also still only available on an annual basis. Formally we can state that:

$$\text{Index}_{\text{Real GDP}} = \text{Nominal GDP/Real GDP}$$

Figure 2.8 shows the implicit GDP deflator. Comparing Figure 2.8 with Figure 2.6, we see substantial differences in measured inflation. Between 1985 and 2009, estimated inflation averaged twice as high using the CPI compared to the GDP deflator (this difference is too large to be explained on the basis of differing definitions of inflation); but in recent years, the GDP deflator showed larger inflation than the CPI (again about twice as large). If the GDP deflator has been underestimated (and the CPI is the truer estimate) then China's real GDP growth is being seriously overestimated and in recent years the reverse would be true. Clearly, more work needs to be done to improve one or both measures of inflation in China.

Other Price Indexes

China's other price indexes—such as the retail price index and the industrial and raw materials price indexes—provide price information at production stages before final sale to consumers. As

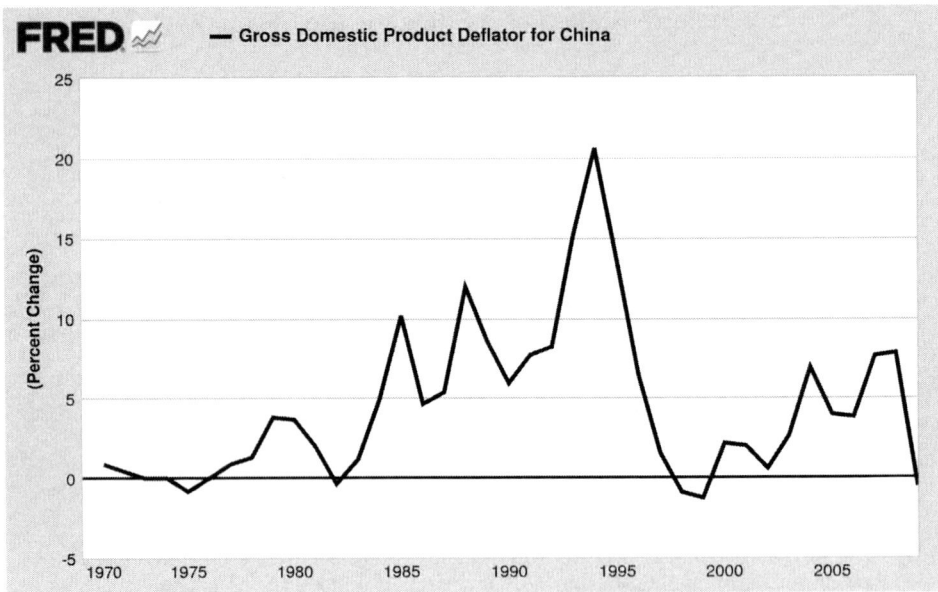

Figure 2.8 China's GDP deflator is still under development and can be derived by dividing nominal GDP by Real GDP.

Source: FRED, Federal Reserve Economic Data, Federal Reserve Bank of St. Louis: Gross Domestic Product Deflator for China; Organisation for Economic Co-operation and Development. 2014 research.stlouisfed.org

such, they are similar to the Production Price Index (PPI)[19] which provides information at crude, intermediate, and finished good production stages in the United States. These indexes differ from the CPI in that they do not cover the prices of services, distribution costs, or taxes at the point of sale to consumers.

Price Index Issues

There are several aspects in which China hopes to improve the accuracy of its indexes. One is by the greater use of chain-type indexes. This would provide more updated market baskets and would take into account the substitution impact of price changes for goods and services. Another goal is to expand coverage of the services sector. Currently, both the CPI and the GDP deflator fall very short in their coverage of services—an area of rapid growth in recent years. Finally, coverage of export and import prices could be improved substantially. The trade sector continues to be treated as a residual measure rather than a sector in and of itself. Ideally, it would be independently measured for price effects.

Case Study 2.4: China's Unemployment Rate

China's official unemployment rate (registered unemployed in urban areas) was 4.1 percent in 2012. Over the past decade, it has not deviated from that number by more than half a percentage point (see Figure CS2.4a). Most analysts believe this number seriously underestimates actual unemployment nationwide. The method of collection is based on the number of people who register themselves as unemployed at local urban employment offices. To register, one needs to be a local resident, holding an official identification card (*hukou*) and many unemployed do not have a local *hukou*, but a *hukou* from their home town or village. Giles et al. (2005) estimate that China's actual unemployment in 2002, for example, was closer to 14 percent (compared to the official number of 4 percent). The correlation between economic growth and the unemployment rate (referred to as Okun's Law) also seems quite low—only about 18 percent (negative)—close to half of the correlation found in the United States. Since 2002, China's economic growth has been quite strong, suggesting a decline in the unemployment rate from the Giles estimate to a number closer to 11 percent today.

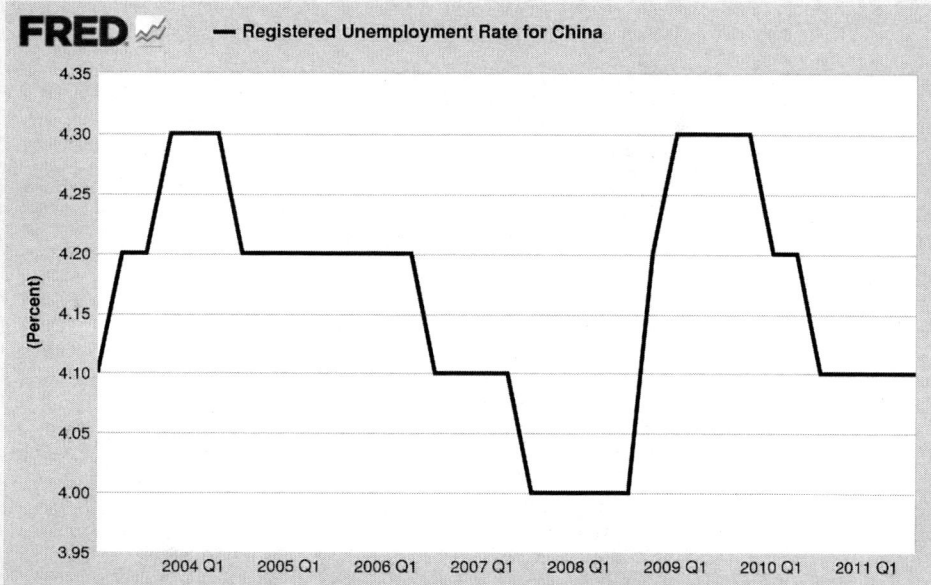

Figure CS2.4a The lack of variation in China's official unemployment rate suggests that it is not a very reliable measure of actual unemployment.

Source: FRED, Federal Reserve Economic Data, Federal Reserve Bank of St. Louis: Registered Unemployment Rate for China; Organisation for Economic Co-operation and Development. 2014 research.stlouisfed.org

A preferable method of collecting unemployment information is through surveys, rather than self-reporting by individuals. The U.S. Bureau of Labor Statistics conducts monthly surveys to collect employment and unemployment statistics. Nevertheless, the number of unemployed in the United States is likely also underestimated due to methodological flaws. In the United States, individuals are asked if they are looking for employment. If they respond that they are not looking for work, then they are not included among the unemployed. Thus, in the United States, "discouraged" workers are undercounted in the unemployment statistics.

We can classify the unemployed into three different types: cyclical, structural, and frictional. Cyclical refers to those who have lost their jobs due to the business cycle; that is, a recession. Structural refers to those who have lost their work due to being in the wrong place or having the wrong skills while the economy is undergoing a fundamental transformation. Frictional relates to those who have left one job but have good prospects of finding another; that is, those who are between jobs. The latter kind of unemployment is actually considered a good thing, in its own way. It is one sign of a healthy labor market to see individuals matching their talents and tastes with evolving job opportunities. Cyclical or structural unemployment, on the other hand, are concerning for governments. Most governments feel pressured to respond to these types of unemployment with short-term or longer-term supply side (structural) policies.

China's causes of unemployment are complex, and often work in complicated ways. For example, the *hukou* system adds a certain structural rigidity, but at the same time allows employers in urban areas to hire workers as part of an informal economy (at lower cost). The massive movement of labor from rural to urban areas represents a frictional source of unemployment, but the movement ultimately (in the long run) reduces the structural unemployment rate. Investment in China remains government-mandated, which reduces the impact of the most volatile source of demand (and unemployment) in advanced economies. China's relatively low level of consumption, however, removes a stable source of demand as a basis for employment—particularly in the area of services. Table CS2.4a summarizes some of these factors which impact China's unemployment rate.

It should be no surprise that China has a relatively high unemployment rate given that it has experienced all types of unemployment, both historically and currently. The massive restructuring of state-owned enterprises (SOEs) in the 1980s and 1990s created a great deal of structural unemployment. The movement from a rural-based economy to the urban-based economy occurring today is another source of structural unemployment. The recent global financial crisis, coupled with the ongoing slowdown in Europe, was an external shock (cyclical) that hit those employed in export-related industries particularly hard. And of course, the great mobility of China's labor force (migrant workers) is an indication of a very liquid labor market—which gives rise to frictional unemployment.

Table CS2.4a China's unemployment rate is a unique combination of frictional, cyclical, and structural factors which work in complex ways both to increase and reduce the number of unemployed workers.

Type of Unemployment	Increases Unemployment Rate	Decreases Unemployment Rate
Frictional	Dynamic economy and "ambitious" labor force, massive labor migration to urban areas	Unemployment benefits do not exist
Cyclical	Continued heavy reliance on exports, consumption levels still low	Strong economic growth, government-mandated investment
Structural	*Hukou* system, monopsony power of firms in labor markets, major shifts from agricultural to services and manufacturing, mismatch between skills	*Hukou* system, absence of a social safety net, highly mobile labor force, "flexible" labor force, skill enhancement through education

Source: Author created.

Alternative Measures of GDP

Unaccounted Output

The United Nation's System of National Accounts (SNA) stipulates that an exhaustive measure of GDP should include all transactions occurring between a willing buyer and willing seller. In addition, not only should output produced for external sale be included, but output for internal use should also be included (e.g., a farmer's consumption of some of his own crop). Nevertheless, some of the output produced in a country is simply never accounted for. This activity is referred to as "the informal economy" or, in China, *fei zhenggui jingji* (非正规经济 meaning "off the radar screen"). In other words, these transactions are not accounted for via a nation's typical data collection infrastructure of the tax collection ministry, central bank, labor ministry, or the central statistical or census bureau. As such, they are not included in GDP.[20]

Unrecorded output is economic activity which takes place but is not recorded in a nation's statistical offices because officials decide that accurate data is too difficult to estimate or survey methods are still too inadequate for better coverage. A good example of unrecorded output is a spouse who stays at home and does housework (a homemaker). While this activity is both valuable (e.g., caring for children) and time-consuming, it is not recorded as GDP since no explicit market transaction allows for its measurement and estimation. Another type of activity is unreported output. In this case, the official data collectors would actually like to record the economic activity, but individuals and corporations choose not to report it. This might be for purposes of tax avoidance or because the activity is illegal. A repairman, for example, who works "on the side," may choose not to report this income so as to avoid paying taxes. A final category of ex-GDP activity is illegal activities. Although GDP attempts to measure "goods and services," according to the SNA's exhaustive GDP definition, "bads" must also be included as long as the participating buyer and seller willingly undertake the transaction. Illegal gambling, drug sales, prostitution, and counterfeiting of goods are all included, even though most countries seek to eliminate these activities and replace them with legal endeavors. In most countries, illegal activities as a share of GDP would be less than 1 percent.

A common strategy for estimating the size of the informal economy is to examine two separate estimates (often by different agencies or ministries) of the same economic quantity, then infer that if a large difference exists, it corresponds to the informal portion of the economy. For example, we could estimate national savings from national income data, but calculate changes in wealth (which amounts to the same things as national savings) from the banking and financial sector. After taking into account various accounting issues, we might infer that some of the difference represents a gap between the mistaken measure and the true measure—that is, the informal economy. Other approaches involve calculating alternate measures of output (such as electricity use) and inferring what actual GDP might be. Another approach examines cash transactions in an economy, since these are often undertaken to avoid taxes and regulation.

In the case of China, there is a wide range of estimates for the size of the shadow economy. Cai Fang et al. (2009) estimate the share of all workers in the informal economy in 2005 at nearly 53 percent. These are mostly migrant workers whose output may actually be recorded in GDP but who are working outside of regulated labor markets. Meanwhile, Schneider (2007) estimates the size of China's shadow economy at a relatively small 17 percent of GDP in 2004–05. This compares with 15 percent for OECD economies, and 8 percent for the United States. In part, the figures in China may reflect the government's direct or indirect involvement in many parts of the economy, which would make "hiding in the shadows" difficult.[21]

MACRO FINANCE INSIGHT 2.4: STAKEHOLDERS IN THE MACROECONOMY

Who exactly are the stakeholders in an economy? That is, which individuals and entities can lay claim to the economic value that is created within an economy?

For a private firm, we make a distinction between shareholders (those who legally own shares in the company and have a claim on its net income or profits) and other stakeholders (those that ultimately have claims on either the revenues or even the products of the company). Specifically, if I own shares in a company, then I am a shareholder. Creditors, employees, the government, and, of course, shareholders are all considered stakeholders. A broader definition of stakeholder for a corporation also includes customers and suppliers. In general, stakeholders include all those who have an economic interest in seeing that the corporation creates value and is successful.

We often argue that a publicly owned company with a broad shareholder base has a number of advantages. One specific advantage is that, it is in the shareholders' interest to see that the other stakeholders are rewarded efficiently. How does this work? Shareholders are the last to receive compensation for their investment in a corporation. Prior to their receipt of dividends or capital gains, they must see to it that the customers are satisfied, workers are content with their wages and benefits packages, that debt-to-creditors are honored, that suppliers are paid for inputs and services, and that the government is paid in taxes. Otherwise, the firm risks losing its workers and suppliers, or going bankrupt. Only then does the residual economic value created get distributed to shareholders. Since shareholders control how the company is managed and are also the last to get paid, they have the ability and the motivation to ensure that the other stakeholders are satisfied efficiently.

Of course, the division of benefits and control is not always neat and well defined. Conflicts of interest can exist between managers (treated here as a sub-category of employees) and shareholders; inside shareholders and minority shareholders, bondholders and shareholders; or workers and their representatives and shareholders. Often, a single stakeholder class may expropriate value at the expense of overall economic value creation of the entity.

Table MF2.4a presents a breakdown of how CMM, our fictional company discussed earlier, provides value at each stage of operations to different classes of stakeholders. Only after all the other stakeholders are satisfied can the main stakeholder, the shareholder, be rewarded with profits and dividends.

Table MF2.4a At each stage of the company's operations, stakeholders have an interest in the company's success. Only after all of those interests are satisfied are the shareholders rewarded with profits. But in China, the government serves several stakeholder roles leading to a conflict of interest.

		Stakeholders	
Revenues	US$2.98 (billions)	Customers	
Domestic sales	$2.94		
Export sales	$0.04		
Costs of production	US$2.27 (billions)		
Materials	$1.4	Suppliers	
Wages, salaries	$0.87	Employees and managers	
Depreciation	$0.20		
Operating income	$0.509		
Interest to bondholders	$0.09	Creditors	
Taxes	$0 (On "tax holiday")	The government	
After-tax profits	$0.42	**Shareholders**	

Source: Author created.

In a modern economy with laws and institutional arrangements, different citizens and different entities have a formal claim on economic value. So who are the stakeholders in an economy? As we have just described, employees in the United States lay claim to a larger share of national income than do employees in China. Conversely, owners of capital receive a greater share of income in China than in the United States. Another difference is that government's share of enterprise ownership remains much higher in China than in the United States. China also is a major stakeholder in its largest banks. As such, the Chinese government is simultaneously a shareholder in the economy, a creditor to the national economy, and a collector of taxes—thus, it has a large role as a stakeholder. Unlike a single individual firm in the United States, which must compete with other firms for labor, supplies, and financing, a large comprehensive stakeholder such as the Chinese government can exert monopsony power over the acquisition of such resources. For example, Dong and Putterman (2000) suggest that, through the 1980s, the Chinese government paid a real wage less than the marginal product of labor—an observation consistent with monopsony power. The Chinese banking system has consistently paid interest rates below the market cost of funds. Also, China's SOEs do have first claims to the resources of suppliers. Thus, monopsony power may lead to overuse of resources in the sectors of the economy where the state has such power, causing broader problems related to equity and fairness.

A vast literature suggests a misallocation of resources at the firm level when principals and agents have inconsistent goals, when conflicts of interest arise, or when there is asymmetric information between shareholders and other stakeholders. In China, optimal allocation of resources can break down due to monopsony power on the part of the government, and conflicts of interest can arise when the government acts as shareholder, creditor, employer, regulator, and taxing authority all at once.

Purchasing Power Parity GDP

Naturally, a country measures its own GDP in its own currency. The United States measures the value of its output in U.S. dollars and China in *renminbi*. But the need often arises to compare or create a more standardized measure of a country's output. This involves applying an exchange rate, for example, US$/RMB, to China's GDP in order to calculate a dollar measure of China's output. Although this may seem straightforward, in fact several distortions can arise. First, the exchange rate, itself, may be overvalued or undervalued. That is to say, its value at the point in time when the GDP conversion occurs may not be the same as its long-run, or fundamental, value. Real economic activity determines the fundamental value of a nation's currency over the long run, but short-run fluctuations (e.g., shocks in financial markets) can cause the exchange rate to deviate from its long-run value. The second problem relates to relative prices in an economy. It is very unlikely that two economies have the same relative prices for all goods and services. For example, the relative price of a haircut to a steak dinner may be significantly different in China than in the United States. Yet in applying a single exchange rate to aggregate GDP, we are implicitly assuming that relative prices are the same between two nations.

Table 2.6 provides examples of how these two problems can create distortions. We first examine output, observing that (in real terms of this hypothetical example), China's output is exactly 75 percent of U.S. output. In U.S. dollar terms, U.S. output is US$15,000 while Chinese output in RMB terms is RMB 93,750. There would only be one exchange rate which would give us a U.S. dollar GDP for China which is 75 percent of US$15,000—RMB 8.33: US$1. If the exchange rate happens to be any other rate (which it might very well be) then we would not have an accurate measure of the two nations' relative real GDP. Even if we allow relative prices to be the same in each country (e.g., allow the price of coal in China to be RMB 500), we would encounter the same problem; in that case, an RMB/US$ exchange rate of 10 would be required.

Let's examine how relative prices make a difference (i.e., 2:1 in the United States and 4:1 in China for the relative price of wheat to coal). Assume that we use an exchange rate that will accurately convert the RMB price of wheat in China into the dollar price of wheat in the United States, i.e., an exchange rate of RMB 10:US$1. This gives a U.S. dollar value of wheat production of US$7,500 or exactly 75 percent of the value of U.S. wheat production. However, if we apply the same exchange rate to coal production, our measure of China's coal production will, in U.S. dollar

Table 2.6 Purchasing power parity GDPs are intended to avoid some pitfalls in comparing GDPs in a common currency. Problems will still arise, however, when relative prices differ substantially—especially for goods that are not traded, such as services.

	U.S. Price	*U.S. Output*	*China Price*	*China Output*
Wheat	US$100	100 bushels	RMB 1,000	75 bushels
Coal	US$50	100 tons	RMB 250	75 tons

Source: Author created.

*hina GDP: PPP Value vs. Actual Exchange Rate Value

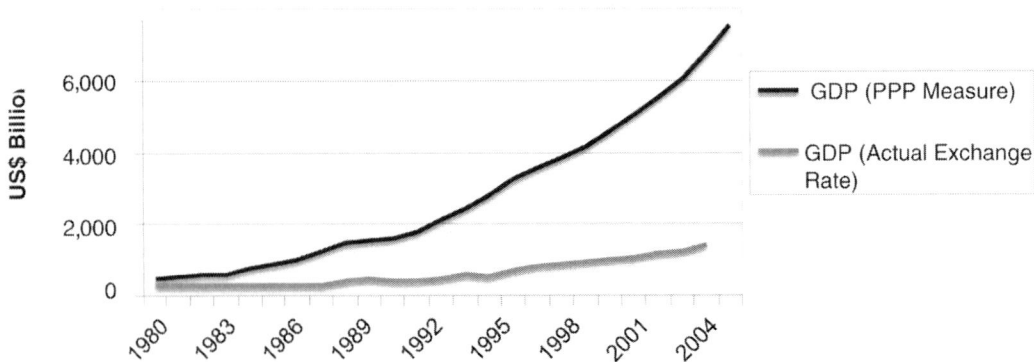

Figure 2.9 China's PPP measure of GDP is substantially higher than GDP converted at the market (official) exchange rate.

Source: National Bureau of Statistics, 2012.

terms, be far too low because of differing relative prices. Ideally, we would apply U.S. dollar prices to China's real output, i.e.,

$$(US\$100 \times 75) + (US\$50 \times 75) = US\$11,250$$

which would result in a measure of China's output that is 75 percent of United States' output. But this can be difficult to achieve, and applying the current exchange rate is unlikely to accomplish this task. Efforts are made, however, at measuring GDP in this ideal way, and the resulting measures are referred to as "purchasing power measures of GDP."

As shown in Figure 2.9, PPP GDP for China is substantially larger than GDP measured at the actual exchange rate. This difference has become larger both in absolute as well as in percentage terms, and reflects both an undervaluation of the RMB relative to the U.S. dollar as well as substantial differences in relative prices. Labor-intensive services, in particular, are substantially lower in price relative to other forms of output in China. When this type of output is assigned prices based on international markets, the U.S. dollar value of Chinese GDP rises substantially. In 2003, estimated PPP GDP for China was about US$6.8 trillion, while GDP based purely on a conversion using the actual exchange rate was only be about US$1.4 trillion. In the former case, China's GDP would be about 62 percent of U.S. GDP, while in the latter, only about 13 percent.

Command GDP

A final measure of GDP to consider is *command GDP*. The conventional measure of GDP used around the world emphasizes the production aspect of GDP rather than the consumption possibilities created by output. This focus probably relates to the tight link between production and employment; and for most countries, employment is a central concern. Specifically, a country that produces output will see the value of that output change depending on how much output it can import (or "command") from the rest of the world. For example, a country which experiences an improvement ʲ⸱ ⁱⁿˢ of trade in domestically grown coffee can now import more foreign machinery for every ʳᶠᵉᵉ that it exports—thus enjoying an improvement in its command GDP. This improve- ᵈ not typically be measured, since traditional real GDP measures negate or offset the improvement so as not to distort the accounting measure of production. In this simple example, the number of coffee bags produced has not changed, but the price of the coffee has improved in world markets. If we wish to shift the focus from production and employment toward consumption and economic well-being, then command GDP offers a preferable measure. Remember, however, under the SNA, command GDP is not given as the main GDP presentation—although some countries do present a separate measure for command GDP.

A country's terms of trade (TOT) can change for two reasons: Either the exchange rate changes between two countries, or the relative price of imports and exports changes. The equation below shows the relationship between the TOT and the exchange rate adjusted for imports and exports. Assume that China exports machinery and imports oil. If either the RMB strengthens—that is, the ratio RMB:US$ falls—or the ratio of the price of oil to the price of machinery falls, then China's terms of trade and command GDP will improve. In other words, China must export fewer machines to acquire each barrel of oil; or alternatively, if it exports the same amount of machines as before, it can import and consume more barrels of oil after the improvement in the terms of trade.

$$TOT_{\frac{MACHINERY}{OIL}} = \frac{RMB}{US\$} \times \frac{P^{US\$}_{OIL\,(IMPORTS)}}{P^{RMB}_{MACHINERY\,(EXPORTS)}}$$

In fact, China's exchange rate has alternated between being fixed for prolonged periods and experiencing a controlled appreciation since 1996, but it has fluctuated against the other major currencies in tandem with the U.S. dollar. In addition, relative prices between China and other countries are not static. One estimate of how the TOT has changed would be to examine a very closely related measure, the real exchange rate.[22] Figure 2.10 provides an estimate of the real exchange rate (weighted by

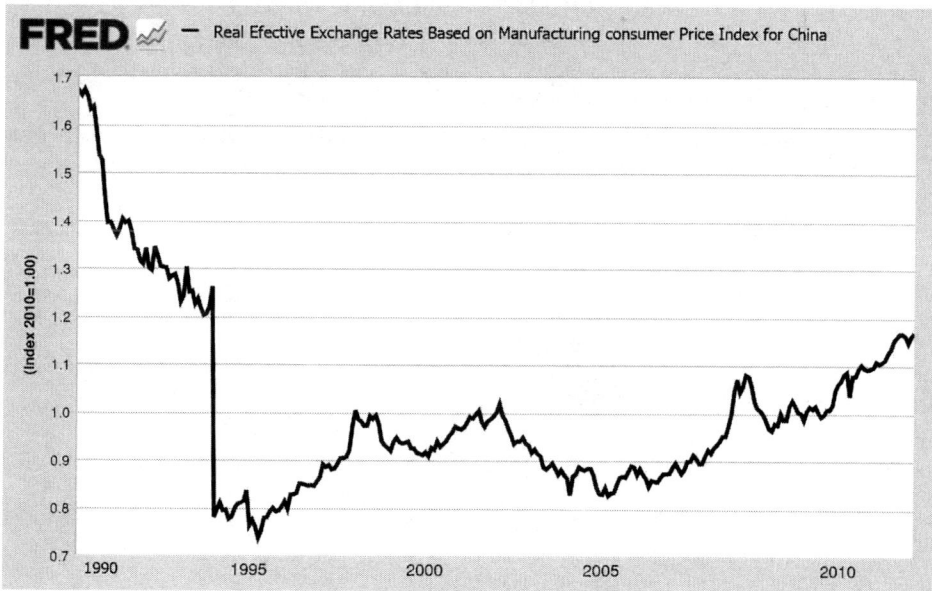

Figure 2.10 In real terms the price of manufactured goods has fallen considerably until 1995. But with the gradual strengthening of the RMB starting in 2005, the real price of China's manufactured goods to the outside world has started to rise. This would imply a larger "command" GDP for China.

Source: FRED, Federal Reserve Economic Data, Federal Reserve Bank of St. Louis: Real Effective Exchange Rates Based on Manufacturing Consumer Price Index for China; Organisation for Economic Co-operation and Development. 2014 research.stlouisfed.org

manufactured goods data) for all of China's major trading partners. The figure suggests a substantial real appreciation of the RMB (a smaller left-hand side in the above terms of trade equation) over the past decade, but with considerable variation. Thus, we can infer that China's command GDP has, in fact, grown faster over this period than China's published GDP.

Challenging Questions for China (and the Student): Chapter 2

1. Go to FRED (the Federal Reserve Economic Database) and find three different measures of Chinese GDP. Define each measure based on its frequency (quarterly vs. annual), basis for measure (e.g., expenditure approach), and whether it is expressed in real or nominal terms.
2. Explain why during an economic downturn, U.S. GDP might actually be underestimated while Chinese GDP might actually be overestimated.
3. Using the table below (mind the footnote at the bottom of the table):
   a. Calculate GDP and GNP based on a method used primarily in China. Identify the method.
   b. Calculate GDP and GNP based on a method used primarily in the United States. Identify the method.
4. Assume that China's entire tertiary sector (services) is non-traded. Use the share of services in China's GDP statistics presented in this chapter to help answer some of the following questions.
   a. Is China's relative price of services to primary and secondary output prices higher or lower than in the United States (use your good judgment)?
   b. Assume that the exchange rate is at purchasing power parity (PPP) for traded goods. If we use that exchange rate to convert Chinese GDP into U.S. dollars, how would that distort your estimate of Chinese GDP given your answer in (a)?
   c. Suggest a better way to approach the problem of converting Chinese GDP into U.S. dollars.
   d. Observe Data (PPPTT2CNA618NUPN) in FRED. How does this approach compare to your answer in (c)? Apply the most recent PPP exchange rate found in this series to nominal Chinese GDP. How much larger is China's US$ GDP compared to when you use the actual exchange rate for the same period?
5. If a 2,000 square foot apartment in New York sells for US$1.5 million, what is its per square meter RMB price and total RMB price. Be sure to use proper Chinese numerical units.
6. Using the table found below:
   a. Explain the classical relationship between other stakeholders and shareholders in a capitalist system.
   b. Explain the relationship among the various stakeholders in China. Compare and contrast to your answer in (a).
   c. Using one of the key drivers for China presented in Chapter 1, explain the difficulties of managing a mixed-market economy such as China's.

Income Statement for a Typical Firm in an Economy*

		STAKEHOLDERS
Revenues	US$ 2.98 (billions)	Customers
Domestic sales	2.94	
Export sales	.04	
Costs of production	US$ 2.27	
Materials	1.4	Suppliers
Depreciation	US$ .20	
Operating income	US$ .509	

		STAKEHOLDERS
Interest to bondholders	US$ .09	Creditors
Taxes	US$ 0 (On "tax holiday")	The government
After tax profits	US$ .42	**SHAREHOLDERS**

*Assume this is a 50/50 joint venture with a foreign company and that inventories decreased during the period by 0.14.

Notes

1. We should not confuse the flow of housing services in a given year with the production of a housing (residential) unit in that year. The latter is included under *I* (an investment). As to whether this suggests double counting, we note that, under a Net National Product measure (NNP), we also depreciate the housing stock. Thus, the difference between the flow of housing services and its depreciation represents a net flow of housing services. The gross measure, however, includes the creation of the residence as a part of GDP and, in the periods that follow, as a housing service under GDP.
2. In this case, we could think of the government both producing and using the good and service.
3. We use the "≡" when presenting a definition or an identity rather than an arithmetically derived relationship.
4. China's data based on 2011; the United States, 2012.
5. In fact, China inherited a measure, the Gross Value of Output (GVO), from the Soviet Union, which did exactly that. This measure is no longer in use.
6. Comparisons of productivities in Figure 2.5 also reveal "comparative advantages" (see, e.g., Krugman and Obstfeld, 2009). Specifically, we see a comparative advantage for the United States in the primary sector and for China in the secondary sector.
7. Though taxes paid by both workers and corporations might be considered as "income" for the government, we are more interested in examining the link between the direct producers of output (the factors of production) and their earnings. For this reason, pre-tax wages and profits are typically used in the Income approach to measuring GDP.
8. As discussed below, input–output tables are one means by which income data for China can be obtained. These tables, however, are only published every five years.
9. Though the product of labor and the wage rate is the total wage bill. If the supply of labor is sufficiently large, the wage will be driven down to the inelastic portion of the demand-for-labor curve, causing total employee compensation to actually decline.
10. In Chapter 5, we discuss this paradox in more detail.
11. This approach continues even today but in a diminished form—China's Five-Year Plans are discussed in later chapters.
12. We include the Income approach, since it is a variation on value-added measurement in which factors of production could be thought of as providing value.
13. Countries with higher per capita incomes can generally afford more leisure time than can low per capita income economies. However, among those high per capita economies, different choices are made with respect to vacation time and hours worked per week, suggesting that sacrificing GDP in favor of more leisure is perceived as welfare enhancing in some but not all economies.
14. The Gini coefficient is an index measuring the gap between a perfectly equal distribution and the actual income distribution of a country. A measurement of 0 would correspond to perfect income equality and a measurement of 1, perfect inequality. For example, in the latter case, a small percentage of the population would be receiving all of the economy's income.
15. From a purely accounting perspective, we could think of the subsidy as the government purchasing part of the good or service on behalf of the consumer or investor. From an economic perspective, however, to the extent that the subsidy distorts production and consumption decisions, our GDP measure would also be distorted.
16. Both in China and the United States, governments not only supply but also purchase—and these purchases are included as government use.
17. Even though the government pays for something based on its cost, the price which that output would command in the market could actually be higher or lower.
18. About 60 percent of China's population is classified as rural; in the United States it is only about 2 percent.
19. The Producer Price Index was formerly known in the United States as the Wholesale Price Index.
20. Theft, for example, would be excluded from a GDP measure since one is not willingly robbed.
21. For both countries, the proportion identified as self-employed remains close to 10 percent. How well this sector's output is measured in each country determines the size of the shadow economy.

22. The real exchange rate takes into account the relative importance of different kinds of imports and exports with different countries. A variety of measures for relative prices are used, including export–import prices, unit labor costs, overall prices, etc. As a result, there are a variety of real exchange rate measures.

References

Boskin, Michael. 1996. *Toward a More Accurate Measure of the Cost of Living (The Boskin Commission Report)*. Washington, DC, December 4.

Cai Fang, Du Yang, and Meiyan Wang. 2009. "Employment and Inequality Outcomes in China." Institute of Population and Labour Economy. China Academy of Social Sciences. http://www.oecd.org/employment/emp/42546043.pdf

Cai Fang, and Meiyan Wang. 2002. "How Fast and How Far Can China's GDP Grow?" *China and World Economy* 5 (May): 9–15.

Chow, Gregory. 2006. "Are Chinese Official Statistics Reliable?" *CESifo Economic Studies* 52(2): 396–414.

Dong, Lihua. 2006. Quarterly GDP Estimation in China, in Series 9 of "Research of Methodological Issues in National Accounts—China," presented at OECD on December 2, 2009. www.oecd.org/std/na/44128807.ppt

Dong, Xiao-yuan and Louis Putterman (2000). "Pre-reform industry and state monopsony in China," *Journal of Comparative Economics* 28(1): 32–60.

Eurostat, International Monetary Funds (IMF), The Organisation for Economic Co-operation and Development (OECD), United Nations (UN), and World Bank. 1993. System of National Accounts. Brussels, New York, Paris, Washington, DC. http://unstats.un.org/unsd/nationalaccount/

Feenstra, Robert C., Hong Ma, Neary, J. Peter, and D.S. Prasada Rao. 2012. "Who Shrunk China? Puzzles in the Measurement of Real GDP." *The Economic Journal* 123(573): 1100–29.

Fernald, John, Israel Malkin, and Mark Spiegel. 2013. "On the Reliability of China's Output Figures." Federal Reserve Bank of San Francisco Pacific Basin Letter, March 25.

Giles, John, Albert Park, and Juwei Zhang. 2005. "What Is China's True Unemployment Rate?" *China Economic Review* 16(2): 149–70.

He, Xinhua. 2010. "Noteworthy Discrepancies in China's GDP Accounting." *China World Economy* 18(4): 88–102.

Holz, Carsten A. 2004. "Deconstructing China's GDP Statistics." *China Economic Review* 15(2): 164–202.

———. 2008. "China's 2004 Economic Census and 2006 Benchmark Revision of GDP Statistics: More Questions Than Answers?" *China Quarterly* 193 (March): 150–63.

Huang, Langhui. 2005. "Compilation Method and Quality Control of CPI in China." Statistical Commission and United Nations Economic Commission for Europe (UNECE), March 10.

Keidel, Albert. 2001. "China's GDP Expenditure Accounts." *China Economic Review* 12(4): 355–67.

Klein, Lawrence R., and Sulyman Ozmucur. 2003. "The Estimation of China's Economic Growth Rate." *Journal of Economic and Social Measurement* 28(4): 187–202.

Koch-Weser, Iacob N. 2013. *The Reliability of Chinese Economic Data: An Analysis of National Output*. Washington, DC: U.S.–China Economic and Security Review Commission, January 28.

Krugman, Paul R., and Maurice Obstfeld. 2009. *International Economics: Theory and Policy,* 8th edn. Boston: Pearson Addison-Wesley.

Lin, Jintai, Da Pan, Steven J. Davis, Qiang Zhang, Kebin He, Can Wang, David G. Streets, Donald J. Wuebbles, and Dabo Guan. 2014. "China's International Trade and Air Pollution in the United States." *Proceedings of the National Academy of Sciences*. doi: 10.1073/pnas.1312860111.

Lin, Z.X. and M.S.H. Shih. 2002. "Earnings Management in Economic Downturns and Adjacent Periods: Evidence from the 1990–1991 Recession," Working Paper. Singapore: National University of Singapore. http://papers.ssrn.com/sol3/papers.cfm?abstract_id=331400

Liu, Fujiang. 2000. "Brief Introduction on Labor Force, Retail Sales and Price Statistics of China." Workshop on Key Economic Indicators in China, Bangkok, May 22.

Maddison, Angus, and Harry X. Wu. 2008. "Measuring China's Economic Performance." *World Economics* 9(2 April–June): 13.

National Bureau of Statistics of China (NBS). 2012. Table 2.1 and Tables 2.16–2.18. In *China Statistical Yearbook*. Beijing: China Statistics Press.

Organisation for Economic Co-operation and Development (OECD) Working Group on Privatization and Corporate Governance of State Owned Assets. 2009. *State-Owned Enterprises in China: Reviewing the Evidence*. OECD Occasional Paper, January 26.

Orlik, Tom. 2012. *Understanding China's Economic Indicators*. Upper Saddle River, NJ: FT Press.

Ou, Pao-san. 1946. "A New Estimate of China's National Income." *Journal of Political Economy* 54(6): 547–54.

Prasad, Eswar, ed. 2004. *China's Growth and Integration into the World Economy: Prospects and Challenges*. Occasional Paper 232. Washington, DC: International Monetary Fund.

Rawski, T. 2001. "What is Happening to China's GDP Statistics?" *China Economic Review* 12(4): 347–54.

Schneider, Friedrich. 2007. "Shadow Economies and Corruption All Over the World: New Estimates for 145 Countries." *Economics—The Open-Access, Open-Assessment E-Journal,* July 24.

United Nations Development Program (UNDP). 2013. Human Development Indicators and Thematic Tables. Statistical Tables from the *2013 Human Development Report*. http://hdr.undp.org/en/data

U.S. Bureau of Economic Analysis. 2009. "National Income and Product Accounts Tables." Washington, DC. www.bea.gov/national/nipaweb/IndexI.htm

Wang, Xiaolu, and Meng Lian. 2001. "A Reevaluation of China's Economic Growth." *China Economic Review* 12(4): 338–46.

Wu, Harry X. 2007. "The Chinese GDP Growth Rate Puzzle: How Fast Has the Chinese Economy Grown?" *Asian Economic Papers* 6(1): 1–23.

Xu Xianchun. 2009. "Zhongguo Guomin Jingji Hesuan Tixi de Jianli, Gaige he Fazhan [The Establishment, Reform and Development of China's National Economic Accounting System]." *Zhongguo Shehui Kexue* [China Social Science] 6: 58–59.

3 China and the United States and the Balance of Payments

积少成多
Many a Little Makes a Mickle

This chapter tackles an issue which is critically important to many aspects of international finance and economics; we will discuss how a country interacts with the rest of the world, and we assess the different tools for measuring that interaction. The balance of payments is the main accounting tool for examining this question. The formal generic definition of balance of payments (BOP) is a record of one nation's transactions with the rest of the world. In other words, it is a record of what a country imports, exports, borrows, lends, invests, and pays, and receives for liabilities and investments outside of the country. For our purposes, as MBA/EMBA/Master's practitioners, we can use a much simpler and more immediately meaningful definition: the BOP simply answers the question, "Is a country getting or losing foreign exchange?"

Why is this latter question so vitally important? Many countries around the world rely on access to foreign exchange as the lifeblood of their economy. By "foreign exchange" we mean the main tradable currencies in the world that are used as a medium of exchange: the U.S. dollar, euro, British pound, Japanese yen, and Swiss franc. The Chinese yuan is on the way to joining this list. Most countries need to import critically important products such as oil, pharmaceuticals, and spare parts for machinery. Meanwhile, diplomatic missions abroad need to be funded. All these activities require foreign exchange as defined above because most countries' local currency is simply not acceptable as a means of payment.[1] The seller wants to be paid in a currency that is liquid and used widely around the world. For example, payment for oil imports is typically made in U.S. dollars. It is therefore critical that each country has access to some of the main tradable currencies. Some countries experience chronic shortages of foreign exchange; others experience a more acute shortage in the form of a balance of payments crisis. Thus, the BOP lets us know whether a country is getting or losing foreign exchange and if that country might eventually run out of foreign exchange.

The Latin American debt crisis of the 1980s, the Mexican financial crisis of 1994, the Asian Financial Crisis of 1997, and the Ethiopian crisis of early 2009 cover the gamut of situations in which countries can run out of foreign exchange. These situations can lead to economic collapse since, for example, the nations involved may not be able to import medicines or oil needed for power, or to replace spare parts for machinery. When this happens, problems can spiral downward toward overall economic collapse.

While the BOP for advanced economies such as the United States may not have the same level of drama as a depletion of foreign exchange reserves in developing economies, foreign exchange and BOP problems for mature countries can also be pernicious and disruptive. In the United States, for example, chronic BOP deficits in the 1960s and early 1970s ultimately led to the abandonment of the gold standard and a succession of depreciations of the U.S. dollar against other currencies.

Case Study 3.1: China's Cautious (Wise) and Staged Liberalization of the Capital Account

While many economists support economic liberalization, most academic economists and international organizations such as the IMF are more circumspect when it comes to a country opening up (liberalizing) its capital account to foreign financial flows.* Ill-conceived financial liberalization on the capital account has, in the past, led many countries to experience large capital inflows, an appreciating currency, current account deficits, a net loss of foreign exchange reserves, and a financial crisis. In the twentieth century, Argentina, Mexico, Peru, and Egypt all allowed for financial liberalization on the capital account, then experienced a financial crisis triggered by volatile capital flows. Similarly, in Thailand during the Asian Financial Crisis in 1997–98, massive capital inflows in the context of a weak regulatory framework led to bad investments and financial collapse. Figure CS3.1a (Reinhart and Rogoff, 2009) illustrates the long-term relationship between capital flows and financial crises. We need to emphasize that international capital flows in and of themselves serve a useful economic purpose. Problems can arise when these flows are allowed to occur in a system that lacks sound regulations, sound economic fundamentals, or unexploited arbitrage opportunities related to residual and isolated regulations. Scholars such as Guillermo Calvo have highlighted the role of policy credibility, international capital flows, and crises triggered by "sudden stops" of foreign capital.

Chinese policymakers, being well aware of the problems identified above, have been both cautious and prudent in their approach to liberalizing the capital account. Specifically, the following stages have been undertaken in that process:

1. Allowing foreign investment into China via special economic zones (1980s).
2. Liberalizing most FDI flows into all of China (1988).

Capital Mobility and the Presence of Banking Crisis: All Countries, 1800–2007

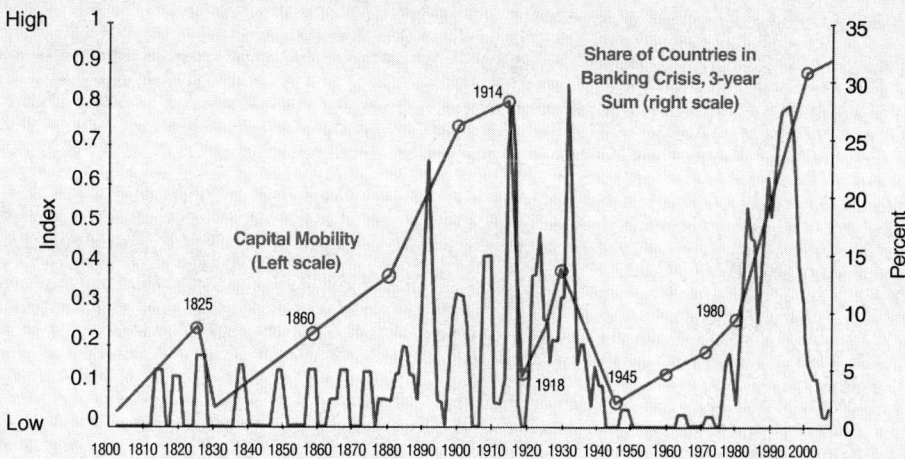

Figure CS3.1a Increased international capital mobility and financial crises appear to be linked. China has restricted capital mobility but has been gradually loosening controls in recent years.

Source: Reinhart and Rogoff, 2009.

*See for example, Diaz-Alejandro, 1985.

3. Initially limiting capital inflows to large foreign institutions that were permitted to invest in China's A-share market through qualified foreign institutional investors (QFIIs) programs (2002).
4. Accepting Article VIII of the IMF Charter for full current account convertibility (1996).
5. Issuing the first RMB denominated bonds (2007).

Since 2007, capital account liberalization has picked up speed with efforts at the internationalization of the RMB. Nevertheless, as suggested above, full capital account convertibility will only be achieved when the authorities feel confident enough to take these steps:

1. Allow the RMB exchange rate to float (with all that would entail).
2. Allow the domestic banking system to manage all risks associated with international capital flows.
3. Declare the regulatory framework to be sufficient (after stress-testing over time).

Balance of Payments

The BOP for China and the United States are presented in detail in Tables 3.1 and 3.2. Given that the main purpose of the BOP is to indicate whether a country is getting or losing foreign exchange, we can use a very simple rule to determine this: Any transaction that leads to a country receiving foreign exchange can be recorded as plus (+) on the BOP; any transaction leading to a loss of foreign exchange will be recorded as a minus (−). For example, the purchase of a dress made in China by a U.S. consumer would result in a negative contribution since it would trigger either a loss of foreign exchange on the part of America (loss of RMB), or a receipt of foreign exchange on the Chinese side (a gain in US$). Similarly, if a Chinese bank lends an American company US$ or RMB, the result is either a reduction in Chinese holdings of foreign currency or an increased holding of RMB by Americans (depending on the currency of the loan). Either way, the loan would be recorded as a plus on the American BOP and a minus on the Chinese BOP.

Table 3.1 China: Balance of Payments 2012.

Item		Balance	Credit	Debit
		Units: 100 million US$		
I.	Current Account	1,931	24,599	22,668
	A. Goods and Services	2,318	22,483	20,165
	Goods	3216	20569	17353
	Services	−897	1914	2812
	Transportation	−469	389	859
	Travel	−519	500	1,020
	Communication Services	1	18	16
	Construction Services	86	122	36
	Insurance Services	−173	33	206
	Financial Services	0	19	19
	Computer and Information Services	106	145	38
	Royalties and License Fees	−167	10	177
	Consulting Service	134	334	200
	Advertising and Public Opinion Polling	20	48	28
	Audio-visual and Related Services	−4	1	6
	Other Business Services	89	284	196
	Government Services	−1	10	10
	B. Income	−421	1,604	2,026
	Compensation of Employees	153	171	18
	Investment Income	−574	1,434	2,008
	C. Current Transfers	34	512	477
	General Government	−31	9	40
	Other Sectors	65	503	438

		Units: 100 million US$	
Item	*Balance*	*Credit*	*Debit*
II. Capital and Financial Account	−168	13,783	13,951
A. Capital Account	43	45	3
B. Financial Account	−211	13,738	13,949
Direct Investment	1,911	3,079	1,168
Abroad	−624	234	857
In China	2,535	2,845	311
Portfolio Investment	478	829	352
Assets	−64	237	301
Equity Securities	20	120	100
Debt Securities	−84	117	201
Bonds and Notes	−49	110	159
Money Market Instruments	−35	7	42
Liabilities	542	593	51
Equity Securities	299	348	49
Debt Securities	243	244	2
Bonds and Notes	173	175	2
Money Market Instruments	70	70	0
Other Investment	−2,600	9,829	12,429
Assets	−2,316	1,402	3,718
Trade Credits	−618	4	622
Long-term	−12	0	12
Short-term	−606	4	610
Loans	−653	244	897
Long-term	−568	0	568
Short-term	−85	243	329
Currency and Deposits	−1,047	1,027	2,074
Other Assets	3	127	125
Long-term	−100	0	100
Short-term	103	127	25
Liabilities	−284	8,428	8,712
Trade Credits	423	503	80
Long-term	7	9	1
Short-term	416	494	78
Loans	−168	6,480	6,648
Long-term	102	543	440
Short-term	−270	5,937	6,207
Currency and Deposits	−594	1,339	1,933
Other Liabilities	54	106	51
Long-term	47	47	1
Short-term	8	58	50
III. Reserve Assets	−966	136	1,101
Monetary Gold	0	0	0
Special Drawing Rights	5	7	2
Reserve Position in the Fund	16	16	0
Foreign Exchange	−987	112	1,099
Other Claims	0	0	0
IV. Net Errors and Omissions	−798	0	798

Source: China State Administration of Foreign Exchange and National Bureau of Statistics.

Although there are many detailed items on the BOP, the simplified version of the BOP in Table 3.3 shows that there are only a few main categories. The first block of items in Table 3.3 lists current account transactions. The current account represents trade in actual goods and services, such as the shipment of steel or the consulting services of an attorney. Specifically, the trade balance represents trade in goods while the non-factor services are those that are currently consumed or used (e.g., the provision of education or a tourist visit from one country to another). Meanwhile, factor services represent income generated related to a loan or investment, or for a foreign resident in a country who has some type of legal visa-granted status in that country and is paid for services

Table 3.2 United States: Balance of Payments (Millions of US$) Bureau of Economic Analysis.

Line {credits+;debits-}	2012
Current Accounts	
1. Exports of goods and services and income receipts	USD$2,986,949
2. Exports of goods and services	2,210,585
3. Goods, balance of payments basis	1,561,239
4. Services	649,346
5. Transfers under U.S. military agency sales contracts	18,520
6. Travel	126,214
7. Passenger fares	39,360
8. Other transportation	43,855
9. Royalties and license fees	124,182
10. Other private services	294,527
11. U.S. government miscellaneous services	2,688
12. Income receipts	776,364
13. Income receipts on U.S.-owned assets abroad	770,079
14. Direct investment receipts	470,233
15. Other private receipts	297,891
16. U.S. government receipts	1,954
17. Compensation of employees	6,286
18. Imports of goods and services and income payments	−3,297,677
19. Imports of goods and services	−2,745,240
20. Goods, balance of payments basis	−2,302,714
21. Services	−442,527
22. Direct defense expenditures	−24,734
23. Travel	−83,451
24. Passenger fares	−34,654
25. Other transportation	−55,445
26. Royalties and license fees	−39,889
27. Other private services	−201,227
28. U.S. government miscellaneous services	−3,127
29. Income payments	−552,437
30. Income payments on foreign-owned assets in the U.S.	−537,815
31. Direct investment payments	−176,747
32. Other private payments	−233,336
33. U.S. government payments	−127,732
34. Compensation of employees	−14,622
35. Unilateral current transfers, net	−129,688
36. U.S. government grants	−46,090
37. U.S. government pensions and other transfers	−3,685
38. Private remittances and other transfer	−79,913
Capital Accounts	
39. Capital account transactions, net	6,956
Financial Accounts	
40. U.S.-owned assets abroad, excluding financial derivatives (increase/financial outflow{-})	−97,469
41. U.S. official reserve assets	−4,460
42. Gold	0
43. Special drawing rights	−37
44. Reserve position in the international Monetary Fund	−4,032
45. Foreign currencies	−391
46. U.S. government assets, other than official reserve assets	85331
47. U.S. credits and other long-term assets	−8,202
48. Repayments on U.S. credits and other long-term assets	2,546
49. U.S. foreign currency holdings and U.S. short-term assets	90,987
50. U.S. private assets	−178,341
51. Direct investment	−388,293
52. Foreign securities	−144,823
53. U.S. claims on unaffiliated foreigners reported by U.S nonbanking concerns	−25,723
54. U.S. claims reported by U.S. banks and securities brokers	380,498

Source: United States Commerce Department, Bureau of Economic Analysis.

Table 3.3 Balance of Payments United States and China (2011) (US$ Millions).

	United States	China
Exports of goods	US$1,288,699	¥1,581,417
Imports of goods	−1,934,555	1,327,238
Balance of Trade	−645,856	254,180
Exports of non-factor services	548,878	171,203
Imports of non-factor services	−403,048	193,321
Balance of Non-Factor Services	145,830	−22,118
Export of factor services	663,240	144,622
Import of factor services	−498,016	114,242
Balance of Factor Services	165,224	30,380
Net Transfers	−136,095	42,932
Current Account Balance	−470,897	305,374
Capital Transactions	−152	4,630
Financial Transactions	−93,631	221,414
Net financial flows	21,493	96,484
Net foreign direct investment	−115,124	124,930
Errors	216,761	−59,680
Balance of Payments	−347,919	471,739
Change in Official Reserves	347,919	−471,739

Source: Author's estimates.

rendered. In other words, factor services include interest on debt, as well as dividends paid on an investment or salaries paid to expatriate workers.

The financial account represents financial flows between borders that, in turn, imply a gain or loss in foreign exchange.[2] As such, the capital account includes loans (short term and long term), the sale and purchase of bills and bonds, and portfolio investment in equity and foreign direct investment (FDI).[3] Errors or statistical discrepancies are a measure of the difference between the above accounts and how much the country actually gained or lost in foreign exchange.

The overall BOP can be measured using different methods but the international norm is to determine the total foreign exchange assets actually gained or lost by the central banking authorities. The United States uses increased holdings of foreign exchange by the Federal Reserve System and nets out official dollar reserves held by other central banks around the world. In China, the measure includes not just China's central bank, the People's Bank of China (PBC), but the banking system as a whole. This is appropriate since, for most Chinese banks, the Chinese government is still the principal shareholder. In the end, it is critical to determine how much control a country's central banking authorities have over the foreign exchange accumulated in its economy. In China, that control remains substantial; in the United States, less so.

Thus, we see that the balance of payments follows a very simple form, as outlined in the equation below, but with many detailed items:

Current Account + Capital Transactions + Financial Account = **Balance of Payments**

We can learn several interesting things about China and other emerging market countries by taking a look even further "below the line" of the BOP. That is, we can ask how are those balances used if they are positive or how are they financed if they are negative?

Current Account + Capital Transactions + Financial Account = **Balance of Payments** = Change in Foreign Exchange Reserves of the Central Bank (or in China's case, banking system)

If we have a BOP surplus, it becomes a part of the banking systems' holdings of foreign exchange reserves; the BOP is a flow, and foreign exchange reserves are the stock into which they accumulate. For example, China had about US$470 billion surplus in 2010. Given end-of-2009 foreign exchange reserves of US$2.45 trillion, we can estimate China's end-of-2010 foreign exchange reserves as US$2.45 + 0.47 = US$2.92 trillion.

What happens if a country has a negative number for its BOP and is losing foreign exchange? Take the United States, for example. The United States has the luxury of simply issuing more of its currency to settle its imbalance (a solution which, we will show cannot be used over a prolonged period of time). But what happens in a small emerging economy such as Uruguay? Uruguay in 2010 had a BOP deficit of approximately US$400 million. In that case, its reserves served as a buffer used to finance (pay for) the BOP deficit. But what about a country in which reserves are insufficient to pay for a BOP deficit? The expression below suggests that "exceptional financing" may come into play:

Current Account
+ Capital Transactions
+ Financial Account
= Balance of Payments
= Change in Foreign Exchange Reserves of the Central Bank (or in China's case, banking system)
+ IMF Loan
+ Debt Restructuring
+ Default
= Financing Gap

Case Study 3.2: How Did China Accumulate Over US$3 Trillion in Foreign Exchange Reserves?*

China's Current Account Surpluses

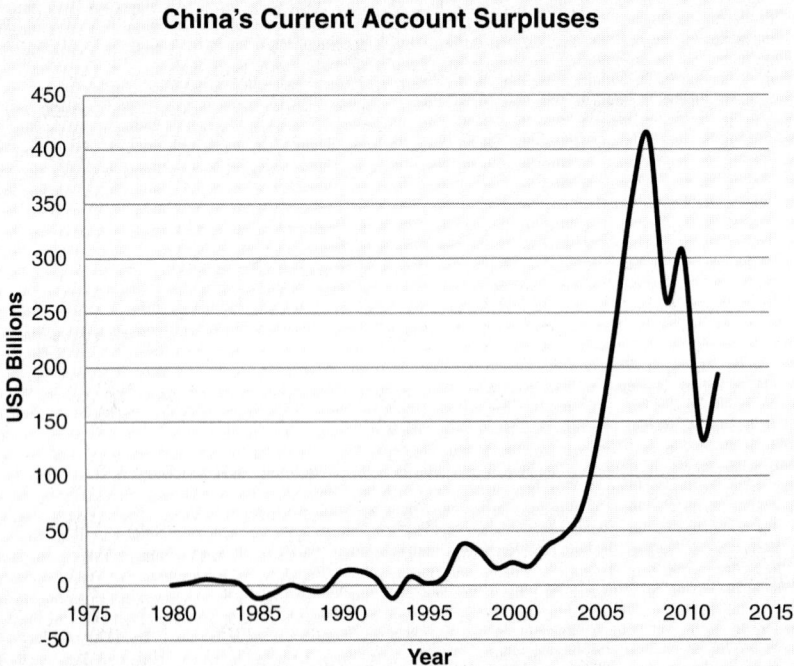

Figure CS3.2a China has become the world's export powerhouse.

Source: FRED, Federal Reserve Economic Data, Federal Reserve Bank of St. Louis: 2014
research.stlouisfed.org

Since the BOP is just another way of measuring a country's change in foreign exchange reserves, we might ask how China came to accumulate a stock of foreign exchange reserves now over US$3 trillion. Let's look at a graph of China's current account surpluses over the years (Figure CS3.2a). The current account has greatly influenced China's overall BOP in recent years—since capital account mobility has been (and continues to be) highly circumscribed around FDI. If we take the sum of the surpluses in Figure CS3.2a (the integral beneath the curve), we have a total of almost exactly US$2 trillion. If we add one major capital account positive item—foreign direct investment for the same period—we have an additional surplus of about US$1.3 trillion. Taken together, we come up with a virtually complete explanation as to how China has accumulated close to US$3 trillion in foreign exchange reserves.† As suggested earlier, on a net basis, a large part of China's current account surplus is explained by the deficit that the U.S. runs with China; the FDI surplus for China presents a more mixed picture. Scholars such as Maurice Obstfeld (2012) show that the former remains a key factor when it comes to macroeconomic stability. The latter elements (FDI and other gross asset positions) have added another layer of complication over the past several decades for economic policymakers.

*Since the time this was written, the level of foreign exchange reserves has moved closer to US$ 4 trillion!

†Of course to be exact, we would need to know other specific line items such as outflows on the capital account and capital gains/losses on the reserve holdings themselves.

A country with a BOP deficit but insufficient foreign exchange reserves to support that deficit may need exceptional financing to "plug" the gap. (Thus we use the positive sign to indicate an addition to the available pool of resources.) We call this "exceptional financing" because this financing is made available not on any market-based, profit-making motivation, but rather as emergency financing. In effect, it is a situation that both lenders and borrowing countries prefer to avoid. An International Monetary Fund loan comes with terms of "conditionality," which injects outside policy control from the IMF in order to improve the recipient country's BOP. Most countries prefer not to surrender such autonomy in terms of macroeconomic policy.[4] Debt restructuring is another possibility but involves rescheduling promised commitments on external debt that are located above the BOP line. Again, implicit and explicit penalties—such as loss of reputation, higher borrowing costs or equity exchanges—may be imposed on the country. Default is a unilateral decision (often politically motivated) not to pay and may have severe short-term consequences, especially in the area of trade finance.

MACRO FINANCE INSIGHT 3.1: THE ROLE OF THE INTERNATIONAL MONETARY FUND

China's historically conservative approach to managing its balance sheet has enabled it to avoid externally related financial crises such as have been experienced by many other emerging economies around the world (see Reinhart and Rogoff 2009 for an extensive catalog of crises in Latin America, Africa, Eastern Europe, and the advanced economies). The IMF has been involved in many of these crises. In fact, among some 188 IMF member countries, more than half have enjoyed some type of loan from the IMF, either via balance of payments support or "structural support." Neither China nor the United States (key members of the Fund) has ever found it necessary to seek such support.

The IMF was created in 1944 along with its sister institution, the World Bank. While the latter has focused on long-term development including everything from developing health and welfare to road-building, the IMF has focused on its mandate of macroeconomic management. Specifically, the IMF assists countries with weak international balance sheets that are at risk of running out of foreign exchange.* In return for buttressing a country's foreign exchange holdings through its various lending programs, the IMF negotiates with the borrower to develop macroeconomic measures to avoid further international financing problems going forward. This is referred to as "conditionality," and is often at the center of any discussion of the costs and benefits of IMF involvement with member countries.

Typically, the IMF makes a loan when commercial and even government lenders are no longer willing to finance a country's balance of payments deficit. Needless to say, this can prevent severe harm to the borrower's economy and its citizens in the short run. But both the IMF and the World Bank (as well as other supranational lenders) take on a senior creditor status after making the loan—that is, they usually insist on being paid first before any other lender is paid. An open question is whether the benefits of the Fund loan and/or macroeconomic improvements from conditionality and the implicit seal of approval for a country undertaking a loan outweigh the costs. Specifically, new lenders must take on a junior status to the Fund and World Bank senior creditors. Will they withhold loans or charge a higher interest rate in the medium term because of their diminished rank in the payoff order?

*In the years between 1944 and 1973, the IMF viewed its primary role as the protection of the fixed exchange rate system with the U.S. dollar at the center of that system. Being a liquidity provider of foreign exchange was a key tool for the Fund in guarding the system. With the move to floating exchange rates in the early 1970s, the role of guardian of the foreign exchange system vanished. The expertise that had been developed in conditionality and international coordination, however, allowed the Fund to still wield the powerful tool it had used in the past—the provision of foreign exchange liquidity—to ease crises centered around countries' balance of payments.

If, after breaching all of these below-the-line thresholds, the country still finds itself unable to finance its BOP deficit, it is left with a hole, or "financing gap." At this point, the country is forced into "import compression"—an extremely difficult situation in which it cannot, for example, import oil, pay to keep its power plants maintained, or pay for its employees at diplomatic missions abroad. In effect, the country goes into "shutdown" mode, from an external trade and finance perspective. By the time it reaches the default stage, the country has a "liquidity" event and is effectively bankrupt.

MACRO FINANCE INSIGHT 3.2: CHINA'S EXTERNAL BALANCE SHEET AND CAPITAL STRUCTURE

The standard presumption for a company is that capital structure does not matter. Whether debt finance or equity finance is used or not, the weighted average cost of capital remains unchanged and the value of the firm does not change. The fact that the assets side of a firm's balance sheet remains the same irrespective of financial structure drives this key result commonly known as Modigliani–Miller I. When taxes, bankruptcy, and agency costs come into play, capital structure can affect value. Recall, for example, that taxes on interest payments are expensed while dividends are not, thereby creating a tax benefit to debt over equity finance.

We can examine China's capital structure vis-à-vis its relationship with external investors in Table MF3.2a. What is striking is China's very conservative financing on the Liabilities side of the balance sheet and its very conservative holdings on the Assets side. We see that, within an estimated US$3.5 trillion in assets, only about 16 percent is financed via debt or international borrowing. The remaining assets are financed via equity finance, split between FDI (37 percent) and Owner's equity (48 percent). A typical company operating with 30–40 percent financing from debt might still be considered operating at a level of safe leverage. On the assets side, we see China still holding an extremely high level of its foreign assets in a relatively liquid form—"foreign exchange reserves" at 91 percent, with the remaining assets held as FDI in other countries.

Being conservative has both costs and benefits. A conservative policy reduces the risk of default and financial crises. As stated above, in our discussion of staged capital account liberalization, Chinese policymakers have followed a well-thought-out policy strategy by encouraging FDI, but heavily restricting international borrowing.* The cost, however, has been a lower return on the more liquid assets and a more expensive cost of capital of equity versus debt finance. Whether the risk-adjusted costs of equity and finance are the same is an open question.

Under the Capital Asset Pricing Model (CAPM), a cornerstone of modern finance, the more a company uses debt finance, the more it amplifies the non-diversifiable risk of the firm (its equity). In turn, the cost of equity finance rises with greater leverage. But in the case of China, capital markets are not integrated—which calls into question the applicability of CAPM at least under standard assumptions. Returns on Chinese-denominated assets are far less correlated with international markets because of capital controls. Under standard CAPM, equity returns on Chinese assets should be correspondingly lower. But in a survey of U.S. firms operating in China, for example, 88 percent reported profit margins that were higher in China in 2009 than in the rest of the world. In summary, it would appear that China, at least until recently, has provided both less risk and higher returns to the foreign investor! Furthermore, the large short-term asset position provides a further cushion of safety. The legacy of encouraging FDI at the expense of loans appears to have significant costs; China could likely benefit by shifting its capital structure (external sector balance sheet) away from equity and toward debt finance.†

Table MF3.2a China's capital structure as measured by its external balance sheet can be described as very conservative with a corresponding low return. There is very little external borrowing and a substantial amount of cash holdings.

Assets End 2011 (US$ billions)		
Foreign exchange reserves	3,180	91%
Foreign direct investment	318	9%
Total assets	3,498	

Liabilities End 2011 (US$ billions)		
External debt	549	16%
FDI	1,279	37%
"Owner's equity"	1,670	48%
Total liabilities and equity	3,498	

Source: Author's estimates.

*Technically, national statistics bureaus around the world include both debt and equity finance when measuring FDI. Even under this broader definition, China still relies mostly on the equity form of FDI.

†Another benefit accruing from agency theory may be that countries with some indebtedness may feel greater pressure to invest funds more parsimoniously.

MACRO FINANCE INSIGHT 3.3: THE PECKING ORDER THEORY

The pecking order theory suggests that, because of asymmetric information between firms and potential investors, firms tend to rely first on internal sources of finance (retained earnings), then debt, and finally (as a last resort) equity. The idea here is that outsiders know less than insiders and are therefore an expensive source of capital since they charge a premium in the face of greater uncertainty regarding investment. This is particularly true of an equity investment since this requires an outright valuation of the underlying assets of the firm. In contrast, debt finance is determined more on the basis of a binomial question: Will the borrower pay the amount owed or not? Less information is required to answer this question than what is involved in equity valuation.

The above suggests that countries normally rely on internal savings before seeking outside finance. This conclusion is consistent with an early study done by Feldstein and Horioka (1980) which shows a high correlation between nations' levels of savings and investment; that is, a disproportionate reliance on internal versus external finance. Our conclusion is consistent with China's flow of funds, in which domestic investment is financed mostly by domestic savings. In terms of debt vs. equity finance, however, the results for China seems to differ. China has shown a clear preference for a particular form of equity investment as opposed to the alternative form of external finance taken by many emerging market countries—debt finance. This interesting macro deviation from the pecking order theory is consistent with the common complaint heard among Chinese policymakers: FDI is a very expensive form of external financing.

Current Account Balance from Four Angles

We can look at current account balances from four different perspectives. These perspectives are fully equivalent in an accounting sense, but each provides a unique insight or policy angle explaining why a country might run a current account surplus or deficit. This is particularly important in the context of China and the United States since so much emphasis has been placed on the former's surplus and the latter's deficit. We will later discuss how these imbalances are really two sides of the same coin, but for now let's focus on different ways of thinking about current account deficits.

Approach #1: Current Account Balance by Definition

The simplest approach for discussing the current account balance is to rely on its definition: the difference between the goods and services which a country exports and those it imports:

Current Account Balance = XGS – MGS

In 2010, the current account balance for the United States was a deficit of about US$471 billion, while China had a surplus of about US$305 billion. As described above, these amounts included goods, factor services, non-factor services, and grants. In using the definitional approach to current account balance, we focus closely on trade results. "Correcting" a current account imbalance using this approach would rely on trade-related policies. Thus, to counteract a current account deficit, one might focus on tariffs (taxes) or quotas on imports, or subsidies on exports.[5] Furthermore, countries might try to streamline relevant regulations and approvals for exporting or importing. Or policymakers might seek to adjust exchange rates if they felt their currency was misaligned and was the cause of a current account surplus or deficit.

Approach #2: Current Account Balance and Absorption

Using our second approach, we view the current account balance as the difference between a nation's **supply** (GDP) and **demand** (*C + I + G*). (Note: Here, *C, I,* and *G* denote Consumption, Investment, and Government demand.) If more is being demanded than supplied, those goods and services must come from outside the country (i.e., from abroad). Conversely, if more is supplied than demanded, the excess goods must go somewhere (i.e., exported abroad).[6] We can formally state that:

Supply – Demand or
Sources – Uses or
GPP – (C + I + G)
= Balance in Goods and Non-Factor Services

Recognizing that:

GNP = GDP + Net Factor Income (Factor Services)

We can say:

GNP – $(C + I + G)$ = Current Account Balance.

This approach emphasizes the need for demand and supply management to correct current account imbalances. For example, a country running a current account deficit may take steps to reduce Demand (Consumption or Government or Investment[7]). Alternatively, the country may need to improve productivity or its product mix to increase supply (GDP or GNP).

Case Study 3.3: China and the United States—Two Sides of the Same Coin

That there is a significant financial and economic relationship between the United States and China is well known. The BOP serves as the key nexus in which that relationship can be examined. We see in Table 3.3 that the United States has a balance of trade deficit of close to US$650 billion while China has a surplus of over US$250 billion. The opposite signs reflect in large part substantial Chinese exports to the United States (of at least US$350 billion) and relatively small U.S. exports of goods to China (around US$85 billion). In other words, the U.S. trade deficit with China alone can fully explain China's substantial trade surplus. On the non-factor services we see a reversal of signs that also, in large part, can be explained by the services such as shipping and insurance or legal and consulting services; areas in which the United States has a comparative advantage and tends to export to China. Both countries run a positive balance on factor services, but again the relationship is significant. The large holdings of U.S. dollar reserves by China earn a positive, albeit very low, income (interest payments); the substantial amount of foreign direct investment in China by U.S. firms earns a positive and large income (in the form of retained earnings). On the capital account, we see substantial outflows on foreign direct investment from the United States; but only a small fraction of these flows end up in China.*

*And only about 3 percent of all FDI into China comes from the United States. Most of the FDI into China comes from Asia—specifically, Hong Kong, South Korea, and Japan. Since Chinese exports come mainly from these sectors with heavy foreign investment, we could view a substantial amount of U.S. imports from China as actually imports from greater Asia— capital owned by outside Asians, but utilizing Chinese labor.

Approach #3: Current Account Balance and the Gap Between Savings and Investment

While Approach #2 highlights the imbalance between the supply and demand for goods and services, the **Savings/Investment** approach examines the imbalance between a nation's source of funds (savings) and its use of funds (investment). This is also known as a *flow of funds approach*. The gap between the two represents how a current account deficit is financed or, in the case of a current account surplus, how much is lent abroad. The subscripts "$_P$" and "$_G$" represent the private sector and government sector.

We recall that:

$$Y_{GNP} = C_G + C_P + I_G + I_P + \text{Current Account Balance}$$

And that

$$S_P + C_P = Y_{GNP} - \text{Taxes} + \text{Transfers}$$

where S_P represents private savings.
Defining government saving as[8]:

$$S_G = \text{Government Savings} = \text{Taxes} - (C_G + \text{Transfers}) \text{ or Revenues} - \text{Current Expenses[9]}$$

We have:

$$\text{Current Account Balance} = (S_G - I_G) + (S_P - I_P)$$

In other words, the current account balance is the difference between national savings and investment at both the government level and private sector level. We could state this in an even simpler form by saying:

Current Account Balance = $S - I$
(Note: Private sector and government sector savings and investment have been "collapsed" into the terms S and I.)

Although this approach toward the current account is less intuitive than the earlier two, it provides highly useful insights. It makes clear that a country that saves a lot is producing while not consuming (since savings cannot exist without first producing something). Production that is not being consumed domestically must be going somewhere. Since the "I" term takes into account production being used for investment (e.g., roads or plant property and equipment) and inventory accumulation, then the only place production must be heading to (or coming from) is abroad.

The Savings/Investment approach allows us to focus on a fundamental cause of current account deficits or surpluses. If a nation does not save enough, or invests too much, it will run a current account deficit. If a nation saves too much or invests too little, it runs a surplus. For example, if the United States wishes to reduce its current account deficit, it must either increase national savings (increase private savings or reduce dissaving in the budget deficit) or reduce investment. Since investment in the United States is not high by international standards, the goal of improving the savings rate would appear to be a more reasonable path. Similarly, in order for China to decrease its current account surplus to more sustainable levels, it must either decrease savings (or increase consumption in the private or public sectors) or increase investment. Since China's investment is already extraordinarily high by international standards, a similar focus on less saving and more consumption (but in the opposite direction to the United States) seems reasonable.

Approach #4: Current Account Balance and External Debt

If we imagine the current account as simply "trading in tangible goods," ignoring trade in services for the moment, then we could think of a current account deficit as "purchasing more tangible goods from the rest of the world than we sell to the rest of the world." What would our trading counterpart receive to settle the balance due? Clearly, the counterpart would need something if our own goods are not settling the imbalance. Some type of financial obligation (more graphically a piece of paper, or an IOU) would be needed. That financial obligation might take the form of currency, a debt instrument, or an equity instrument. One way or another, we need to offer sufficient value to offset our shortfall in exports to imports. Thus, we can think of the current account balance as a change in our net external debt position. When we run a current account deficit, we need to finance that deficit via a financial instrument or via the counterpart's willingness to hold our own currency.[10] When we run a surplus, we increase our own holdings of foreign financial obligations, decreasing our net debt or increasing our net creditor position. If foreigners settle the difference using our own currency—U.S. dollars—then our net external debt position falls or our net creditor position rises.

Formally:

Current Account = Change in Net External Debt (−) for a *CA* surplus; (+) for a *CA* deficit.

This perspective on the current account highlights the notion that a deficit must be financed (via the financial account or reserves) and this act of financing alters our net external debt position. From a policy perspective, it tells us that countries which cannot obtain external finance (i.e., borrow from abroad) will be constrained in running a current account deficit. Countries which experience current account surpluses, such as China, are simultaneously (by definition) lending to the outside world. For other countries whose creditworthiness is in question, the inability to finance a current account deficit leads to painful "import compression" as discussed earlier.

MACRO FINANCE INSIGHT 3.4: WHAT IS THE CASH FLOW FOR AN ENTIRE ECONOMY?

In corporate finance and financial accounting, a central question relates to the cash flow of a company. Both finance and accounting have different answers to this fundamental question. As we shall see, we can ask the same question regarding a country as a whole. The balance of payments and current account discussion above provides some useful tools for evaluating the cash flow for an entire country. The balance of payments is conceptually close to an accounting measure of cash flow, since it includes both operations (the current account) and financing items (the financial account). We now proceed to show how to measure a country's cash flow from the perspective of finance or valuation.

Measuring a Company's Cash Flow

Recall that, when measuring a company's cash flow, we are interested in identifying outflows and inflows in actual cash. Specifically, we want to look beyond the income statement and balance sheet, although these tools help answer an investor's fundamental question, "Is this company generating or losing cash?" After all, investors give cash to the company and their principal question is, "When and how much will I get paid back in cash?" Net income, assets, turnover ratios, etc. are all useful accounting terms but do not directly translate into a measure of cash generated. Reviewing the basic steps for determining free cash flow (FCF) for corporate valuation purposes, we calculate:

NOP (Net Operating Profit) = EBIT(1 − Tax Rate)

where EBIT is earnings (net income) before interest and taxes are deducted. We can then estimate FCF for any given year using:

FCF = NOP − Change in NFA − Change in Working Capital

where NFA is the firms' net investment in plant, property, and equipment and

Working Capital = Current Assets − "Excess Cash" − Non-Interest Current Liabilities*

Moving from the Corporation to the Nation

One critical insight into creating cash flow for a nation is that national savings comes partly from corporate profits, while the rest come from personal savings and government savings (surpluses or deficits in the case of dissaving). Similarly, corporate investment is a critical part of national investment. Our approach then is to build up net income in a very natural way.

We let earnings before interest and taxes (EBIT) or net operating profits (NOP) correspond to the S in the S − I macro accounting framework, and I (Change in NFA) corresponds more broadly to corporate investment, government investment, and individual investment. In dealing with such elements as taxes and payments, we recognize that national level intra-sector payments of interest and taxes are netted out and sum to 0. It is only when these payments are made abroad that they would affect national cash flow. Finally, we note that the BOP "change in reserves" bottom line is equivalent to the accounting "statement of cash flows" bottom line. Instead, here we are measuring cash flows from the valuation perspective of corporate finance.

Table MF3.4a presents a highly simplified correspondence between measuring cash flows at the financial level and the macro (national) level. A number of basic assumptions are made, particularly with regard to the working capital component.

Given the simplified correspondence between measures of financial cash flow and macroeconomic cash flow, we can say that a measure of macroeconomic cash flow consists of a refinement of $S - I =$ Current account. Instead, we use the relationship based on GDP and not GNP to define macro cash flow†:

Macro Cash Flow = $S - I$ = Trade Balance plus Non-Factor Services Balance

As we can see in Figure MF3.4a, from the 1990s to the present, the United States' negative cash flow has grown increasingly large as a share of GDP. This negative cash flow has been financed from abroad via the financial account broadly defined to include the holding of U.S. dollar reserve assets abroad. We will discuss the sustainability of this pattern and its implications for the valuation of the United States later. The reverse picture holds for China, as shown in Figure MF3.4b. Here we see a positive cash flow in virtually all years since 1990. And just as the U.S. saw negative cash flows surge in the 2000 decade, positive cash flows surged in China during that time.

Table MF3.4a Correspondence between corporate cash flow and national cash flow.

Financial Cash Flow	*Macroeconomic Cash Flow*	*Row*
Net operating profits	Domestic Savings (S) = Corporate + Private + Government	A
Change in net fixed assets	Gross Investment (*I*) = Corporate + Private + Government	B
Inventory accumulation	Included in Gross Investment above	C
Accounts receivables – Accounts payable	Constant at 0	D
Necessary cash holdings	Constant at initial months of sales or imports	E
Other current assets	Constant at 0	F
Other non-interest liabilities		

Source: Author created.

US: Macro Cash Flow as a Share of GDP

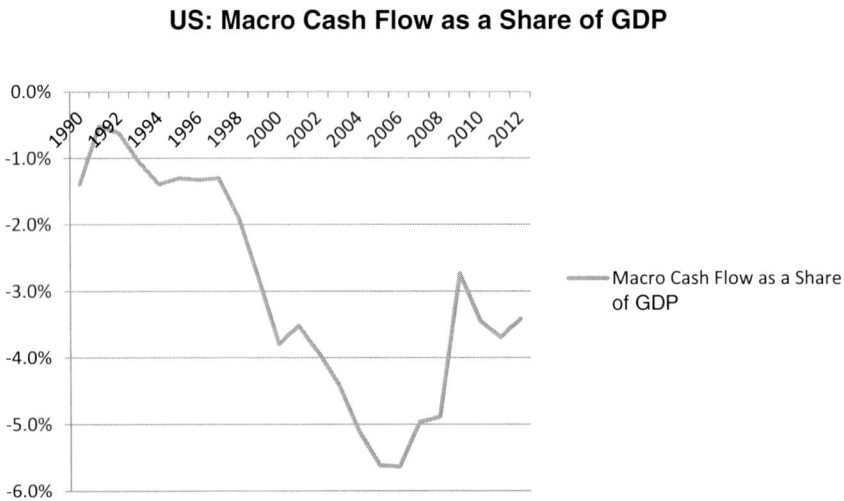

Figure MF3.4a Cash flow for the United States has been negative for many years primarily as a result of the low savings rate.

Source: Author created.

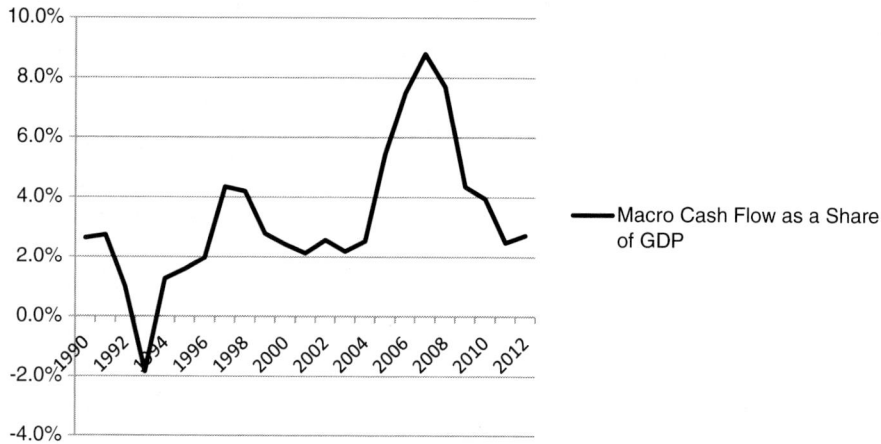

China: Macro Cash Flow as a Share of GDP

Figure MF3.4b Cash Flow for China has been largely positive over the past twenty years notwithstanding China's high rate of investment; the large flow of savings has been the key factor.

Source: Author created.

* Current Assets − Excess Cash = Necessary Cash Holding + Accounts Receivable + Inventory + Other Current Assets

† We are assuming here that any factor service savings due to foreign workers are available as cash flow to the home country.

Challenging Questions for China (and the Student): Chapter 3

1. Go the Federal Reserve Economic Database and update China's current account balances and foreign exchange reserve holdings both graphically and numerically. Determine the implied value of China's financial account + capital account + errors for the most recent three years.
2. Explain why the chapter argues that China's foreign exchange capital structure has been "conservative" in recent decades. Relate this to questions of capital mobility and financial crises.
3. Consider the current account balances for China and the United States:
   a. Explain the four different ways of looking at a current account deficit.
   b. Discuss: If China stopped buying U.S. Treasury bills, the U.S. current account deficit would shrink. Which of the four views of a current account deficit is useful in this context?
4. Choose among the four different ways of looking at a current account deficit or surplus and explain why China has run a historically large current account surplus and the United States has historically run a current account deficit.
5. Discuss:
   a. The balance of payments is a measure of a country's accounting cash flow while the current account is a measure of a country's financial cash flow.
   b. In recent years, the United States has had a negative financial cash flow while China has had both a positive financial and accounting cash flow. The opposing balances are related.
   c. We should not worry about cash flows for either China or the United States since a country is not a company and having too much or too little cash flow is not important.
6. Determine the cash flow of the United States and China based on Table 3.3. Then update the data using FRED.
7. Explain why as a conventional accounting measure, the balance of payments is equivalent to "the statement of cash flows," while for financial valuation purposes the current account is almost the same as "financial cash flow."

Notes

1. We see in Table 3.1 that China's balance of payments is measured in US$ rather than RMB. Most countries will provide a US$ presentation for their BOP. This highlights the central role that foreign exchange plays in the BOP.
2. A confusing set of definitions involves the capital account and the financial account. The latter used to be known as the former! The capital account now represents a rather insignificant item which takes account of such transactions as land sales to foreigners.
3. The distinction between what constitutes portfolio investment and foreign direct investment is definitional. Foreign direct investment entails a degree of ownership and control; a rule of thumb cutoff between portfolio and FDI defines more than 20 percent of the company owned by a group of foreign investors as FDI.
4. Emergency lending could also come from outside governments or, for example, the European Union. But again, such loans are granted with policy strings attached or "conditionality."
5. Most economists since at least the time of David Ricardo in the nineteenth century would agree that such policies are more likely to cause harm than good.
6. Note that we exclude the possibility that excess goods fall into inventory accumulation since such inventory accumulation is already accounted for by the "I" term in $C + I + G$.
7. Keep in mind that investment includes housing—an acute source of excess demand in the United States pre-financial crisis.
8. Government savings is the same concept as a budget deficit or surplus.
9. Note consistent with accepted corporate accounting practices, we do not include I_G as a current expense. Fiscal accounting practices around the world do, however, include this I_G in the definition of the budget deficit or surplus.
10. Holding of our own currency by another nation is a legal obligation of our own country to provide something of value in the future and in this sense constitutes a debt-like obligation.

References

Calvo, Guillermo. 2005. *Emerging Capital Markets in Turmoil: Bad Luck or Bad Policy?* Cambridge, MA: MIT Press.

Diaz-Alejandro, Carlos. 1985. "Good-Bye Financial Repression, Hello Financial Crash." *Journal of Development Economics* 19(1–2): 1–24.

Eichengreen, Barry. 2011. "The Renminbi as an International Currency." *Journal of Policy Modeling* 33(5): 752–59.

Feldstein, M., and C. Horioka. 1980. "Domestic Savings and International Capital Flows." *Economic Journal* 90(June): 314–29.

Glick, Reuven, and Michael Hutchison. 2009. "Navigating the Trilemma: Capital Flows and Monetary Policy in China." *Journal of Asian Economics* 20(3): 205–24.

Greenwood, John. 2008. "The Costs and Implications of PBC Sterilization." *Cato Journal* 28(2): 205–17.

Knight, John, and Wei Wang. 2011. "China's Macroeconomic Imbalances: Causes and Consequences." *World Economy* 34(9): 1476–1506.

Mundell, Robert. 2012. "U.S. and China in the World Economy: The Balance of Payments and the Balance of Power." *Journal of Policy Modeling* 34(4): 525–28.

Myers, Stewart C., and Nicholas S. Majluf. 1984. "Corporate Financing and Investment Decisions When Firms Have Information That Investors Do Not Have." *Journal of Financial Economics* 13(2): 187–221.

National Bureau of Statistics (NBS). 2012. Table 2–32. In *China Statistical Yearbook*. Beijing: China Statistics Press.

Obstfeld, Maurice. 2012. "Financial Flows, Financial Crises and Global Imbalances." *Journal of International Money and Finance* 31(3): 469–80.

Reinhart, Carmen, and Kenneth Rogoff. 2009. *This Time is Different: Eight Centuries of Financial Folly.* Princeton: Princeton University Press.

Ryan, Vincent. 2011. "China's Currency Conversion." *CFO Magazine,* July 15.

Tang, Guoxing. 2000. "A Model Study of Balance of Payments and Money Supply of China." In *Econometric Modeling of China,* eds. Lawrence R. Klein and Shinichi Ichimura, 9–65. Singapore: World Scientific.

Zhang, Liqing. 2004. "Coping with China's Balance of Payments Surplus: Why and How?" *China and World Economy* 12(4): 79–87.

Zhu, Yiping. 2010. "Trade, Capital Flows and External Balance: Is China Unique in Two Hundred Years of Globalisation?" *Journal of Chinese Economic and Business Studies* 8(1): 1–22.

4 Long-Run Economic Growth

冰冻三尺，非一日寒
Only a Long Winter Yields Thick Ice—Beijing Was Not Built in a Day

We now turn to one of the most important and challenging questions in macroeconomics: What determines the long-run growth of an economy? Long-run growth refers to the secular real growth in GDP that occurs over decades after smoothing out (filtering) short-run business cycles. While macroeconomic analysis often focuses on the latter (for good reason), it is long-run growth that ultimately determines the economic well-being of a nation's citizens. More immediately, we are interested in the question: Why does China consider a growth rate of 7.3 percent as disappointing while the United States considers growth rates of 4 percent to be extraordinarily good? How sustainable is China's growth rate and how do we know that, over time, China's rapid growth will gravitate toward the same rates found in the United States and other advanced economies?

A careful analysis of what determines long-run growth is warranted for at least three reasons:

1. Small differences in growth rates can make huge differences in standards of living over a relatively short time. For example, a real GDP growth rate that is just twenty-five basis points higher (.0025 points) in Country A than in Country B will result in one's grandchildren having a standard of living approximately 20 percent higher in Country A. In 1980, China's nominal GDP was only 11 percent of U.S. GDP; by 2011, it had reached 50 percent of U.S. GDP. That ascent reflected real GDP growth for the period of around 10 percent and 2.6 percent, respectively. In Figure 4.1, we see that China's purchasing power parity per capita income has moved from under 5 percent of United States levels to over 20 percent during the same time span.
2. Higher long-run growth allows for the economic pie to expand over time, which reduces potential conflict among society's various stakeholders (government, companies, investors, and citizens). In China during recent decades, this has allowed a consensus to form among society's stakeholders regarding a broad range of policies.
3. Any discussion of economic growth allows us to introduce key macroeconomic concepts and definitions including: average productivity, technical progress, and value-creating growth. Furthermore, through comparing China and the United States, we gain a deeper insight into what it means to categorize China as "labor intensive" and the United States as "capital intensive."

Figure 4.2 shows growth in the United States and China from 1970 to 2011. Despite the considerable short-run fluctuations, we can see China's long-term growth rates rising significantly above U.S. growth rates from the late 1970s (beginning with the period of economic reform), then a dramatic widening from 1990 to the present (reflecting substantial rises in productivity). In this chapter, we discuss the causes and meaning of these differences. Part I presents the standard Solow accounting framework, the Solow–Swan growth theory (Solow growth theory), then various extensions and theoretical challenges to the Solow model. Along the way, we will examine specific examples related to China's

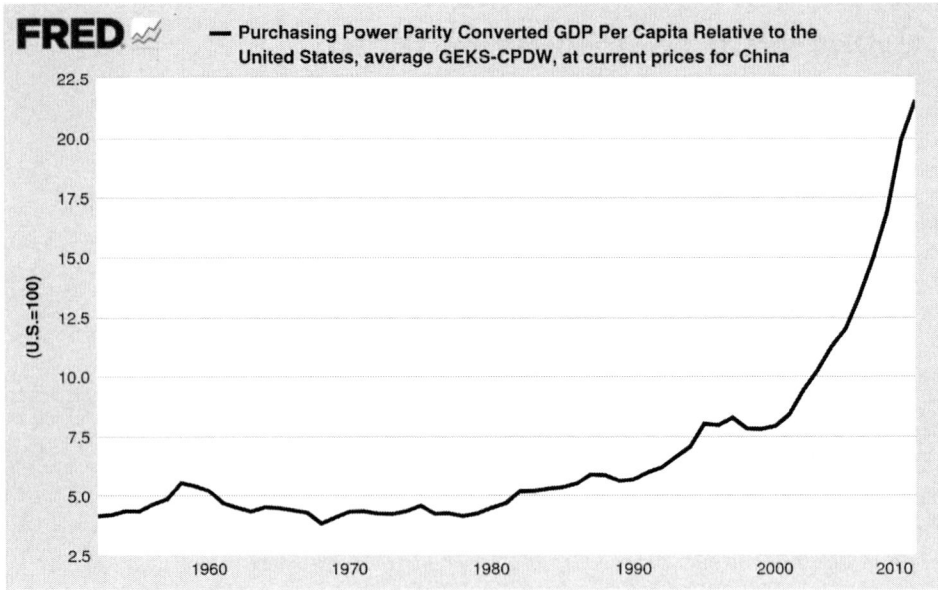

Figure 4.1 China's spectacular growth since the start of the reform period (1978) has resulted in per capita income rising from less than 5 percent of U.S. levels to over 20 percent.

Source: FRED, Federal Reserve Economic Data, Federal Reserve Bank of St. Louis: Purchasing Power Parity Converted GDP Per Capita Relative to the United States, average GEKS-CPDW, at Current Prices for China; University of Pennsylvania. 2014 research.stlouisfed.org

Figure 4.2 Real GDP growth in China, an emerging economy, has far exceeded that of the United States, a mature economy, for a prolonged period.

Source: FRED, Federal Reserve Economic Data, Federal Reserve Bank of St. Louis: Constant Price Gross Domestic Product in China, Gross Domestic Product by Expenditure in Constant Prices in U.S. 2014 research.stlouisfed.org
Note: Shaded areas indicate U.S. recessions.

astounding GDP growth and gain insights into the future outlook. Part II examines the related and important question of "quality of growth" in China, borrowing concepts from corporate finance.

Part I: Economic Basis for Long-Run Growth

The Accounting Framework

A good starting point for any discussion of economic growth is the Solow accounting framework, which decomposes growth into component factors of production including: capital (K), labor (L), and an exogenously determined factor referred to as "technological progress" (A). Since long-run equilibrium growth in these neoclassical models is determined by assumed outside forces (such as population growth), they are commonly referred to as "exogenous growth models."

For now, we assume (in our accounting decomposition) a closed economy, full employment of resources, and the absence of short-run business cycle fluctuations such as recessions and recoveries. (We can always relax these assumptions to add specific relevance.) Let's assume only two factors of production: capital (K) and labor (L). These factors are needed to produce goods and services in the economy, including capital, itself. Thus, we can say, Equation 1:

(1) $Y = A \times f(K,L)$

in which, as always, Y represents GDP or output. Here, we combine capital and labor in our economy somehow in order to get output or GDP. This combination will be adjusted based on how much technology (A) we have at our disposal. Further, we can make each variable dependent on time (t), where t represents one year, and give more specificity to Equation 1, as seen in Equation 2:

(2) $Y(t) = A(t) \times K^\alpha(t) \times L^\beta(t)$

Here, α and β can be interpreted in three different ways: (1) returns-to-scale, when we increase K and L in tandem; (2) elasticities of output (Y) with respect to inputs K or L; or (3) in the case of constant returns-to-scale, shares of national income received by the two factors as compensation for their contribution to national income. These interpretations are more clearly seen if we take the natural logarithm of each side of Equation 2, yielding, Equation 3:

(3) $Ln(Y(t)) = Ln(A(t)) + \alpha Ln(K(t)) + \beta Ln(L(t))$

For example, if we increase K and L by 1 percent, output increases by ($\alpha + \beta$) percent. (For now, we are assuming that A grows exogenously over time, allowing us to focus on the path of Y, K, and L.)

Taking the first derivative of Equation 3, with respect to time and using Δ to indicate change, we have, Equation 4:

(4) $\Delta Y(t) / Y(t) = \Delta A(t) / A(t) + \alpha \Delta K(t) / K(t) + \beta \Delta L(t) / L(t)$

Equation 4 provides an obvious but important finding: economic growth relies on growth in inputs and the degree to which technological progress [$\Delta A(t) / A(t)$] occurs. Simply put, if we consistently lack sufficient capital or labor, it will be difficult to increase output. This is true both when we measure growth and output over time as well as against a cross-section of countries. Small countries tend to have small GDPs, while large countries (such as the United States and China) have large GPDs; this outcome results from the pool of available inputs. However, we must always acknowledge the important role of technology (A) in qualifying these results.

Case Study 4.1: China's Growth Since the 1978 Economic Reforms

Beginning in 1978, China embarked on a dramatic new course for economic management. Moving from the dirigiste Communist-bound tradition of central planning to a market-based system of economic organization (termed as either "Socialism with Chinese characteristics," "Socialist Market Economy," or "Capitalism with State Planning and Intervention"), China's economic landscape had been transformed. From the death of Mao Zedong (in 1976) and the return of Deng Xiaoping in 1978, initial reforms began in the agricultural sector across locations ranging from Sichuan to Guangdong Provinces. Lin (1992) discusses this process, which began by reforming agricultural pricing structures, as well as production.

Under China's new household responsibility system (家庭联产承包责任制), peasants were allowed to grow and sell their output using land leased from the local municipality, rather than working on collectivized plots of land. Rather than central planners deciding key inputs such as how much fertilizer to order, farmers were permitted to make these decisions on their own. In this way, individual incomes quickly became linked to the individual farmer's efficiency and efforts, and the reforms reduced the role of the state and enhanced the role of markets in agricultural production.

During the 1980s, privatization moved into the industrial sector (Chow 1993). Since China's state-owned enterprises (SOEs) were at the time the main source of output, they became the new target for reform. Ever greater autonomy was given to SOEs in terms of employment, wages, investment, and inputs, and the retention of profits. Special economic zones (experimental geographic areas in which government intervention in markets was vastly reduced and foreign investment was encouraged) flourished in certain provinces including Guangdong, Jiangsu, Zhejiang, Shanghai, and other areas in Eastern China.

During this time, China's town and village enterprises (TVEs)—partnerships between local governments, local managers or company founders, and local workers—served as bridges between the previous Communist system and the emerging corporate structure. These very dynamic enterprises, which also were located in Eastern China, in cities such as Wenzhou, became very profitable and important sources of foreign exchange earnings from exports. Other reforms included increased openness to foreign direct investment, and liberalization of international trade—which culminated in China's accession to the World Trade Organization (WTO) in 2001. Institutional reforms in corporate governance, regulations, and the law continued in the early part of the new millennium. Financial reform involving the evolution of China's "Big Four" state-owned banks into true financial institutions also began in the late 1990s.

What was the impact of this massive effort at economic and institutional reform in China? A number of authors including Lin (1992), Hu and Khan (1996), and Chow (1993) have employed the Solow accounting framework to address this question. Table CS4.1a uses a Solow accounting perspective to present representative results of China's spectacular growth. These results show an incredible 60 percent increase in economic growth rates during the post-1978 reform period versus the prior decades of state intervention and planning. While much of this growth was due to the greater use of a key input—capital—in production, the results also suggest that total factor productivity or technical progress played an even more important role. By these estimates, close to half of the growth rates or all of the increment in growth can be attributed to this factor alone.

Table CS4.1a Estimates of the sources of China's growth.

	Hu and Khan (1996)		World Bank (1997)
	1953–78	1978–95	1978–95
Growth rates (% per annum)			
Output	5.8	9.3	9.4
Contribution to growth (%)*			
Physical-capital input	3.8	4.2	3.5
Labor input	1.0	1.2	0.7
Human-capital input	NA	NA	0.8
Total Factor Productivity	1.0	3.9	4.3

Source: Francis, Painchaud, and Morin, 2005.
*Percentages are rounded and therefore do not add up to 100.

Table CS4.1b Total factor productivity (TFP) growth has been a major source of China's economic growth since reforms began in 1978. A key component of this source was the movement of labor from agriculture to manufacturing and construction.

Estimates of Sources of TFP Growth in China

	Heytens and Zebregs (2003)				
	1971–78	1979–94	1985–89	1990–94	1995–98
Total Factor Productivity	−0.53	2.78	2.11	2.81	2.30
Structural reform	0.38	0.94	0.76	0.83	0.39
Labor migration out of primary sector	2.34	2.01	1.52	2.15	2.08
Exogenous trend	−3.25	−0.17	−0.17	−0.17	−0.17

Source: Francis, Painchaud, and Morin, 2005.
*Percentages are rounded and therefore do not add up to 100.

Other researchers provide a more nuanced explanation. Alwyn Young (2003), for example, estimates growth in total factor productivity in this period in the industrial sector was only 1.4 percent, with labor productivity rising 2.6 percent.* He suggests that these growth rates, while significant, are no different from those of other East Asian emerging economies during economic reforms. Young's careful analysis of the data suggests that increased labor participation rates, enhanced human capital, plus agricultural reforms which freed up labor for industry were the key drivers for economic growth in the industrial sector (see Table CS4.1b).

Table CS4.1b illustrates the drivers behind China's increased total factor productivity. Here, we see that labor migration played an important role. The process of agricultural reform allowed many workers with previously low productivity to shift into the higher productivity industrial sector. Furthermore, the reorganization of work around a market-based system allowed the agricultural sector itself to grow at an unprecedented pace. Agricultural reform allowed productive workers to increase output sufficiently while releasing non-productive workers to move into high-margin activities. We can now understand the very broad impact of "technical progress" referred to as "*A*" in the Solow framework. Not only does it include education, new technology, and the results of R&D, but it also dictates how the work is organized and managed.† Lin (1992) estimates that nearly half of the increase in China's early reform output was triggered by the new Household Responsibility System. For example, shifting into a more market-based system is a significant form of technical progress. A similar phenomenon was observed during the Enclosure Movement of the seventeenth to nineteenth century, when European agricultural land was permitted to be fenced off for private rather than communal production. The above results are also consistent with a number of academic studies on the U.S. economy (Denison, 1974).

* Young also estimates a lower growth in industrial output for a similar period.
† Of course, this is the very notion that professors of management teach in their courses.

The term, $\Delta A(t) / A(t)$, is commonly referred to as "technological progress," "total factor productivity," or "the Solow residual." Historically, we can estimate economic growth (the left side of Equation 4 above) as well as deriving estimates of how fast our factors of production (such as K and L) have grown. This allows us to infer or estimate the term, $\Delta A(t) / A(t)$; it serves as a "catch-all" for any growth that cannot be explained by factor of production (K and L) growth. Economic growth is caused not only by the raw accumulation of inputs but the "other" factor which we call "technological progress." In fact, it may also be called "ignorance" since the $\Delta A(t)/A(t)$ term reflects whatever remains unexplained by our accounting model, (i.e., everything we have left out). In other words, it really serves an accounting "plug." Since close to half of economic growth is represented by this term, optimists say that broadly defined technology is vital to economic growth, while skeptics say there is much we do not know about why economic growth occurs.

Accounting for Growth in Labor Productivity

In competitive markets, the entire economy benefits from improvements in labor productivity, and each worker benefits from his or her enhanced productivity. With that premise in mind, we now examine the factors that determine growth in labor productivity from a growth accounting framework. We can define average labor productivity as seen in Equation 5:

(5) $y = Y / L$

or total output divided by the size of the workforce. Growth in y is the growth in the ratio of *Y/L*. The growth in this ratio is approximately, Equation 6:

(6) $\Delta y / y = \Delta Y / Y - \Delta L / L$

This is growth in labor productivity, a key metric in understanding how (in a material sense) individuals in society are improving.[1] We will now assume that the economy exhibits constant returns-to-scale, or that $\alpha + \beta = 1$, or that we can substitute in Equation 4 for β the expression $1 - \alpha$, that is, Equation 7:[2]

(7) $\beta = 1 - \alpha$

Combining Equations 4, 6, and 7, we arrive at an accounting for average labor productivity growth, as seen in Equation 8:

(8) $\Delta y / y = \Delta A(t) / A(t) + \alpha[\Delta K(t) / K(t) - \Delta L(t) / L(t)]$

Equation 8 shows that growth in labor productivity depends on two key factors: technological progress and growth in capital relative to growth in the labor force. This intuitive result implies that the more equipment and the better technology each worker has to work with, the more productive he or she will be.

From Solow Accounting to Solow Theory

Solow accounting, in and of itself, is a valuable tool for decomposing growth into its constituent components. As soon as we begin to make assumptions, we move from the realm of accounting to theory. We now discuss a theoretical framework for growth (the neoclassical framework) that has a long history in economics (see Domar, 1946). In this basic version (Solow–Swan), we make several assumptions:

1. Constant returns-to-scale or, as in above: $\alpha + \beta = 1$.
2. An economy that is closed to international trade and capital flows (can always be relaxed).
3. Exogenous population growth, assumed to grow at a rate of $\Delta L / L = \eta$; this is the same growth as the labor force.
4. Savings rate (as a share of income) that is exogenous at "*s*," and a depreciation rate for capital that is exogenous at "*dep*."
5. The Solow accounting framework is a valid accounting of economic growth.

We will continue the convention of defining small letter variables to represent per capita versions of the corresponding capital letters. So:

$y = Y / L$
$k = K / L$

and to repeat:

- s = the savings rate such that $s \times Y$ and $s \times y$ yields national savings, S, or per capital savings S/L
- η = rate of population and labor force growth
- *dep* = the rate of depreciation of K and k.

Employing our constant returns-to-scale assumption and Equation 2 above, we have Equation 9:

(9) $Y(t) = A(t) \times K^{\alpha}(t) \times L^{(1-\alpha)}(t)$

Expressing this in per capita terms, we divide Equation 9 by labor (L) to say in Equation 10:

(10) $y = A \times (k)^{\alpha}$

Figure 4.3 shows the relationship in Equation 10 between y and k. It is concave downward because, under our assumed production function (with constant returns-to-scale), increasing the ratio of capital to labor (k) causes diminishing returns.[3] Once again, we can use the relationship between the growth rate of a ratio and the numerator and denominator of that ratio analogous to Equation 6. Equation 11:

(11) $\Delta k / k = \Delta K / K - \Delta L / L = \Delta K / K - \eta$

We will refer to Equation 11 as **STEP 1**.

Secondly, we note that the ΔK is the net increase in the capital stock or net investment. Net investment is the difference between gross investment and depreciation, shown in Equation 12:

(12) $\Delta K = I - dep \times K$

where I is gross investment.

We note that in a closed economy, I in Equation 12 equals Savings or $S = I$. We note further that $S = s \times Y$. Combining these definitions and Equation 12, we can say, Equation 13:

(13) $\Delta K = s \times Y - dep \times K$

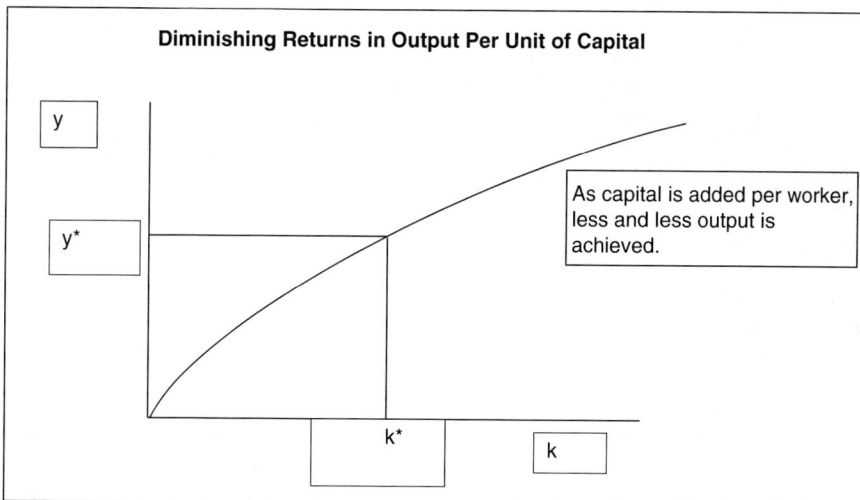

Diminishing Returns in Output Per Unit of Capital

y

y*

As capital is added per worker, less and less output is achieved.

k*

k

Figure 4.3 Adding more capital per worker will increase output but with diminishing returns.

Source: Author created.

We will refer to Equation 13 as **STEP 2**.

Substituting ΔK from STEP 2 in Equation 13 into STEP 1 in Equation 11, we have, Equation 14:

(14) $\Delta k = s \times y - (\eta + dep) \times k$

or

Δk = sources of capital − uses of capital

In other words, if we hope to increase the amount of per capita capital (how much capital each worker works with), we must ensure that per capital savings exceed the uses of capital. Savings are a source of capital because savings are the part of output not consumed (or exported in an open economy). Thus, the remainder can be used as capital. Depreciation (*dep*) is clearly a "use" of capital, but what about population growth (η)? Population growth is akin to the notion of shareholder dilution in finance; the larger the workforce (analogous to the greater the number of shares), the less capital with which each worker can work (or the less valuable a fixed set of assets per share). Population growth dilutes the pool of capital; thus, in this sense, population growth is a "use" of capital (on a per capita basis) and has the same mathematical effect as depreciation.

Case Study 4.2: China's Population Controls

In 1978, China began a set of policies to control the growth of its population. One year later, the government's family planning policy (more commonly called the "one child policy") was instituted and included, as its centerpiece, the limitation of one child per urban family.* The policy was a response to the strain on resources (ranging from food and water to energy) caused by China's vast population.† By 1978, China's population had reached almost 1 billion people. Despite an overall decline in birth rates between the founding of the People's Republic of China in 1949 and 1978, China's population had actually grown during this period due to greater life expectancy (which, in part, reflected lower infant mortality rates). The family planning policies of 1978 were the government's response to the overall growth. Figure CS4.2a depicts a corresponding deceleration of population growth beginning in 1978. From 1978 to 2010, the population grew at a compounded rate of about 1 percent per year—virtually identical to that of the United States in the same period. While much of the U.S. population growth has been (and is) fueled by immigration, China's population growth reflects a number of exemptions to the one child policy.‡ Rural families and ethnic minorities, for example, were allowed to have more than one child. In addition, the greater freedom to move from one part of the country to another has led to the one child rules being flouted due to a lack of ability to track births.

Originally, the policy was intended to last only one generation. As often happens with well-intentioned government policies, the law of unintended consequences has come into play; a preference for male heirs has led to an imbalance in the population toward boys. In addition, as discussed in Chapter 5, the one child policy has led to an ever-aging population in China. These outcomes have caused the government to rethink the program and, in recent years, to grant further exemptions. By late 2013, the authorities began allowing parents who were themselves both single children to have two children. The upshot of these policies, from a Solow perspective, was to reduce the "uses of savings" slope (η + dep) as indicated in Figure CS4.2b

Figure CS4.2b shows the initial steady state at A (with a relatively high rate of population growth), then B (in which population growth has slowed). At the steady state B, we have a higher level of per capita income in the long run. However, as with all steady states in the Solow framework, growth of overall output $\Delta Y / Y$ equals growth in population (i.e., a slower rate of output growth). This is paradoxical: higher per capita income but slower long-run growth. The key to understanding this is to realize that countries that ultimately increase the ratio of capital (or other key factors) to the labor force have a higher standard of living. But when one key input (such as labor) grows more slowly, this eventually causes a bottleneck that reduces growth in output. In other words, over time, China's family planning policy will surely make the population better off, but just as surely force down China's current double-digit nominal growth rates.

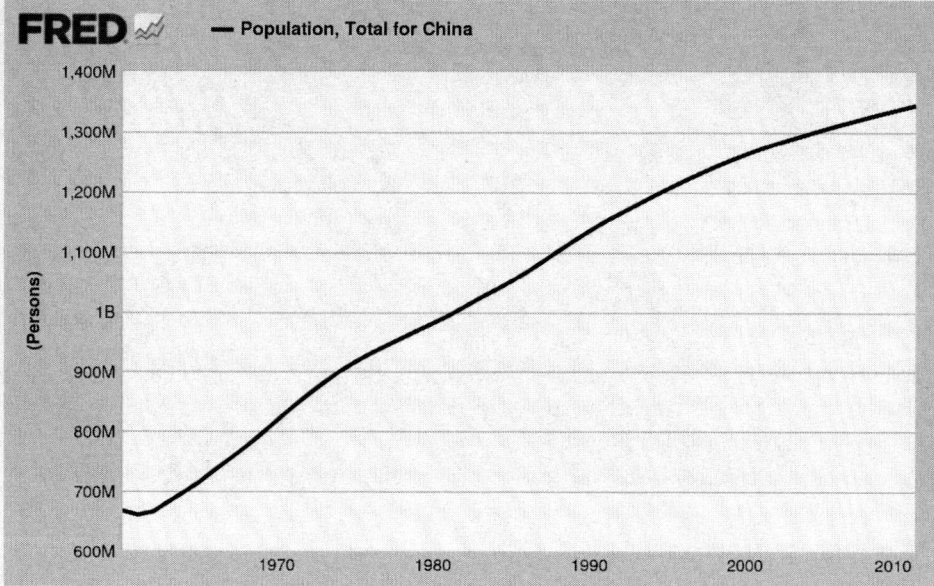

Figure CS4.2a China implemented a set of policies to limit population growth in the late 1970s.

Source: FRED, Federal Reserve Economic Data, Federal Reserve Bank of St. Louis: Population, Total for China; World Bank. 2014 research.stlouisfed.org

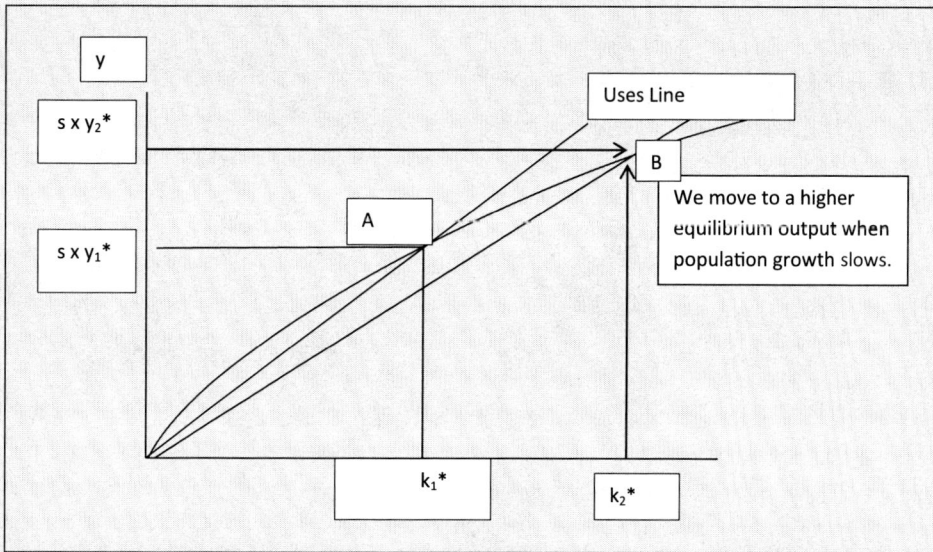

Figure CS4.2b The effect of slower population growth in the Solow framework is to increase per capita output but decrease growth of total output in the steady-state.

Source: Author created.

In the above discussion, we have focused on China's overall population growth, however some significant sub-trends in the actual labor force are or will become important. First is China's increase in labor force participation in the industrial sector, which resulted from the nation's massive agricultural reforms. Second is China's changing population demographics from working age to old age—a shift in the dependency ratio that will reduce the availability of workers.

*A complementary policy was to create a minimum marriageable age in China of twenty years of age for women and twenty-two for men; this is the highest regulated marriage age in the world.
†One measure of this demand on resources is that, in China, the ratio of people-to-acres of arable land is about 6.6 times higher than in the United States.
‡There are an estimated twenty-two different exemptions to China's one child policy (see *New York Times*, July 23, 2012).

With Equation 14 established, we can now find a steady state. The steady state is the point at which sources just equal uses in Equation 14 and $\Delta k = 0$. We call this a "dynamic equilibrium" because it is a point at which the system is stable and toward which the economy gravitates. If $\Delta k = 0$, then we can also see from Figure 4.4 that y will also be unchanging. The equilibrium is dynamic in the sense that, although y and k are constant, the variables that lie beneath y and k are still changing (i.e., Y, L, and K). Setting $\Delta k = 0$ in Equation 14, we have the conditions for a steady state in our simple growth model, as seen in Equation 15:

$$(15) \qquad s \times y = (\eta + dep) \times k$$

In Equation 15, we have a critical result, stating that the long-run destination of an economy is the point at which the sources of capital just equal its uses. Significantly, at that point, y and k will be

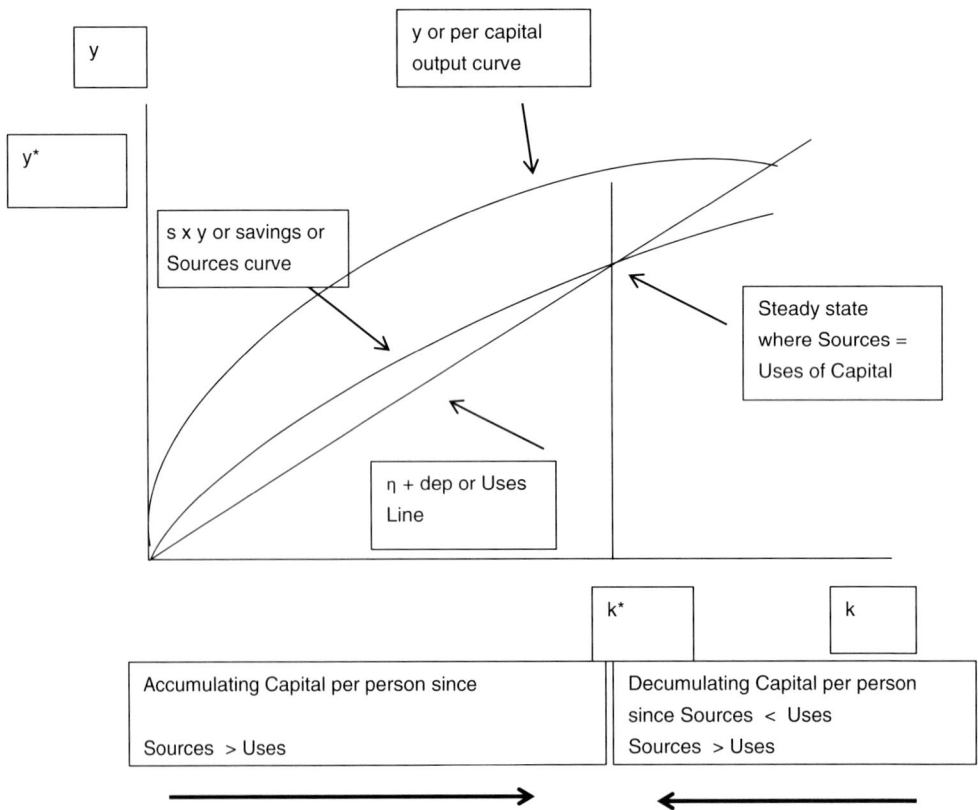

Figure 4.4 In the Solow framework, the steady state is where the sources of capital (savings) just equal its uses (population growth and depreciation).

Source: Author created.

unchanging; therefore, we have specific solutions for y and k which we can call y^* and k^*. Figure 4.4 shows such a possible combination. Given that $y = Y/L$ and $k = K/L$, and that y and k are constant at y^* and k^*, and that labor (L) is assumed to be growing at a constant rate (η), we reach another key result. At the steady-state equilibrium, Equation 16:

(16) $\Delta Y/Y = \eta = \Delta K/K$

That is, at the steady-state equilibrium (the point where we believe the economy will end up), the growth in output and the capital stock will equal (or be constrained by) our assumed growth in the labor force (η). This key result is worth restating: assuming that a key input into the production process—such as labor (L)—is limited or grows within limits, then it is natural to assume that this will ultimately hinder economic growth. In other words, the economy cannot grow much faster over the long run than one of its key inputs.[4]

What drives this result in an economic sense? Three key factors "drag" an economy down to its steady-state equilibrium:

1. As more capital is accumulated in the face of constant growth in the labor supply, diminishing returns set in.
2. As an economy increases its capital stock, more of its sources of capital (savings), are used just to cover the depreciation of the ever-larger capital stock.
3. As an economy increases its per capita capital stock, each new entrant (labor force member) requires more capital just to maintain the same level of per capita income as the previous cohort of workers. A key use rises.

One critical assumption in this simple model of growth is the constant growth rate of the labor force. Despite the limitations of this assumption, we have some critical insights into the causes of very rapid economic growth and what, over time, constrains that growth.

Case Study 4.3: Solow Theory and Why China is Growing Far Faster Than the United States and Europe

We now have some basic tools for assessing why a country such as China can grow at three to four times the rate of the United States for a number of years. Figure CS4.3a shows the algebraic results of our analysis, depicting our sources (savings) and uses (population growth and depreciation) of capital lines. In addition, we also see our per capita income, or y-line. Recall that both the savings and income line are concave downward due to diminishing returns. The point at which the sources and uses line intersect is a key point: the "steady state." Beneath this point of intersection, lies Equation 16, in which growth in capital and output (total, not per capita) just equals population growth. This point represents "dynamic equilibrium."

China, like all emerging economies, lacks the legacy of a large capital stock. Even though capital has steadily been added to the economy (especially infrastructure) since 1978, per capita capital still remains well below industrialized economies such as the United States. As shown in Figure 4.3a, China is well below its steady state (to the left of k^*). Since 1978, and continuing in the decades to come, China is moving rightward in the direction of the steady-state point of $s \times y^*$, y^*, and k^*. Thus, both y and k are growing.

Since y and k are Y/L and K/L, respectively, and since y and k are rising, we can infer that Y and K are growing faster than the labor force (L). Thus, growth in capital, labor force participation, and technological progress will be the key drivers of growth. Meanwhile, as a mature economy, the United States is already at or near its steady state. Its growth has been dragged down by the forces of depreciation, diminishing returns, and the need to bequest an ongoing high standard of living to each additional entrant into the population. In the United States, growth in the labor force and technological progress will be key drivers of growth.

Beyond China's ability to accumulate capital while avoiding some of the constraints seen in the United States, other key factors come into play. Although China's savings rate is higher than that of the United States (as discussed in Chapter 5), and China has been creating, adopting, and adapting technology from all

y

y*

y or per capital
Output curve

s x y or savings or
Sources curve

United States is a
mature economy
operating near its
steady-state.

η + dep or Uses
Line

Accumulating Capital per person since
Sources > Uses; this is where **China**
is operating.

k*

k

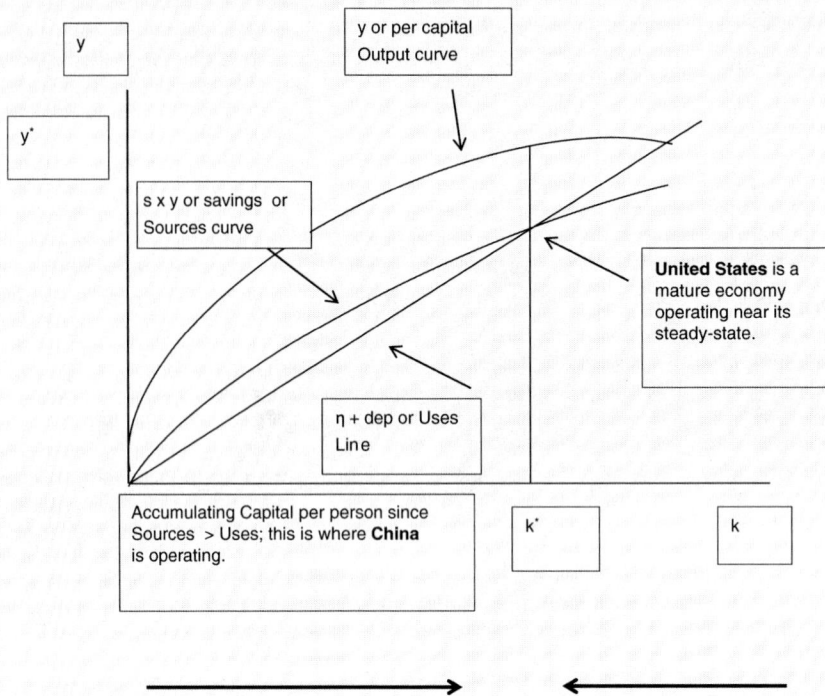

Figure CS4.3a China is well below its steady state and as such is still accumulating capital at a rapid
rate. The United States has matured closer to a steady state where sources of capital are
offset by uses of capital.

Source: Author created.

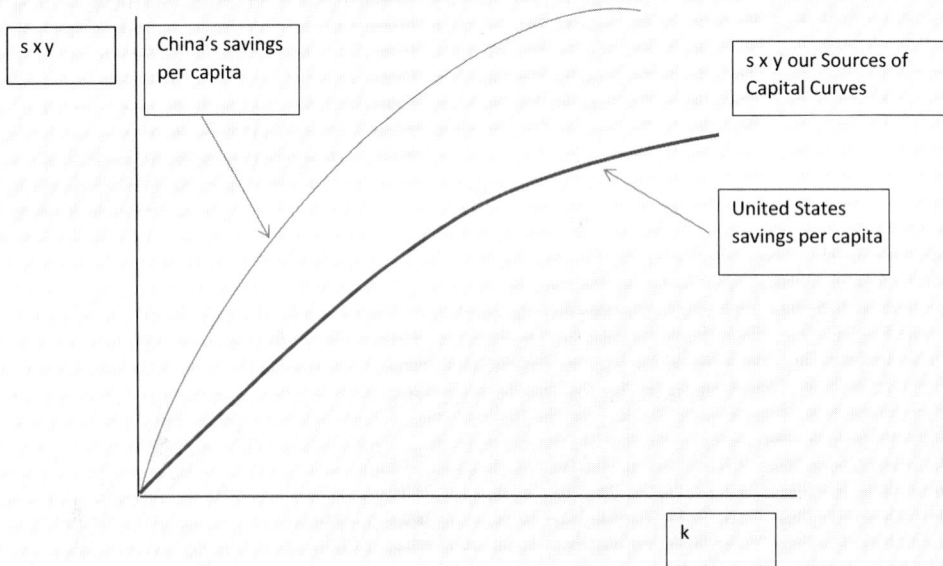

s x y

China's savings
per capita

s x y our Sources of
Capital Curves

United States
savings per capita

k

Figure CS4.3b China's per capita savings is still well below the United States even though its long-run
savings curve is above that of the United States.

Source: Author created.

Table CS4.3a We see an extraordinary buildup of capital in China when we examine the unweighted growth rate of capital in the latter part of the twentieth century. That buildup actually accelerated over the most recent decades.

	Real Growth Rates 1978–98	
	United States	China
Output*	3.0%	10.6%
Capital	2.1%	9.8%
Labor†	1.6%	2.9%

Source: Author created.
*Growth in output in manufacturing sector in the United States and non-agricultural sector in China.
†U.S. labor force growth and China non-agricultural employment growth.

over the world (causing the *y*-curve and *s x y*-curve to shift upward over time), its per capita savings is still one-third the U.S. rate. This is caused by China's larger population and the fact that it has not yet reached the steady state. In other words, although China's long-run savings curve is above that of the United States, it must move to the right along that curve for some time (likely several decades) before matching the per capita savings ratio of the United States (see Figure CS4.3b). In the future, given a higher per capita savings rate and technological progress, China will accumulate capital (*K*) faster than the United States, and growth rates will be even higher. It will take time, however, for China to be able to create as much capital per person as the United States.

Tables CS4.1a and CS4.3a illustrate the rapid buildup of capital in the industrial sector in China versus the United States following the 1978 reforms.* In both China and the United States, growth in output exceeded growth in production factors, reflecting the impact of technological progress. China relied more heavily on the growth in its capital stock, while the United States relied relatively more on technological progress. As mentioned earlier, China's employment growth in the industrial sector represented a shift from agricultural to manufacturing. As a result, employment growth exceeded population growth for the same period. Another important factor was a demographic shift in China as more of the population reached working age in the 1980s and 1990s. In the United States, meanwhile, the constraints of the Solow steady state seem to be at work; both capital and labor are growing at relatively low rates.

* The numbers differ between tables mainly because Tables CS4.1a shows weighted growth rates (by α and β) while growth rates in Table CS4.3a are unweighted.

Case Study 4.4: Are China's Provinces Converging?

One conclusion from the Solow growth theory is that if countries have access to similar technology (similar production functions), population growth rates, availability of savings, and factors of production, then they will all converge (over time) to similar levels of per capita income or development.* This is based on the notion that countries with low levels of capital grow faster than those with a lot of capital and which are already at a steady state. Prima facie, this conclusion is false. The twentieth century appears to show greater divergence between clusters of countries (i.e., Europe and North America, Southern Hemisphere economies, or Asian Tigers such as Singapore, South Korea, and China versus Southeast Asian economies). Instead, economists speak of conditional convergence—that is, convergence that depends on factors including education levels, openness to trade, political systems, or even religious tradition such as Christianity, Hinduism, and so forth (Barro, 1991; Sala-i-Martin, 1997).

Regional convergence is more likely to occur at the state or provincial level, since labor and capital tend to be mobile across state or provincial boundaries, and because access to technology is similar. Furthermore, many of the "conditional" factors—such as culture or religion—are similar within a

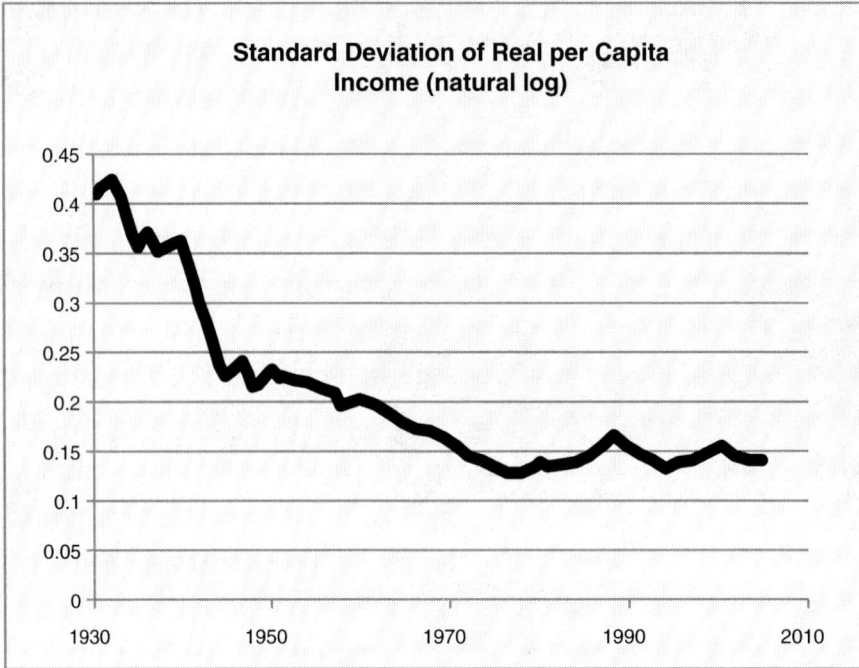

Figure CS4.4a Since 1930 there has been substantial convergence of individual incomes across the United States reflecting urbanization and rapid income growth in the southern states.

Source: DiCecio and Gascon, 2008.

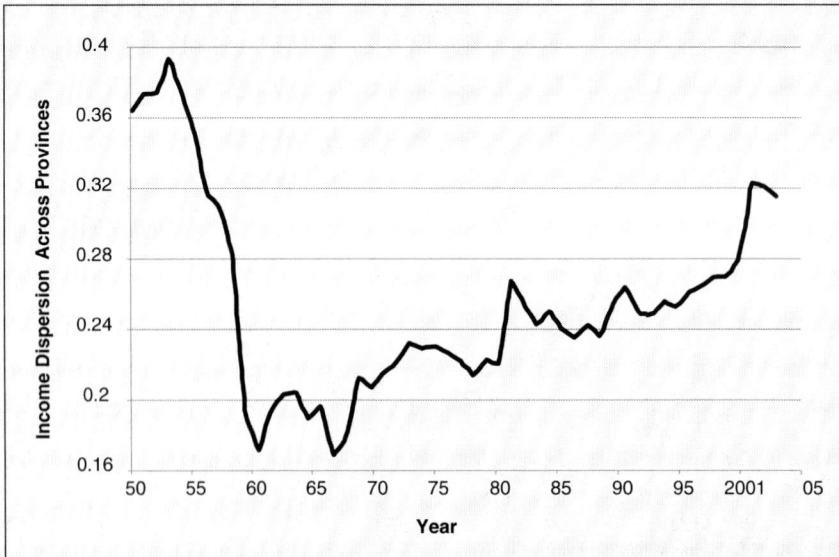

Figure CS4.4b Economic reform has been accompanied by widening income disparity across provinces in China. The charts shows the provincial dispersion of income over time.

Source: Lau, 2010.

country. Figure CS4.4a shows convergence patterns based on U.S. states since 1930 by measuring the standard deviation of per capita real income across states. As we can see, divergence by this measure has decreased from about 0.4 to 0.14. Much of this convergence is due to more rapid growth in per capita incomes in the southern United States. Other authors (DiCecio and Gascon, 2008) suggest that U.S. state convergence is far less important than the convergence of individual incomes in the country, irrespective of state boundaries. Their research points to urbanization in the United States (from rural to urban areas) as the key factor driving individual incomes to converge. Urbanization of the labor force allows for higher productivities, better paying jobs, and (in turn) individual income convergence.

By contrast, since the start of major economic reforms in 1978 (the post-reform period), China has seen increased divergence rather than convergence across provinces (Lau, 2010). Before reforms began, China experienced a tendency toward convergence (see Figure CS4.4b). Clearly, the post-reform divergence indicates that not all provinces have benefitted equally from economic reform. Specifically, the urbanized eastern and southern seaboard benefitted from a resurgence of manufacturing, comparative advantages, and exports while western China's remained mired in outdated modes of agricultural production. This suggests that, before any country can expect convergence, it may first see some regions (clusters) surge ahead. In other words, in order to converge, some successful "pace-setters" must first take the lead.

While the pattern of divergence in post-reform China has been both dramatic and possibly troubling (in terms of social stability), there is good news on the horizon. The research of DiCecio and Gascon (mentioned earlier) suggests that urbanization has played a key role in creating individual economic convergence in the United States. The relaxation of China's *hukou* system (explained in other chapters), coupled with the massive urbanization now under way, suggest that China will eventually experience much greater convergence—at least at the individual level, and likely at the provincial level.

*Even if savings rates differ across countries, access to international capital (global savings) allows for similar levels of per capita domestic product (though different per capita gross national incomes). An analogous concept from international trade theory states that workers in different countries with the same technology and labor force skillset will earn the same wage in a system of free trade in goods and services.

Further Insights into Long-Run Growth

Within the Solow model described above, an economy stabilizes at a steady state (long-run equilibrium) when per capita income is constant and no longer grows. Given the experience of the industrialized economies, in which per capita income experiences positive growth even after these economies have matured, this result (from the base Solow framework) seems too limiting. In fact, in the Solow framework, long-run per capita income can grow if there is technological progress, that is, if

$$\Delta A(t) / A(t) > 0$$

Up to now, we have assumed no technological progress, i.e., this term equals 0. We can see this result in Equation 8, in which the term $(K(t) / K(t) - \Delta L(t) / L(t)) = 0$ in the steady state. As long as $\Delta A(t) / A(t) > 0$, we can still have per capita income growth in the long run (which is consistent with what actually happens in many countries). In this case, the growth rate per capita stabilizes (rather than per capita income stabilizing at a constant ratio) at the rate of technological progress.

Although this result gets us closer to the reality of long-run economic growth, it still does not answer the question: What determines technological progress? Some researchers (Romer, 1994) have found the "exogenous" explanation still wanting and have attempted to find endogenous explanations for long-run growth in the steady state. One focus has been the possibility that the economy experiences increasing returns-to-scale. Figure 4.5 shows how capital is continuously accumulated during economy-wide increasing returns-to-scale, which in turn trigger growth in per capita income. Other approaches rely on "spillovers" of knowledge creation. For example, as firms in a certain industry invest more in R&D, the entire industry benefits from the fruits of such research.

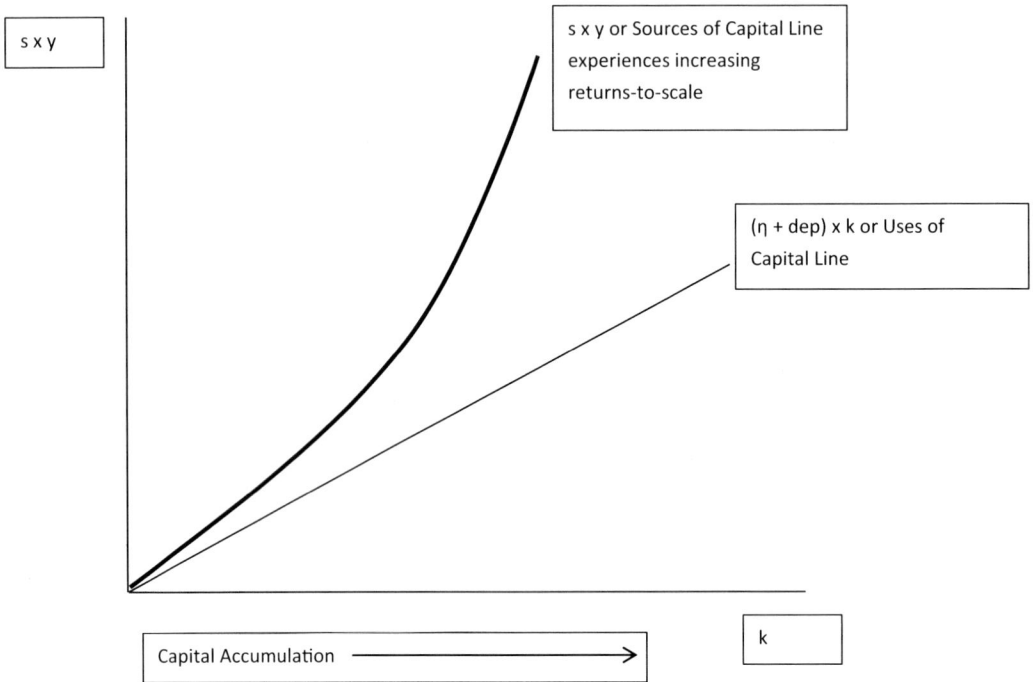

Figure 4.5 In the case of increasing returns-to-scale an economy can experience continued economic growth for a prolonged period without being "trapped" at a steady-state level of per capita income.

Source: Author created.

Case Study 4.5: Increasing and Decreasing Returns-to-Scale

After the death of Mao Zedong in 1976, China entered a brief period of high uncertainty regarding economic policy; should the nation continue following the same interventionist policies promoted by Mao, or move toward a more open economy based on market incentives? The year 1978 was a critical one in which economic reformers took the helm and (among other things) began opening the economy to foreign direct investment.

Under the theory of the firm, a common assumption is that firms first experience increasing returns-to-scale (IRS), then constant returns-to-scale (CRS), then decreasing returns-to-scale (DRS). This is the basis for the U-shaped long-run average cost curve for firms in a competitive industry. What if we applied this theory to an entire economy instead of a single firm? Figure CS4.5a shows a sources line with all three returns-to-scale, in which the uses line intersects the sources line in the CRS region.

In this example, there are three possible steady states: A (famine), B (unstable/intermediate), and C (feast). A country which finds itself initially at B, if bumped slightly to the left (by an economic shock or by bad policy decisions) will tumble inexorably to a very bad steady state at A. Uses will continuously exceed sources of capital, and things will only get worse. On the other hand, a country at B which is slightly bumped to the right by a positive shock (e.g., economic reforms) will move to a very good new steady state at C. This simple example provides a basis for aggressive policy intervention in emerging markets, allowing them to achieve more feast-like steady states instead of heading into famine. Given China's unprecedented growth since 1978, Figure CS4.5a suggests that very good policy decisions were made at the time—and that a much worse alternative path was possible.

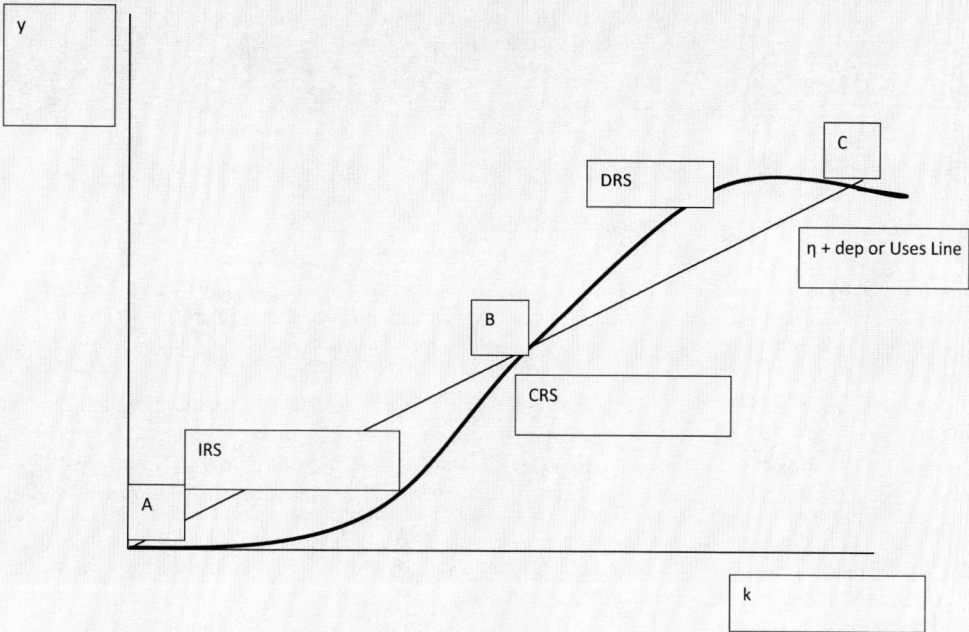

Figure CS4.5a If countries were to resemble firms with increasing (IRS), constant (CRS), and decreasing (DRS) returns-to-scale, there would be two stable steady states in the economy and one unstable one. Depending on policies, a country may end up in a "famine" steady state (A) or a "feast" steady state (C).

Source: Author created.

Other models with "learning by doing" (where workers learn from undertaking higher level tasks) posit that capital accumulation serves dual purposes: the traditional goal of serving as a factor of production, and, just as importantly, the goal of building up human capital. In other words, when new equipment is introduced into the workplace, workers are transformed through acquiring the new skills necessary to operate that equipment. Consider that a new computer is not only a new tool, but also a form of education for the user. By using this new technology, the worker is positively transformed. In the process, capital accumulation triggers an even greater impact than was envisioned in the traditional Solow framework, thus allowing positive per capita income growth in the long run.

**MACRO FINANCE INSIGHT 4.1: SUSTAINABLE GROWTH I—
NATIONAL RETURNS ON CAPITAL**

We can gain insight into which growth rates and returns on investment are sustainable over the long run by using either the Solow model or another simple model borrowed from finance: the Dupont model. Let's first examine sustainable growth and returns using the Solow model.

Figure MF4.1a shows our standard framework but at the optimal level of consumption. By "optimal level of consumption," we mean a particular savings rate and corresponding steady state that maximizes steady-state consumption given all of our other parameters (e.g., technology, population growth rate, and depreciation rate). The steady state that maximizes consumption always corresponds to a point along the uses line $(\eta + dep) \times k$. Consumption will be measured as the difference between savings and income wherever our steady state ends up along the uses line. The maximum point of consumption (the largest gap between the uses line and y) will occur at the point where the slopes of the uses line ($\eta + dep$) and the y-curve ($f'(k)$) are the same. This occurs at point A on Figure MF4.1a. Maximum steady-state consumption (y-c) is measured as the distance between the y-curve and the uses line vertically downward.

We can now state that the optimal steady state in the Solow framework (or the point where consumption is maximized) occurs when, Equation 17:

(17) $f'(k) = \eta + dep$ or $f'(k) - dep = \eta$

However, $f'(k) - dep$ in Equation 17 is simply the real return on capital. Thus, in the base Solow framework, the real return on capital (or assets or investments) is anchored and constrained by a country's population growth, just as GDP growth is locked in by population growth. This is an important benchmark for both China and the United States. Ultimately, the bottleneck for growth and returns is the growth of one key factor—the labor force—over the long run. The significance of this result cannot be overstated for a country such as China, in which (as discussed earlier) the labor force is shrinking. But this is a base case. Changing the dimensions from the long-run overall economy to the shorter-run specific industry dimension, we see other factors can come into play, specifically:

1. Technological progress allows economic growth to surpass the population growth rate, breaking the bottleneck constraint both in the short and long run.
2. Countries including China, although still far below the steady state, can see growth rates and returns surpass population growth for a long time period.
3. Specific economic sectors (e.g., real estate or manufacturing) can reward investors with a risk premium, thus exceeding the economy's overall return on capital.
4. Those parts of the economy that experience increasing returns-to-scale need not be constrained by population growth.

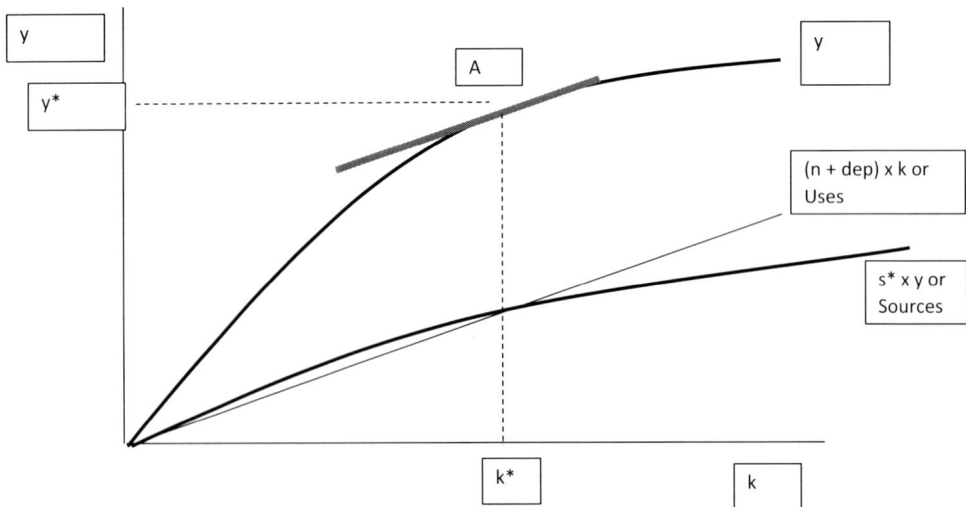

Figure MF4.1a At point A the distance between per capita savings and per capita income is maximized; in other words, per capita consumption is maximized in the steady state—a desirable outcome.

Source: Author created.

5. Monetary and fiscal policies can have an impact on both nominal and real returns in the short run.

Summarizing these results, we find that short-run real return on capital can be expressed as:

Real Return = f (k, population growth, distance from steady state, technological progress, economies of scale, risk, and monetary and fiscal policies)

All of this being said, it is important to keep in mind the benchmark case: the growth rate of an entire economy and the overall real return on capital are unlikely to stray far from each other or from the growth of a fundamental factor of production—its labor force.

Case Study 4.6: Cautionary Tale of Two Cities—Singapore vs. Hong Kong

As shown in Tables CS4.1a and CS4.3a, a key driver for China's growth has been the accumulation of capital (which has been growing at double-digit rates in tandem with GDP). China has the world's largest share of GDP devoted to investment in plant, property, equipment, and infrastructure. Is this necessarily good for China? We addressed a related issue in Chapter 2 on GDP accounting: the question of growth versus value creation. The experiences of Hong Kong and Singapore shed light on these questions. We will use our growth framework to highlight the key issues (Young, 1992).

Both Hong Kong and Singapore are small island economies linked to greater Asia through China or Malaysia. Both are former British colonies with large ethnic Chinese populations. Both have a tradition of open international trade and capital mobility. And both have moved successfully from trade to manufacturing to high-end industries, including banking and finance. Finally, both economies have enjoyed extraordinary growth rates; between 1960 and 2010, Singapore's per capita real income grew at 5.5 percent while Hong Kong's grew at 5.1 percent.

Despite these similarities, there are major differences between the two economies related to economic policy. Hong Kong has relied mainly on a laissez-faire economic policy. The city simultaneously built strong legal and regulatory frameworks while allowing industries and firms substantial leeway in terms of microeconomic choices. Singapore, meanwhile, played a more direct part in encouraging its industries—by targeting key areas for development and, at a macro level, requiring a high level of savings via a mandatory pension plan. In part, these differences reflect Singapore's later start in industrialization and its desire to "catch up" to Hong Kong.

These policy differences have led to dramatic differences in macroeconomic balances. For example, primarily due to its pension scheme requirements on savings, Singapore's savings rate has been at least 50 percent higher than Hong Kong's (45 percent of GDP versus 30 percent from 1998 to 2010). By the late 1990s, Singapore's savings rate exceeded 50 percent of GDP—a rate that compares to recent levels in China. The flip-side of the savings coin was that Singapore's investment shares reached nearly 40 percent of GDP compared to "only" 20 percent of GDP in Hong Kong. In the growth theory context, Hong Kong achieved similar growth to that of Singapore through technological progress, while Singapore relied heavily on the raw accumulation of capital. Meanwhile, per capita annual national income (in dollars) reached US$56,000 in Singapore and US$48,000 in Hong Kong; both countries appear to be close to the same steady state.

Figure CS4.6a provides a stylized, bare bones description of these differences. To highlight the differences in savings rates and technology, we assume that both countries have similar rates of depreciation and population growth; Singapore shows higher savings, while Hong Kong shows greater total factor productivity. On balance, we assume the two effects offset one another such that they have the same sources $(s \times y)$ curve but different per capital output curves, y.

At A, we see identical steady states in terms of capital stocks. But one key difference lies in the measured levels of per capita consumption: $y - (s \times y)$, or output minus savings. In Hong Kong, the difference at the steady state is $(C - A)$, while in Singapore, the distance is $(B - A)$. Clearly, Hong Kong enjoys

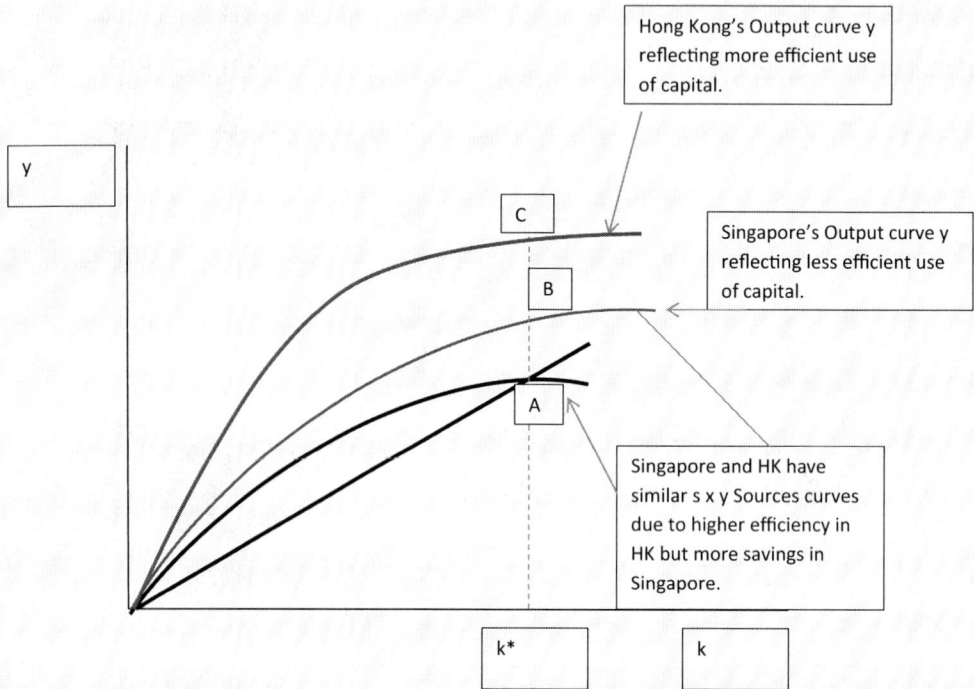

Figure CS4.6a Hong Kong and Singapore are similar but a key difference is Singapore's forced high savings rate which results in a steady-state level of consumption (B–A) which is below Hong Kong's (C–A) and sub-optimal.

Source: Author created.

much greater consumption than does Singapore, despite sharing the same steady state. Why is this? Again, by relying so heavily on capital growth rather than efficiency improvements, Singapore suffers from diminishing returns, depreciation, and the need to bequest to the next generation.

Several studies support these results. An examination of returns to capital and corresponding returns to public pensions shows Singapore as lacking when compared to other developed economies worldwide. By the 1990s, the Singaporean government had recognized the problem of overreliance on a rapid buildup of domestic capital. Singapore's Central Provident Fund (its mandated savings and pension plan) has increasingly looked beyond its borders for international investment opportunities. While this reduces the problem of diminishing returns, the other two problems still remain.

The lessons for China should be clear: relying too heavily on savings and investment as vehicles for growth creates problems later, as an economy moves closer to its steady state.* In particular, savings grow too large, and consumption—a key measure of economic well-being—falls too low. In this scenario, we see a merging of two of China's Five-Year Plan Goals: the need to stimulate short-run demand via consumption and the need to accomplish long-run economic well-being.

*We can argue that economies including Hong Kong and northern European countries such as Germany have found the "Goldilocks" levels of consumption and savings. Their savings rates are above the sub-optimal levels of the United States and other parts of Europe but below those supra-optimal levels of Singapore and China.

Part II: Financial Basis for Long-Run Quality Growth

Part I of this chapter dealt mostly with the question of raw economic growth without looking deeply into the question of the "quality" of growth. In Part II, we apply a finance-based approach to our country growth analysis in order to analyze the quality of growth more carefully. First, we examine the equilibrium relationships between returns on capital and cost of capital. Next, we discuss measuring the return and cost of capital independently.

Using ROIC and WACC to Evaluate the Quality of Growth

Two related formulas from financial valuation link together a firm's weighted average cost of capital (WACC): the return on invested capital (ROIC) and growth rate (*g*). Equations 18 and 19 below show that a firm only creates value (economic profits, defined as profits above and beyond the opportunity cost of), Equation 18:

(18)   Economic Profits = (ROIC − WACC) × Invested Capital

Meanwhile, Equation 19 links long-run firm value with ROIC, WACC, and firm growth, Equation 19:

(19)   Long-Run Firm Value = Operating Profits × (1 − *g* / ROIC) / (WACC − *g*)

In Equations 18 and 19, we see that if ROIC is high and the cost of capital (WACC) is low, the firm's value is larger.[5] In this scenario, growth can only increase value. Importantly, however, if the cost of capital is greater than the returns to capital, then growth actually **destroys** value, and the firm's long-run value is negative. As we emphasize many times throughout this text, high growth rates do not imply value creation. Only when ROIC exceeds its opportunity cost does growth lead to value creation. And even this assumes that the ROIC is truly measuring value—something we discuss below.

In terms of a country's economy, Equations 18 and 19 show that economic growth is good if it occurs when the opportunity cost of growth (foregone consumption) is less than the returns from investments currently undertaken. Later, we will present estimates of WACC and ROIC at a national (country) level.

Measuring ROIC and the Cost of Capital à la Wicksell

Figures 4.6 and Figure 4.7 show Swedish economist Knut Wicksell's explanation for how an economy-wide interest rate is determined through the flow of available savings and investment (the supply of loanable funds and the demand for loanable funds) in a closed economy. (The equilibrium interest rate is described as the natural or long-run interest rate.[6]) We could think of the natural rate as the base rate that determines the equilibrium cost of capital and returns-on-investment in each country. The equilibrium (i.e., the intersection of the savings and investment curves) shows the natural or base rate in a closed economy for each country. In contrast the solid flat line depicts identical equilibrium rates in economies that are fully integrated to capital flows. In Figure 4.6 (which corresponds to the U.S. situation), the base rate exceeds the integrated world rate (*A* > *B*). In Figure 4.7 (which represents China) the base rate is below the world natural interest rate or the integrated rate (*C* < *D*), illustrating the hypothetical rate in an economy completely open to international capital flows. By implication, the base rate is higher in the United States than in China. How can we know if these two figures accurately reflect the relative rates between the two economies?

Recall that the gap between savings and investment represents how much each country is borrowing or lending to cover a current account surplus or deficit. Since the United States is running a current account deficit with China (the gap between savings and investment at some world rate) and China is running a complementary current account surplus, we can infer that the U.S. base rate is above the world rate while China's is below that rate.

One critical problem with the Wicksellian approach, however, is that it assumes market-based decision making regarding capital flows. In fact, capital flows from China to the United States have been traditionally invested in U.S. Treasury instruments at the behest of SAFE (China's State

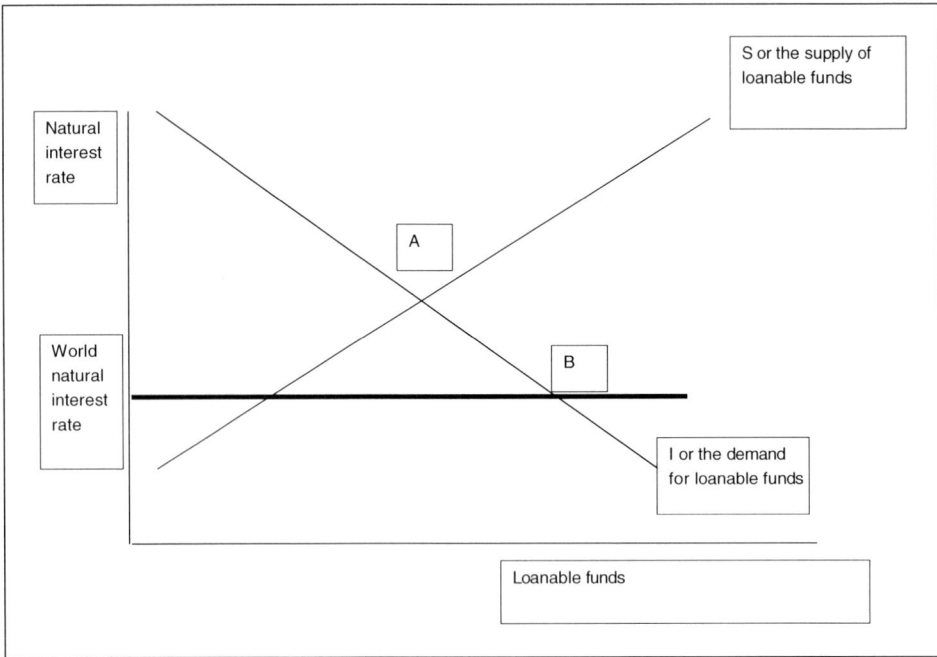

Figure 4.6 A closed economy would have an equilibrium between national savings and investment at A. In an open economy such as the United States where substantial international borrowing occurs, the borrowing rate is at B, well below what would be the rate if the U.S. did not have access to foreign capital.

Source: Author created.

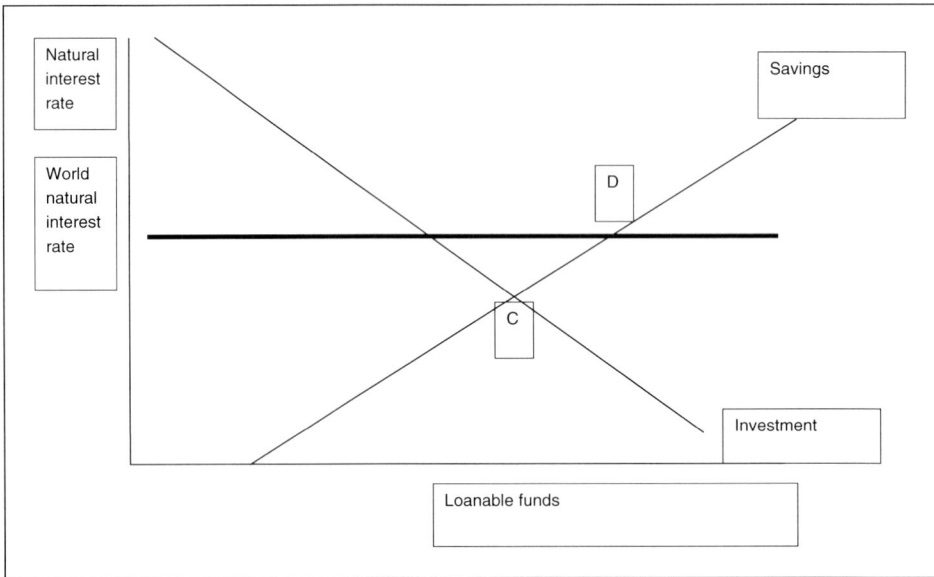

Figure 4.7 In an economy such as China (where controls on capital flows still exist) the equilibrium is somewhere between C and D. China is a net lender to the rest of the world and savings exceeds investment.

Source: Author created.

Administration for Foreign Exchange) and the People's Bank of China (PBC). The Wicksell model is incomplete when examining China and the United States. This analysis does show, however, that current account deficits must be financed, and when financed, they tend to push interest rates lower than they would otherwise be in the borrowing country and higher than otherwise in the lending country.

In summary, China's base rate for cost of capital and investment returns would be lower than the United States' if China were truly closed in terms of lending and borrowing internationally. The fact that China can lend abroad (specifically to the United States) acts as a "relief valve" which has, in recent years, kept China's overall interest rates higher and U.S. rates lower. Despite China's enormous demand for loanable funds (via its vast investment effort), its supply of savings is even more substantial. In fact, a large portion of those savings find their way into the U.S. market for loanable funds—especially funds representing U.S. government credit demands.

Measuring Returns on Capital

We now examine the ROIC which corresponds to the demand for loanable funds or the investment curve.

The Solow Approach and ROIC

One approach to measuring the return on capital economy-wide is to use Equation 4 in the Solow accounting framework itself. Consider Equation 20:

$$(20) \qquad \Delta Y(t) / Y(t) = \Delta A(t) / A(t) + \alpha \Delta K(t) / K(t) + \beta \Delta L(t) / L(t)$$

Maintaining the usual assumption of constant returns-to-scale (CRS), we have $\beta = (1 - \alpha)$. Recall that the coefficients α and $(1 - \alpha)$, when summed in Equation 20, represent either: (1) returns-to-scale (one in this case, since the sum of α and $(1 - \alpha)$ is 1); (2) elasticities of output with respect to input; or (3) shares of national income received by the factors of production (capital and labor). Using interpretation 2, we see that, Equation 20a:

$$(20a) \qquad \alpha = (\Delta Y(t) / Y(t)) / \Delta K(t) / K(t)$$

which in turn can be rearranged as, Equation 20b:

$$(20b) \qquad \alpha = MP_K \times K(t) / Y(t)$$

in which MP_K is our gross marginal product of capital—or, more importantly, our gross return on capital in a competitive market. With a little effort, we can determine the gross return to capital (since Equations 20 correspond to gross domestic output), then subtract out depreciation to determine the real return to capital.[7] Note that we also need to know the capital-to-output ratio.

Bai, Hsieh, and Qian (2006) use a similar approach to estimate returns to capital in China since 1978 in the range of 30 percent (see Figure 4.8) but declining in recent years. This figure represents economy-wide fixed investment, excluding urban housing.[8] Since the shares of income to labor and capital sum to one, the basic approach is to identify income not accruing to labor as accruing to capital. Figure 4.9 shows returns if we include the important non-fixed asset—inventories. During the 1990s, including inventories would have reduced China's average returns by as much as 10 percentage points. The difference in returns between Figures 4.8 and 4.9 highlights an area in which Chinese companies could continue to make improvements: the management of working capital, especially inventories.

Percent a year

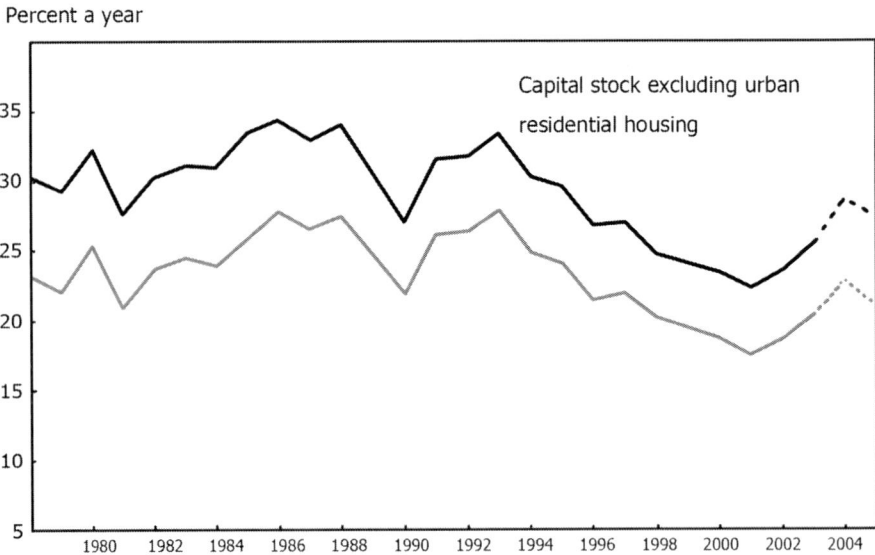

Figure 4.8 China's returns on capital using a Solow-like framework have been historically high but edged down from rates near 30 percent in the early years of reform. The light gray line is the base case benchmark rate of return for China.

Source: Bai et al. (2006).

Percent a year

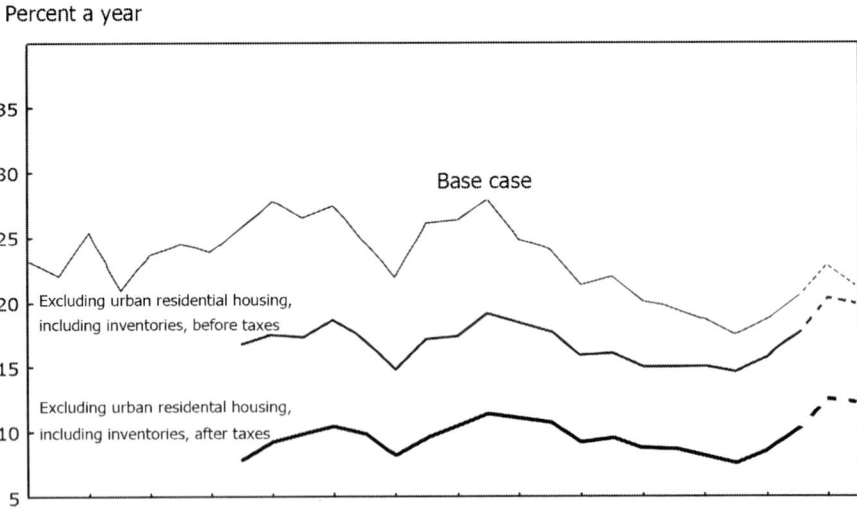

Figure 4.9 China's returns on capital using a Solow-like framework are lower when including China's notoriously high inventories as an asset.

Source: Bai et al. (2006), based on NBS data.

A similar economy-wide business estimate for the United States shows after-tax real returns of 6 to 8 percent—not far below comparable figures in China as seen in Figure 4.9.[9] In summary, regarding fixed assets, China's returns appear to be substantially higher than the United States'. Once inventories are included, returns in each country grow closer.

MACRO FINANCE INSIGHT 4.2: RETURN TO CAPITAL—ROIC AND ICOR

In looking at questions of the efficiency of resource utilization and diminishing returns to capital, a common ratio used in the macro-growth literature is the ICOR (the incremental capital to output ratio). More formally:

ICOR = (Real Investment / Real GDP) / Real GDP Growth

Or more intuitively:

ICOR = ΔK / ΔGDP

The ICOR ratio describes how much additional capital is required in order to increase real GDP—all measured in constant dollars. The ratio is, in effect, the inverse of the marginal productivity of capital measured at a national level. The lower the ratio, the more likely that additional units of capital will be value-creating.* Through the mid-2000s, China's ICOR was relatively low compared to other countries, suggesting room for efficient investment of capital. Our own estimates show an ICOR for China during 1980 to 2011 of 2, and for the United States, of 3.1—a 65 percent difference in favor of China. While China may be entering a transitional phase of diminishing returns to capital, the data for recent years suggest an actual decline in the ICOR. Furthermore, China's ICOR is substantially lower than that of neighboring Asian economies.

ICOR Shortcomings

ROIC as a Measure of Returns Compared to ICOR

A literal but not technical rearrangement of the ICOR is the ROIC (the return on invested capital), which we have already introduced as a concept borrowed from finance. ROIC can be defined and decomposed into the following components, Equation 21:

(21)   ROIC = NI / Assets = Sales / Assets × NI / Sales

Stated in words, we have:

ROIC = Asset Efficiency × Profit Margin

We can immediately see some shortcomings of ICOR when we compare it to the ROIC.

The ROIC does contain one element—asset efficiency—that is similar to the factors measured by the ICOR.† But ICOR does not take into account the other element—profit margins. Equation 21 highlights both a weakness and a danger in using ICOR alone to measure asset efficiency, particularly in making cross-country comparisons. We are leaving out a key term—profit margin—that is just as important a measure of value creation. No matter how much we produce with our assets, a second critical question remains: How much value are we creating? Profit margin is intended to answer that question.

Moving from corporate finance to macro finance, we can think of GDP as the counterpart to corporate revenues, or sales and national savings as the counterpart to corporate (and private) income (profits). Thus, we note a dichotomy between growth and value-creating growth. The fact that the ICOR does not include national savings over sales (profit margins) is critical. Under certain conditions, we can achieve large increases in output with relatively little cost in terms of adding (incrementing) capital (a low ICOR), but still enjoy a very low return on assets. This would occur if firms were not creating value (ROIC) or net income; possibly even destroying value. Countries which grew rapidly (such as the former Soviet Union) or at a company level (such as General Motors) may have favorable ICORs but also low ROICs. Similarly, countries that are producing efficiently in very competitive industries (zero or negative economic profits) may show favorable ICORs, and at the same time, low ROICs.

Cross-Country Comparisons and ICOR

Country-to-country comparisons also present challenges since an ICOR that is considered efficient for one country may not be efficient in another. In equilibrium, a country with high wage costs relative to low labor productivity will use more capital in production and, in turn, have a higher ICOR.‡

Solow and Other Factors Impacting Productivity and ICOR

The ICOR has another serious shortcoming that is highlighted by the Solow framework: ICOR does not take into account (or is not conditioned upon) other key factors such as labor inputs and technological progress. In isolation, ICOR really does not tell us about capital's contribution to value creation since we have not segregated out the contribution of these other key factors.

*Of course, the cutoff for value creation will depend on the opportunity cost (diminished consumption) incurred by adding a unit of capital.

†Besides being the inverse of the other, they differ in two other critical ways: (1) The ICOR is marginal (or increment) in the numerator and denominator, while the ROIC's asset efficiency term represents the average. (2) Sales in ICOR represent final sales plus inventories and indirect taxes rather than revenues (as typically used in the ROIC sales measure for a firm or industry).

‡This would be true if technologies differed between countries, and if trade in goods across borders were impeded. The Heckscher–Ohlin theorem (from international trade) implies that—in the long run—marginal productivities and returns will be equalized between trading countries due to free trade and identical technologies.

Actual Profits and ROIC

A more direct approach in measuring returns is to measure profits (net income) and the assets of companies, and then measure the implied return on assets. Hodge, Corea, Green, and Retus (2012) of the U.S. Bureau of Economic Analysis use this method (Figure 4.10 shows their results). They find recent pre-tax returns for U.S. non-financial corporations at 8–10 percent. These returns are based on fixed assets and inventories of these companies. When comparing returns from the United States to those of China remember that the U.S. data exclude the agricultural sector, infrastructure, and residential housing. As such, they are most comparable to the middle line in Figure 4.9, in which Bai, Hsieh, and Qian show returns of 15 to 20 percent.

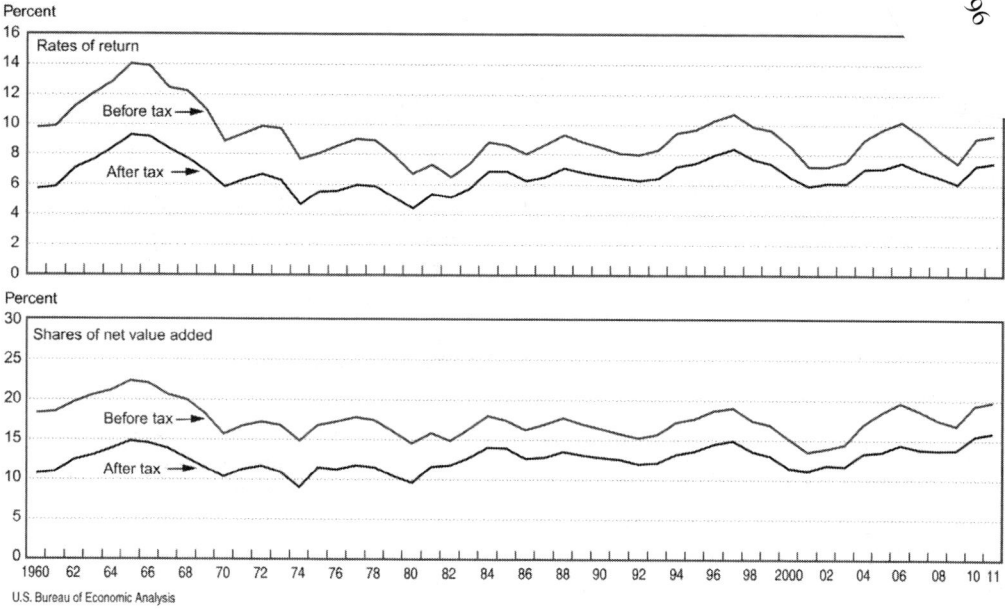

Figure 4.10 Pre-tax rates of return on assets seen in earlier charts show significantly higher returns than those seen below in the United States.

Source: U.S. Bureau of Economic Analysis, *Survey of Current Business.*

The above comparison is largely based on the business sector. We see a ROIC that is greater than the cost of capital in both countries (as discussed below), and ROICs in China that are higher than those of the United States. ROIC across the two economies moves closer when we exclude residential housing but include inventories in our measure of assets. Including residential housing substantially lowers returns in the United States while including inventories substantially lowers returns in China.

A Broader Measure of ROIC: The Dupont Model and Macro Aggregates

We can implement the Dupont model (expressed in Equation 22 and discussed in Macro Finance Insight 4.3) using macroeconomic data for each country. Recall that we proposed using national savings as the counterpart for company income and GDP as a measure of sales. Estimates for a nation's assets are based on annual measures of investment in each country and models of perpetual depreciation. Both the U.S. Bureau of Economic Analysis and China's National Bureau of Statistics provide sufficient data for authors such as Hodge et al. and Bai et al. to come up with estimates for assets, Equation 22:

(22) $ROIC = NI / Assets = Sales / Assets \times NI / Sales$

Or in words,

$ROIC = Asset\ Efficiency \times Profit\ Margin$

In the context of macro analysis, we can tweak the corporate finance concept (Equation 22) into a more appropriate form for our purposes, as Equation 23:

(23) $\text{ROIC} = \text{GDP} / \text{Fixed Capital} \times \text{Gross Savings} / \text{GDP}$[10]

Equation 23 shows the amount of capital needed to produce output (the first term on the right-hand side in the equation) and the profit margin equivalent. The ROIC being measured is then gross savings/fixed capital. Unlike more common measures (i.e., in the Solow formula or ICOR), the numerator contains a savings measure rather than a GDP measure. We suggest here that, when analyzing the returns to an economy, factoring in savings is more appropriate in terms of finance, accounting, or policymaking.

At a financial and accounting level, Equation 22 measures corporate profits or net income. When shifting to a national level, that same measure is included in national savings. To be consistent, we should also include corporate savings as an appropriate measure for national returns. But this also suggests that we should include the "profits" of households (or what is described in national income accounts as "personal savings"). We consider that, although individuals do earn income, the portion of income used for consumption is clearly the counterpart to a firm's cost of doing business and needs to be netted out. In other words, a household's expenditures on food, shelter, and transportation are all inputs into the household production function, and that production function yields a net return—savings.[11] We thus include corporate savings and personal savings, as well as government savings (dissavings), as a measure of a macroeconomy's returns. Using savings as a measure of return is consistent (in an accounting sense) with the accumulation of capital for the firm and, more broadly, the accumulation of wealth for the entire economy.[12]

In elaborating further on the parallels between profitability and national savings, we must recognize that corporate income already makes up close to half of the national savings in both China and the United States. Government savings (deficits or surpluses) are also already included. Including personal savings is a natural extension of the accounting concept. Some economists might argue that we should look at disposable personal income (DPI) as the appropriate counterpart to value creation or net income in addition to the corporate and government savings. Because economics is the study of how to match society's unlimited wants with its limited resources, some would argue that DPI can be considered the means to that end, and therefore is a more reasonable measure of returns.

But DPI is a different metric from savings; savings is the difference between revenues and costs, while disposable personal income is more closely aligned with revenues (which is already included in Equation 23). One interpretation is that personal savings can be included as a measure of value creation, given the assumption that the goal of a household is to create residual value. If our goal is wealth creation (the building up of equity) then all savings in the nation— business, government, and personal—must be consistently taken into account. In Chapter 5, in particular, we highlight why this view is more consistent with Chinese rather than Western households.

Figures 4.11 and Figure 4.12 decompose Equation 23 into return on fixed capital and savings margins, consistent with our approach. The ratio of output to fixed capital has remained more or less steady over the past thirty years, with China's ratio being higher than the United States'—a result consistent with our earlier ICOR measures. This result is also consistent with the Solow framework (see Figure 4.3) in which a ray drawn from the origin to the y-curve has a slope equal to the output/capital ratio. As we move from the left of the x-axis to the right (China's location to the United States) that ray becomes flatter, representing diminishing returns as the output to capital ratio declines. This in no way contradicts the fact that the United States has a higher **per capita** capital ratio than does China and, in turn, higher per capita income.

Ratio of Output to Capital China and the United States

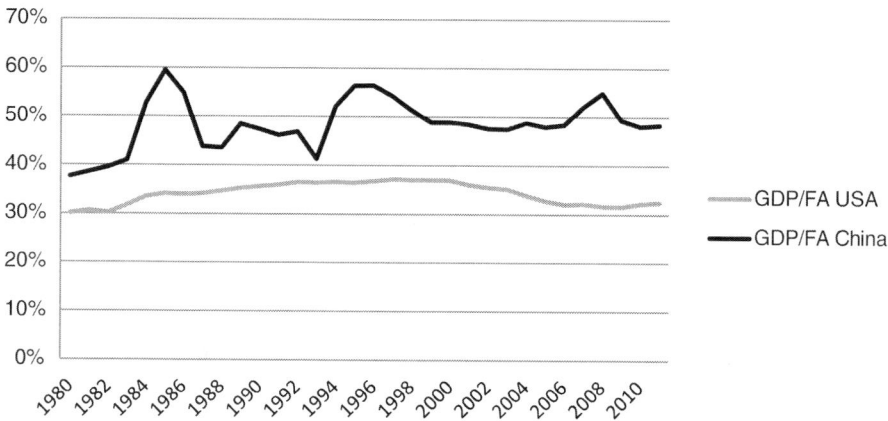

Figure 4.11 Using the Dupont model, we see China's output to capital ratio higher than in the United States—something expected for an emerging economy.

Source: Author created.

Gross Return on Capital China and the United States

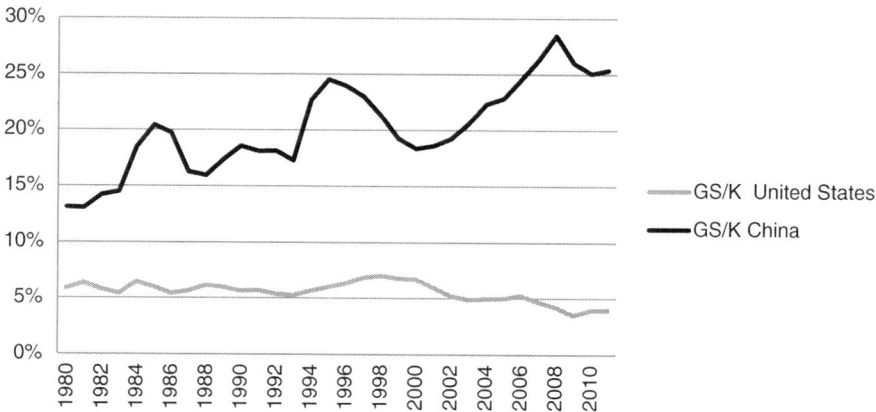

Figure 4.12 Using the Dupont model and savings as a measure of returns, we see China's nominal returns on capital substantially higher than in the United States.

Source: Author created.

Examining the savings/GDP ratio, we also see that China's ratio is substantially higher than the United States' and that, in recent years, it has been rising in China but falling in the United States. Combining the two right-hand side terms in Equation 23, we see that gross returns on capital and real returns on capital have been (and continue to be) higher in China than in the United States. In fact, during that time period, real returns in the United States (using our measure) are barely positive, compared to China's national returns of 8.6 percent. When we compare returns in just the corporate sector (as indicated earlier), we see relatively high U.S. returns. Why, then, are overall returns in the United States so low (by our savings measure) as compared to the corporate sector or to other studies of United States' returns or when compared to China's returns?

A number of factors contribute to this large discrepancy between U.S. returns and Chinese returns:

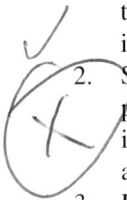

1. Each economy is located at different points along the Solow growth curve. Thus, it should be no surprise that China (an emerging economy) has both higher growth and higher returns than the United States (a more mature economy)—particularly when both economies are segmented in terms of international capital flows.

2. Since we are measuring returns according to savings (not GDP, or sales), we must also consider personal savings (not just corporate savings). Personal savings in the United States has been incredibly low, which has acted as a heavy weight dragging down the overall U.S. rate of return as measured here.

3. Unlike China, a very large share of the overall capital stock in the United States represents housing. We have included the returns to housing in our overall measure of returns for the United States and Chinese and these returns are negative in real terms in the United States.

The above discussion suggests low and possibly negative real returns on the overall United States capital stock in recent years (See Figure 4.13). Consequently, overall wealth in the United States has barely changed or has even declined. On the surface, this latter result may seem counterintuitive; however, it is consistent with the record of current account deficits in the United States over the last several decades—much of which has been used to finance home-building.

In China, although the picture appears more positive, we must remember that most of the nation's savings has been used domestically as investment—just as a company would use retained earnings to finance its capital expenditure. Whether these investments create more

Real Net Returns China and the United States

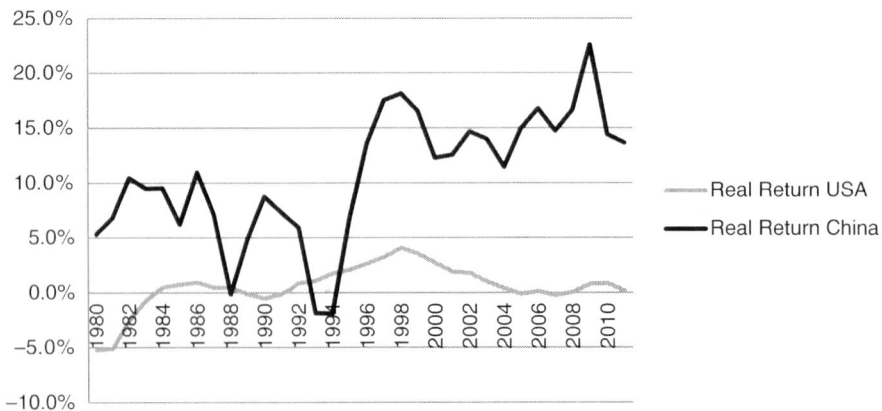

Figure 4.13 Using the Dupont model and savings as a measure of returns, we see U.S. real returns on capital hovering around 0 over the past several decades. The broad measure of returns includes returns on residential housing.

Source: Author created.

value than the U.S. housing stock investment remains to be seen in the coming years.[13] This point highlights another level of important inquiry in measuring the quality of growth. Not only are we asking whether ROIC > WACC, as seen earlier in Equations 18 and 19, but we are also asking a deeper question: When items produced and measured are considered as investment goods (i.e., housing in the case of the United States, and plant, property and equipment (PP&E) in the case of China), can we be sure that the real economic value of these goods is being measured properly? In other words, when measuring ROIC, it is far more difficult to measure the economic value of an investment good than a consumption good which is actually purchased and used by consumers.

MACRO FINANCE INSIGHT 4.3: SUSTAINABLE GROWTH II—THE DUPONT MODEL

The sustainable growth model used in finance describes the rate at which we expect a company to grow sustainably. By "sustainable" we mean that the following conditions are met:

1. No additional equity (outside finance) is raised.
2. The capital structure remains the same (debt as a share of assets is unchanged).
3. Constant returns-to-scale (i.e., if we increase all our inputs by the same proportion, our sales will likewise increase).
4. The payout ratio, R, or dividends as a share of net income is 0. (Note: we can relax this assumption later.

What is the basis for this set of assumptions in the corporate context? Raising outside finance in the form of equity can be expensive and impacts control of the company—particularly between outside and inside shareholders. Relying on debt (increased leverage altering the capital structure) can be risky, even leading to bankruptcy. Constant returns-to-scale (CRS) are assumed (as in the Solow framework), which serves as a useful, empirically based benchmark.* Altering the payment of dividends or changing the retention ratio, R, is bounded from below by 0 and from above by 1. This serves as a constraint in helping us define what is sustainable.† Given CRS, if sales grow by 10 percent (for example), then assets must also grow by 10 percent. However, since the capital structure on the firm's liability side of the balance sheet cannot change, then debt and equity must grow by 10 percent. Recall that, for a firm:

Change in Equity = Net Income + New Equity Raised

And since new equity raised by assumption is 0, then:

Change in Equity = Net Income

And dividing the above equation by assets, we have:

Change in Equity / Assets = Net Income / Assets

Since we know that the change in equity over assets is 10 percent from the previous equation, then the return on assets is also 10 percent. (Note that ROA is the same as Net Income / Assets.) We have just shown that, if we assume sustainable growth as defined, then a sales growth of 10 percent must equal the return on assets of 10 percent.

Translating this into a macro context, GDP growth (sales growth) will be sustainable as long as it is consistent with return on assets (savings/assets). If GDP is growing faster than ROA, then one of three scenarios will emerge: ever-increasing borrowing from abroad, lower dividends from firms to individuals (in or outside the country), or more outside (foreign direct investment) equity. If employed on an ongoing basis, all of these outcomes are fraught with problems and thus are unsustainable. For example, increased borrowing will lead to a financial crisis, and relying on ever-increasing foreign ownership (equity) of one's country is usually not politically feasible.

If sales are growing slower than ROA, then increased deleveraging of an economy occurs, turning it into an ever-larger creditor. In turn, the payout ratio must increase and greater ownership of foreign assets occurs. Though this path does not lead to bankruptcy, it is also not sustainable since the same problems and issues described above will emerge but in the rest of the world.

If ROA does not equal GDP growth, then we can turn to our Dupont model to see how an economy can be rebalanced over the long run:

ROA = GDP / Assets × Savings / GDP

An economy must either alter the efficiency in which it uses its assets or alter its return on assets to allow ROA to again equal GDP growth. If these cannot be adjusted for some reason, then growth in GDP must be shifted either upward or downward to accommodate ROA.

It is interesting here to note that, both Solow and the Dupont sustainability result require that GDP growth be consistent with returns on capital or assets. Solow takes us deeper in the direction of labor force growth as a key driver; the sustainability approach takes us deeper in the direction of asset efficiency and the savings margin as key drivers.

Once again, we see China and the United States at opposing but connected ends of the same economic financial relationship. The above analysis suggests China's ROA is unsustainably high compared to its current rate of economic growth; while the United States' ROA is below long-run economic growth. China's divergence, in part, is clearly related to the fact that the nation remains far from its steady state (which will self-correct over time). But an important example of the divergence, for both economies, is the difference in the savings/GDP rate—which is too high for China, and too low for the United States. China must channel more of its corporate savings into the hands of citizens and, in turn, boost consumption. The United States will need to increase savings, particularly at the personal level, and boost the value of GDP to assets—which may, in part, come from a diminished role for housing as a national asset.

*Do not confuse this assumption also found in Solow with the law of diminishing returns, in which only one input (capital per person) is increased, and output or sales increase at a diminishing rate.

†Of course, firms do buy back shares which, in effect, moves *R* to a negative number. We relax the constraint on *R*.

Measuring the Cost of Capital

Now that we have spent some time on the returns to capital in each country, we next turn to the cost of capital. Nan Geng and Papa N'Diaye (2012) provide estimates for both WACC and ROIC in each country. Based on data for Chinese listed firms (virtually all have the Chinese government, directly or indirectly, as a majority shareholder), the authors find the real cost of capital to be significantly lower in China than in the United States.[14] Real WACC is comprised of borrowing costs of around 3 percent (compared to nearly 4 percent in the United States) and a real cost of equity of about 5 percent (compared to about 10 percent in the United States). The authors stress that China's low payout ratio on dividends—(around 18 percent) compared to a global average of 33 percent and a U.S. average of roughly 20 percent—is an important factor in their cost of equity calculation.

Our own calculations, however, suggest that, at least prima facie, the cost of capital between two countries in fact is quite similar—perhaps only slightly higher in the United States. Table 4.1 shows real interest rates for China and the United States over the past decade on: bank deposits (one year), the prime rate (United States), base lending rates for one-year loans (China), and rates on loans of either AAA-rated companies in the United States (thirty-year maturity), or corporate loans in China (minimum fifteen-year maturity).[15] These rates come close to measuring base interest rates since they represent loans to the most creditworthy borrowers.[16] For Chinese floor lending rates, we have applied an 80 percent discount since regulations in China typically permit lending at a discount to the floor rate. Even after this discount in China, interest rates seem surprisingly close to U.S. rates.

While China's legally mandated base rates come close to the U.S. prime rate, it would be wrong to conclude that the distribution of interest rates is similar. In fact, particularly for Chinese SOEs, access to credit at a below market rate is common. The difficulty in assessing credit quality for the full spectrum of China's SOEs means that many entities which would otherwise face higher borrowing costs from the banks in China (BBB-rated or even C-rated firms) receive rates close to or even below the base rates found in Table 4.1. It is evident that these SOEs would not receive any loans if purely commercial criteria were the sole determinant of credit access. This phenomenon is accentuated by the close links between state-owned banks and borrowing SOEs (OECD, 2005).

If some borrowers are receiving below-market interest rates, some borrowers inevitably face above-market borrowing costs. Estimates of an underground lending market (shadow banking) are as high as RMB 4 trillion.[17] Lin and Schramm (2009) estimated that up to one-third of China's savings is channeled through an informal market. Some estimates indicate borrowing costs in certain cities as high as 180 percent (Ma, 2011). These numbers are in stark contrast to the base lending rates shown in Table 4.1. But the fact that depositors face very low deposit rates while SOE borrowers face low lending rates creates an arbitrage opportunity that, in turn, fosters China's underground market. If access to credit is restricted to SOE firms in the formal market, an overflow of demand for credit in the underground market will be created. Both depositors in the formal market and those

Table 4.1 Real interest rates on deposits and loans in China and the United States in recent years have been relatively low and within the same range.

Real Interest Rates on Deposits and Loans

	Deposit Rates on One-Year Deposit	Loan Rates on One-Year Working Capital Prime Rate	Loan Rates on Long-Term AAA (30 year for U.S. or > 5 years for China)
United States	−0.5%	2.6%	3%
China	0.2%	3.4% (2.7%)*	3.3% (2.6%)*

Source: Author's estimates.
*Assumes a rate that is 80 percent of the base/floor borrowing rate.

Table 4.2 Price earnings (PE) ratios in recent years for Chinese and U.S. firms suggest that the cost of equity is in fact relatively high in China if one takes into account perceived growth opportunities.

	Outright PE Ratio	Future Growth Scenario	PEG Ratio
United States	18	2.6%	692
China	27	7%	386

Source: Author's estimates.

with access to credit at below-market rates in the formal market eventually exit this market—taking with them their demand for credit and their access to credit. They enter the informal market as a way to arbitrage between a market with price controls and one that does not contain such controls.

On the cost of equity side, we can take an alternative approach to that of Gang and N'Diaye in measuring the cost of equity. Gang and N'Diaye measured cost of equity based on current earnings and dividends payout. This approach is problematic in China since growth is an essential part of the pricing equation for equities and the cost of capital. Furthermore, parsimonious dividend payments in China obfuscate other types of obligations of firms when the principal investor is a government entity.[18] Table 4.2 highlights this and suggests that the cost of equity is actually not as low as suggested in their paper—in fact, it may be higher than in the United States. We use the price earnings (PE) ratio as a rough measure (in which the higher the ratio, the lower the cost of capital). Comparing China's PEs for the past decade to U.S. historical norms, the cost of equity appears to be low in China. After adjusting these PE ratios for growth rates (known as "PEGs") based on projected real GDP growth rates, however, we get very different results. Taking into account the strong growth potential for China in the coming years, the cost of equity actually looks higher (corresponding to a lower ratio) than that of the United States. That is to say, a Chinese company issuing equity would feel that it is a relatively expensive way of raising capital given the anticipated growth rates in earnings and/or dividends.

Summary of China, the United States, and the Cost of Capital

In summary, when we look at the cost of debt and the cost of equity in China and the United States, we find that the costs of capital (a weighted average of debt and equity) are surprisingly similar. Why is this? As with many comparisons between China and the United States, the story is "complicated." Several factors seem to be at play:

1. While we may expect China's vast savings to keep the cost of capital low, we must also remember that the demand for savings in China is extraordinarily high—both savings (supply of loanable funds) and investment (demand for loanable funds) take up about 50 percent of China's GDP. This is a simple story of supply and demand.
2. Although China's sources of funds (savings) are greater than its uses of funds (investment), the excess is shipped out (lent) to the United States. This triggers both lower U.S. interest rates and higher Chinese rates, as shown in Figure 4.6 and Figure 4.7.
3. We may have overreached a bit in our conclusions regarding relatively costly debt and equity in China. The loans of the banking system in China tend to cluster around the floor rates, leading borrowers (a disproportionate number are SOEs) to receive the same loan rates. Thus, for those SOEs with access to bank credit, the average borrowing cost may in fact be quite low. In other words, in China, a C-rated borrower may very well receive a rate quite close to that of a AAA-rated borrower. This is caused by the lack of a reliable rating system for China's SOEs, and the continued preferences they enjoy in borrowing. In contrast, corporate borrowers receive the entire spectrum of interest rates in the United States, thus making borrowing costs higher for approximately half of the borrowers. China's risk-adjusted borrowing rates, then, may still be substantially lower than U.S. rates. In China, interest rates tend to spike around the floor, while in the United States, the distribution is more even.[19]
4. On the equity side, we have only provided information on listed companies. Companies that are not publicly traded in China and do not have access to retail investors (but rather the wholesale intra-company investment market) are likely to experience even higher cost of equity.
5. Credit in China is still very much a matter of segmented markets. Those with access to bank credit (especially SOEs) can tap into the vast pool of Chinese individual savings (available at a low-ceilinged interest rate). Those outside of this market (such as Small and Medium-Size

Enterprises (SMEs)) face a much higher cost of funds. Another level of segmentation is between the private intra-company financing market, in which returns and the cost of funds can be extraordinarily high, and the *lao bai xing* (common man) market in which risk-adjusted returns are relatively low (bank deposits, the stock market, and real estate). It remains difficult for the common man to tap into the higher returns offered by private companies seeking finance.

In Summary, while Points 1 and 2 provide a compelling macro story for convergence of the cost of capital in the United States and China, examining the question at an industrial organization/micro level shows that the cost of capital may either be distorted to too low a level or, in the dynamic private market segment in China, may be too high. In the SOE segment, the cost of capital is too low (both in absolute terms and relative to the United States). In other words, underperforming firms appear to have access to relatively inexpensive credit—which undermines China's more value-creating private firms.

MACRO FINANCE INSIGHT 4.4: GROWTH AND COMPETITIVE ADVANTAGE

Michael Porter has suggested a framework of advanced and basic factors for the competitive advantage of nations (Porter 1998). We can think of economic growth in the same terms, building on our earlier discussion of value-creating growth compared to growth for growth's sake. Table MF4.4a provides a list of factors that tend to create basic economic growth as compared to intermediate or advanced economic growth. "Basic growth" refers to raw economic growth that may or may not create value, while "advanced growth" refers to sustainable, value-creating growth. "Intermediate growth" represents economies with more sustainable growth rates than basic, but in which economies are unlikely to achieve the per capita income levels found in the industrialized economies.* Some countries (e.g., North Korea) have not even achieved basic growth, due to enormous political and institutional constraints.

As we move from basic to advanced economic growth, we shift to more sophisticated, rule-based, research-intensive economies (what Porter calls "advanced factors"). Importantly, we are moving toward societies in which institutions provide the levels of trust and security necessary to allow for ever-more complex economic transactions and relationships. Countries that have achieved basic economic growth may encounter bottlenecks to achieving more sustainable economic growth if legal and regulatory frameworks are not present. In effect, we are moving from basic economies with the necessary "hardware" for economic growth to more advanced economies that have the necessary institutional "software." Economies including the United States have achieved advanced economic growth but are always wary of slipping back into lower stages. Meanwhile, China arguably is at an intermediate economic stage and is working to develop the institutional "software" to move to a higher, more sustainable growth path.

Table MF4.4a We could classify all countries at different stages of economic growth. China is at the intermediate stage, having achieved most of the benchmarks of basic growth; the United States is at the advanced and sustainable stage.

Basic Growth	*Intermediate Growth*	*Advanced (Sustainable) Growth*
Political stability	*+ Basic growth factors*	*+ Intermediate growth factors*
Macroeconomic stability	Solid national savings rate	Sophisticated financial system
Microeconomic freedom	Solid national investment	Transparency
Rule of law	Basic education	Strong regulatory framework
	Open trading systems (international)	Strong legal system
		Strong universities with advanced degrees

Source: Author created.

*In the context of the growth and convergence literature, we are identifying growth clusters or growth leagues.

Summary of the Returns and Cost of Capital

By applying several concepts from finance at the macro level, we can qualitatively identify differences between China and the United States. China's growth in the near to medium term is likely to be larger than U.S. growth for reasons already described. As an emerging economy, China is still likely to have an ROIC greater than its cost of capital, especially if we measure China's return on a national savings basis, à la the Dupont model. On an ongoing basis, if we examine Equation 22 or 23, we see that, in the future, China is more likely to be creating value than the United States.

Given what we now know about the cost of capital from our discussion above, we see that there is still room for expansion of the capital stock and continued growth in both China and the United States (but particularly China). There are two main factors clearly at play in China's gap between investment opportunity and realization:

1. Adjustment costs involved in building up capital at too rapid a pace may require a slower pace of growth in the capital stock.
2. The segmented nature of China's capital markets, combined with restrictions on capital inflows, hinder development of the most productive segments of the economy—the dynamic private sector.

The positive portrayal of investment opportunities for China comes with some serious caveats, particularly related to how we measure the value of an investment. Since so much of output in China is in the form of investment, we really need to understand the quality of that investment more deeply and whether the cost of that investment is truly reflective of its economic value. We return to this question in Chapters 5 and 6.

Challenging Questions for China (and the Student): Chapter 4

1. Go the Federal Reserve Economic Database (FRED) table "Purchasing Power Parity Converted GDP Per Capita Relative to the United States, average GEKS-CPDW, at current prices for China" (http://research.stlouisfed.org/fred2/series/PGD2U2CNA621NUPN). Update and explain the graph found here and in the chapter.
2. Explain using the Solow framework why China's economic growth will inevitably slow in the coming years. Pay particular attention to what factors "drag a country" down to the slower growth steady state.
3. Using the standard Solow framework, explain how China's one child policy of the past affects per capita incomes in the short run and the long run. Explain how it will affect economic growth in the long run.
4. Urban residents from one child families can now have two children in China. Discuss this policy and how it will affect the growth of the labor force in China in the coming years à la Solow.
5. Using the World Bank estimates in Table 4.1 and the estimates for 1978–98 in Table 4.3, provide an estimate for the Solow alpha and beta we discuss in the growth accounting equations in the chapter.
6. Link the Solow framework with real returns on capital:
   a. Using the Solow framework, explain why faster population growth would increase the real returns to capital in the long-run steady state.
   b. At China's current stage of development, what are the factors that make its returns to capital so much higher than that of a mature economy such as the United States.

7. Utilizing the Solow growth framework:
   a. Explain the sources of economic growth for China in the past and what the sources will be in the future using the following equation:

$$\Delta Y(t) \,/\, Y(t) = \Delta A(t) \,/\, A(t) + \alpha \Delta K(t) \,/\, K(t) + \beta \Delta L(t) \,/\, L(t)$$

   b. Explain why we say that surely China's growth rate will slow in the future.
   c. Explain why China's high savings rate is an unlikely source of sustainable growth.
8. In as detailed a manner as possible, discuss the quality of China's growth compared to the quantity of China's growth. Use equations, facts, and data in your discussion.
9. We discussed different stages of growth for economies around the world—from basic growth to advanced growth. Provide different periods in China's recent economic history which might correspond to the different phases. Include what will happen in the future. Be specific about the necessary ingredients for each stage.
10. Provide the intuition behind the Dupont model of sustainable growth which specifically links the growth in GDP (sales) to a nation's return on assets. Is this consistent with what is happening in China and the United States?

Notes

1. In continuous time under certainty, Equation 6 is exact; in discrete time, it is an approximation.
2. A common assumption across economics which we discuss below.
3. Note the subtle difference between diminishing returns and decreasing returns-to-scale; the former holds an explicit input constant (as demonstrated above) while in the latter case, all explicit inputs increase in proportion but output increases by a smaller proportion (due to some implicit background constraint).
4. In chemistry, the same idea applies to chemical reactions. Le Chatelier's Principle states that the speed of a chemical reaction is constrained by the slowest "link" in the chain of the necessary chemical reactions needed to progress.
5. Operating profits are also described as EBIT or earnings before subtracting out interest and taxes.
6. As opposed to the short-run rate, which is determined by the demand and supply of money, where the supply of money is determined by monetary policy.
7. We assume that K/Y is a ratio of two real numbers measured using the appropriate deflators for each, thus obviating the need to convert our gross return from a nominal to a real number.
8. It includes fixed capital in the manufacturing, mining, infrastructure, and agricultural sectors. As such, it includes government investments in fixed capital (such as buildings and roads). Excluding the agricultural sector does not alter the data much.
9. See various issues of the U.S. Commerce Department's Survey of Current Business.
10. In place of GDP, we could use retail sales (which does not include inventory accumulation as in GDP but unfortunately excludes most investment, government spending, and net exports). In place of gross savings, we could also use net savings (which is net of depreciation). In place of fixed assets (which includes inventories), we could use all assets of the economy. Choices among all of these depend mainly on what national data are actually available for each country and what definition is most useful for a specific interpretation.
11. One might exclude expenditure on recreation and leisure, and include these with savings.
12. We will later show a much broader measure of a nation's wealth or assets.
13. If we substitute fixed capital with a broader measure of all wealth (produced, natural, and human) devised by the United Nations (Inclusive Wealth Report, 2012), we see a negative real return of close to 5 percent for the United States and a positive return of close to 6 percent for China. Again, this assumes savings is an appropriate metric for measuring national returns on assets.
14. The authors typically compare China to the "Developed Americas," which includes the United States and Canada.
15. Over the years, China has had both ceilings and floors on interest rates for bank deposits and loans; what economists call financial repression. As one tool in its efforts to enhance bank profitability and bank capital, it has removed the ceiling on interest rate loans and installed a floor on those rates, while putting a ceiling on what could be paid on deposits. This, in turn, has created a large sizeable profit margin for Chinese banks. Note: China's largest banks still have, as their principal shareholder, the Chinese government.

16. Certainly, high-quality borrowers in China would be borrowing very near the floor for bank loan interest rates. But lower-quality borrowers in China may also be borrowing at these lower rates (see the section on "Measuring the Cost of Capital" for this discussion).
17. In the 2011 lending crisis in Wenzhou, a dynamic center for economic growth and exports in Zhejiang Province, borrowers defaulted on loans with interest rates estimated to range from 14 percent to 70 percent (Martin, 2012). "China to Control Shadow Banking and Private Lending," BBC, October 19, 2011.
18. In the past, SOEs were required to provide some of the traditional services that governments typically provide, such as health, education, and other community services. Although these obligations have largely vanished, the majority shareholder (usually the government) may demand other forms of compensation—when a majority shareholder transfers assets of the firm to itself at the expense of minority shareholders, we refer to this as *tunneling*.
19. Net interest paid to the large banks (e.g., ICBC, BOC, ABC, and CCB) are relatively close to the base lending rates in Table 4.1, suggesting such clustering.

References

Bai, Chong-En, Chang-Tai Hsieh, and Yingyi Qian. 2006. "The Return to Capital in China." NBER Working Paper 12755. Cambridge: National Bureau of Economic Research, December.

Barro, Robert J. 1991. "Economic Growth in a Cross Section of Countries." *Quarterly Journal of Economics* 106(2): 407–43.

Chow, G. 1993. "Capital Formation and Economic Growth in China." *Quarterly Journal of Economics* 108(3): 809–42.

Denison, Edward F. 1974. *Accounting for United States Economic Growth*. Washington, DC: The Brookings Institution.

DiCecio, Ricardo, and Charles S. Gascon. 2008. "Income Convergence in the United States: A Tale of Migration and Urbanization." Working Paper 2008–002C. St. Louis: Federal Reserve Bank of St. Louis, December.

Domar, Evsey. 1946. "Capital Expansion, Rate of Growth, and Employment." *Econometrica* 14(2): 137–47.

Francis, Michael, Francois Painchaud, and Sylvie Morin. 2005. "Understanding China's Long-Run Growth Process and Its Implications for Canada." *Bank of Canada Review* 2005 (Spring): 5–17.

Geng, Nan, and Papa N'Diaye. 2012. "Determinants of Corporate Investment in China: Evidence from Cross-Country Firm Level Data." IMF Working Paper No. 12/80. Washington, DC: International Monetary Fund, March.

Heytens, Paul, and Harm Zebregs. 2003. "How Fast Can China Grow?" In *China Competing in the Global Economy*, eds. Wanda Tseng and Marjus Rodlauer. Washington, DC: International Monetary Fund.

Hodge, Andrew W., Robert J. Corea, James M. Green, and Bonnie A. Retus. 2011. "Returns for Domestic Nonfinancial Business," *Survey of Current Business* 91(6): 24–28.

Hu, Z., and M. Khan. 1996. "Why Is China Growing So Fast?" IMF Working Papers, 96/75. Washington, DC: International Monetary Fund.

International Human Dimensions Programme on Global Environmental Change (UNU-IHDP) and United Nations Environment Programme (UNEP). 2012. *Measuring Progress Toward Sustainability*. Inclusive Wealth Report. Cambridge. Cambridge University Press.

Lau, Chi Keung Marco. 2010. "New Evidence About Regional Income Divergence in China." *China Economic Review* 21(2): 293–309.

Lin, G., and R. Schramm. 2009. "A Decade of Flow of Funds in China: 1995–2006." In *China and Asia: Economic and Financial Interactions*, eds. Y.W. Cheung and K. Wong. London: Routledge.

Lin, Justin Yifu. 1992. "Rural Reforms and Agricultural Growth in China." *American Economic Review* 82(1): 34–51.

Ma, Guangyuan. 2011. "What Do We Have for Wenzhou's Rescue?" *China–U.S. Focus,* November 16.

Martin, Michael E. 2012. *China's Banking System: Issues for Congress*. CRS Report for Congress 7–5700, R42380. Washington, DC: Congressional Research Service.

Organisation for Economic Co-operation and Development (OECD). 2005. *Economic Survey of China* 2005(13): 19, 40.

Pedroni, P., and J.Y. Yao. 2006. "Regional Income Divergence in China." *Journal of Asian Economics* 17: 294–315.

Porter, M.E. 1998. *The Competitive Advantage of Nations: With a New Introduction*. New York: Free Press.

Romer, P.M. 1994. "The Origins of Endogenous Growth." *Journal of Economic Perspectives* 8(1): 3–22.

Sala-i-Martin, Xavier X. 1997. "I Just Ran Four Million Regressions." NBER Working Paper No. 6252. Cambridge, MA: National Bureau of Economic Research.

Solow, Robert M. 1956. "A Contribution to the Theory of Economic Growth." *Quarterly Journal of Economics* 70(1): 65–94.

Swan, Trevor W. 1956. "Economic Growth and Capital Accumulation." *Economic Record* 32(2): 334–61.

Szamosszegi, Andrew, and Cole Kyle. 2011. *An Analysis of State-Owned Enterprises and State Capitalism in China.* Washington, DC: U.S.–China Economic and Security Review Commission, October 26.

Wicksell, J.G. Knut. 1898/1936. *Interest and Prices,* trans. R.F. Kahn. London: Royal Economic Society.

World Bank. 1997. *China 2020: Challenges in the New Century.* China 2020 Series. Washington D.C.

Wu Jinglian. 2005. *Understanding and Interpreting Chinese Economic Reform.* Mason, OH: Thomson/South-Western.

Young, Alwyn. 1992. "A Tale of Two Cities: Factor Accumulation and Technical Change in Hong Kong and Singapore." *NBER Macroeconomics Annual 1992,* eds. O.J. Blanchard and S. Fischer, 13–54. Cambridge: MIT Press.

———. 2003. "Gold into Base Metals: Productivity Growth in the People's Republic of China during the Reform Period." *Journal of Political Economy* 111(6): 1220–61.

5   Consumption and Savings in China and the United States

大富由天小富由俭
Great Wealth Comes from Plain Luck, Plain Wealth from Great Thrift

China has the highest savings rate in the world, currently estimated at over 50 percent of GDP.[1] China's share of GDP saved exceeds even that of some of its high-saving neighbors such as South Korea (32 percent) and Japan (22 percent); and vastly surpasses the United States (16 percent, pre-crisis). Figure 5.1 shows China's consistently high national savings rate over the past four decades and how it has increased to even higher levels over the last decade. Since savings is the absence of consumption, we will take dual perspectives on China's high savings rate or low rate of consumption. The earlier sentence could just as correctly have been written to say: China has the lowest rate of consumption among the world's major economies. As a share of GDP, Chinese consumption has been only around 36 percent over the past decade—a rate far below the global average of 61 percent and the U.S. average of over 70 percent. (See Figure 5.2 for Chinese household consumption share compared to the United States.) Household consumption rates in the United States and China were approximately equal in the early 1970s, then diverged in the years to follow. Note that those earlier years of high consumption rates for China are typical for most early stage emerging economies in which incomes are low and just sufficient to support subsistence consumption.

Today, China's high level of savings is a **key driver** for other salient features of its economy, such as its current account balance and rapid economic growth. Beyond China's borders, its high savings rate has implications for global imbalances on current and capital accounts in the balance of payments, world interest rates, and inflation and commodity prices. It is therefore very important to understand the factors behind China's high savings rate and how those factors are likely to evolve in the coming years. Examining China's savings rate will also allow us to look at the role that credit markets, corporate governance, and demographic factors (just to name a few) come to play.

China's Current Savings Rate

China's 2011 savings rate of around 51 percent of GDP is equivalent in U.S. dollar terms to approximately US$580.7 billion.[2] China's savings rate has for decades been high but, beginning in 2003, surged even higher and continued to increase as seen in Figure 5.1. Meanwhile, in the United States, gross national savings has declined as a share of national income from about 25 percent in 1965 to around 18 percent in 2013. Figure 5.2 shows the corresponding trends in consumption for each country over the past half century. While the data discussed here generally refer to national savings, we will focus our discussion on savings of the private sector, broadly defined to include savings of individuals (households), non-government organizations (NGOs), and businesses (enterprises). Specifically, we will not attempt to explain in this chapter government savings or dissaving—this is covered in the chapters on fiscal policy. We focus mainly on households and enterprises because they make up the lion's share of savings in China and because these sectors' savings patterns can be

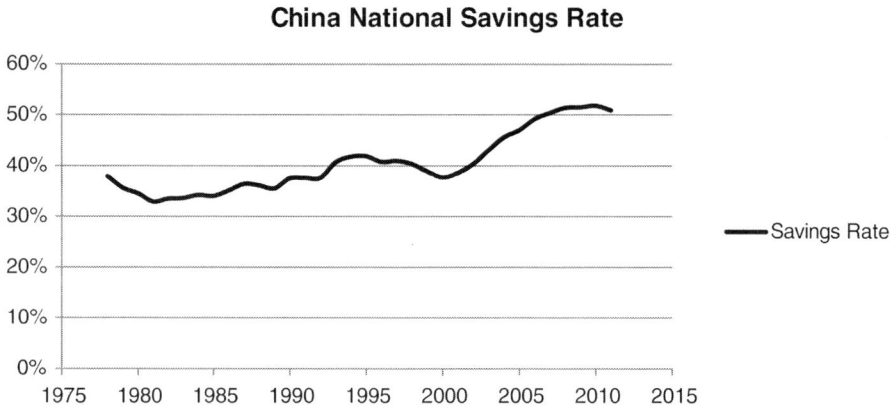

Figure 5.1 China's savings rate has continued to rise.

Source: National Bureau of Statistics of the People's Republic of China.

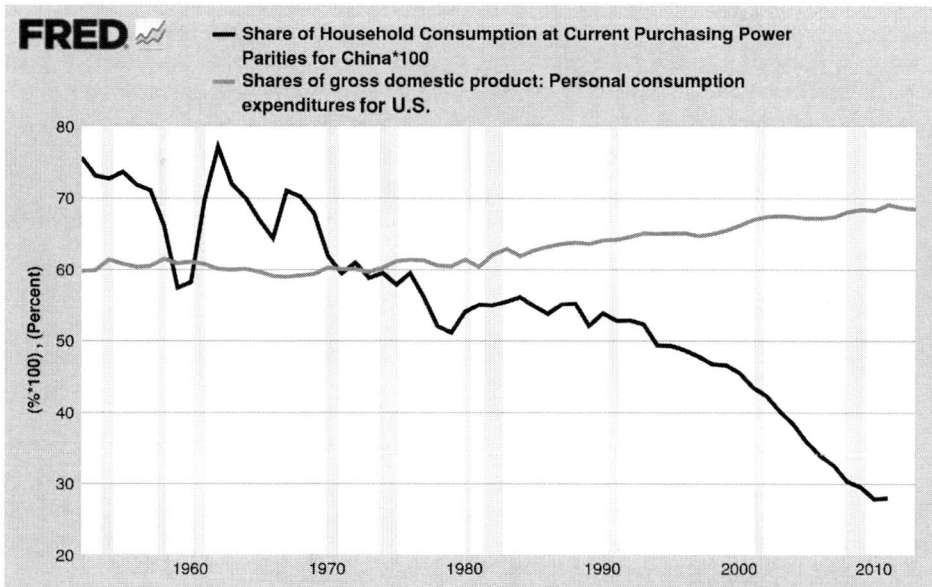

Figure 5.2 China's share of personal consumption out of GDP is low compared to the United States.

Source: FRED, Federal Reserve Economic Data, Federal Reserve Bank of St. Louis: Shares of Household Consumption at Current Purchasing Power Parities for China, Shares of Gross Domestic Product: Personal Consumption Expenditures for U.S. 2014 research.stlouisfed.org

Note: Shaded areas indicate U.S. recessions

explained more easily by economic fundamentals—government budget surpluses and deficits often result from policy-based decision making—an area of expertise for political scientists. It is important to note that, for the United States, government budget deficits (dissavings) have been larger than private savings in recent years.

Table 5.1 provides a breakdown of the sources of savings in both countries. Here, we examine where savings come from. There are three possible sources: households (personal), businesses

Table 5.1 For both China and the United States corporate savings are a significant source of national savings.

	China	*United States*
Sources of Gross Savings		
Business	42%	71%
Government	10%	3%
Households	48%	26%
Total	100%	100%

Source: NBS, Flow of Funds, Table 2–30 for China. BEA, United States.

(corporate profits), and government (budget deficits and surpluses). Some interesting results and comparisons emerge. In both countries, a significant share of savings come from the business sector,[2] which includes both companies producing goods and services and financial institutions. For the United States, this has traditionally been the largest source of savings. Notwithstanding high household savings rates in China (20–30 percent of disposable income), disposable income still remains a relatively low share of national income in China—thus limiting the possible contribution of household savings. We return to this point later in the chapter. Meanwhile, corporate income has been relatively high.[3]

In contrast, in the United States, household savings as a share of personal income has been in the single digits for most of the post-World War II era, while personal income has a substantially heavier weight in national income. On balance, businesses—not households—are the main source of savings in the United States. In China, governments contribute to the savings pool, while in the United States the contribution is barely positive and in fact becomes negative once depreciation is included.

While the above discussion has focused on savings as a share of GDP, we can get a broader perspective by looking at per capita savings. Consider the following identity and corresponding ratios for each country:

Savings / GDP × GDP / Population = Per Capita Savings
China: 0.51 × US$5,420 = US$2,764
United States: 0.16 × US$51,197 = US$8,192

Even though the United States saves much less as a share of GDP, on a per capita basis it saves three times as much as China. Clearly, the difference is in the much larger U.S. GDP and the much larger Chinese population.[4] In terms of creating individual wealth and individual investment, the Chinese may view their savings rate as too low! As we discussed in Chapter 4, this paradox is resolved once we consider that each country is at different points along the path of long-run economic growth.

In both countries, investment including new homes, plants, property, and equipment, and infrastructure is the primary use of savings. Some of China's savings are lent to the world; the United States has had to borrow other countries' savings in order to cover its own investment and consumption needs.

Theories of Savings

The theories below apply mainly to households. But for the United States, the largest contributor to national savings is the corporate sector (71 percent of savings in the United States is corporate savings) and for China the corporate sector combined with the government sector is the largest contributor. To the extent that the corporate sector is profitable, national savings will, of course, be higher. We return to this in the last half of this chapter. Another component of national savings is government savings or dissavings. For China, this factor is positive. For the United States, budget deficits are a large negative factor.

Disposable Income, Consumption, and the Interest Rate

In discussing different theories of savings, we begin with the accounting identity for the household:

Personal Savings $\equiv$ Disposable Personal Income $-$ Personal Consumption

Given the accounting identity above, a change in disposable personal income would exactly be matched by a change in savings for any given level of consumption. Moving from accounting to theory, the Keynesian approach posits consumption being positively related to disposable personal income as is savings. As we shall discuss later, from a theoretical perspective, savings and consumption are more likely to be directly related to disposable personal income when constraints exist on spending current wealth, or borrowing against current wealth or future income. Classical economists had earlier emphasized the role of interest rates in determining savings since income was generally taken as a given at full employment. In the event, disposable personal income, interest rates, and consumption are three key variables that both theoretically and empirically help to determine the level of savings.

Life Cycle, Permanent Income, and Wealth Effects

More modern theories emphasize the role of savings as a means to an end—where the ultimate goal is a smooth pattern of consumption over either a finite horizon (typically an assumed lifetime) or an infinite horizon for a representative agent. These theories of savings emphasize savings in its role as smoothing consumption either in the short term or the longer term. In other words, savings act as a buffer to either unanticipated shocks to income or anticipated long-run changes in income. Most important to consider are the types of income (temporary or permanent) and the actual or projected income earned by different demographic groups for a given economy. This approach allows for more comprehensive theories of savings. Temporary changes in income have a smaller impact on consumption than do permanent changes (Friedman's permanent income hypothesis (PCH)) and so, for example, a temporary increase in income will tend to be saved—so as to maintain a smooth (balanced) consumption pattern over time. This approach helps explain the smoothing of consumption over the short run when income experiences random shocks.

In Modigliani's life cycle hypothesis (LCH), an individual recognizes three ages of man—youth, working age, and retirement.[5] Before retirement, we save money; during retirement, we dissave. Roughly speaking, the saving that is undertaken during our employment years matches the consumption undertaken during years of retirement. Youth (e.g., a student reading this text), neither earns nor saves—only consumes and dissaves. Clearly, LCH suggests a strong role for age distribution and the dependency ratio (defined below) within a society in determining the savings rate.

Figure 5.3 illustrates a typical consumption/savings pattern for an adult whose life cycle is L years. For simplicity, we assume that the interest rate is 0, but income grows at a constant rate for $L - N$ working years until retirement date (N). Savings during the working years must sum to the ($L - N$) years of consumption during retirement. This simple model explains the smoothing of consumption across the long run where income fluctuates predictably.

Both the permanent income hypothesis and the life cycle hypothesis, in emphasizing some type of planning horizon, suggest an important role for wealth in determining consumption. Here, wealth is broadly defined to include both accumulated wealth-to-date for an individual as well as the present

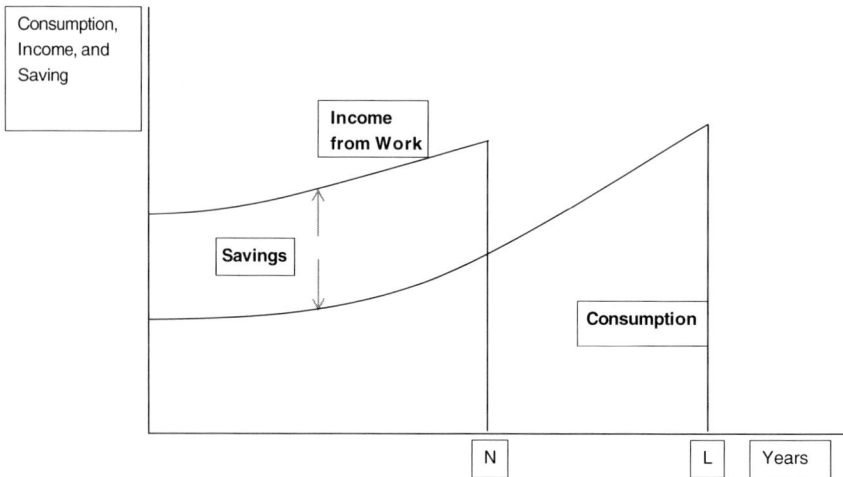

Figure 5.3 Life-cycle savings and consumption.

Source: Author created.

value of future income, that is, the lifetime budget constraint. We now consider two situations: one in which an individual is not permitted to accumulate wealth (not save) and one in which the individual is permitted to save.

Figure 5.4 shows two cases where an individual has average income over his/her working years of RMB 100,000 but can only expect government transfers (such as social security payments) of RMB 20,000 per year in retirement. Assume he/she is constrained to consume all income in each period—no more and no less. Point A, with the accompanying indifference curve, shows this situation. Suppose, instead, the individual is now given the opportunity to save RMB 28,000 per year and to invest it in a pension fund. The assumed return on his/her investment will now permit consumption of RMB 72,000 in the working years and RMB 72,000 in the retirement years (Point B)—a smoother pattern and a higher level of utility. The higher the return on savings, the greater the consumption possibilities across both periods. Savings is the key element in allowing income to be smoother and utility higher across both long-term income imbalances and short-term income fluctuations. While governments may not impose restrictions on savings as in Point A, policies which discourage savings or which make savings risky (e.g., an unstable banking system) may have the same effect.

From the LCH, we can also infer an increase in the savings rate in periods where economic growth accelerates from the norm. Here, the desire to smooth consumption (either absolutely or relative to an anticipated growth in income) causes one to save a disproportionate share of income earned from growth surges in order to maintain higher levels of consumption in retirement. Conversely, if growth is anticipated to surge (decelerate) in the future, then current consumption will rise (fall) in anticipation of the future higher income. Other research attempts to show that the rapid growth in East Asia and in China specifically (Modigliani and Cao, 2004) is central in explaining the high savings rates found there. Modigliani and Cao incorporate the unique aspect of the one child policy begun in the late 1970s in China, which reinforced the need for savings by the working generation. No longer could the working generation anticipate the cultural norm of support from several offspring during retirement.[6]

Case Study 5.1: Is Consumption (消费) a Bad Word?

Cultural differences are often cited as a reason for generally higher rates of savings. We note that China's one child policy that began in the late 1970s tends to force the current generation of workers to save rather than rely on the earnings of several offspring. Even in the absence of this policy there still exists a cultural bias toward saving (even the Chinese characters for consumption *xiao fei* 消费 suggest waste and loss). Furthermore, an inter-generational simultaneity form of savings exists which no longer exists in the West. Consider that a typical urban worker in China has recently migrated from the countryside. He/she tends to have an unskilled job. Housing and food consumption are often part of the wage package and covered by the employer. These recent unskilled workers save and remit a large share of their income (even though it is low) to their parents in the countryside. Meanwhile, the parents—whether working or retired—save their income as a bequest to the very same children who are saving for them! Such symbiotic savings helps keep China's savings rates high.

Liquidity/Borrowing Constraints

Liquidity and/or borrowing constraints represent another major determinant with respect to savings. This is similar to the situation we just examined in which savings or wealth accumulation is not permitted. In the presence of a binding liquidity or borrowing constraint, consumption cannot exceed the flow of income. In other words, savings cannot be negative. *Liquidity constraints*, and *borrowing*, or *capital market constraints* are terms often used interchangeably but, in fact, are different. Liquidity constraints represent the inability to convert accumulated wealth (non-human capital wealth) into purchasing power with ease, for example, from penalties for early withdrawal from a retirement account or a certificate of deposit. Capital market constraints represent the inability to easily borrow against accumulated wealth or future income (human capital wealth). The impact of either constraint, when it is binding, is that individuals consume up to their income (in contrast to consuming potentially up to their wealth—human and financial capital. For these individuals, savings and consumption are a function of income; in other words, these variables move in tandem with the constraint's relaxation. It has been suggested that these types of constraints are more likely to occur in developing economies where wealth is low and capital markets undeveloped. Therefore, consumption and savings as a function of disposable income (as opposed to wealth) may be an appropriate description of savings and consumption for these emerging economies.

Liquidity or borrowing constraints will tend to force individuals to begin saving and to stop dissaving. These constraints have a particularly important impact in home, automobile, or other high-cost durable goods purchases.[7] Individuals typically must save for the down payment or purchase price of these items in the absence of a financing option. In the case of autos or other durables, purchases may simply not occur which by definition reduces consumption and increases the savings rate.

We note that liquidity constraints in the absence of borrowing constraints would still allow for dissaving or consumption above income. Borrowing constraints in the absence of liquidity constraints, on the other hand, tend to encourage savings (while ultimately permitting dissavings) since individuals understand that wealth accumulation is the only means for making large purchases. Furthermore, shocks to income that cannot be financed externally must be financed from savings. This suggests a higher savings rate. In a symmetrical fashion, shocks to consumption—a healthcare emergency, for example—will also need to be paid for out of savings when financing is not available.

To the extent that constraints on lending by financial intermediaries (e.g., usury laws) reduce returns to depositors, savings could be negatively impacted. Those with savings may choose to

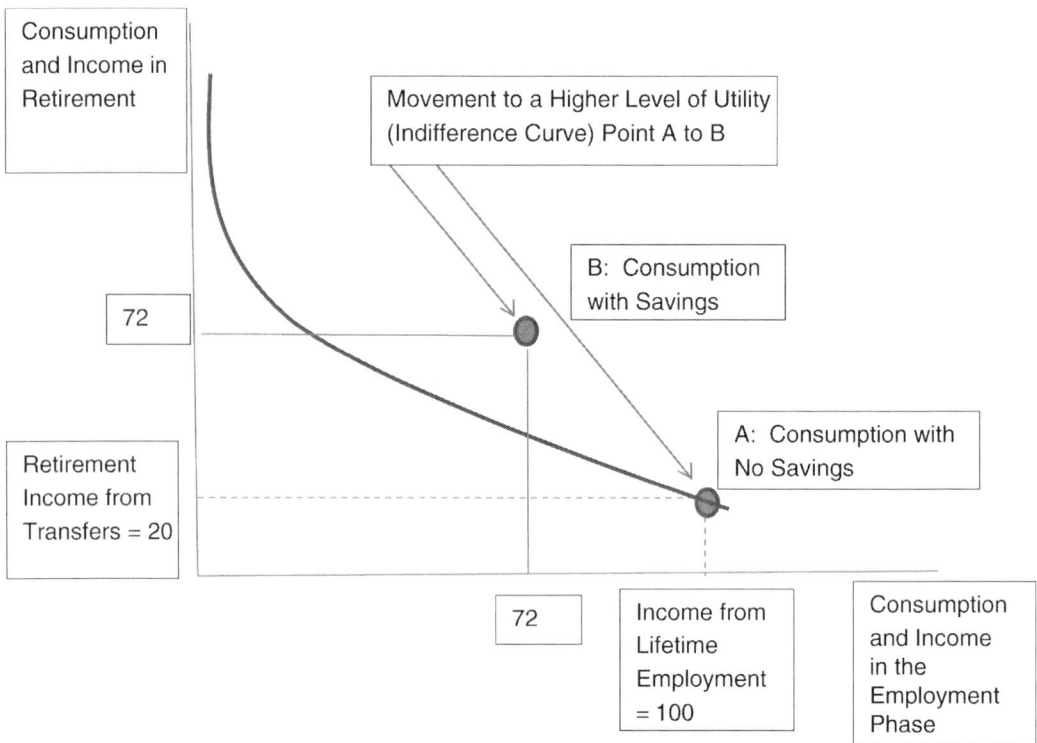

Figure 5.4 Savings and consumption with and without constraints on wealth accumulation.

Source: Author created.

increase their own purchases of automobiles or durables, since their savings cannot be profitably intermediated to an outside borrower.[8] Furthermore, in the presence of both liquidity and borrowing constraints (such as the situation in some developing economies) combined with negative real interest rates, one may choose to consume and not save at all—since the benefits of saving are small, if not negative.

Figure 5.5 shows the supply and demand for savings in the presence of a constraint on lending or financial intermediation between household and corporate savers and household borrowers. Instead of lending taking place at the equilibrium level of *S*, it occurs at *S'*. Credit rationing is more likely as the demand for loans increases.[9] Empirical work suggests that the presence of lending or borrowing constraints increases the national savings rate. Specifically, increases in current income increase consumption, suggesting the presence of liquidity/borrowing constraints (Hall, 1978; LeBaron (2006)).

Precautionary Motive for Savings

Similar to the Friedman (1957) argument, uncertainty in income is an additional factor impacting savings—the so-called precautionary motive. As we have seen above, uncertainty in the presence of liquidity or borrowing constraints will increase savings for the individual. Aggregating to the national savings rate, a key question is how open the economy is to financial and trade flows. A national income that is highly variable—for example, due to exchange rate (terms of trade) shocks in which international trade is important—may or may not be able to buffer those shocks through international borrowing and diversification. In summary, shocks that cannot be buffered due to either liquidity or capital market constraints (including the ability to diversify) at both the domestic and international levels will generate a higher level of national savings. Feldstein and Horioka (1980) conclude that, in

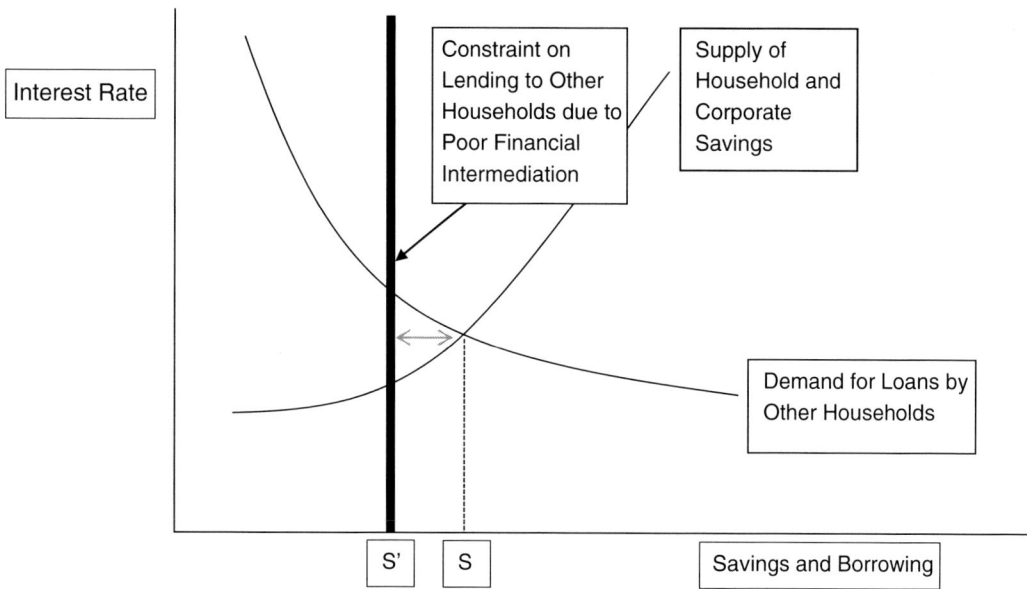

Figure 5.5 Impact of lending constraints on national savings. Constraints on lending will tend to decrease loans
to the household sector resulting in lower consumption and higher savings.

Source: Author created.

fact, markets still remain largely segmented. This implies that countries must, in effect, self-insure
against shocks to real income via higher savings rates.

At the macroeconomic level, the presumption is that increased uncertainty increases savings;
however, the microeconomic foundation for this conclusion is less clear. Uncertainty has a dual
effect—an income effect and a substitution effect. The income effect is the same as the precautionary motive discussed above; the certainty equivalent of our income is lower in future periods when
there is greater uncertainty, so we need to save more. The substitution effect states that, since future
consumption (and happiness or welfare) is less certain, we should "live for today." That is, consume
now and save less for the uncertain future. Which one of these effects dominates will determine savings at the microeconomic level.[10]

Specific Savings Motives

In an interesting empirical work based on survey data, Horioka and Watanabe (1997) examine the
motivation for savings by Japanese households. They find that the motivation for gross savings, in
order of importance, are: retirement, housing, peace of mind, illness, education, marriage, consumer
durables, leisure, bequest, business, and tax purposes. Most of these motivations can be subsumed
under the broader theories discussed above.

Why Has China's Savings Rate Risen So High?

China's Precautionary Motive

In the case of China, perhaps the most commonly cited explanation for the high savings rate is the
precautionary motive—the desire to save as a precaution against uncertain fluctuations in income.
Beyond the normal uncertainties of an agrarian society confronted with a rapidly rising population, blight and drought, we see a rather amazing series of political events in China over the past

200 years, which clearly impacted its ability to produce income.[11] (See Case Study 5.2.) These events have combined with a still-weak social safety net (health insurance, unemployment insurance, retirement benefits, as discussed in Chapter 9) to generate a clear need for significant personal savings.

Case Study 5.2: Recent Chinese History and the Precautionary Motive for Savings

Over 200 years of turmoil in China undoubtedly has resulted in large precautionary savings. The intensifying encroachment of foreign powers into China in the nineteenth century reached a climax with the Japanese seizing large parts of the country. The clash between Chinese imperial society, Western powers, and Japan served as a backdrop and then set the stage for a number of specific catastrophic events and movements. To name just a few, the Opium Wars (1839–42), the Taiping Rebellion (1850–64), the Boxer Rebellion (1900–01), the collapse of a two-millennia-old system of dynastic rule in the fall of the Qing (1911), a period of warlordism and civil war between the Communists and the Guomindang (1911–49), the Japanese progressive seizure of most of modern China (1915–45), the massacre of Nanjing (1938), establishment of a Communist government (1949), the Great Leap Forward (1958–60), the Cultural Revolution (1966–69), and finally the movement toward a market economy beginning in 1978. Most of these events have become more or less a part of the vocabulary of anyone familiar with China. But the enormity of their impact on individuals living through these periods is difficult to fathom.

Never in the history of humanity have so many citizens of one country suffered such a series of disruptive events over such a prolonged period. Needless to say, to sum up the loss of life across this stretch of misery would total in the millions. Similarly, the loss of income for those who managed to survive the famines and other conflict-related hardships was enormous. Given the relatively recent movement toward a system in which individuals in China can actually save on their own, it is no surprise that those savings would be huge and would reflect the need to buffer against potential fluctuations in income which in the past had led to outright starvation.* By way of comparison, volatility of real GDP in China from 1952 to 1977 (pre-Deng Xiaoping reform) was 10.5 percent per year. Volatility in the industrialized economies over an overlapping period was about 2.5 percent, diminishing to 1.5 percent by the 1990s, according to the OECD.

But the events described above are of diminished significance to China's younger generation—especially those born after 1978. Table CS5.2a gives the projected percentage of the population expected to be born post-1978 by year in China.

Table CS5.2a Share of Chinese population born after the turbulent pre-1978 era.

Year	Chinese Population Born After 1978
2000	37%
2025	61%
2050	78%

Source: United States Census Bureau, IDB Database.

By 2025, a majority of China's population will have been born after 1978 and presumably the events pre-1978 will become increasingly a matter of history rather than personally meaningful. In turn, one would expect that the precautionary motive for savings will have been dampened.

*Prior to 1978, any savings or surplus was extracted from individuals as part of the central plan.

Examining China's official GDP growth estimates during 1952–78 against the post-1978 (reform) period, we see a large drop in GDP variance, from 10.5 percent to about 3 percent per annum. The former number is not far above the output variability of the OECD economies. If the set of impressive reforms which began in 1978 continues, the variability of output is likely to remai and this would tend to reduce the level of precautionary savings. But the kinds of uncertainty that existed in the past were essentially caused by fundamental political upheaval—as opposed to economic fundamentals.

An alternate view is that post-1978 growth has created a different kind of uncertainty. According to Chamon, Liu, and Prasad (2010), high growth rates are accompanied by greater fluctuations and uncertainty regarding the future sustainability of growth.[12] They find that, the greater uncertainty accompanying growth and structural shifts in the economy explains roughly 4 points of the 20–25 percent savings rates for twenty- to thirty-somethings. Taking a life cycle approach, they also find that pension reform implemented in 1997 effectively reduced retirement income (after the age of sixty) by about one-third. This has resulted in a higher savings rate among older Chinese workers on the verge of retirement. As growth rates move to more sustainable levels and the social safety net is both widened and deepened, savings rates are expected to diminish with higher rates of consumption.

The Life Cycle Hypothesis and the Dependency Ratio

Since the life cycle hypothesis posits that individuals save based on their age, it is important to examine the current demographic structure of China. A particularly useful metric is the dependency ratio—the ratio of those considered either too old or too young to work (over sixty-four and under fifteen years of age) to those of working age (fifteen to sixty-four). The higher the ratio, the lower the expected savings rate. Those between the ages of fifteen and sixty-four have both disposable personal income **and** consumption in the equation below. Those outside this range have mostly consumption and very little income from current employment, and this pushes savings and savings rates down.

Personal Savings = Disposable Personal Income – Consumption

China's dependency ratio in 2013 (according to the World Bank) was 36 percent, which is substantially lower than that of the United States (50 percent). Both of these numbers compare favorably with the dependency ratio found in most low-income economies (59 percent, according to the World Bank). Table 5.2 shows that the dependency ratio in OECD economies was as high as 84 percent. No doubt this bulge in the working-age population in China plays a significant role in the high national savings rate.

China's retirement age of between fifty and sixty years of age is significantly lower than that of the United States (between sixty-two and sixty-seven).[13] This has two offsetting effects. First, China's dependency ratio is higher. Second, given China's average life expectancy of about seventy-four years, the shorter working period necessitates greater savings to cover the longer retirement.[14] Since, at present, the demographic balance is still weighted more heavily toward those under fifty, we have the second positive effect outweighing the first negative effect.[15] From a life cycle approach, the lower dependency ratio ought to have a positive impact on the savings rate of China.

Demographic Factors in the Coming Years

Figures 5.6–5.8, indicate that China's population during the next fifty years will become, on average, older. By 2050, about 24 percent of the population will be over the age of sixty-four compared to only about 6.8 percent today. We see a corresponding shrinkage in the under-fifteen age group. A quick snapshot can be taken by observing that the largest cohort in 2000 was the ten- to fourteen-year-old group, which implies that, in 2050, the largest cohort will be the sixty- to

Table 5.2 Labor force and economic dependency ratios in OECD countries (projections) for 2000–50 show an aging population.

Country	Labor Force			Economic Dependency Ratio		
	2000 (thousands)	*2050 (thousands)*	*Variation (%)*	*2000*	*2050*	*Variation*
Austria	3,881	3,579	−7.8	0.67	0.95	0.28
Belgium	4,167	3,805	−8.7	0.84	1.13	0.29
Denmark	2,903	2,785	−4.1	0.62	0.79	0.17
Finland	2,647	2,234	−15.6	0.68	0.94	0.26
France	25,949	24,037	−7.4	0.79	1.09	0.30
Germany	38,261	31,188	−18.5	0.69	1.01	0.32
Greece	4,268	3,902	−8.6	0.82	1.23	0.41
Ireland	1,429	927	−35.1	0.84	1.51	0.67
Italy	23,375	16,538	−29.2	0.80	1.30	0.50
Japan	65,574	44,248	−32.5	0.61	1.13	0.52
Luxembourg	173	212	22.4	0.81	1.04	0.23
Netherlands	7,647	7,368	−3.6	0.68	0.95	0.27
Portugal	4,776	4,490	−6.0	0.67	0.98	0.31
Spain	16,494	12,538	−24.0	0.77	1.30	0.53
Sweden	4,444	4,819	8.4	0.72	0.83	0.11
United Kingdom	29,014	26,593	−8.3	0.71	0.91	0.20
United States	142,424	161,628	13.5	0.66	0.86	0.20

Source: McMorrow and Roeger, 1999.

sixty-four-year-old age group. The implication for national savings is downward—but by how much? McMorrow and Roeger (1999) estimate that for every single percentage point increase in the dependency ratio, the average propensity to consume (1 minus the average savings rate) increases by about a quarter of a percentage point. Using the traditional definition of the dependency ratio, we see that between 2000 and 2050, China's dependency ratio is expected to rise from about 49 percent to 65 percent. This suggests a decrease in the savings rate of about 4 percentage points. If we examine the increase in the traditional dependency ratio out to the nearer horizon of 2025, we see a much smaller drop in the savings rate, of about .75 percentage points (for a retirement age of sixty-five) and of .05 percentage points (for a retirement age of fifty-five). Clearly, China's policy regarding retirement will be a critical factor in determining savings. As long as the typical retirement age of sixty for men and between fifty-five and sixty for women remains in place, the more dramatic the drop in the savings rate will be due to demographic factors. Another factor in the coming years will be the impact of relaxing China's rules related to family size (see Case Study 5.5). In all scenarios, however, the direction of average savings (from a demographic perspective) is downward.

As we noted above, another implication of the life cycle approach is that higher growth rates today relative to the future will result in higher average savings rates today. China's average growth rate in real GDP between 1978 and 2003 has been above 9 percent. As discussed, when the ratio of increments to income are so large, a larger portion is saved so as to smooth out consumption over the retirement period (Modigliani and Cao, 2004).

Finally, the life cycle hypothesis implies that consumption will be determined by the level of wealth. We approximate private wealth in China was at US$0 in 1978, then it rapidly increases thereafter (see Figure 5.9). The World Bank estimates per capita produced wealth in China at US$4,633 and in the United States at US$49,294 in 2008—an update to Figure 5.9 (UNU-IHDP 2012).[16] We can infer that China still remains far from a steady-state level of wealth accumulation. Wealth accumulation is based on savings and if China's citizens hope to become as wealthy as Americans on average (see Case Study 5.3) a continued pattern of high savings will be needed.

China:2050

MALE   FEMALE

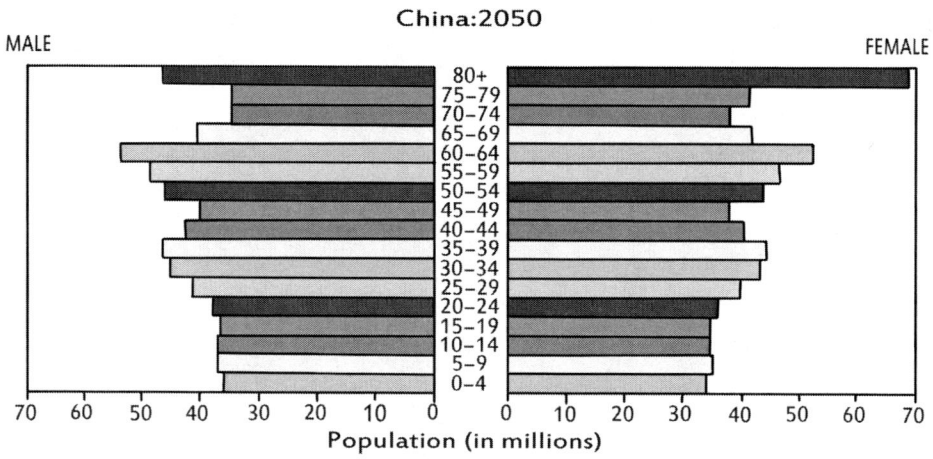

Figure 5.6 China's retired population becomes very large in 2050.

Source: United States Census Bureau International Data Base.

Growth of Working-Age Population (In percent)

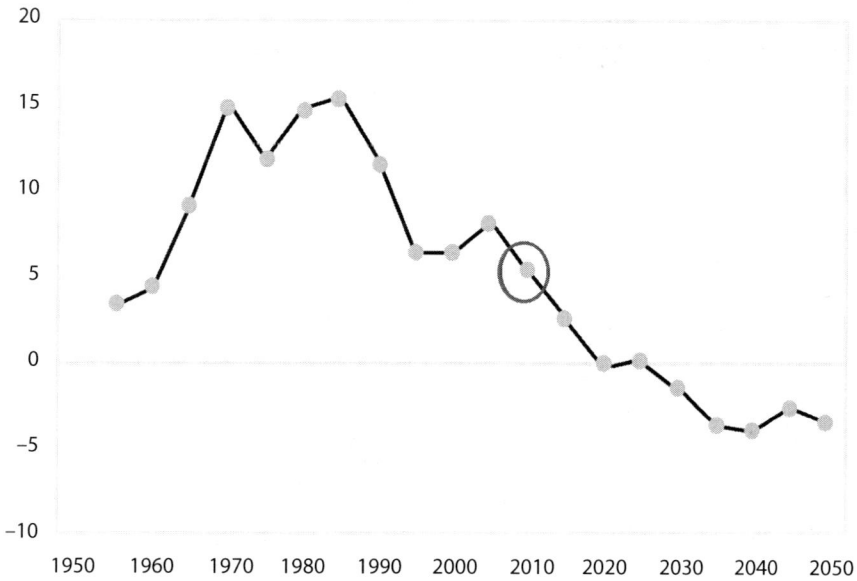

Figure 5.7 China's Shrinking Working Age Population

Source: Estimates from IMF data. (Das, Mitali, and Papa N'Diaye. 2013a.)

Demographic Pressures
(In millions)

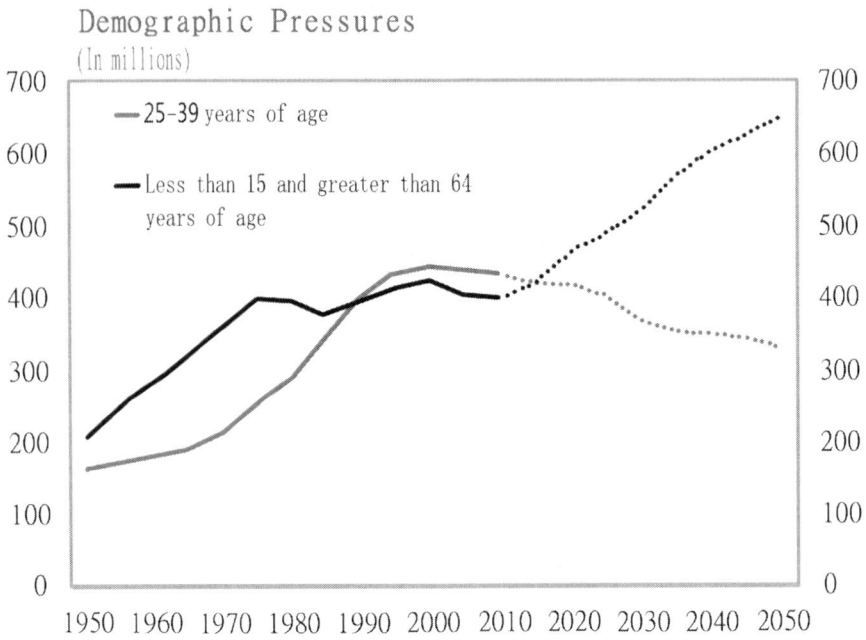

Figure 5.8 A rising burden for those of marriageable age in China.

Source: UN Population Database and IMF staff estimates. (Das, Mitali, and Papa N'Diaye. 2013b.)

CHINA: HOUSEHOLD WEALTH PER PERSON: 1978–2000

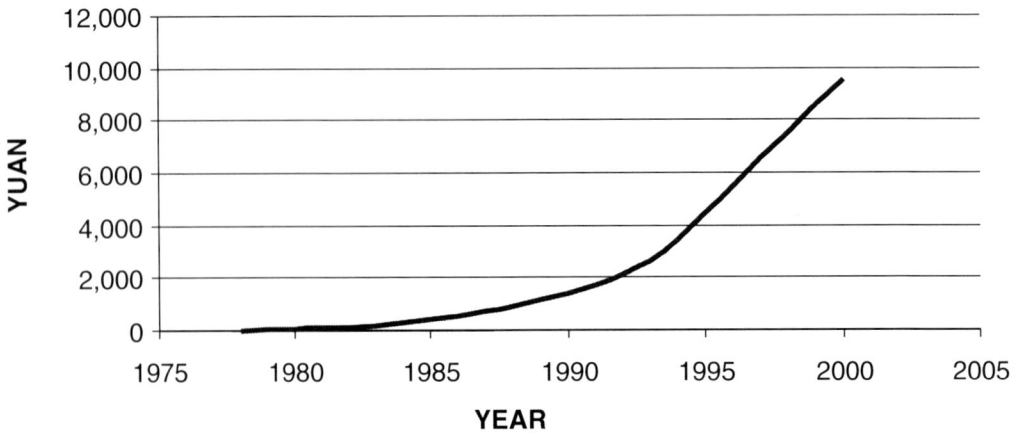

Figure 5.9 Per capita private wealth has increased dramatically in the reform era.

Source: Author created.

Case Study 5.3: Keeping Up with the Wangs (Joneses): Unbalanced Income Distribution

It has been argued that one of the reasons for high consumption rates in the United States has been the "keeping up with the Joneses" phenomenon, a colloquial formulation of the relative income hypothesis of the Harvard economist, James Duesenberry (1949). Specifically, individuals try to maintain consump-

Variation in China Provincial Per Capita GDP

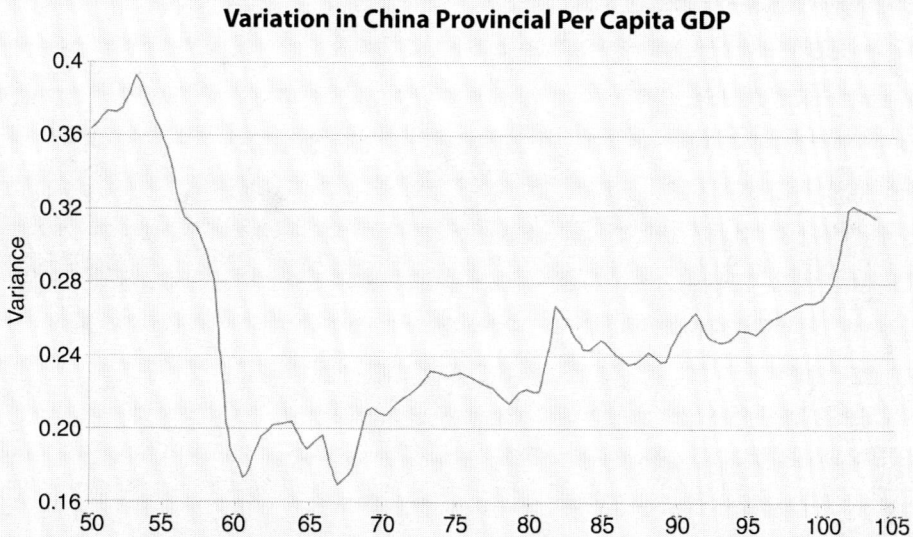

Figure CS5.3a Economic reform in China has come at the cost of increasing income disparity.

Source: Lau, 2010.

tion levels consistent with their neighbors and their own past peak levels of consumption. Besides having a remarkably prescient relationship to modern behavioral finance notions of anchoring and benchmarks, the theory also provides a unique twist on the Chinese citizen's behavior. What if Chinese citizens, rather than trying to match their neighbors' consumption, try to match their neighbors' (higher) wealth? When income distribution becomes unequal, such a desire necessitates significantly higher savings on the part of those (large numbers in the case of China) at the lower end of the income distribution.

Figure CS5.3a shows an increasingly unequal income distribution in China. China's Gini coefficient in recent years has been estimated to be as high as 0.47 (the United States, is estimated at 0.41). This puts China in league with Latin American economies known for their unequal income distribution.* Since 1978, China's income distribution (virtually equal in 1978) has been growing ever-more unequal alongside economic growth. In the United States, conspicuous consumption is the counterpart to China's conspicuous wealth—lavish homes and a foreign education for one's children are all ways of attaining status and "having face." These symbols of wealth do not go unnoticed by those on the lower rungs of income distribution; advertising and the media provide ready access to the rich and famous. In an insightful paper by Jin, Li, and Wu (2011), the authors find that the widening gap in income has, in fact, led to increased savings by those at the lower end, particularly by those furthest down the income scale and by younger households. The one exception (remarkably consistent with what we know about China) is with respect to education. Those at the low end of the scale tend to increase spending on education— defined by GDP accountants as consumption, but in reality an investment in human capital.

*The estimate of 0.47 is for 2012 and was included in the Article IV consultation of the IMF with China for 2013.

Borrowing/Lending Constraints and Consumer Credit in China

Consumer credit is a critical area for reform in China as government officials move to spur consumption demand to provide an alternative to exports and investment as the primary drivers of short-term economic growth (see Case Study 5.4). Consistent with low levels of consumption, consumer debt (defined here to include everything from home mortgages to loans for a vacation or a credit card purchase of an expensive watch) is also well below that found elsewhere around the world. In Figure 5.10, we see that overall credit to the private sector in China is substantially lower than in the United States. But even this understates the actual situation related to consumer credit.

Firstly, in China, about half of credit represents bank credit and most of this is directed to large companies—the large banks still have as their principal shareholder the Chinese government (we discuss this further in Chapter 7, which describes China's monetary institutions). In the United States, credit is provided by private lenders to private borrowers. Secondly, but related to the first point, only about 15 percent of total credit in China goes to the household sector—the lion's share of credit (about 65 percent) goes to the corporate sector. Thirdly, the private sector as defined in China includes many enterprises which still have the government as a major shareholder.

Notwithstanding the above qualifications, credit to households in China has surged in recent years from 30 percent of disposable personal income to close to 50 percent. This figure is still well below the U.S. rate (100 percent) or even that of China's Asian neighbors.[17] Following the global financial crisis, this ratio has been growing in China and shrinking in the United States. An estimated RMB 15 trillion in personal debt now exists in China. In part, this reflects liberalization in the credit markets, as discussed below. The trend also reflects the growth of peer-to-peer (PTP) lending in China. We discuss some specific areas where credit market activity is particularly important. Table 5.3 provides typical terms on major classes of consumer loans (including mortgages) in China.

Peer-to-Peer Lending

PTP lending, often Internet based, is part of the broader world of micro finance lending. Entrepreneurs directly link those who wish to lend with those who wish to borrow. This is a different model

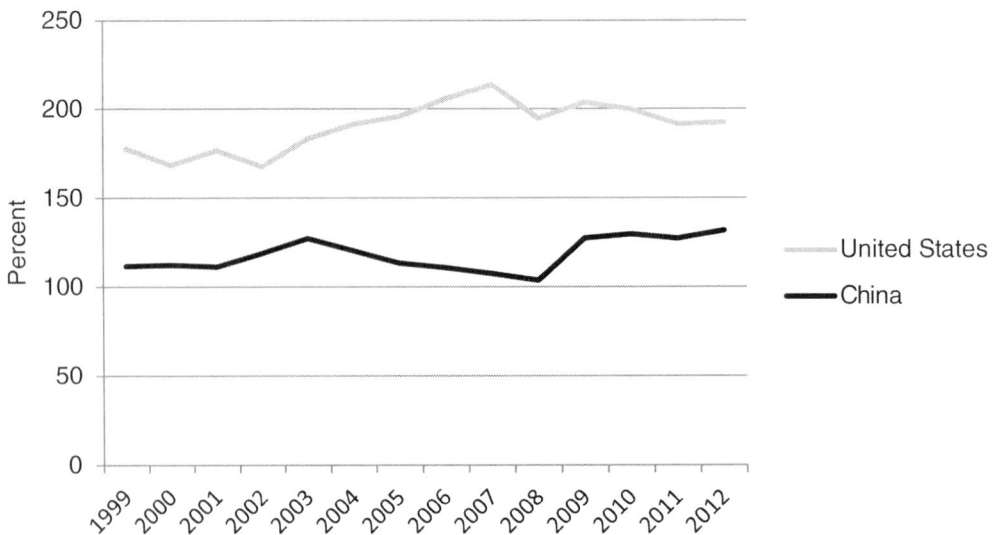

Figure 5.10 Domestic credit to the private sector as a share of GDP is one measure of a more sophisticated financial system in the United States.

Source: World Bank Databank.

Table 5.3 Typical terms for consumer loans in China.

Type of Loan/Term of Loan	Interest Rate	Maturity	Limit
Housing	Set by PBC	30 year maximum	70% value of underlying
Automobile	Set by PBC	5 year maximum	80% value of underlying
Education	Set by PBC	10 year maximum	Each student per year is RMB 6,000 maximum
Home remodeling	Set by PBC	70 year maximum	70% Value of underlying
Travel/Vacation	Set by PBC	10 year maximum	Maximum of RMB 1 million
Consumer durable	Set by PBC	10 year maximum	80% of cost maximum up to RMB 2 million
Secured personal	Set by PBC	3 year maximum	Maximum of RMB 25 million
Small consumer loans	Set by PBC	5 year maximum	Maximum of RMB 30 thousand

Source: Industrial and Commercial Bank of China (November 2013).

from the traditional financial institution model of pooling deposits into a fungible source of funds for making loans. At least 200 PTP lenders now exist in China—a market with threadbare regulation. In fact, PTP might be described as part of a new and rapidly growing shadow banking system (see Chapter 7) creating yet undetermined risks. The critical risk management question related to PTP lending is: how much of their own capital do PTP shareholders (owners) actually have at risk? At present, very little information is available about the financial situation of these lenders.

Home Mortgages

An important area of credit to individuals, both in the United States and China, is the home mortgage market. Home ownership in China (mentioned earlier) is among the highest in the world, with 80 percent of households owning a home. U.S. home ownership peaked at 70 percent pre-financial crisis and is now down to around 65 percent. Owning more than one home is not uncommon among China's middle class—a key investment in an economy with limited investment choices. In Case Study 5.5, we can see that home ownership brings both status and possibly a spouse. Thus the importance of owning a home should not be underestimated.

While home ownership is high, only about a fourth of homes are purchased with mortgages in China. Home mortgage value represents about 15 percent of GDP in China and over 80 percent in the United States. Usually, those who can tap into the formal credit market are in the upper echelons of the income distribution. Furthermore, a down payment (cash payment required to obtain a mortgage) is typically 30 percent of the value of the purchase price, significantly higher than in the United States.[18] The upshot is that individuals still need substantial savings to acquire a home. Although low as a share of GDP, mortgage loans still make up the bulk of all consumer loans in China. As a proportion of all consumer loans, mortgages make up 78.6 percent in China versus 76 percent in the United States. This likely reflects not only the cultural factors mentioned earlier but also China's policy of supporting mortgage lending on the part of banks. In the absence of a sophisticated private credit rating mechanism, it is no surprise that consumer loans are geared toward this highly collateralized product.

Student Loans

The student loan market is also still relatively small in China. Although higher education is an important symbol of status and a stepping stone to marriage, most students find it difficult to obtain loans. In Table 5.3 we see that Chinese banks do offer student loans, but for most families in China, tapping into this source of funding remains difficult. Only an estimated 10 percent of students partic-ipate in the two available government-sponsored loan programs. As one measure of the difference, average student debt in the United States is close to US$30,000; in China, under US$1,000. Between 2008 and 2012, the size of the student loan market in China, albeit relatively small, increased by a factor of ten.

A number of factors combine to limit the size of the market. Most students are still assigned to state-run universities based on a national test (the much-feared 高考 *gaokao*), where the tuition is quite low. Furthermore, information on credit scores, collateral, and cross-province enforcement of loan agreements all hinder an active credit market from developing. In China, student loan programs are targeted mostly to very low-income families. Once again, the contrast with the United States is remarkable: there, most students borrow through publicly or privately financed loan programs in pursuit of a higher education.

Case Study 5.4: Credit Reforms as an Example of a Program Rollout

In late 2013, China's Banking and Regulatory Commission (CBRC) announced that its Consumer Finance Company pilot program would be expanded to cities including Chongqing, Guanzhou, and Qingdao. The program had already been introduced in Beijing, Shanghai, Tianjin, and Chengdu. The new policy allows for non-bank financial institutions with assets over RMB 80 billion to make consumer loans locally. This excludes loans for automobiles and home mortgages (unlike in the U.S., where mort-gage loans are still the purview of regulated banks).

Consumer finance has been a relative latecomer in China's post-1978 reforms. In May 1998, the People's Bank of China (PBC) issued "Methods of Management of Personal Housing Loans," which detailed regulations related to interest rates, maturity, and eligibility in the home mortgage business. In 1999, the PBC issued "Guidelines for Conducting Personal Consumer Credit," opening the way for commercial banks to provide consumer credit across the board.

In 2003, the CBRC allowed companies with total assets of RMB 4 billion and registered capital over RMB 500 million to set up auto financing businesses. This allows the auto financing market to move outside the banking system, particularly to the major auto manufacturers themselves. Earlier reforms included allowing banks to make consumer loans and to issue debit cards and credit cards. Today, Chinese financial institutions have issued an estimated 3 billion debit cards and 300 million credit cards, the latter seeing rapid growth in recent years. These various steps are all part of an ongoing process for freeing up and transforming China's vast savings into consumption demand.

That the recent reforms were first introduced in a few cities, then rolled out to an even broader number of Chinese cities, is unique to China and virtually identical to what a company would do with a new product being tested in the market. This method provides an opportunity to experiment and learn what "bugs" exist in the program, and then recalibrate and improve for the final broad market introduction. This approach has worked remarkably well for China in a number of areas, including allowing farmers to sell their produce at market prices in the late 1970s; the creation of special economic zones in the 1980s as a stepping stone to opening up all of China to foreign direct investment; the development of an interbank market in foreign exchange; the development of a corporate bond market; and plans to intro-duce special economic zones for allowing full convertibility of the RMB against other currencies. This methodical approach has served China well and contributed to its spectacular economic performance in recent decades.

Progress in Consumer Credit Markets

Clearly, a major relaxation of borrowing and liquidity constraints is under way in China (see Case Study 5.4). The extent to which this will impact consumption and its mirror image of savings is an open question. Whether or not China will ever develop a borrowing culture is also unclear. Credit constraints may be lifted but the demand for credit may remain muted. Recent liberalization in credit markets suggests that Chinese consumers will indeed increase borrowing and spending. But China will still need some institutional developments in order to foster credit market growth while minimizing the risks of a consumer-led credit crisis. Specifically, progress must be made in the following areas.

Lack of Credit History

Because individuals have only recently begun borrowing for personal use, China lacks credit history data and rating agencies for individuals. Information is "the coin of the realm" in finance. Anathema to all of finance is asymmetric information which leads to the "lemons problem," in which credit is restricted due to the absence of good information on borrowers (who have perfect information on their own creditworthiness); the end result is that the market collapses and credit availability drops to zero.

Enforcement

When borrowers default, lenders need an orderly and legal mechanism for compensation and for penalizing borrowers. Perhaps collateral is seized by the creditor or a new payment schedule is established. Perhaps borrowers are excluded from the credit market in the future or, as in some countries, even imprisoned. China has yet to develop an orderly process. Even when courts do make a determination regarding a default, enforcement of the ruling (collection) remains problematic. This opens up the real possibility of non-legal, arbitrary, and sometimes criminal methods for collecting bad debts.

Other Factors Impacting China's Savings Rate

Policies Promoting Investment and Exports

If we consider the fundamental accounting identity in an open economy, we have:

National Savings ≡ National Investment + Current Account Balance

In an accounting sense, this identity suggests that the higher the level of the current account surplus or level of investment, the higher the level of savings.[19] Alternatively, and more intuitively, the higher the level of exports and production of investment goods as a share of some total fixed output, the less available for consumption. Thus, as a result, savings must be higher. Chairman Mao's policies in the 1950s, which followed the Soviet model of massive investment in infrastructure and heavy industry while at the same time isolating the economy internationally, effectively put China on a path of high national savings. In terms of the landscape of production, this was similar to the United States' New Deal—a period of massive public works projects. Of course, a major difference was the forced conscription of labor for China's projects. An economy directed from above (the central government) to produce investment goods will be constrained in its production of consumer goods. After 1978, China's policymakers shifted to opening up the external sector but with an emphasis on the export of goods. Again, in an accounting sense, the production of consumer goods would be squeezed.

Implicit Insurance of Savings Deposits

The real return on savings will impact a nation's propensity to save over the long run. These deposits become, in effect, debt free if the government implicitly guarantees the principal on savings deposits within the state-owned banks. Confidence in China's government-backed guarantee has played a key role in its continued savings even in the face of the ongoing banking crisis. One could imagine other outcomes, including a financial panic or a surge in the purchase of consumer durables. The history of financial crises worldwide is filled with such situations, but China has managed to avoid this problem due, in large part, to its ever-growing national wealth and to an implicit government guarantee.

Case Study 5.5: Love and Marriage—Unbalanced Sex Ratios

In an interesting piece of research, Wei and Zhang (2009) cite the current imbalance in the ratio of males to females in China as an explanation for half of the increase in China's savings rate since 1995. They argue that, in order for sons to find a marriage partner, parents need to save more for what is, in effect, a reverse dowry—to make their son an attractive candidate. Potential bridegrooms similarly save more in order to purchase a home.

China's one child policy, which commenced in the late 1970s, combined with a strong traditional preference for sons, has led to the current unbalanced sex ratio. One would normally expect about 106 boys for 100 girls in any given population—in China that ratio likely now exceeds 124 to 100. For those age twenty-five in 2005, there was an estimated excess number of males relative to females amounting to 30 million—the population of Canada! Examining data from 122 rural counties and 70 cities, the authors find a strong link between sex ratios and savings rates. An interesting question not fully answered is why families with just one daughter do not save less. In the meeting of the Third Annual Plenum of China's top leadership, it was announced that the one child policy would be relaxed. If at least one parent came from a one child family, then those parents would be allowed to have two children. Needless to say, this has led to much "soul-searching" combined with economic calculations regarding the value of a second child; a second child brings both joys and significant additional costs.

Summary of China's Personal Consumption and Savings

In an insightful paper, Guo and N'Diaye (2010) suggest that notwithstanding all of the above interesting arguments, there is in fact nothing "special" about China's pattern of consumption and savings when compared to a cross-section of thirty-nine countries. In effect, these authors find that disposable income in China is substantially lower as a share of national income—a fundamental difference that explains at least one-third of the difference in consumption and savings. For example, China's disposable income as a share of GDP has fallen below 60 percent in the past decade; in the United States that figure remains around 72 percent. Rather than asking, "Why is consumption so low in China?" the authors suggest that a better question would be, "Why is disposable personal income so low in China?" The answer, of course, relates to a lower share for labor income as opposed to business income, lower returns on investment (particularly from the financial system), and (as discussed in Chapter 10 on public finance) lower transfer payments, particularly from the government.

Guo and N'Diaye assert that the above differences point toward a means to achieving greater consumption in China beyond the ones mentioned earlier. Those include: greater service sector employment, in which the ratio of labor income to corporate income (corporate savings) is higher, further financial market reform with liberalized interest rates, and higher returns on investment for savers (as discussed earlier and below.)

Corporate Savings and Investment

As we survey the above sections, we get the sense that **almost any theory of consumption can lay claim to explaining China's large savings rate on the part of individuals or households**—and there are many theories of consumption.[20] But this focus on consumption in explaining savings is, to some extent, misguided since the larger part of China's savings comes from institutions rather than private individuals. That is to say, the sum of profits of SOEs and private companies and government budget surpluses are larger than individual savings. If we consider that rural and urban households on average save about 30 percent of their disposable income, we realize that it is nearly impossible to explain China's national savings rate of over 50 percent through savings and consumption by individuals alone. Consider the following identity:

$$\frac{S}{DPI} \times \frac{DPI}{GDP} = \frac{S}{GDP}$$

where S is savings by individuals and DPI is disposable personal income. In recent years, China's ratio of savings to DPI has been about 30 percent, while DPI to GDP has averaged around 60 percent. This suggests that individual savings as a share of GDP is at the most 20 percent. China's national savings as a share of GDP is over 50 percent, further suggesting that, at most, 40 percent of China's savings comes from individuals while 60 percent comes from institutions. For individuals to account for over half of national savings either the DPI/GDP ratio would have to be over 80 percent, or private savings out of disposable income would have to be close to 40 percent, or some combination of these two ratios. This is not consistent with recent data on savings and disposable income.

In the United States, a similar relationship holds true with respect to private savings and corporate savings (but not with government budgets, because the United States runs budget deficits at the federal level). About 70 percent of private savings is attributed to businesses; the remaining 30 percent comes from households. Fortunately, there are some reliable relationships and frameworks which permit us to look at corporate savings (earnings) in depth. We will examine corporate net income and retained earnings from two different angles to compare the two economies. First, we will examine the determinants of net income based on the Dupont model to see why the source of corporate saving or net income may differ. Second, we will examine dividend policy to examine the wedge between net income and retained earnings (i.e., the measure included in corporate savings).

Sources of Profitability

A shorthand accounting of profits, the Dupont model, provides insight into differences between profitability and returns in China and the United States. As an identity, the Dupont model decomposes return on equity (ROE) into three components: productivity of all assets (sales/assets), profit margin (net income/sales), and financial leverage (assets/equity). We can write this identity as follows:

$$\frac{NI}{Equity} = \frac{Sales}{Assets} \times \frac{NI}{Sales} \times \frac{Assets}{Equity}$$

Table 5.4 provides an estimate of these ratios for the manufacturing sectors in China and the United States for 2010 and highlights some likely differences in profitability between the two countries. Overall, it appears that Chinese firms are more profitable (17 percent compared to 14 percent). This difference is consistent with China's faster growth as an emerging economy and helps explain China's higher rate of overall savings. Behind this difference, the Dupont model suggests that China produces a greater amount of output per asset than does the United States. This can likely be explained by China's enormous substitution of labor for capital. In other words, labor plays a much larger role as an input in China as compared to fixed assets. As a result, the ratio of output to fixed assets employed is higher.

Table 5.4 Dupont model: Explaining national savings from the corporate sector perspective.

Dupont Model	China	United States
Manufacturing Industries		
Sales/Assets	118%	78%
Net income/Sales	6%	8%
Assets/Equity	236%	226%
Net income/Equity (ROE)	17%	14%
Net income/Assets	7%	6%

Source: Author created.

Meanwhile, profit margins are higher in the United States—a larger share of sales goes to corporate profits. This in part reflects the pricing power that U.S. firms have—especially in the context of branding and a strong market share. Financial leverage overall seems quite similar.[21] The greater profitability of Chinese firms is just one contributing factor to a higher savings contribution from the business sector. The ratio of overall business income to disposable personal income is substantially higher in China than in the United States (almost by a factor of four)—and this diminishes the weight that high personal savings has in China.

We next turn to the question of share of profits returned to shareholders in each country (dividends) and those not saved (retained) by companies.

Dividend Policy

In any discussion of corporate and domestic savings, we must examine dividend policy. Dividends paid out to shareholders are the wedge (the difference) between net income and retained earnings. A business entity with a high payout ratio (dividends to net income per period) no longer has access to that share of net income paid out to shareholders. In turn, the marginal propensity to consume or save on the part of shareholders will then determine how much of what they receive in dividends goes out to domestic consumption or savings. We formally summarize this in the following relationships:

PR = Dividends / Net Income where PR is the Payout Ratio
Retained Earnings = Net Income − Dividends = $(1 - PR) \times$ Net Income
MPC = Marginal Consumption / Dividends

And so:

$PR \times MPC \times$ Net Income = Marginal Consumption[22]

The payout ratio, the marginal propensity to consume, and corporate income will all determine consumption. Haldane (2010) estimates that for 2009, the average dividend payout ratio in the United States was 40 percent, with fewer than 25 percent of listed firms paying no dividend at all. Meanwhile in China, the average payout ratio was 18 percent with more than half of listed firms paying no dividends at all. Assuming consumption rates of 70 percent and 95 percent for Chinese and U.S. consumers respectively, the product of the first two terms, *PR* and *MPC* would be 0.13 and 0.38. In other words, for every U.S. dollar (or RMB) of corporate profit in each country, consumption created is three times greater in the United States than in China. Since dividend payments in China have been substantially lower than in the United States, it is important to discuss why such a difference exists. In doing so, we can understand more deeply why corporate savings in China is relatively higher, and in turn why domestic savings in China is higher. We do so in the following section.

MACRO FINANCE INSIGHT 5.1: WHEN DIVIDENDS ARE A PROBLEM

Most of China's listed companies still continue to have the state as a major shareholder. One example highlights the difference this type of structure makes in terms of dividend policy. Shares were issued to various SOEs at only a fraction of their true value. However, a number of restrictions have been placed on the shares in terms of resale (when they can be resold, at what price, and to whom, i.e., another SOE). In response, shareowners have sought ways to somehow "cash out" of the shares at something closer to market (higher) valuations. Establishing a generous dividend policy or high payout ratio has proven to be a creative solution. This has been described as a form of "tunneling"—a process whereby non-state minority shareholders see their ownership stake clandestinely and unfairly transferred.* In this and in many other ways, we see traditional "agency" theory turned on its head in China. One normally thinks of dividends as a solution to—not a cause of—an agency problem, and as discussed, dividends are generally too low in China, except for those lucky enough to be a majority shareholder!

*While this does provide the means for such a cash event transfer to occur, in fact, the legal transfer occurred long before, when the initial underpriced shares were issued.

Theories of Dividend Policy

Just as different theories exist as to why consumers choose to save; there are different theories as to why corporations choose to retain earnings (save) instead of releasing some share of net income to shareholders. Central to this discussion is the notion that businesses assess their own opportunities for reinvesting net income into their own or related businesses versus returning some of the net income to shareholders (for them to consume or reinvest on their own). If a company, for example, has access to many investment opportunities with high returns and low risk that shareholders do not have access to, then profits should be reinvested by the company for the benefit of all stakeholders. But if the company only has the same opportunity set for investments that shareholders face, then the company should return a large share of net income to shareholders for their own use. Layered onto this approach is the notion that the firm may have better information regarding opportunities and is more likely to be exposed to the "real options" that are available than would be the shareholders.

The above paragraph hints at the notion of a growth company versus a more stable, mature company. The former tends to conserve cash for investing in ever-growing opportunities. The latter, while still profitable, returns net income to its shareholders. Microsoft, in its first eighteen years of operation, paid no dividends—its opportunities were too great. Only as it reached a more mature stage in its life cycle, in 2004, did it begin to pay dividends.

If we assume that a company reinvests up to the point where its returns just equal the opportunity cost of capital from the market (shareholders), then in the absence of tax and bankruptcy issues, the dividend policy of corporations is irrelevant. In other words, what is paid out as dividends does not impact the company's share price. This is known as the *dividend irrelevance theory* (Modigliani and Miller, 1958). In perfect capital markets, any payment of dividends to current shareholders results in an exactly offsetting share dilution as the firm raises new capital through share issuance. Alternatively, original shareholders can themselves raise the same amount of cash as provided by a dividend through selling some of their shares.

Alternate Views

Though Modigliani–Miller dividend irrelevance serves as a benchmark—a null hypothesis if you will—regarding whether dividend payments matter, we will briefly highlight other theories that are particularly relevant in the China–United States context:

Bird-in-Hand Theory (BIH)

Authors such as Graham and Dodd (1934) have argued that, both conceptually and empirically, it is preferable to receive a dividend now rather than letting management reinvest income. The former is risk free while the latter is merely a promise of a higher return or capital gain resulting from reinvestment. The former is safe; the latter risky and nebulous. Conclusion: firms should have a high payout ratio.

The Presence of Taxes

Both in the United States and in China, dividends are taxed more heavily than capital gains. In the United States, for example, a high-income individual could pay a tax rate as high as 35 percent on dividend income but as low as 15 percent on capital gains. In China, the highest tax rates are 45 percent for individuals and 25 percent for corporations, respectively. This should create a bias toward not paying dividends. Furthermore, there is greater flexibility (discretion) for shareholders in terms of when they reap capital gains as opposed to a business-determined dividend payment. Conclusion: firms should have a low payout ratio.

Pecking Order

This approach states that firms tend to pay fewer dividends because retained earnings are the preferred source of finance for firms that need funding. It is argued that retained earnings are a cheaper source of finance than, for example, new share issuance. The latter cost difference results from asymmetric information. While a firm may have inside information regarding a good investment opportunity, that may not be understood by those providing external sources of finance. Share issuance may also be interpreted by external markets as an indication that managers view the current share price as being overvalued. As a result, new share issuance can be more expensive relative to the use of retained earnings. Conclusion: firms should have a low payout ratio.

Agency and Misappropriation of Funds

This theory suggests that dividends are likely to be paid when management cannot be trusted to use retained earnings wisely. More specifically, a more rigid requirement on dividend payments will put pressure on management to ensure that the dividend target is met, and as a result not waste company resources. Conclusion: firms should have a high payout ratio.

Dividends as a Signaling Device

Dividends also may support share prices as a way of communicating that a company believes that its cash flow going forward is sufficient to cover operations and investments. Otherwise, those dividends would be held as cash balances in anticipation of either profit losses or constraints on outside sources of finance. Companies that unexpectedly halt dividend payments often suffer a drop in share price because investors view this as a signal that the company is generating insufficient cash flow to meet capital expenditure and investor needs. Conclusion: firms should maintain a high payout ratio, if possible.

Table 5.5 summarizes the relevance of each theory for China versus the United States. For example, tax differentials on income vs. capital gains suggest that dividend payments are disadvantageous to shareholders. This is more important in China where such differentials are substantial especially taking into account taxes on short-term capital gains in the United States.

Table 5.5 Relevance of different theories of dividend payouts for China and the United States.

Theory	Implication for Dividend Payment	China Significance	U.S. Significance
MM irrelevance	Neutral	Low	Medium
Growth opportunities	Low payout	High	Low
Bird-in-hand**	High payout	Low*	Medium
Tax differentials	Low payout	Medium	Low
Pecking order	Low payout	High	Medium
Agency issues**	High payout	Low	High
Signaling**	High payout	Medium	High

Source: Author created.
*Depends on type of business; for SOEs the effect is High in a perverse way.
**Less relevant for companies that are not held broadly by the public.

The dividend irrelevance theory is probably less relevant for China than the United States since the theory relies on perfect capital markets—especially the ease with which companies and shareholders can raise cash through a share sale. Transaction costs are substantially lower in the more mature U.S. financial markets.

High-growth opportunities clearly exist in China compared to the United States. In Chapter 4 which deals with economic growth, we show that overall macroeconomic growth is closely related to business returns. Clearly, emerging economies such as China's enjoy substantial growth opportunities, and companies in such economies require financing in order to take advantage of both growth and the presence of real options. As such, the payout ratio tends to be lower for Chinese companies which need to retain earnings to invest further. Just as significantly, the opportunity cost to shareholders of retained earnings in China is extremely low. Shareholders in China currently have very few methods for holding their wealth and earning a positive real interest rate. Regulated ceilings on the interest rate paid by banks on bank deposits make for negative real returns, while real estate valuations that are speculatively high make the retention of earnings by shareholding companies attractive.

The flip-side of the argument for growth opportunities is the *pecking order theory*. Chinese companies that are not large nor state-owned continue to face great difficulty borrowing from banks. Banks continue to have the state as their largest shareholder and therefore, both as a matter of policy and convention, find it easier to lend to state-owned enterprises. The vast majority of Chinese firms find it difficult to access bank credit—especially small- and medium-sized firms.[23] The corporate bond market also remains limited as a source of finance. The primitive information on credit histories for most companies is a significant barrier for arms-length finance—bank or bonds. Regional pools of informal finance, such as in Wenzhou, have become available (as discussed earlier) but these are neither cheap nor consistent sources of finance. The very presence of these pools is an exception that proves the point. The upshot of these limitations is that most firms understand that they will need to rely on their own retained earnings or the retained earnings of a small circle of other firms for finance. The dividend payout ratio, as a result, tends to be low.

While the BIH, agency, and signaling explanations seem directly relevant to the circumstances in China, they are not completely relevant. This is because most Chinese companies are not listed. At present, some 2,300 companies are listed on Chinese exchanges while more than 450,000 companies in China have revenues greater than RMB 5 million. Many of these companies are larger than those listed. For most of these companies, especially those that are private or otherwise closely held, the incentives between management and owners are closely aligned. In other cases, where non-listed companies have either minority or non-state shareholders, their stake is too small to impact dividend policy.

The tax bias toward capital gains over dividends appears to be more pronounced in China than in the United States and this also suggests a lower payout ratio. In summary, though some theories point to a higher payout ratio, these are not directly relevant in China while those pointing to a lower payout ratio are directly relevant. Therefore, we can conclude that there are some financial and economic fundamentals at work causing Chinese firms to disburse less of their net income to shareholders. As a result, corporate savings is higher, personal income lower, shareholder consumption lower, and China's domestic savings greater.

Ultimately, a new set of theories on agency and signaling will evolve related to China's unique SOEs situation. Recent policy proposals for growing consumption and reducing savings (in addition to the factors mentioned above, which seem to be supporting such results) include:

- Further relaxation of dividend policy for private and state-owned enterprises beyond the 2007 reforms, which allowed some dividends to be paid. Putting money in the hands of shareholders and local governments would lead to greater consumption since companies do not consume, but save and invest. In fact, China's Third Plenum announced (in November 2013) that SOEs would be required to raise their current regulated payout ratio of 5–15 percent to 30 percent by 2020.
- A broad range of new policies, from greater empowerment of labor unions to enhanced minimum wage laws that redistribute corporation profits to workers. Currently, China has one of the highest ratios in the world of national income accruing to capital as compared to labor (see Chapter 4 on long-term growth).
- Finally, scholars such as Nabar (2011) have recommended paying higher interest rates on savings deposits—arguing that Chinese savers have a savings target in mind and that the faster that target is reached, the sooner consumption will accelerate. Alternatively, the income effect of increased interest must outweigh the substitution effect from consumption to savings. This argument (perhaps justifiably) is counterintuitive. Nevertheless, Nabar finds some empirical support for the proposition.

A more promising path for China (one that it is slowly following) is the introduction of a wider range of assets for citizens to hold beyond the current mix of cash, bank deposits, home ownership, and stock market investment. Specifically, developing the corporate bond market, consumer credit (allowing individuals to sell short their wealth), and the ability to hold short positions in equity would be major steps forward. Allowing a broader range of assets, both in terms of instruments and underlying assets, would allow savers to diversify and, in turn, hedge their portfolios more efficiently (in the sense of different portfolios for different individual preferences). Because wealth would be better protected against adverse shocks in a hedged portfolio, individuals would not hold as much wealth and would not need to save as much to meet the needs of an uncertain future. Furthermore, the increased competition for funds would force companies to engage in a more "investor friendly" policy. In Chapter 7 (on monetary policy) we show the stark differences in the way Americans and Chinese currently hold wealth.[24] Without a doubt, the overweighting of money holdings in the typical Chinese portfolio relates to the lack of a broader range of investment opportunities.

Challenging Questions for China (and the Student): Chapter 5

1. Go the Federal Reserve Economic Database (FRED), and using the relationship: National Savings – National Investment = Current Account Balance, determine China's savings as a share of GDP over the past decades. Hint: Use the data in FRED for China's "Gross Capital Formation."
2. Explain why China's savings rate is so high and why the United States savings rate is so low.
3. In terms of its impact on savings:

   a. Discuss which is more relevant for China: liquidity constraints or borrowing constraints.

   b. Discuss which is more relevant (liquidity or borrowing constraint) for each of these activities:

      i. Purchase of a product at Carrefour or Wal-Mart.

     ii. Use of a debit card.

    iii. Use of a credit card.

    iv. Loan (mortgage) for the purchase of a new home.

     v. Restrictions/penalties on sale of stock/equity holdings before a specified holding period has expired.

4. Select some theories that we discussed and explain what will happen to China's consumption and savings in the coming years. Be specific about which theory you are using.

5. Discuss whether decreased uncertainty about the future will cause Chinese to save more or to save less. Rely on the discussion about the precautionary motive and the substitution effect.

6. Estimate the impact on China's overall savings rate if the dividend payout ratio (PR) rises in China to U.S. levels.

7. Pick one of the theories of dividend policy in Table 5.5 and discuss why you think it is more relevant to China than this book suggests.

8. A major theme in corporate finance is that when firms have "excess" cash they should pay it out to their shareholders.

   a. What are the interpretations/implications of this concept for China's dividend policy and national savings and consumption?

   b. How might Chinese firms' excess cash holdings lead to greater consumption even if dividends do not increase? Hint: Who is another major stakeholder in a company other than shareholders?

9. Why are savings not the likely path for China to increase its citizens' standard of living in the long run? Using a Solow approach, what then is the likely path for long-run sustainable improvements in China's standard of living?

10. Are symbiotic savings important in the United States? Explain what factors make them important in China.

Notes

1. Saudi Arabia is a close second with 50 percent saved.

2. This figure includes household, business, and government sector savings.

3. Table 5.1 uses flow of funds data for China, which gives a significantly higher figure for household savings than does census estimates. In part, this reflects the difficulty in China of segregating very small-scale business profits (savings) from personal savings.

4. The calculation was done using the average market exchange rate. But the result would qualitatively hold for any reasonable PPP-based exchange rate.

5. For Shakespeare, there were seven ages: The whining infant, the schoolboy, the lover, the soldier, the wise and just man, the old slippered man, and the child again. This would be far too complex a life for the economist to model.

6. There are, however, problems of simultaneity or spurious correlation—higher savings clearly will impact growth rates.

7. We note that under national income accounting, an individual's purchase of a home or business using accumulated wealth would not impact the savings rate during that period. Instead, it would represent merely a shift in assets from one type of wealth (e.g., a savings account in a bank) to another kind of investment (a home or business).

8. Note that the purchase of an automobile or other durable is treated as consumption (thus reducing savings) while a loan for the construction of a new home leads to an investment—the counterpart to that investment is a use of savings.

9. Figure 5.5 represents the market between household and corporate savers and household borrowers only. Although these savings may not flow to other households due to lending constraints, we can assume that savings can still flow to corporate borrowers, the government, as well as externally. To the extent that the demand for these loans is high, relative to the household market, the constraint on household lending will

not be binding. In turn, the total level of savings will not be reduced by the constraint effect described in this figure.

10. The result depends on the shape of the individual's utility function—a concept known as *prudence* (Kimball, 1990).

11. Of course, China's long history affords a discussion of many periods of dramatic and devastating change, but the last 200 years seem particularly harsh.

12. The study is based on census data from the China Health and Nutritional Survey (CHNS), a randomized sample from 4,400 households in nine provinces, comprising 19,000 individuals. Survey years are 1989, 1991, 1993, 1997, 2000, 2004, and 2006.

13. The precise age for retirement in China depends on both gender and whether you are employed in the government or private sector. In the United States, retirement ages are less determined by economic sector than on a particular employer's retirement policy.

14. The current life expectancy at birth in the United States is about six years longer than China's. Given a ten-year lead in retirement age, the Chinese would need to save for an additional four years of live retirement compared to the Americans.

15. In the United States, those over the age of sixty-five spend about 15 percent more than their income (most income comes from retirement benefits); whether the thrifty Chinese retiree manages to spend less is a question for further research.

16. Produced wealth or capital includes wealth created through production or labor; it excludes human capital, health, and natural resources of wealth—a much larger figure for both countries.

17. This difference gets magnified when we consider that personal income in the United States as a share of GDP is nearly twice that of China.

18. Given the recent history of defaults on zero-down-payment mortgages in the United States, this is probably a good thing.

19. Here, we are referring to physical investment in plant, property, and equipment, housing, or inventory accumulation.

20. The multitude of theories of consumption no doubt relates to the central role for consumption in recessions and recoveries identified in the early work of Keynes and scholars who built upon his basic framework. Furthermore, in most economies worldwide, with China as one important exception, consumption represents the largest component of macroeconomic demand. Keynes's approach continues to spawn much interest in how consumption, a key component of economic demand, is determined.

21. These results are based on aggregate sales, net income, assets, and equity for each country. Results differ substantially if we look at "typical" or median firms for each country. Aggregation gives a much heavier weight to very large firms in each country.

22. We assume tax rates are 0 without loss of generality.

23. This is certainly true in the United States as well; the government-sponsored Small Business Administration, with its provision of small business loans, attempts to alleviate this problem.

24. The financial crisis beginning in 2008, in which the financial sector had grown to an unprecedented share of the national economy, suggests that Americans may have developed too many ways of holding their wealth. Meanwhile, the surge in stock and housing prices in China suggests that Chinese citizens may have too few. The latter effect has been further exacerbated by a rapid growth in the money supply discussed in Chapters 7 and 8.

References

Chamon, Marcos, Kai Liu, and Eswar S. Prasad. 2010. "Income Uncertainty and Household Savings in China." NBER Working Paper No. 16565. Cambridge, MA: National Bureau of Economic Research.

Das, Mitali, and Papa N'Diaye. 2013a. "The End of Cheap Labor." *Finance & Development*. June Vol. 50, No. 2. Washington DC: International Monetary Fund.

———. 2013b. "Chronicle of a Decline Foretold: Has China Reached the Lewis Turning Point?" IMF Working Paper WP/13/26. June. Washington DC: International Monetary Fund.

Duesenberry, James Stemble. 1949. *Income, Saving, and the Theory of Consumer Behavior*. Cambridge: Harvard University Press.

Federal Reserve Board (FRB) of Governors and U.S. Commerce Department. 2014. Federal Reserve Statistical Release. Bureau of Economic Analysis. Flow of Funds Accounts. Table Z.1. www.federalreserve.gov/releases/z1/current/data.htm

Feldstein, M., and C. Horioka. 1980. "Domestic Saving and International Capital Flows." *Economic Journal* 90(358): 314–29.

Friedman, Milton. 1957. *A Theory of the Consumption Function: A Study by the National Bureau of Economic Research*. Princeton: Princeton University Press.

Graham, Benjamin, and David Dodd. 1934, *Security Analysis*. New York: McGraw-Hill Professional.

Guo, Kai, and Papa N'Diaye. 2010. "Determinants of China's Private Consumption: an International Perspective." IMF Working Paper No. 10/93. Washington, DC: International Monetary Fund.

Haldane, Andrew G. 2010. "Global Imbalances in Retrospect and Prospect." Remarks given at: Global Financial Forum, Chatham House Conference on The New Global Economic Order, November 3, London, England. http://www.bis.org/review/r101223f.pdf

Hall, Robert. 1978. "Stochastic Implications of the Life Cycle-Permanent Income Hypothesis: Theory and Evidence." *Journal of Political Economy* 86(6): 971–87.

Horioka, Charles Yuji, and Wakö Watanabe. 1997. "Why Do People Save? A Micro-Analysis of Motives for Household Saving in Japan." *The Economic Journal* 107(442): 537–52.

International Human Dimensions Programme on Global Environmental Change (UNU-IHDP), and United Nations Environment Programme (UNEP). 2012. *Inclusive Wealth Report 2012: Measuring Progress Toward Sustainability*. Cambridge: Cambridge University Press.

Jin, Ye, Hongbin Li, and Binzhen Wu. 2011. "Income Inequality, Consumption, and Social-Status Seeking." *Journal of Comparative Economics* 39(2): 191–204.

Kimball, Miles S. 1990. "Precautionary Saving in the Small and in the Large." *Econometrica* 58(1): 53–73.

Lau, Chi Keung Marco. 2010. "New Evidence About Regional Income Divergence in China." *China Economic Review* 21(2): 293–309.

LeBaron, Blake. 2006. "Agent-based Computational Finance." *Handbook of Computational Economics,* eds. L. Tesfatsion and K.L. Judd, 1187–1233. New York: Elsevier.

McMorrow, K., and W. Roeger. 1999. "The Economic Consequences of Ageing Populations (a Comparison of the EU, US and Japan)." *Economic Papers* No. 138. EU Commission (Working Document), November, Brussels.

Modigliani, Franco, and Shi Larry Cao. 2004. "The Chinese Saving Puzzle and the Life-Cycle Hypothesis." *Journal of Economic Literature* 42 (1): 145–70.

Modigliani, Franco, and Merton H. Miller. 1958. "The Cost of Capital, Corporation Finance and the Theory of Investment." *American Economic Review* 48(3): 261–97.

Nabar, M. 2011. "Targets, Interest Rates and Household Saving in Urban China." IMF Working Paper No. 11/223. Washington, DC: International Monetary Fund.

National Bureau of Statistics. 2012. *China Statistical Yearbook,* Table 2–30. Beijing: China Statistics Press.

UNC Carolina Population Center. N.d. China Health and Nutrition Survey. www.cpc.unc.edu/projects/china (accessed April 8, 2014).

U.S. Census Bureau. International Programs. International Database. www.census.gov/population/international/data/idb/informationGateway.php (accessed May 8, 2014).

Wei, Shang-Jin, and Xiaobo Zhang. 2009. "The Competitive Saving Motive: Evidence from Rising Sex Ratios and Savings Rates in China." NBER Working Paper No. 15093. Cambridge: National Bureau of Economic Research, June.

6 China's Path of Investment

欲速则不
Haste Makes Waste

The tremendous growth in savings in China has been matched by an equally significant increase in gross fixed investment over the past decade. When discussing investment in this chapter, we are referring to physical investment, that is, the accumulation or flow of new plant and equipment, housing, and inventories.[1] This is in contrast to *financial investment*, which is more commonly used in everyday discussion; the latter refers to the channeling of savings into different asset classes such as savings accounts, stocks, and bonds. Although the two concepts are clearly related, we must keep in mind that investment (in the context of this chapter) involves actual current production of output (investment or capital goods) that will be used to produce more output in the future. In contrast, financial investment may not result in any current production of output at all. Gross fixed investment refers to investment in plants, equipment, and housing, but excludes inventory accumulation (also known as stock-building); total investment includes the latter.

Figure 6.1 shows the acceleration of real investment in China in the post-1978 reform period. The figure also suggests that the increase in investment was not solely an artifact of economic growth; instead, investment took up an increasing share of economic output. Figure 6.2 shows the much smaller share of economic output devoted to investment in the United States. China's share of GDP devoted to investment in recent years has reached nearly 50 percent—the highest rate worldwide for any large economy. We can compare that level to other middle-income economies, in which the share of investment reaches only around 25 percent, and to the United States, where the share is approximately 16 percent.

Figure 6.3 shows a fourfold increase in foreign direct investment (FDI) into China over the past decade. In the same period, however, overall investment increased by a factor of six. Even at its peak in 1994, FDI contributed only about 17 percent of China's total investment; by 2011, the amount fell to 7 percent. Meanwhile, as the share of FDI declined after 1994, overall investment in China actually rose from about 36 percent of GDP to close to 50 percent of GDP.[2] That China's creation of new fixed capital on an annual basis (gross fixed investment or gross capital formation) moved from just RMB 160 billion in 1980 to RMB 22.5 trillion by 2011 has implications not just for the types and level of economic activity in those intervening years, but also for economic growth in the years to follow.[3] Such a massive accumulation of capital raises questions about which economic agents were involved in the decision to invest, what were their motivations, and what can be inferred about the quality of investment taking place. In other words, will these investments yield returns sufficient to offset their initial costs, and who are the potential beneficiaries (or losers) from such investment? Finally, we note that, in developed market-oriented economies, investment has played a critical role in short-run economic fluctuations (i.e., the business cycle). Of the various components of demand for these economies, investment is, by far, the most volatile. Comparing Figures 6.1 and 6.2 shows that investment in the United States as a share of GDP has been far more volatile than in China. Table 6.1 presents the volatility of various components of GDP in each country. Given China's movement

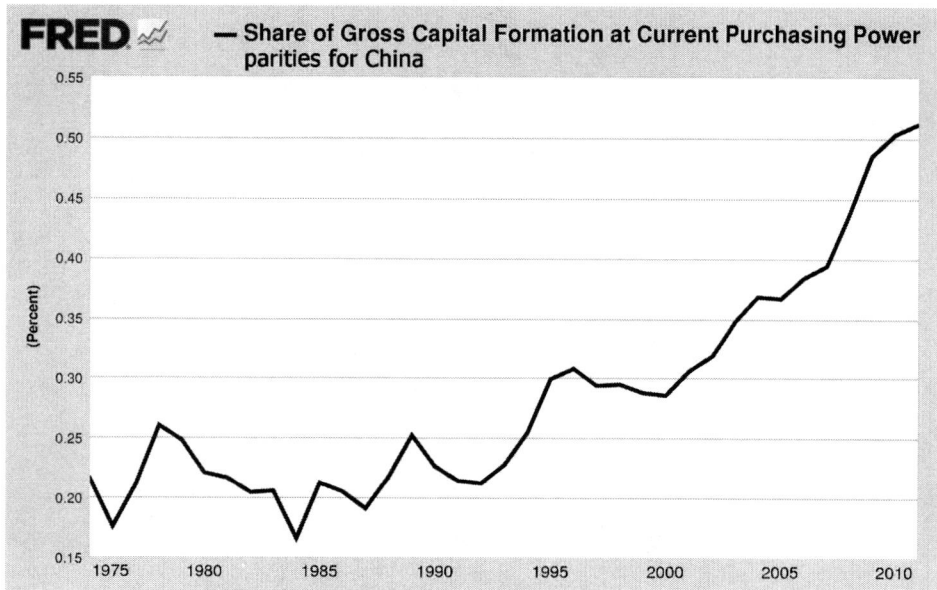

Figure 6.1 Investment as a share of GDP in China has hovered around 50 percent in recent years—the highest ratio in the world among large economies.

Source: FRED, Federal Reserve Economic Data, Federal Reserve Bank of St. Louis: Share of Gross Capital Formation at Current Purchasing Power Parities for China; University of Groningen. 2014 research.stlouisfed.org

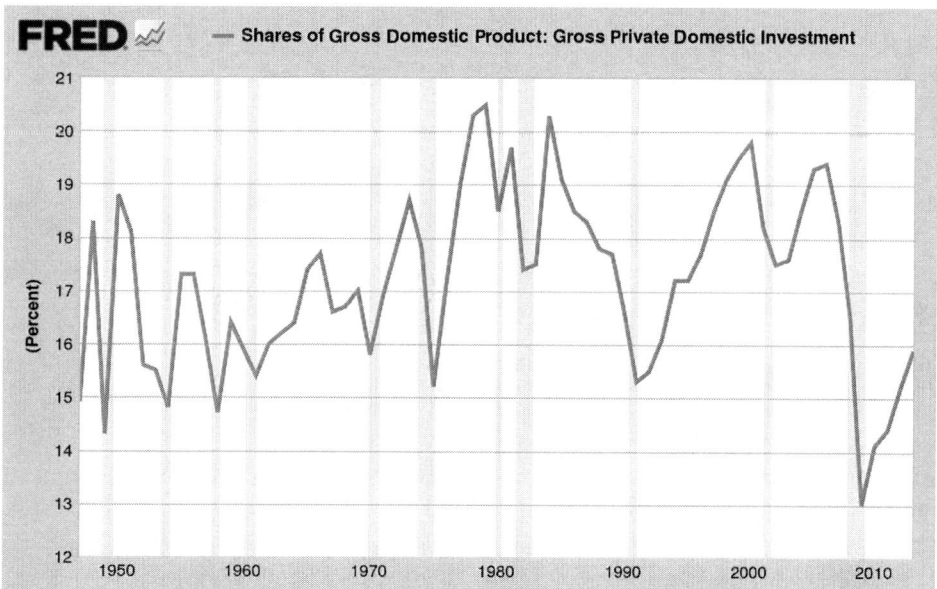

Figure 6.2 U.S. investment as a share of GDP has been highly variable and about a third of China's ratio.

Source: FRED, Federal Reserve Economic Data, Federal Reserve Bank of St. Louis. 2014 research.stlouisfed.org.

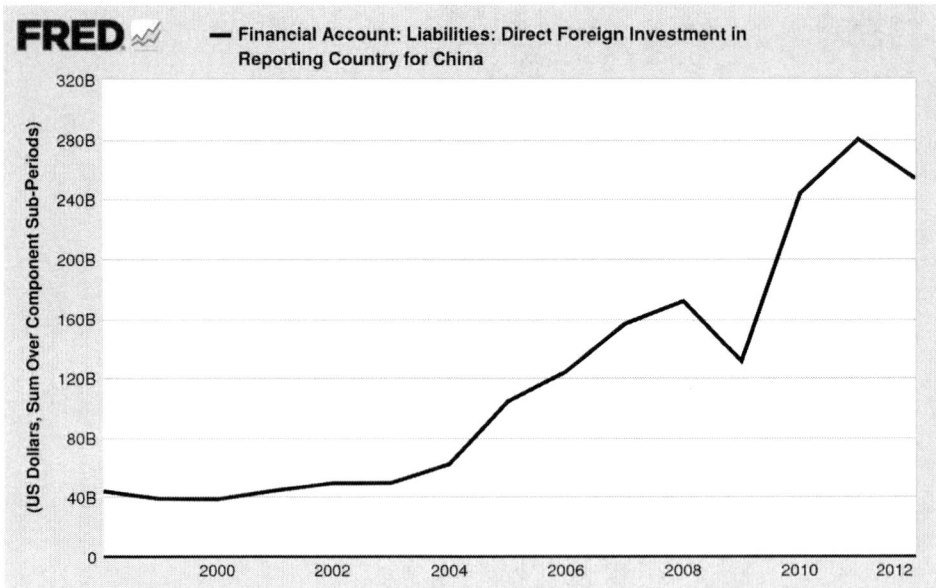

Figure 6.3 Foreign direct investment into China has also grown rapidly but is an ever-decreasing share of total Chinese investment.

Source: FRED, Federal Reserve Economic Data, Federal Reserve Bank of St. Louis. 2014 research.stlouisfed.org

Table 6.1 Growth in China's investment has been both more rapid and less volatile than in the United States in recent years.

		China	*United States*
a.	Real GDP growth %	10.8%	3.1%
b.	Volatility of GDP growth	2.9%	1.8%
c.	Coefficient of variation b/c	27.1%	56.5%
d.	Real investment growth %	12.0%	5.9%
e.	Volatility of investment growth	1.7%	4.4%
f.	Coefficient of variation e/d	14.5%	75.1%

Source: Author created.

away from a planned to a market-based economy, we must understand the implications for investment both in the long run and short run. We address each of these questions in this chapter.

China's Investment: Uses and Sources

Uses

It is worth repeating that in a macroeconomics accounting context, investment, consumption, and government and export spending or demand are defined by their **use,** rather than their **source**. If something is used by the government sector, for example, as a consumable item (such as food), we define that product's use as *government* even though the product was produced in the private sector for the purpose of consumption in a colloquial sense. Similarly, a washing machine purchased by a consumer is defined as *consumption* whereas had it been purchased by a commercial launderer, it would be classified as an *investment* good. Residential housing, meanwhile, is treated as an investment good (even though a consumer is "using" the house) and the homeowner is classified as an investor. Police or fire department services provided by a municipality are included as government spending (as are military services) since they are *public goods* that are in effect demanded by the government. In the latter case, for developed economies, the interesting nexus of classification is between consumption and investment uses.

In China, however, more interest is placed on the government and investment nexus. Investment represents a relatively large fraction of China's GDP. Historically, however, most of the decision making on investment took place at the behest of the government. A further complication is that many investment goods have been produced by state-owned enterprises (SOEs) that are owned by the government. In developed economies, much of that same production would be undertaken by the private sector.[4] Given these differences, our definition of investment as a use becomes an important tool.

Fixed investment includes both business fixed investment and residential fixed investment (housing). Business fixed investment includes new plant or property and equipment (but excludes land) as well as software development. Another type of investment that is not considered "fixed" is the flow of new inventory (stock-building). In summary, investment includes gross new plants, property (including residential housing) and equipment, business software development, and inventory accumulation.[5]

Table 6.2 provides a comparative breakdown of investment types in China and the United States. In order to make such a comparison, we must identify the share of investment undertaken by the government in demanding investment goods. In the case of China, it is difficult to separate out investment demand by the government since a substantial part of investment is undertaken by SOEs. Some of this investment will ultimately be used by the government sector, but much of it will be used by the private sector.

Table 6.2 assumes that government investment demand or use is limited to those investment activities that are formally part of the central, provincial and township, and village government budgets; that is to say, they represent spending by those government entities and are financed by either taxation or public borrowing. As a share of GDP, China's gross investment is two to three times larger than that of the United States. Across all major categories, investment is higher by similar orders of magnitude. In both countries, non-residential investment makes up the lion's share, and this was also true before the 2008 global financial crisis. Non-residential investment includes investment in plant, property, and equipment—mostly on the part of companies, but also includes some infrastructure investment. Residential, government, and inventory investment categories are all disproportionately larger in China than the United States. Even in the pre-financial crisis, residential investment in the United States never reached the share of GDP that it currently holds in China.

Table 6.2 Though residential investment in the United States has often been a popular topic for discussion in the United States, it is relatively more important as a share of GDP in China.

	United States 2012 (US$ billions)	Percent of GDP	China 2011 (RMB 100 million)	Percent of GDP
Gross investment total	3,094.2	19.0%	225,007	47.6%
Non-government, fixed gross investment	2,409.2	14.8%	167,411	35.4%
Non-residential	1,970	12.1%	134,198	28.4%
Residential	439.2	2.7%	33,213	7.0%
Government gross investment	618.9	3.8%	45,631.8	9.6%
Change in inventories	66.1	0.4%	11,964	2.5%
GDP	16,244.6		472,881.6	

Source: Author created.

Case Study 6.1: Is There a Housing Bubble?

A *financial bubble* is an increase in an asset price unrelated to fundamental factors, such as a higher anticipated return or cash flow, or a decrease in the cost of capital. Rather, a bubble is defined as price increases based solely on the expectation of further price increases. Here, we ask one of the most popular questions in China related to finance: "Do housing prices today represent a bubble?" A classic bubble example comes from the South Sea Company (1718–21), one of the earliest attempts to securitize debt—in this case, the national debt of the United Kingdom. Although lacking in actual income, the Company was able to attract investors, so much so that the price of the stock rose from around 100 pounds sterling to close to 1,000. One investor, who bought the stock at around 700 and sold closer to 300 (and missed selling at the peak of 1,000), was the great physicist Isaac Newton. He lost close to US$3 million in today's dollars in the venture, leading him to famously state: "I can calculate the movement of stars but not the madness of men." There are two well-known characteristics of bubbles: (1) they are unsustainable, and (2) they are notoriously difficult to identify in terms of their existence and the timing of their collapse. Or, as the great economist (and investor) John Maynard Keynes said, "Markets can remain irrational longer than investors can remain solvent."

Over the past ten years, housing prices in China have risen in real terms by over 150 percent (or about 10 percent per year) but in a highly volatile fashion. During the same period, land prices have risen by an extraordinary factor of nine in Beijing and in a single quarter of 2013 (the first quarter) land prices nearly doubled in Shanghai. Since residential housing represents about 20 percent of national investment (or about 10 percent of GDP), the impact of a bursting bubble would be significant in China—likely triggering a contagion effect on financial markets, investment, and consumer demand. The recent U.S. financial crisis serves as a "poster child" for such a possibility.

From the founding of the PRC through 1978, land and property in China has been state owned. In 1979, limited privatization of housing began, mainly in cities along the East Coast. The government took another important step toward privatization in the 1988 Constitutional amendment allowing for seventy-year leases of land for residential purposes. The government continues to own all land in China, but individuals can "lease" homes in seventy-year time slots. Another critical year was 1998, as work units (*danwei*) were no longer responsible for the direct provision of housing. Instead, it became the responsibility of individual citizens to rent or purchase their own housing. This was the start of a truly private housing market.

On the supply side, from 1998 to 2008, China saw its available residential floor space more than triple. In some cities, more than half of the housing construction taking place during the past decade was completed by SOEs. These enterprises, as discussed in Chapters 4 and 7, have access to bank finance at subsidized borrowing costs. The high involvement of SOEs raises the question: "Are China's housing price increases driven by supply-and-demand fundamentals, or non-market irrational factors?"

On the demand side, we have seen massive urbanization (i.e., the movement of the population from rural to urban areas) encouraged by policy announcements and Five-Year Plan mandates. In fact, in 1978 less than 18 percent of China's population lived in urban areas; by 2011, over half of the population lived there—a change of about half a billion people. Alternatively, since 2000, about 230 million people have moved into urban areas; meanwhile, only about 50 million single-family housing units were added since then. In the same period, per capita income in U.S. dollar terms increased by more than a factor of six. These factors point to housing shortages conditional on location and family income. Comparing China's situation with that of the United States suggests that the problem may persist long into the future: 50 percent of Chinese citizens still live in rural areas, while only 15 percent of Americans live in rural areas and only 2 percent of the population works in agriculture. Thus, it is likely that China's urban migration will be a long-term phenomenon.

In examining house-price-to-annual-rent ratios (a form of price-earnings ratio), Wu et al. (2011) find that, in seven large Chinese cities, ratio estimates range from 25 to 45.* In the United States, the range would be 16 to 20. They employ an approach suggested by Poterba (1984) to see if the ratios in China make economic sense:

User Cost = $(1 - t)(r + p) + m + \delta + \beta - \pi e$

Here, we employ a specific form of the "user cost" (defined as *the cost of owning a home, per home price*). In the equation above, t is the individual tax rate (and so home interest deductibility benefit), r is the borrowing or financing cost, p is property tax rate, m is maintenance fee, δ is depreciation rate, β is the risk premium on home ownership (in percent), and πe is the expected appreciation rate of the property (home price increase). In theory, this cost should just equal the rental rate or the inverse of the price-earnings (PE) ratios mentioned above.

China's parameters for the above relationship differ fundamentally from those of the United States. It is useful to discuss these differences qualitatively. Interest on mortgages is not tax deductible in China, but is in the United States. Property taxes clearly exist in the United States but not yet in China (though there are plans to implement them). Maintenance fees are generally quite low in China, resulting, in part, to a higher depreciation of property. Home ownership is probably viewed even more as a secure asset in China than in the United States, thus β is likely lower. Finally, if expectations are formed adaptively (i.e., based on what has happened in the past), then China will continue to see high expectations of home price appreciation. Wu et al. (2011) find that the structure of some of these parameters renders current PE ratios unsustainably high (i.e., actual home price appreciation is far from what is expected—implying a possible collapse of China's housing prices in the near term).

The authors also examine home-price-to-annual income measures, but here (as suggested above) the picture is more mixed. Given the factors discussed above, Wu et al. (2011) and others suggest that China's housing market prices do reflect an asset pricing bubble.

Our view, however, is that current prices do not necessarily represent a bubble, but may instead represent fundamental economic factors which have driven prices astronomically high in the short run. Specifically, much of China's rapid increase in prices no doubt reflects an inelastic supply of land in the cities where much of the population is migrating.†

Basic microeconomics clearly segregates short-run from long-run prices. In the former, prices can surge, but ultimately prices will moderate in the long run with new entrants and new supplies into the market. What both "bubblists" and fundamentalists do agree on is that, in both situations, those who invest and assume that current high prices and price increases are sustainable will lose money. The rational investor is able to observe the market fundamentals, understand that other cities may offer opportunities for quality urban living, and thereby moderate demand and price increases. In contrast, those in the bubble economy irrationally ignore fundamentals and, thus, economic outcomes tend to be worse.

Finally, we note that China's real estate market has a different financial structure than did the United States pre-crisis. In China, fewer mortgages are granted and those which are granted require large (20–30 percent) cash down payments. Many Chinese buyers save and acquire a home fully with a cash payment, not relying on any mortgage at all. Employee-based savings plans have also been institutionalized by the government (housing provident plans). In summary, while China's home prices are likely far above their long-run equilibrium value, the housing market also appears to be driven by basic (short-run fixed) supply and measurable fundamental demand, rather than only by champagne fizz (a bubble).

*For an eighth city, Hangzhou, the recent ratio was 65.

†As we noted earlier, part of this may be artificial due to the participation of state-owned, bank-financed SOEs.

Sources

The largest share of investment in China is still undertaken by SOEs, at 35 percent of total investment. This share, however, has been in continuous decline over the past two decades; in 1995, the share of SOE investment was close to 44 percent (Lin and Schramm, 2009). Today, other important investment categories include: private companies (20 percent of all investment) followed by foreign firms (7 percent). The remainder is either undertaken by government (20 percent), individuals, or other legal corporate structures (such as collective enterprises). Both in China and the United States, non-financial corporations rely overwhelmingly on internal funds (retained earnings or profits) to finance investment. In China, despite its substantial investment, the very profitable production sector has been a substantial lender to other sectors—including indirectly financing the U.S. current account deficit with China. In the United States, in recent years, the non-financial corporate sector has used its ample profits to finance its relatively low levels of domestic investment, and has used the surplus funds to finance other economic sectors, including FDI into China. In the United States, companies in recent years have been buying back rather than issuing new equity.[6] In contrast, Chinese firms have been net issuers of equity, and have been borrowing from banks despite their strong cash flow from operations. No doubt some of these funds are recycled (via China's shadow banking system) into other firms with low or negative cash flows. Some of the funds borrowed, however, may simply represent the arbitrage opportunity that SOEs enjoy through borrowing from state-owned banks at low rates, then investing in outside opportunities including foreign investments.

As Lin and Schramm (2009) point out, a key difference between the United States and China, in terms of investment and production, is China's use of SOEs in the production process. The Chinese National Bureau of Statistics provides definitions of the broad types of production units still found in China.

Definitions of Entities Involved in Production of Output in China

STATE-OWNED UNITS

State-owned units (SOUs) are economic units whose assets are owned by the state. This includes various governmental bodies at all levels of government, state-owned enterprises (SOEs) at both the national and provincial levels, and social organizations. Excluded from this definition are collective-owned enterprises.

STATE-OWNED ENTERPRISES

Over 100,000 entities that have not been incorporated which are engaged in the production of goods and services both of a public and private nature, but whose assets are entirely owned by the state, are *state-owned enterprises* (SOEs). Most SOEs are owned by provinces and localities. Over 100 SOEs are owned by the central government and these entities are both large and economically significant.

COLLECTIVE-OWNED ENTERPRISES

Economic units where the assets are owned and operated by members of a group are referred to as a "collective" (collective-owned enterprise, COE). Typically, the collective would represent residents of a town or village—the definition therefore comprises town and village enterprises (TVEs). The collective leadership decides on how revenues of the enterprise are to be distributed among the collective members and any outside stakeholders. Management typically receives some fixed percentage of profits. One type of COE is the cooperative enterprise in which capital is contributed mainly by the workers of the entity. COEs have a great deal of independence in terms of management decisions and strategic direction of the entity as well as distribution of profits and wage remuneration.

PRIVATE AND QUASI-PRIVATE ENTERPRISES

Economic entities that have assumed either a limited-liability corporate structure, shareholding corporate structure, individual proprietor structure, or some type of foreign-funded investment structure are *private* or *quasi-private enterprises* (PEs). Included in this group are shareholding companies that are listed on stock exchanges but whose principal shareholder remains the Chinese government (former SOEs that have been listed).

This is not so much an issue in terms of assigning roles for GDP—for example, whether goods and services are consumer goods or government goods. This classification (as discussed in Chapter 2) is based on the user of the end product, not the producer. Thus, in principle at least, an SOE producing consumer goods would correctly have its output included in consumption, under GDP measurement methodology.

Difficulties arise in deciding how to assign SOE surpluses (profits) or deficits (losses) when measuring flows of funds (the sources of funds for investment (savings) versus its uses (investment)). Are SOE gains or losses assigned to the government sector (particularly at the local level) as deficits or losses, or are they kept off of the government's balance sheet? A similar question arises when we try to assign the amount of investment undertaken by the government: should SOE investment be included or excluded? In recent years, with the declining importance of SOEs in the overall economy, investment attributed to the government in China has risen commensurately. At least anecdotally, the investments previously undertaken by SOEs (such as for health, housing, and general welfare) are now being picked up by all levels of government in China.

Investment Demand Theories

How an investment decision is made is a complex issue in any nation, but especially so in China. Macroeconomics research has provided a variety of models which explain the investment level in an economy, both theoretically and empirically. This work has a long tradition, dating back at least to the beginning of the twentieth century. The neoclassical models are truly at the center of a capitalist framework, in which owners of capital (capitalists) make rational decisions on how much capital to accumulate within a firm.

As we have seen above, however, a disproportionate share of investment in China has been undertaken by the government and SOEs at the behest of the government. In the past, much of this investment was financed either by grants or with "soft" loans (i.e., loans whose payment terms are either more favorable than market rates or which, in effect, become grants, and are never actually required to be serviced or repaid). When investment is determined by government decision makers, there may be an entirely different set of objectives than a private value-creating capitalist might have. This section is set in this context, and analyzes the question: "To what extent can the mainstream (traditional) models of investment behavior explain China's investment behavior?" Given that investment is notorious for its variability, and given its reputation for being at the center of business cycle fluctuations in the short run and economic growth in the long run, the issues covered here are critically important.[7] In China's economy today, we see two extremes. At one end of the spectrum, we see investment undertaken by the central government which, although serving a public policy purpose, may have little or no relation to the mainstream model assumptions and outcomes. Meanwhile at the other end of the spectrum, we see investment undertaken by private entrepreneurs (including foreign ones), which fits very comfortably within the confines of these very same models.

Models of Investment Behavior

Neoclassical Model

If we begin to consider investment at the firm level, we can examine the standard model for decision making on the part of the firm. Here we imagine managers who have a range of possible projects that will yield incremental increases in profits (Π) over some future horizon.[8] The manager must weigh the anticipated benefit (more profit) against the incremental cost of achieving these profits. The incremental cost includes the ongoing cost of financing the investment needed for the project. That cost (r) includes either the opportunity cost of using the owner's own funds or someone else's funds for the project—in other words, what those funds could have earned in their best risk equivalent alternative use during each time period. An additional cost to factor in is depreciation of the fixed investment during each time period, either as a result of wear and tear or because the investment has lost value due to obsolescence. The opportunity cost of these funds plus the depreciation must be compared with the anticipated profits in order to see if the investment should be undertaken. We refer to the sum of opportunity costs and depreciation as the "user cost of investment."

In summary, at the firm level, greater anticipated profits (Π) can be associated with increased investment, while higher opportunity costs (r, often defined as the "cost of capital") are associated with lower levels of investment. This relationship is summarized in the following equation:

$$\text{Net Present Value} = -I_0 + \Pi_1 / (1 + r) + \Pi_2 / (1 + r)^2 \ldots$$

where I_0 represents the initial outlay for investment. The term *net present value* (NPV), in effect, measures the difference between the increased profits and increased cost of undertaking the project. A positive value suggests that the investment should be undertaken. In the Macro Finance Insight 6.1, we establish a link between marginal productivities of capital and cash flows.

MACRO FINANCE INSIGHT 6.1: OPTIMAL INVESTMENT, NEOCLASSICAL MODEL, AND PROJECT EVALUATION

A basic microeconomics course establishes the following equilibrium condition between the cost of capital and returns to capital in a competitive economy:

$P \times MPK$ = rental cost of capital or r

where P is the price a firm receives when selling its output, MPK is the marginal product of capital (or the extra output derived by adding one unit of capital), and r, the rental cost of capital is an all-inclusive measure of the opportunity cost of using one more unit of capital. Sensibly, this means that a firm should add more capital, up to the point at which the extra benefit just equals the extra cost. Implementing this rule in practice has many formulations. For example, we could identify the left-hand side of the above equation with the return on invested capital (ROIC) and the right-hand side with the weighted average cost of capital (WACC), restated as:

$\text{ROIC}(K) = \text{WACC}(K)$

If the left-hand side is greater than the right-hand side, then one should continue investing, creating more and more value, until they are equal.

Similarly, the neoclassical model discussed here can be simplified and rearranged by defining I or investment as ΔK, and assuming a perpetually level cash flow that can increase as a result of an increase in capital. Thus we have:

$$\text{NPV} = -\Delta K + \sum_{1}^{\infty} \frac{CF(K)_i}{(1+r)^i} = -\Delta K + \frac{CF(K)}{r}$$

To maximize, with respect to K, we set

$\Delta(\text{NVP}) / \Delta K = 0$

which yields

$0 = -1 + [\Delta CF(K) / \Delta K] / r$

which yields

$P \times$ MPK = rental cost of capital or r

Here, *MPK* can be defined as the increment to perpetual cash flow from an increase in one unit of capital today.

Researchers examining the efficiency of investment in China use these various measures to examine the efficiency of China's investment decisions. As discussed above, many economists find distortions related to both the right-hand side and left-hand side of this fundamental condition for optimal investing in China.

Profits are the difference between revenues and expenditures. Anything which might increase profits will increase net present values and result in more investment. Since firms seek to ensure that marginal revenue equals marginal cost, any factor that either increases marginal revenue or decreases marginal cost will increase profits—which, in turn, will increase output and increase investment. What we have just established is a positive link between output and investment. While it may seem obvious that more output requires more investment, the subtle point is that increased output derives from either lower anticipated costs or higher anticipated revenues. Meanwhile, that in turn, changes (increases) profits, the optimal level of output, and the optimal level of investment.

In summary, the equation above shows that a higher opportunity cost, a higher rate of deprecia-tion, and an anticipated permanent increase in profit-maximizing output will lead to greater invest-ment. We can summarize this result in a linear equation (where a is a constant term and B and C are sensitivities of investment to the opportunity cost and anticipated output:

Investment = $a - B \times$ (opportunity cost) + $C \times$ (anticipated output)

Of course, other factors—such as exchange rates, the price of capital, and how quickly new capital can be added—must be included in such an equation when we actually attempt to estimate coef-ficients using econometric techniques.

Tobin's Q

An alternate but equivalent approach to the neoclassical model is to examine the relationship between how financial markets value a firm's investment prospects compared to the purchase price (also referred to as the replacement cost) of new capital. We refer to this as "Q theory" or "Tobin's Q." Tobin's Q is defined as *the ratio of the firm's market value to the replacement cost of the firm's capital.*[9] The firm's market value is the market value of the sum of debt and equity issued by the firm. The Q theory states: if the firm's market value is high relative to the replacement cost of capi-tal, it would be worthwhile for firms to issue new debt or equity, and to purchase even more capital. For every share issued with a value of one dollar, less than a dollar would be used to purchase new capital without any dilution of current shareholder value; the residual would reflect the added value that the market believes the firm can contribute when employing the new capital. Clearly, such an expansion of financing and new capital is worthwhile for current shareholders. Thus, Tobin's Q is a theory based on the ratio Q. If Q is greater than 1, we expect to see an increase in fixed investment on the part of firms in the economy; if it is less than 1, the reverse happens.[10]

Referring to the equation above, we recall that profits (Π) are a function of both revenues and costs. Optimal long-run revenues, costs, and (in turn) profits will only expand if output expands. Long-run output will only expand if capacity or fixed investment expands. In summary, profits (Π)

will increase as a function of investment (*I*). We can formalize the Q theory, then, by using the following equation and assuming (for the moment) that net present value = 0 at the margin. Thus, the firm has invested up to the point of optimality. We have:

$$I_0 = \Pi_1 / (1 + r) + \Pi_2 / (1 + r)^2 \ldots$$

In the above equation, the left-hand side represents the replacement cost of capital while the right-hand side represents the market valuation (given the market's opportunity cost and profit expectations). The ratio of the right-hand side to the left-hand side is, of course, Tobin's Q, and is equal to 1 in this special case. If the ratio is greater than 1, then the net present value of the investment would be positive and we would expect the investment to be undertaken.[11]

Is China's Investment Too High?

The fact that China's level of investment as a share of GDP is so high naturally raises the question of whether or not it is *too* high. As we saw in the chapter on economic growth, emerging economies on a sustainable path to growth will naturally have high levels of investment. That is because the marginal productivity of capital (the slope of the production function in a Solow framework) is much greater than that of advanced economies, which have moved further along the development curve. But what constitutes too high a level of investment relative to some optimum level? Economists have broken this question into different parts, logically looking at the marginal product of capital in China (its return), then comparing that to the opportunity cost of capital (its cost). Figure 6.4 shows an equilibrium in which the demand for more capital (investment) corresponds to a declining marginal product of capital. The supply of greater capital (investable funds) only willingly increases with higher returns.

A related question regarding China's massive investment described above is: "To what extent has this investment been determined by market forces, and to what extent by government decision making?" In the former case, we can use a variation on the models mentioned above to explain China's investment; in the latter case, we must identify the government's possibly diverse motivations for investing. This latter set of motivations is more complex as they range from the traditional public good approach to developmental approaches to purely political motivations.

As discussed in other chapters, analyzing investment in China presents additional layers of complexity beyond these questions. Specifically, when measuring the returns on investment, much of production (close to half of GDP) is an investment good rather than a consumer good. Determining the value of an investment good requires us to assume that our estimate accurately reflects the value of goods and services which investment goods will yield in the **future**. In contrast, an investment good used to produce consumer goods and services can be valued based on our knowledge of what consumers willingly pay for that good or service **currently** an easier task. Regarding the cost of capital (discussed in Chapters 4 and 7 on economic growth and monetary policy), China's capital markets are segmented both domestically and internationally. Identifying a cost of capital that truly reflects all risks with opportunity costs is very difficult.

Authors such as Bai et al. (2006) look at aggregate data and find China's marginal productivity of capital still high but declining. Consistent with that notion, Figure 6.5 from the IMF shows an increasing ICOR for China but at levels still below the United States and neighboring economies in Asia. Qin and Song (2009) examine investment across provinces and find evidence of both inefficient allocation of capital across sectors of the economy and inefficient use of capital once it is put in place. They find greater efficiency along the eastern and central regions of China compared to the western regions.

Other authors examine disaggregate data at the firm or industry level to determine cash flows and marginal productivities. Ding et al. (2010) examine more than 100,000 firms in China and find that overinvestment is pervasive across both private firms and SOEs; they find that one-third of China's

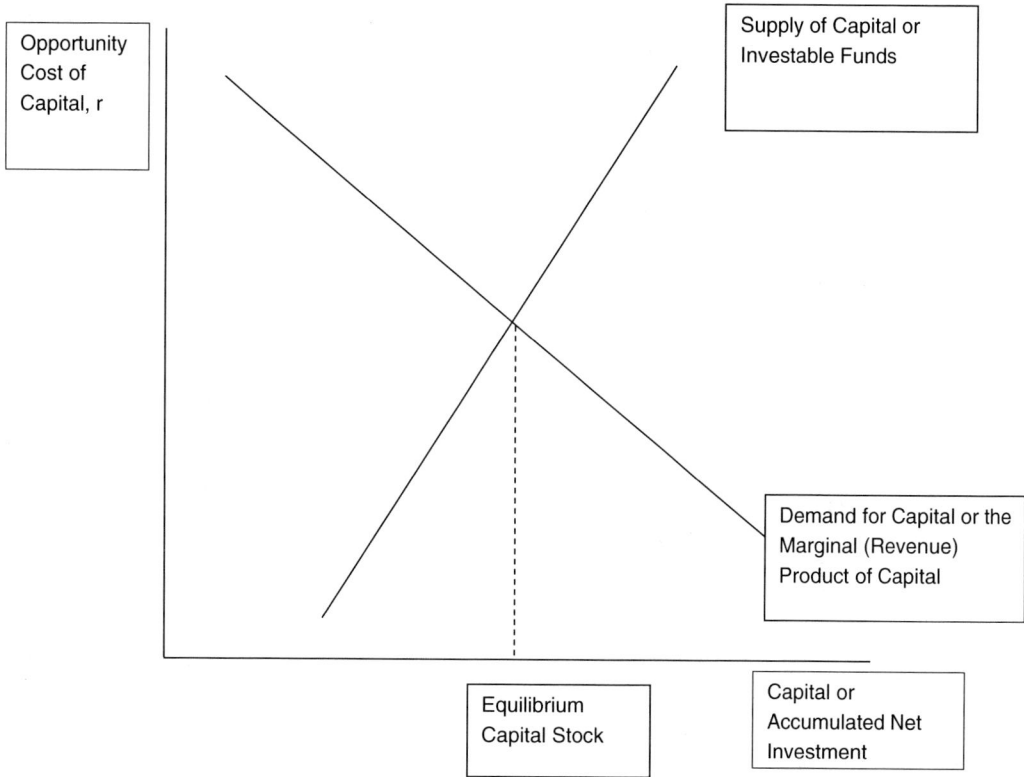

Figure 6.4 In a neoclassical framework the supply of loanable funds and the demand for capital (based on capital's marginal product) will determine an equilibrium level of capital.

Source: Author created.

firms overinvest, and those which do so have capital that is too large by a factor of about 25 percent. The authors suggest that private firms overinvest because of the presence of excessive cash flow and an absence of outside stakeholders—in particular, a lack of private bondholders. SOEs tend to overinvest because of easy access to credit from the banking system, which is lacking in screening and monitoring capabilities.

Lee et al. (2012) take a comprehensive look at investment using both a neoclassical approach and a model of dynamic optimization. They find that, in China, actual investment as compared to optimal investment has been consistently too high—and may now be up to 10 percentage points too high (i.e, as a share of GDP investment, it should be closer to 40 percent rather than 50 percent).

A simple approach to answering the question of whether China's investment is too high is to examine what steady-state investment would be for a country such as China and then compare this to the actual level. Recall our simple Solow steady-state condition used in Chapter 4:

$$s \times y = (n + dep) \times k$$

In other words, sources of capital (on a per capita basis) equal uses of capital. We can transform this to a condition in terms of savings per output and capital per output (rather than per capita); if we allow for the accounting identity of Savings ≡ Investment, and assume future economic growth to equal population growth, we have:

$$i = (g + dep) \times k$$

**ICOR
(Investment/Change in Y)**

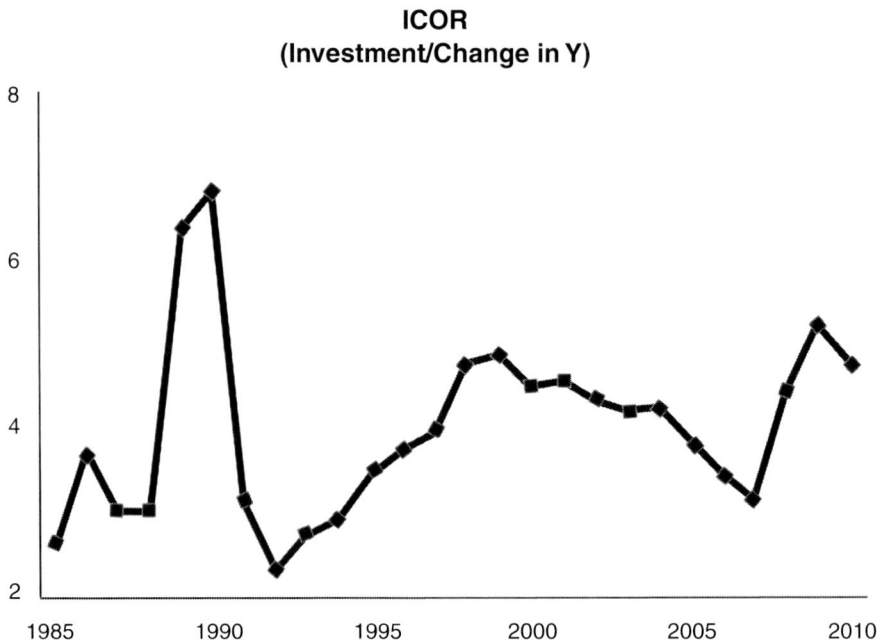

Figure 6.5 China's ICOR has trended upward over the past two decades—one indication of diminishing returns
        to investment.

Source: International Monetary Fund Estimates.

where i and k are investment-to-output and capital-to-output ratios. Currently, China's capital-to-output ratio is around 2. Let's assume China ultimately achieves the United States' steady-state ratio of around 1.8. Furthermore, let's assume a steady-state growth for China of around 3 percent and a depreciation rate close to 11 percent. The equation above shows steady-state investment for China in the neighborhood of 28 percent of GDP. This is close to the level of some of China's Asian neighbors, and suggests that the gap between today's investment rates and steady-state levels in China is too large. It also suggests that U.S. investment as a share of GDP is too low.

    The theoretical models above are rooted in the neoclassical framework in which rational firms and investors respond to market forces when making investment decisions. A number of studies have examined this approach econometrically. Specifically, authors such as Lee at al. (2012), Geng and N'Diaye (2012), and Song et al. (2001) have attempted to estimate the responsiveness of investment in China to real interest rates (the cost of capital), real economic growth, the real exchange rate, and availability of credit—just to name a few variables. Overall, the data suggest that, in fact, investment in China does respond to market forces in a predictable way. Recent policy developments show that the role of market forces should become ever more important. Further research is needed to prove whether or not such changes are taking place in a meaningful way.

Financial Repression

While the above models are increasingly useful in showing how future investment will be determined, the reality regarding a significant share of investment determination in China (especially before 1998) is that the key determinant has been government decision making. Through its control of virtually all financial intermediation in the post-reform period—especially its control of lending decisions by the four major banks (which manage most of the nation's loanable funds)—the government has been the ultimate decision maker in the level, patterns, and types of investments made. The term *financial repression* describes a set of policies which, in effect, remove most of the market-based mechanisms we expect to operate in financial markets. Specifically, financial repression refers to an institutional arrangement in which the following conditions apply: profitability is not the main objective of financial institutions; there is an absence of competition among financial institutions; lending and borrowing rates are not determined by supply and demand conditions; and where lending and borrowing decisions are not based on anticipated net present values (as suggested in the models above), but rather by other criteria, e.g., a social or public good objective. We can still describe China's financial system as "financially repressed" but rapidly transforming into a market-based system. In Chapter 7, we look more deeply into some of these issues. Under a financially repressed system, one does not see the usual supply curve of loanable funds, as in Figure 6.6. Rather we see, for example, interest rate ceilings below the equilibrium level and rationing of credit (investable funds) to select borrowers.

The fact that investment has been determined by lending policies (which in turn reflect government decision making) is only half the story. The other half is control over the real economy and investment at the firm and industry level. China's central government has, at times, felt the need to directly control investment spending in the aggregate and, at other times, in specific industries in which a perceived overinvestment (bubble) is occurring. The government accomplishes this by restricting specific industries to specific levels of investment. Thus the government can and has directly controlled investment both at the financing (lending) end and at the industry (decision-making) end.

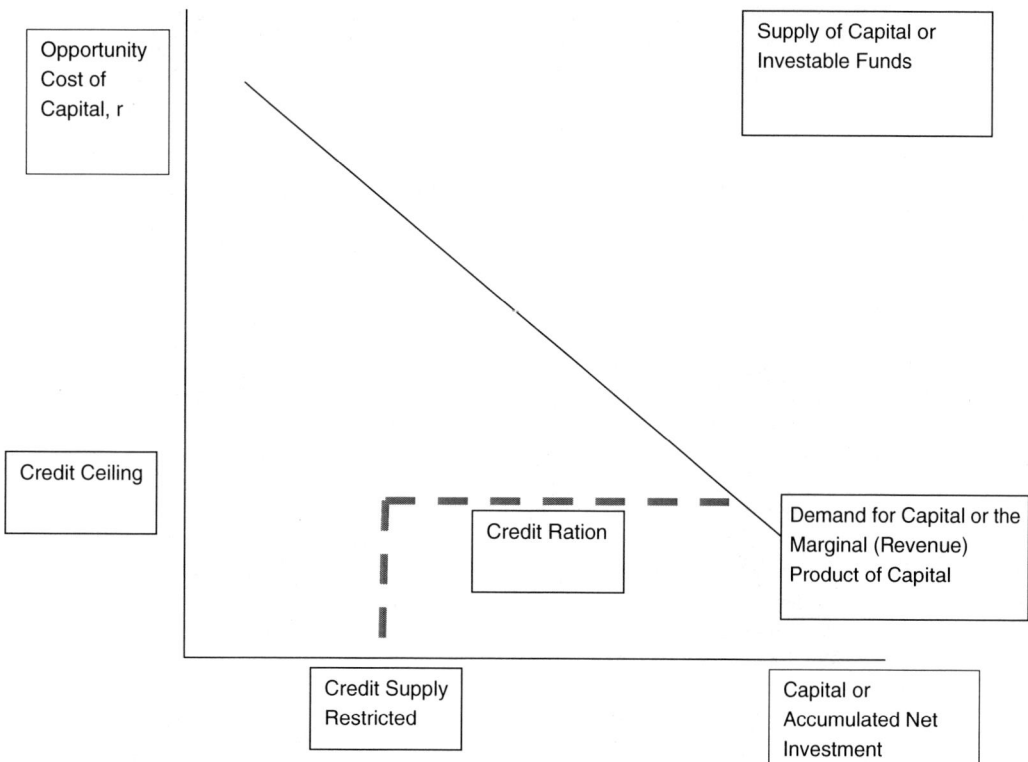

Figure 6.6 Credit ceilings in the market for capital result in credit rationing.

Source: Author created.

A Growing Periphery

In contrast to the processes described above, a growing periphery of newly introduced investor classes (such as venture funds and private equity funds) and small businesses have emerged on the investment scene. These new entrants are still guided by China's Five-Year Plans in making sectoral investment decisions, but likely base specific investment decisions on financial criteria. The new set of investors, however, represents only a sliver of China's total investment activity.

On the positive side, relatively small private firms now make up over 90 percent of the productive units in China. We can assume that, for this group, the models presented earlier in this chapter have become more relevant. As in the United States, small businesses now represent China's most dynamic sector. Furthermore, since 1998, new policy loans to SOEs have been substantially cut back and, in turn, SOEs, goals have also changed in a way consistent with our market-based models.

China Case Study: 6.2. China's Development Bank: A Fannie Mae Freddie Mac Redux?

One institution at the center of the Chinese government's investment effort is the China Development Bank (CDB) founded in 1994.* Its mandate is to finance the vast collection of infrastructure projects that result from China's Five-Year Plans. Owned by the central government, half of its capital comes from the Ministry of Finance and the other half from Central Huijin Investment Corporation and the nation's social security fund—all government-owned entities. A good fraction of the CDB's loan portfolio is for public highways, subways, airports, power, and other large infrastructure projects across China and in developing countries (Figure CS6.2a). The Three Gorges Dam and Shanghai's Pudong International Airport were financed primarily with funds raised by the CDB as were deluxe sports complexes and hotel resorts both inside and outside of China. Many of its loans are to provincial and local governments (Chapter 10 provides some context for this). Its main source of funds is through the issuance of bonds with maturities ranging from short term (under one year) to over ten years. It is the second largest issuer of bonds in China after the Ministry of Finance itself.

By the end of 2012, its assets (loans and other investments) had totaled RMB 7.5 trillion (over US$1.2 trillion), an amount that was nearly double its 2008 portfolio. In tandem, its outstanding negotiable instrument liabilities (bonds, etc.) had nearly doubled, reaching RMB 5.3 trillion. In 2012, the CDB lent over US$140 billion. By comparison, the entire World Bank Group had provided new financing commitments in 2012 totaling US$53 billion. CDB was responsible for funding 4–5 percent of all investments undertaken in China in 2012 and about 20 percent of all Chinese government investment. About 19 percent of its investment portfolio is for foreign projects—particularly in Africa. With these foreign loans, an interesting question going forward is who will take senior creditor status should borrowers encounter difficulties in repaying their debt: China or the World Bank?†

Since the CDB issues debt with an implicit government guarantee, its debt instruments are considered risk free—it has been able to borrow at a lower cost than would an institution without such support. One of its principal sources of finance is the large state-owned banks (the Big Four) that hold the vast savings of China's citizens. A natural question to ask when governments are so heavily involved in both borrowing and lending for projects at such a break-neck pace is whether or not a crisis is brewing. Are there echoes here of Fannie Mae and Freddie Mac and the supercharged lending for residential construction that occurred in the last decade in the United States (and other parts of the world)? At a macro level, government-mandated borrowing and lending has a very different set of goals (e.g., employment) than the traditional one of explicit value maximization. This can and has led many intermediating financial institutions into trouble around the world. At a microeconomic level, access to an eager lender can lead

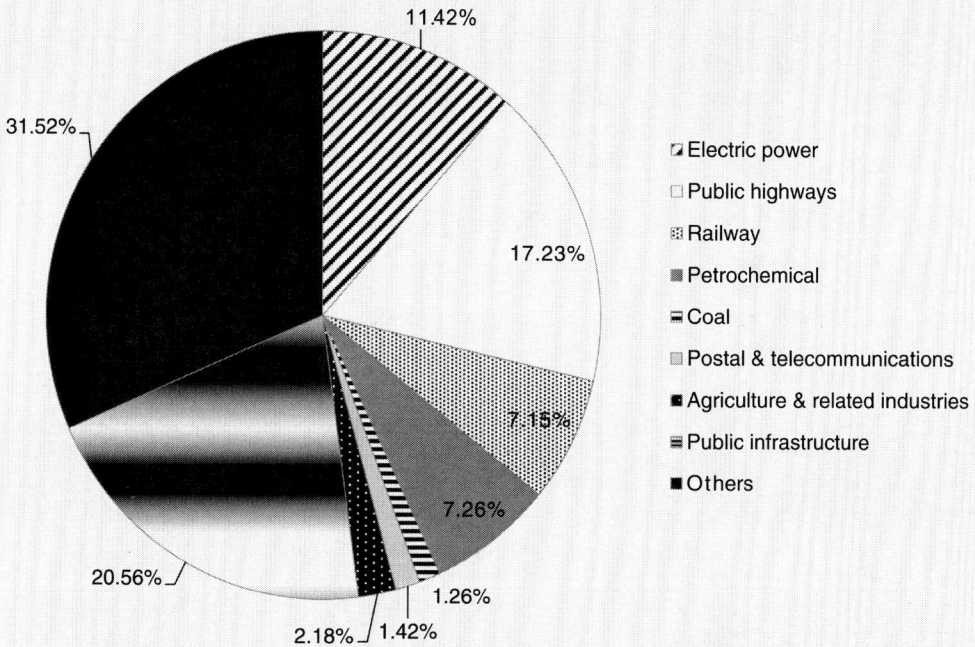

Figure CS6.2a A good fraction of the China Development Bank's loan portfolio is for public highways, subways, airports, power, and other large infrastructure projects across China and in developing countries.

Source: China Development Bank, 2012.

to slack project evaluations and corruption as seen in the 2008–09 U.S. financial crisis. But most of CDB investment is not for residential construction, but rather for infrastructure.

Various key financial ratios such as CDB's return on assets (.92 percent), or the capital adequacy ratio (close to 11 percent), or non-performing loan ratios (.30 percent) compare quite favorably to the major private U.S. banks today. One way of quickly assessing whether CDB is a value-creating entity is to examine how well its investors are doing. Equity holders (the government) who provide about 10 percent of the Bank's capital, earn a nominal return of over 13 percent. Lenders, however (including the Big Four banks), who provide the remaining 90 percent of its finance, have earned 3.7 percent or less; inflation, meanwhile, has averaged around 3.6 percent in recent years. It would appear the real return to lenders may be close to zero, if not negative. In 2013–14, the interest rate charged to CDB by creditors rose by almost 50 percent to close to 6 percent; could this be a risk premium tacked onto new CDB borrowings—a sign of insider knowledge and worry among its lenders? Or is it just a sign of tight credit markets? Only after a better understanding of each project's merit will we be able to understand the answer to these questions. Good projects will yield social returns which taxpayers will gladly pay for via the low returns on their savings; bad projects will weigh heavily on the real returns anticipated but never received by China's thrifty citizen-savers.

*Other major government banks with a mandate for development include the Agricultural Development Bank of China (ADBC), the China Export Import Bank (CEXIM), and the Guangdong Development Bank (provincial level); their names suggest their role in development.

†Both the IMF and World Bank view themselves as the senior creditor to countries.

Summary

The long-term future of China's citizens and all its stakeholders depends heavily on the investment decisions of China's production sector. The medium-term return to households on their financial investments and real estate investments are likewise dependent on these decisions. The huge scale of China's investment relative to other components of GDP reinforces these points. In any society, the ability to generate investment depends on a number of steps working in a synchronized fashion:

$$I = \text{efficiency} \times (\text{Investing} / FI) \times (FI / S) \times (S / Y) \times Y - \text{Rate of Depreciation} \times K$$

On the left-hand side, we have actual investment; on the right-hand side, we have a nation's savings (S) out of GDP (Y) being channeled to financial institutions (FI), which in turn make loans and invest. How efficiently the productive entities use those funds will determine the true size and value of the investment taking place (I). In contrast to the United States, China has a vast pool of internal savings relative to GDP (S / Y). This is both a blessing and a curse. It allows for a great deal of leeway in terms of how those funds are used—in the short run, mistakes can be made without being noticed and those mistakes can accumulate into large economic losses. Furthermore, academic research suggests that, at the corporate level, the greater the availability of funds, the more likely that they will be used inefficiently. Meanwhile, the United States has a much more sophisticated financial system ("efficiency") than does China but has less savings to work with (overconsumes). This tendency has likely led to underinvestment. The United States' capital stock is significantly larger than China's, which is also a blessing and a curse. While a higher standard of living results, the absolute amount of capital depreciation is that much higher, and diminishing returns act as a drag on economic growth.

Investment is not only important as a source of future output, but also as a source of demand for economic output in the short run. Over half of China's GDP growth can be attributed to investment demand growth. Fortunately for China, it is not as volatile a demand component as found in the United States; fluctuations in investment demand are often the major contributor to business cycle fluctuations. Once again, though, the silver lining for China comes with a cloud. When investment is that stable, we can question the extent to which market forces, rather than government mandate, are driving China's investment decisions.

Challenging Questions for China (and the Student): Chapter 6

1. Go the Federal Reserve Economic Database (FRED) and update Chinese investment as a share of GDP.
2. In terms of measuring the size of the government sector in China, explain why it is important to understand how GDP's components of *C*, *I*, *G*, and *NX* are being measured in a GDP accounting sense.
3. In this chapter we derived: $P \times MPK$ = rental cost of capital or r
    a. From the cash flow valuation approach, assume that cash flows are growing at a rate of g. Derive the above equilibrium condition in this case.
    b. Based on your answer in (a), explain in a neoclassical sense why China's investment rates are so high compared to the United States.
4. When investment is a large fraction of GDP output, as in China, why does this present special challenges in measuring the quality of economic growth as compared to the quantity of economic growth?
5. Discuss the neoclassical framework as it relates to decision making on Chinese investment:
    a. Provide the neoclassical framework for investment and link that to the traditional cash flow Net Present Value approach.

    b. Discuss whether the approach in (a) is applicable to China. Is it more relevant for some sectors instead of others? Which sectors of the economy?

    c. Why are the questions in (a) and (b) vitally important for China in the coming years?

6. Explain the costs and benefits of providing public works projects (infrastructure) via the financing mechanism of the China Development Bank as compared to a taxation mechanism for public works (let's say a property tax or personal income tax) in China.

7. In this chapter we discussed the user cost of capital and PE ratio (the home price to annual rental ratio): where user cost $= (1 - t)(r + p) + m + \delta + \beta - \pi^e$ where t is the personal tax rate, r is the borrowing cost of financing a home, p is the property tax rate, m is the cost of maintenance, β is the risk premium on property, π^e is the expected appreciation of property values, and δ is the depreciation rate on residential property (all expressed in nominal percent).

    a. If in the United States home prices are expected to increase by 3 percent, $r = 4$ percent, the tax rate is 25 percent, property tax is 1 percent, the maintenance fee is 0.5 percent, depreciation is 3.5 percent, and the risk premium is 2 percent, calculate the PE ratio

    b. If some Chinese cities have a PE of let's say 30, calculate the implicit value of π^e. Provide justification for the other numbers that you used in the formula for the China case. Do you think π^e is based on rational or adaptive expectations?

    c. In this chapter, we suggest that the housing market price surge in China represents fundamental factors and not a bubble. Buyers may still end up losing money over the long term, however. Explain using basic supply and demand curves. If we are correct, then why haven't rental rates risen as dramatically as home prices? Are we wrong? Explain.

8. Why can the stability (that it fluctuates so little year to year) of China's investment as a share of GDP be viewed as a "blessing," a "curse," and a worrisome omen?

9. Explain why measuring the "cost of capital" (a difficult task anywhere in the world) is particularly difficult to measure in China.

Notes

1. Also included is investment in software which, in the United States, was first included in 1999.
2. Foreign direct investment (FDI) is defined as both a degree of foreign ownership and control of an economic entity in another country. This contrasts with portfolio investment, which represents a degree of ownership but absence of control. The IMF defines FDI as an investment with a "lasting interest" in the enterprise. Both the IMF and OECD suggest at least a 10 percent voting interest in an enterprise as a necessary and sufficient condition for having a lasting interest.
3. We discuss the link between the accumulation of investment (the capital stock) and economic growth in Chapter 4. For now, it is worth noting that, in recent years, investment demand growth forms over half of China's economic growth rate.
4. In 1995, the World Bank estimated conservatively that approximately 42 percent of state investment could be undertaken by the private sector. Clearly, that would be an upper bound today given the substantial privatization in China since then. Most countries now split government spending into government investment and government consumption. Budget deficits or surpluses (however) continue to be reported after expensing government investments (unlike accounting practices for firms).
5. Generally speaking, if something is permitted to be depreciated under the tax code (as certain software development is now, for example), it can be considered an investment.
6. For example, in February 2014, Apple Computer repurchased US$14 billion of its own shares.
7. In the U.S. post-World War II period, it is estimated that business fixed investment is three to four times more volatile than output.
8. Most important in finance is not accounting profit but cash flow. Cash flow is defined as profits after adding back non-cash expenses (such as depreciation) and certain cash expenses (such as interest payments) while subtracting out the tax benefits accruing from these accounting expenses. Although the accounting treatment of depreciation is not included, investment required to replace depreciated capital is a cash item and is therefore subtracted from profits. In this way, it is included in actual cash flow. In summary, the reference to profits above is actually a reference to all cash revenues and expenditures, as well as new investment.
9. Named after the great Nobel Prize-winning economist, James Tobin.

10. When $Q < 1$, the firm's current capital is worth more than its market values. It should then either sell off some of its physical capital or allow it to depreciate without replacement.

11. In fact, Tobin's Q relates to the existing capital stock and existing opportunities projected off of that capital stock within the traditional valuation approach in finance. In the analysis presented here, we assume that, if valuations exceed the replacement value of the current capital stock, then the same will hold true for the marginal investment opportunity.

References

Bai, Chong-en, Chang-Tai Hsieh, and Yingyi Qian. 2006. "The Return to Capital in China." NBER Working Paper No. 12755. Cambridge, MA: National Bureau of Economic Research.

China Development Bank. 2012. *Annual Report.* www.cdb.com.cn/english/Column.asp?ColumnId=91 (accessed May 8, 2014).

Ding, S., A. Guariglia, and J. Knight. 2010. "Does China Overinvest? Evidence from a Panel of Chinese Firms." Department of Economics Discussion Paper Series. No. 520. Oxford, UK: University of Oxford.

Dong, H., W. Zhang, and J. Shek. 2006. How Efficient Has Been China's Investment? Empirical Evidence from National and Provincial Data. HKMA Working Papers, No. 0619. Hong Kong: Hong Kong Monetary Authority.

Geng, N. and P. N'Diaye. 2012. "Determinants of Corporate Investment in China: Evidence from Cross-Country Firm Level Data." IMF Working Paper No. 12/80. Washington, DC: International Monetary Fund.

Lee, I.H., M. Syed, and L. Xueyan. 2012. "Is China Overinvesting and Does it Matter?" IMF Working Paper No. 12/277. Washington, DC: International Monetary Fund.

Lin, G. and R.M. Schramm. 2009. "A Decade of Flow of Funds in China (1995–2006)." In *China and Asia: Economic and Financial Interactions*, eds. Y.W. Cheung and K.Y. Wong. London: Routledge.

Poterba, James. 1984. "Tax Subsidies to Owner-Occupied Housing: An Asset Market Approach." *Quarterly Journal of Economics* 94(4): 729–52.

Qin, Duo, and H. Song. 2009. "Sources of Investment Inefficiency: The Case of Fixed Asset Investment in China." *Journal of Development Economics* 90: 94–105.

Song, H.Y., Z.N. Liu, and P. Jiang. 2001. "Analysing the Determinants of China's Aggregate Investment in the Reform Period." *China Economic Review* 12: 227–42.

Wu, Jing, Joseph Gyourko, and Yongheng Deng. 2011. "Evaluating Conditions in Major Chinese Housing Markets." NBER Working Paper No. 16189. Cambridge, MA: National Bureau of Economic Research.

7 Monetary Policy and Institutions in China and the United States

钱能通神
Money Allows You to Speak to the Gods

In this chapter, we will define what money is, discuss the supply and demand for money, and learn about Chinese monetary policy. In the process, we will not only understand what money is conceptually, but also institutionally. How money is supplied to the economy is, at its core, an institutional question based on how a country's central bank and banking system operate and are structured. The question of why individuals and institutions in an economy want to hold on to money—the demand for money—raises interesting conceptual and theoretical questions (addressed in Chapter 8). In this chapter, we focus on the institutional framework for monetary policy in both the United States and China. These two large economies make for some interesting comparisons and contrasts both historically and contemporaneously in terms of monetary economics. We care about money not only because of its relationship to institutions and its role as a key asset, but also because the amount of money in an economy has profound effects on inflation, interest rates, short-term economic growth, and employment.

Defining Money (Conceptually)

Money is anything that is generally accepted as a medium of exchange. This broad definition highlights the open-ended possibilities of what constitutes money. As long as individuals willingly accept and make payments with such an instrument, that instrument constitutes money. Tea, black and white shells (wampum), printed deer skin, gold, silver, cigarettes, and pieces of paper have all served at one point or another as money.[1] Not too long ago, the French franc or the Dutch florin represented money for those countries, but by 2001 these currencies had been fully replaced by the euro. Whether the Bitcoin will eventually make it to the class of world monies will ultimately depend on its general acceptability as a form of money.

Case Study 7.1: The Invention of Paper Money

China was the first country to introduce paper money ("flying money," made of mulberry bark, was used as banknotes) in the Tang Dynasty (618–907 CE). The use of printed money (using wood blocks) became widespread in the economically sophisticated Song Dynasty (960–1279 CE). Bronze coins with a square in the middle could be looped around a string and thus easily transported. Spades and knives were also used as money in China and currency later kept the form (but not the agricultural function of these types of money). In nineteenth-century China, centrally issued paper money and copper coins (*wen*) circulated alongside foreign coins of silver and gold and were all used as money. As late as 1995, a separate currency for foreigners circulated alongside the Chinese yuan or RMB. The Foreign Exchange Certificate (FEC) served to control how and where foreigners could spend money in China. Since the FEC's value in terms of actual foreign currency was inconsistent with the official RMB rate of exchange for foreign currency, a black market developed and this led to the elimination of the FEC as a separate form of money in China.

In colonial United States, settlers used wampum to trade with Native American tribes. Gold, silver, and banknotes also served as forms of colonial monies. In the first half of the nineteenth century, a number of banks issued their own paper currency and these forms of payment were not always acceptable across state lines. Eventually hundreds of different kinds of money circulated alongside gold and silver in the United States. By mid-century, the U.S. government refused to accept tax payments in the form of paper money (the Specie Circular specified gold and silver as the only legitimate form of tax payment) and most of these locally issued monies became worthless. In order to help finance the Civil War, the U.S. government (the "North") began issuing United States Notes (greenbacks) in 1862. This launched the creation of a truly national currency—accepted across the nation.

Yuan or RMB have been used interchangeably to describe the Chinese currency since the founding of the PRC in 1949. Yuan is the basic unit in the Chinese monetary system (like the dollar) in which all other coins or denominations are expressed as a fraction thereof. In foreign currency markets, the Chinese currency is the CNY or Chinese yuan and the United States dollar is the USD or US$. The RMB stands for *renminbi*（人民币）or "People's Currency." In Case Study 7.1 we discuss the much longer role of paper money in China.

Defining Money (Institutionally)

The above section provides an overview of what constitutes money at a conceptual and historical level. But how do we define money at a practical level, for the sake of policy and measurement? Countries worldwide use very similar definitions of money. But as we shall see, there are large institutional differences in the types of bank accounts and other financial institutional assets offered in different countries. Every nation attempts to use the conceptual definition above to drill down to an implementable definition of money, but because of institutional differences, countries inevitably come up with the same name for a technically different type of asset and classify it as money. For example, is a savings account with a ceilinged interest rate (as found in China) really the same thing as a savings account with a market-determined interest rate (as found in the United States)? Both will be clumped together in each country's definition of money. Or in the United States, we find money market funds as an important component of the supply of money, while in China, money market funds have yet to become an important asset class.

Table 7.1 shows the different definitions of money used in the United States, China, and virtually the entire world. M1, or narrow money, includes currency in circulation or cash—what most people (who have not taken a macroeconomics course) assume is money. An even larger share of what constitutes money is demand deposits (about 37 percent of M1 in the United States, 83 percent in China—referred to as sight deposits or checking accounts). These typically provide an instant means of payment either via an ATM, debit card, or written check. M2 includes everything in M1 plus time deposits and savings accounts; access to one's savings via these latter accounts may be restricted in terms of withdrawals or making payments for purchases of goods and services. Figure 7.1 shows a steep ascent in M2 in China since the global financial crisis—something we will discuss in Chapter 8.

Table 7.1 Components of M1 and M2 for China and the United States.

United States: Seasonally Adjusted Components of M1 (billions of dollars)			China: Seasonally Adjusted Components of M1 (RMB 100 million)		
Components of M1	% OF M1	% OF GDP	Components of M1	% OF M1	% OF GDP
Currency	1,145.8	44.6%		Currency	50,748.5	17.5%	
Demand deposits	960	37.3%		Demand deposits	239,099.2	82.5%	
Other checkable deposits	466.5	18.1%		Other checkable deposits	N/A	N/A	
Total M1	2,575.9	100.0%	16.4%	**Total M1**	289,847.7	100.0%	61.3%
Components of M2	% OF M2	% OF GDP	Components of M2	%OF M2	% OF GDP
Total M1	2,575.9	23.8%		Total M1	289,847.7	34.0%	
Savings deposits	6,960.70	64.3%		Savings deposits	166,616.0	19.6%	
Small-denomination time deposits	398.20	3.7%		Small-denomination time deposits	352,799.4	41.4%	
Retail money funds	658.80	6.1%		Retail money funds	42,329.7	5.0%	
Total M2	10,818.6	100.0%	69.0%	**Total M2**	851,590.9	100.0%	180.1%
Total GDP/GNP	15,684.80			**Total GDP/GNP**	472,881.60		

Source: People's Bank of China and the Federal Reserve Bank of the United States.

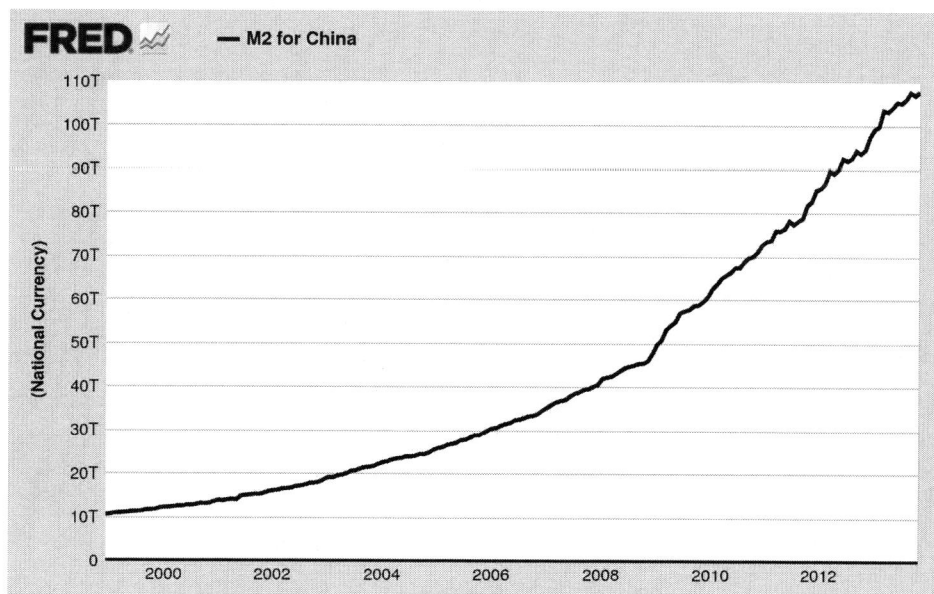

Figure 7.1 Since the global financial crisis the growth of M2 has accelerated in China.

Source: FRED, Federal Reserve Economic Data, Federal Reserve Bank of St. Louis: M2 for China; International Monetary Fund. 2014 research.stlouisfed.org

We can see that, as we move from M1 to M2, we are shifting into forms of money that are less "liquid." We define liquidity as the ease with which we can convert one asset into purchasing power without a loss in that asset's long-term value.[2] Clearly, cash is a very liquid asset since we can buy goods and services without affecting the face value found on either the dollar or yuan. Meanwhile, use of a time deposit to make a purchase may involve some explicit or implicit "transactions costs." For example, we might have to pay a penalty for early withdrawal or may have to physically go to our bank to make a withdrawal. Clearly, assets such as a time deposit, corporate bond, equity, or jewelry are less liquid forms of money than cash.

Another way of looking at the movement from M1 to M2 is that we are moving from more transaction-based motives to a more investment-based motive—that is, a greater focus on return as opposed to liquidity. Most countries around the world, including China and the United States, choose M2 as their main definition of money. M2 can be used for transactions with relative ease and would also be the type of money implicit in the response of a typical consumer or company to the question: "How much *money* do you have in the bank?"

We also need to highlight some of the institutional differences in the definition of money. We have already mentioned interest rate ceilings on bank deposits as one key difference. China's banking institutions, which really only became true financial institutions in the early 1990s, have managed to jump past one of the most common features of banking in the United States—checking. (Checking involves "writing a check" or assigning value that is held in the bank—a checking account—to another party via a signed, legally binding document, i.e., the check.)

Instead, China's demand deposits are used by customers either via an ATM machine (which involves paper money) or a debit card (which does not). Even today, a surprising amount of business in China is transacted in cash—not checks and not debit cards (see Case Study 7.2). Business transactions, especially at the small and medium-size levels, continue to be transacted in cash. Consumer transactions, however, are increasingly conducted using debit and credit cards (especially the former). It appears that China and the United States are converging—at least in terms of consumer use of debit cards. Cash is still used relatively more for retail transactions in China; checks significantly more so in the United States. Figure CS7.2a shows China relying increasingly on debit and credit cards and is now approaching the United States in terms of their relative use. Growth in all non-cash payments in China in recent years has been between 20–30 percent.

Case Study 7.2: RMB Notes by the Carload

The largest currency denomination in China is the RMB 100 note, introduced in 1988. At today's exchange rate, that is worth less than a US$20 bill. The small denomination combined with the continued use of cash for many large transactions lead to some odd situations in China. The *New York Times* reported on the purchase of a new BMW in Shanghai which involved the exchange of US$60,000 at the auto dealership; nearly 10,000 RMB 100 notes stashed into duffel bags (Barboza, 2013). The China Banknote Printing and Minting Corporation employs 30,000 people at the behest of the PBC and prints 40 percent of the world's total currency note output.

Some have suggested that the small denomination is one way that the government discourages corrupt practices such as paying off government officials for special favors. One could say it promotes "transparency" in financial transactions.* Citizens, meanwhile, have limited ways to hold their wealth beyond cash (see the discussion on Walras's Law). Thus, they place greater trust in cash holdings as opposed to other ways of holding wealth. In Chapter 5, we discuss how a limited range of available assets limits diversification possibilities. This in turn creates a need for even greater precautionary savings. The same argument would apply to holding wealth in one of its least risky forms—cash. Figure CS7.2a shows China's use of cash in recent years, relative to debit and credit cards.

**Ratio of Value of Debit and Credit
Card Transactions to Currency in Circulation**

■ China ■ United States

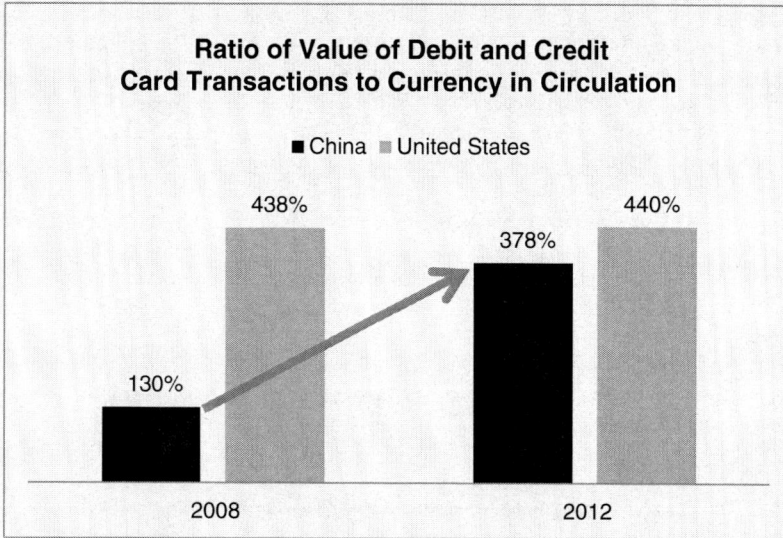

Figure CS7.2a Non-cash modes of payment have been rising by 20–30 percent annually over the past decade. Relative to the level of currency in circulation, debit and credit card transaction values are now approaching the same levels as in the United States.

Source: Author created.

*The "Law of Unintended Consequences" does come into play here—gifts of expensive watches or jewelry then come to fill the same purpose.

What is most striking from what we saw in Table 7.1 is the significantly higher share of GDP that M1 and M2 constitute in China compared to the United States. One would think that, if transactions are the main motive for holding money (as we have defined it), then these ratios should not be too different, and if anything, lower in China since consumer transactions (as we have seen in Chapter 5) are substantially lower. Holding money, however, is also a vehicle to save or to store our wealth—a relatively risk-free but very low-yielding method.[3] China has a very limited array of assets for holding wealth safely and profitably; corporate bonds remain limited, the stock market contains only a fraction of existing companies, government bonds and treasuries remain limited to institutions and not the public, and foreign-based assets are not yet legally available.[4] As a result, Chinese citizens and companies hold a greater share of their wealth (or savings) in the asset that is available via the institutions that do exist—mainly banks. The phenomenon of holding wealth in the bank rather than via a broader range of assets is also reflected in China's lower currency-to-total M1 or M2 ratio. An even more indicative measure of the importance of cash is China's larger holdings of currency as a share of GDP (11 percent) compared to the United States (7 percent).[5]

MACRO FINANCE INSIGHT 7.1: WALRAS'S LAW AND HOW CHINA AND THE UNITED STATES HOLD WEALTH

Walras's Law states that, for a complete set of related markets, the value of excess supply must equal the value of excess demand. Formally, for a set of related markets in which P_i, D_i, and S_i are the price, demand for, and supply of a particular asset, good, or service, then:

$$\sum P_i x \left(S_i - D_i \right) = 0$$

Walras's Law is a form of budget constraint stating that in order to effectively demand something in one market, you must offer something from another market. (Note that money is a key vehicle for doing this.) The acquisition of one form of wealth (e.g., a bond) requires something in exchange (such as cash). Let's assume that the goods market has, on balance, no excess demand or supply, that is, it is in equilibrium. This allows us to focus on the market for financial assets including money, bonds, and stocks, and non-financial assets such as real estate or direct ownership of companies. Some of these markets may have excess demand and some will have excess supply. Walras's Law states that these must balance out to 0. Consider Table MF7.1a for example. Here, we only have two financial assets: money and stocks. The sum of these two assets (US$300) represents our nominal financial wealth. In the short run, the quantity of these assets is fixed, meaning that we cannot have instantaneous IPOs or changes in the money stock. The prices of these assets can change, however, depending on the elasticity of demand.

Table MF7.1a shows an excess supply of money (more than individuals want to hold) of US$40. Where has this excess money gone? The only other available market is equities. Thus, the desire to move US$40 out of money must also be a desire to move US$40 into equities. In other words, the fact that the sum of

Table MF7.1a An excess demand in one financial market implies an excess supply in some other financial market.

	A Simple Example of Walras's Law		
	Supply (in US$)	Demand	Excess demand (−) Excess supply (+)
Money	200	160	40
Stock or equities	100	140	−40
Total assets	300	300	+0

Source: Author created.

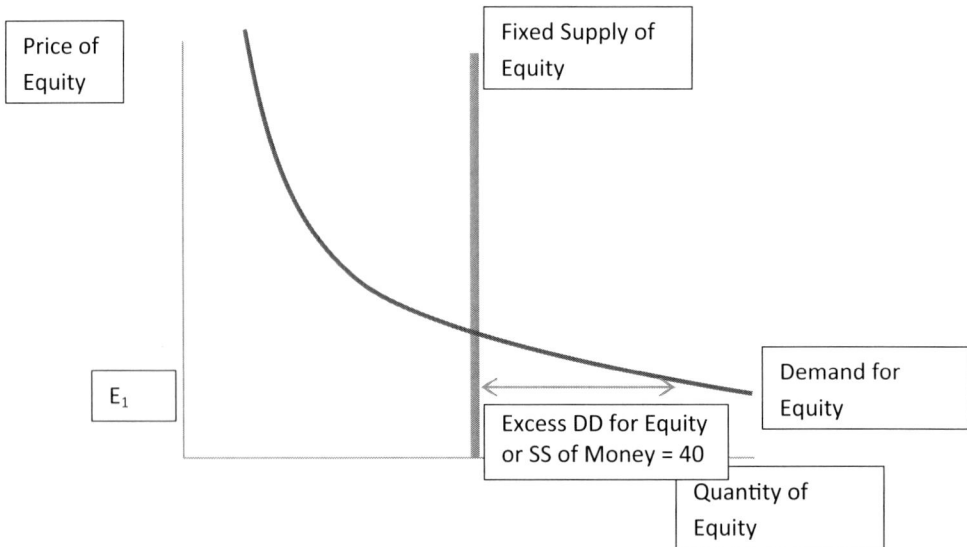

Figure MF7.1a An excess supply of money corresponds to an excess demand for equity.

Source: Author created.

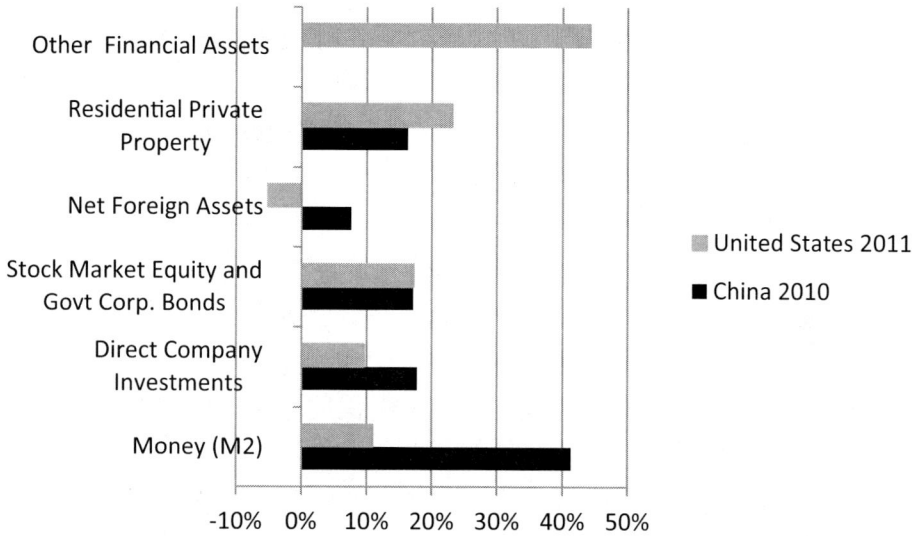

Figure MF7.1b   Walras's Law and how wealth is held.

Source: Author created based on data from NBS, 2012 and Federal Reserve Board of Governors and U.S. Commerce Department, 2014.

40 and −40 is zero is not a coincidence but a consequence of Walras's Law. Because of disequilibrium in the separate markets, either the price of money will fall (not feasible since money has no explicit price) or the price of equities will rise (or the return on equity (ROE), which is the implicit price of money, will fall). Some new nominal wealth will be established if the price of equity rises. Again, we can assume that the quantity of equities or money will not change; however, the nominal value of equity (its price) may change. Figure MF7.1a shows the initial disequilibrium in the money and equity market at a price of E1. The price of equity will have to rise to reach equilibrium in both the money and equity markets.

Looking at the distribution of wealth across different asset classes through the lens of Walras's Law provides some useful insights. Figure MF7.1b shows some rough comparisons regarding how China and the United States hold gross wealth. The chart uses best available data and is thus only roughly comparable; they show values of different asset classes economy-wide in China for 2010 and for U.S. households in 2011.*

The first striking difference is the share of wealth in China held as money compared to that of the United States (43 percent vs. 11–13 percent). This difference is tightly interlinked with two other differences. Firstly, China has fewer available and so holds fewer "other financial assets." Secondly, China's foreign assets holdings (8 percent of all assets) have led to sterilization, an increased money supply, and the absence of "other financial assets." Meanwhile, the United States has net foreign assets of −5 percent of the total. These two percentages, of course, are linked to the fact that China holds substantial assets in U.S. Treasuries as a counterpart to the U.S. liability. The United States' gross foreign asset position is supported by a large stock of foreign direct investment (FDI) worldwide, including FDI in China. These differences in investment holdings create a paradoxical result: while net foreign investment holdings are negative for the United States and positive for China, net foreign investment income is positive for the United States and negative for China. This is a result of the high returns earned on U.S. foreign direct investment in China versus the low returns of Chinese investments in U.S. government assets.

Other financial assets (equities, mutual funds, hedge funds, etc.) represent 38 percent of all assets in the United States and are still relatively insignificant in China. The lack of a broad range of assets available in China is a central theme discussed in other parts of this textbook; both supply and regulatory factors have led to a disproportionate level of money holdings.†

In China, direct company ownership (partnerships, LLCs, etc.) has led to tremendous wealth creation that is not yet publicly traded (19 percent in China vs. an estimated 10 percent in the United States).

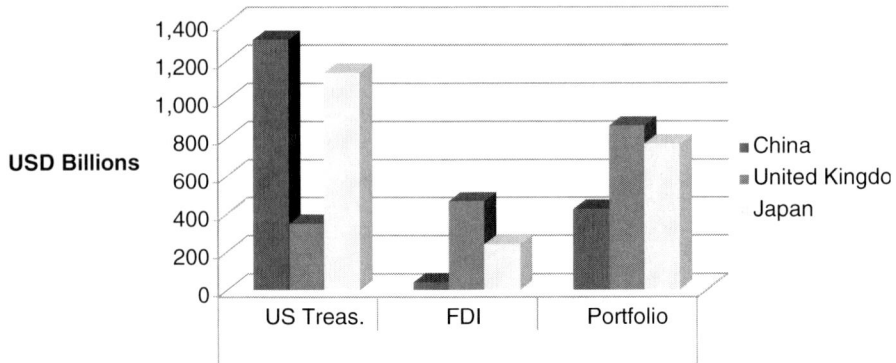

Figure MF7.1c　Foreign Ownership in the United States by asset type with China compared to Japan and the United Kingdom (the main three outside investors into the United States).

Source: Author created.

Residential property as an asset class is larger in the United States than in China by a factor of about 2.5. And the differences do not stop there. Surprisingly, home ownership in China is even higher than in the United States (over 90 percent in China versus 67 percent of households in the United States) (Arora, 2013; FRB of St. Louis, 2013). Ownership in publicly listed shares and corporate bonds were similar in each country, at 18 percent of assets. But that similarity is deceptive, providing for an interesting discussion in the context of Walras's Law. The number of companies traded on China's two main stock exchanges is roughly half of those traded in the United States. But those Chinese companies, in 2010 and earlier years had PE ratios that were double the median found in the United States (around 30 compared to 15). It is this price effect that causes Chinese stocks and bonds to contribute to a significant share of wealth. How can we explain these high valuations? Examining the high relative supply of money (M2), we can argue that such an "excess supply" matched by an excess demand (via Walras's Law) for equities must be worked off via a price adjustment. That price adjustment triggered these high valuations. In the short run, prices for equities rise. But in the long run, this encourages an increased supply of equities or, in real terms, a larger capital stock. China is clearly trying to avoid this latter effect by promoting greater consumption in the output mix. By 2011, the same suggested pattern applied to China's real estate market.

Based on the survey of U.S. households, and assuming that China holds approximately US$1.3 trillion in U.S. treasury instruments, we can estimate that China finances about 2 percent of U.S. household assets. China's holdings represent about 2.2 percent of U.S. household's net worth. Figure MF7.1c shows that these figures are comparable to that of Japan. One key difference is that both Japan and the UK (the world's third-largest asset holder) hold a substantial part of their portfolios in FDI—not U.S. government obligations. Another key difference is that these asset holdings were built up over many decades compared to China's astounding pace over only two to three decades.

*Not included are assets of financial institutions, land, and some government-owned assets. Land is excluded as an asset since the government owns land and leases it out. Thus, we assume that the value of these leases is included in the table. Financial institution assets (loans) are not included since these effectively are already included in the measurement of M2. Direct company investment is a book value. Other assets are market value (estimated) at the end of 2010. The data for the United States shows domestic households. It represents gross assets of U.S. households excluding liabilities to the corporate sector and financial sector. It also excludes the government sector and foreign obligations. Since households are the ultimate owners, either directly or indirectly, of the nation's wealth (i.e., not financed from abroad), Figure MF7.1b provides a reasonable illustration of how national wealth is distributed across different asset classes.

†Some would argue that China has too few ways to hold wealth while the United States presents a confusing array of too many ways to invest in financial securities.

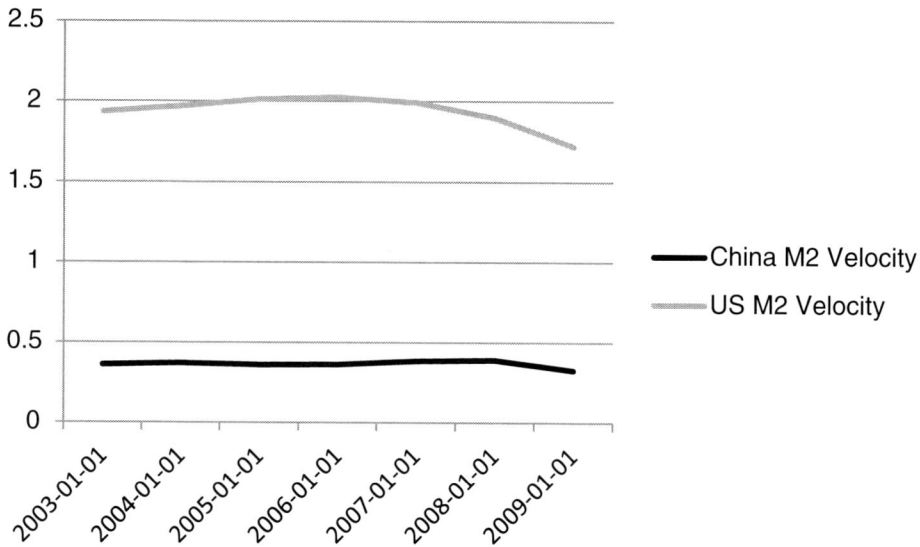

Figure 7.2 China's velocity of money (M2) has been substantially lower than the M2 in the United States because Chinese citizens have only a limited range of assets to invest in.

Source: Author's estimates.

Defining the Velocity of Money

Another way of comparing China's money supply to that of the United States is to look at the velocity of money. *Velocity* is defined as the average number of times the money supply needs to turn over in order to purchase one year's GDP. More formally:

Velocity = Nominal GDP / Money Supply

We can calculate M2 velocity by substituting M2 into the above formula. For 2011, China's M2 velocity was around 0.56, that is, the money supply was more than enough (by almost a factor of two) to purchase all of China's GDP in a single year. For the same year, velocity in the United States was around 1.7—over three times as fast. Do United States financial institutions and individuals really utilize money that much more efficiently than the Chinese or is there another explanation? A likely interpretation is that much of M2 is not held for GDP transactions but rather as a way of savings (as discussed earlier) in China. In other words, the turnover of M2 is significantly higher in the United States because M2 is an asset used more for transactions than as a store of wealth—higher-yielding outside assets serve more of the latter purpose.

Figure 7.2 shows M2 velocity for the United States and China in earlier years where the difference appears even greater. One measure of the sophistication of a financial system is the speed of its velocity. China's velocity of money will trend closer to that of the United States and other financially developed economies as its financial system continues to evolve.

Case Study 7.3: Did the Chinese Invent Velocity, Too?

In his epic work, *Science and Civilization in China*, Cambridge University scientist and historian Joseph Needham details the many early Chinese discoveries and inventions in science and technology, ranging from paper to water pumps for agriculture. No similar work has yet detailed early Chinese contributions in finance and economics. We do note, however, one of the earliest discussions of the velocity of money by Shen Kuo, a finance minister in the Song Dynasty (Chaudhury, 1990). He stated, in 1077:

> The utility of money derives from circulation and loan-making. A village of ten households may have 100,000 coins. If the cash is stored in the household of one individual, even after a century, the sum remains 100,000. If the coins are circulated through business transactions so that every individual of the ten households can enjoy the utility of the 100,000 coins, then the utility will amount to that of 1,000,000 cash. If circulation continues without stop, the utility of the cash will be beyond enumeration

The Money Supply Process

How does money enter into an economy? What you may have observed in Table 7.1 is that most of money (M2) is demand deposits and other types of savings accounts. These vehicles for holding savings can also be used for transactions, but are not created by either governments or central banks. Rather, they are financial instruments created by commercial banks and other financial institutions. While currency (cash) is deposited at these financial institutions, that same currency is re-lent by banks many times over and re-deposited in an ever-growing cascade of checking accounts and other deposits. In this sense, most "money" is actually created by the banking system. While this may seem like an artificial form of money, if one were to ask each depositor how much money they have in the bank, their response would correspond to the value of their checking and various savings accounts. If consumers and investors accept (believe) something is money, and can use it for all the purposes that money is used for, then in fact it **is** money.

The most common way for a piece of paper to become acceptable as money is for a government to create laws making it acceptable. In effect, holding money becomes the same as holding a legal document, such as the title to a home or a land lease giving the bearer a variety of rights. Specifically, governments create "legal tender" which is acceptable for tax payments and legally mandated as acceptable for the settlement of debts. This governmental imprimatur effectively guarantees money's acceptability as a medium of exchange.

But what about cash itself? Who creates that? Of course, that is created by central banks with varying degrees of government involvement. Currency in circulation is called M0. The portion of the money supply that includes currency in circulation, currency held in vaults by banks, and currency on reserve by banks at the central bank is the *monetary base* or *high-powered money*. It is the base from which all the other types of money-like accounts are created by the banking system; as such, it is truly "high-powered."

The monetary base enters the economy through the actions of the central bank as it interacts with the government and the private economy. Central banks can and do print money or issue electronic credits for money, and then trade that money for government, central bank, and sometimes even private securities.

In summary, while central banks create what is traditionally thought of as money (pieces of green or red paper printed with official portraits of current or former leaders and official language), financial institutions, including commercial banks, create most of what constitutes money. The money multiplier (the ratio of M2 to the monetary base) was 3.7 for the United States and 3.9 for China.[6] In other words, the actual money supply (M2) was close to four times larger than what was created by the central bank. But as we shall see, the central bank (in normal or non-crisis times) still exerts almost complete control over the overall size of M2 via the various tools at its disposal.

Monetary Policy Tools

Table 7.2 provides a summary of monetary tools and their uses by the PBC and the Federal Reserve (the Fed). Specifically, we can think of these as instruments or operational tools of monetary policy that the central banks can directly affect. Employing these tools, central banks hope to affect intermediate targets such as the money supply (usually measured by M2), the availability of loans within the banking system, longer-term interest rates such as for mortgages, or corporate borrowing and the exchange rate. In turn, it is hoped that these intermediate economic variables affect final targets such as economic growth, employment, and inflation in a positive way. As we discuss in Chapter 8, the United States and China have monetary policy agendas that differ (at least at this point in each country's development) in terms of the tools employed (e.g., the use of reserve requirements), intermediate targets (monetary growth instead of a targeted overnight interbank rate), and final targets (tolerance for inflation).

Open Market Operations

Open market operations (OMOs) are the most widely used tool by central bankers worldwide. On an ongoing basis, central banks buy and sell securities of short-term maturities, and undertake repurchase agreements ("repos") with financial institutions.[7] When a central bank buys a security, it pays the financial institution with high-powered money or reserves. This increases the money supply. When it sells a security, the money supply shrinks. Repos tend to be short term (less than a month), allowing central banks to both add to and drain liquidity from the economy as needed, at known prices. Open market operations are intended to affect the monetary base or the availability of reserves in the banking system and the interbank market interest rate. In China, the interbank market determines CHIBOR, the interbank interest rate (based on actual transactions for Chinese banks) and SHIBOR (based on a poll of sixteen banks of the estimated cost of overnight funds in Shanghai). Meanwhile in the United States, the interbank rate is called the federal funds rate. When banks lack available reserves (usually due to open market operations of the central bank), they tend to cut back on lending to one another, increasing their own reserves. This impacts interbank interest rates.

Though both China and the United States engage in open market operations, there are some fundamental differences. The first is that the Fed buys and sells via a primary dealer while the PBC deals directly with banks.[8] A second difference reflecting fiscal surpluses and a limited supply of government debt is that the PBC deals mainly in its own central bank bills for open market operations (OMOs) as well as corporate bonds, while the Fed has traditionally used government-issued securities.[9] A final critical difference is that the PBC buys and sells foreign exchange so as to maintain a targeted exchange rate. In the United States, there is no target exchange rate and intervention in the foreign exchange market is rare. On those rare occasions where there is an intervention in currency markets, the Fed and the U.S. Treasury coordinate their activities.

Table 7.2 Monetary policy tools and their use by China and the United States.

Monetary Policy Tools	China	United States
Open market operations	Active	Active
Adjusting reserve requirement	Active	Rare
Discount window lending	Active	Occasional
Window guidance	Active	Rare
Interest rate ceilings	Active	Not used
Directed credit	Active	Rare
Gov't. deposit management	Active	Rare

Source: Author created.

mmary, open market operations in China involve both the sale and purchase of its own bills urities, and foreign exchange while in the United States, open market operations are conducted using securities alone. During the last half of 2012, China's PBC took a major step toward using open market operations as its main tool for implementing monetary policy. Up to that point, the PBC had relied mostly on adjusting reserve requirements to affect the money supply. Via twice-weekly auctions of bills and bond repurchase agreements (repos), the PBC undertook approximately RMB 1 trillion in transactions from July to December of 2012—representing the estimated equivalent of a 1-percent hike in overnight interest rates. Apparently, the flexibility of open market repos compared to the more rigid reserve requirement ratios outweighed some of the cost considerations discussed below.

Discount Window Lending

Discount window lending is targeted to specific banks that borrow short term on collateral in order to meet their reserve requirement Borrowing banks are required to pay an interest rate (the discount rate or rediscount rate) that is above the interbank market rate. The discount interest rate also serves as a clear signal regarding the intent of central bank policy since it is not subject to daily market fluctuations but rather a rate fixed by the monetary authorities. When set above the interbank rate, it serves as an indicator of the upper bound of rates acceptable to the monetary authorities.

China uses the discount window as a tool of monetary policy on a more regular basis than does the Fed. Discount window lending in the United States tends to be for exceptional circumstances, such as when a bank is having difficulty in meeting its reserve requirements—a serious problem suggesting that the bank is lacking adequate liquidity to cover the cash demands of its depositors.[10] Figures 7.3, 7.4, and 7.5 show discount window utilization by financial institutions

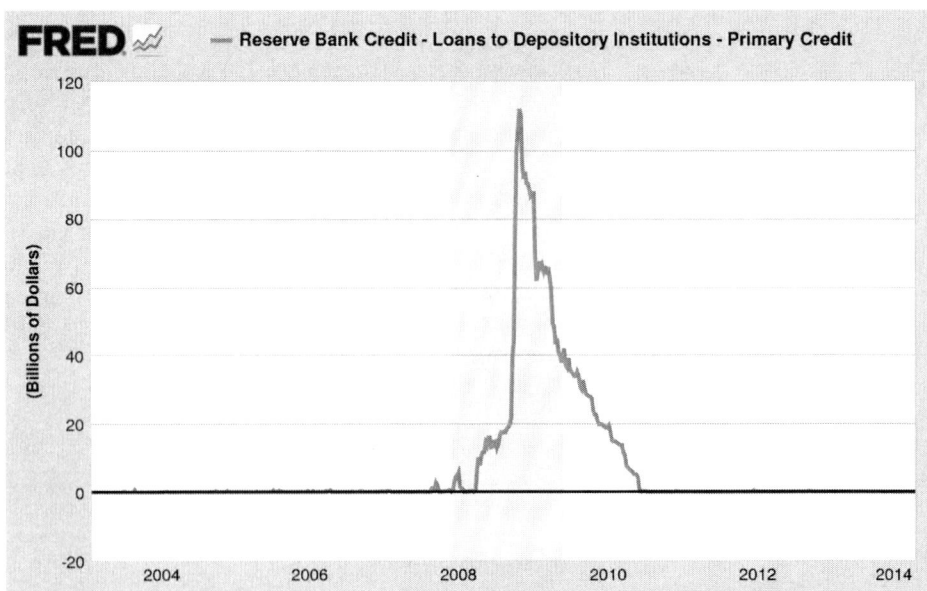

Figure 7.3 Lending through the discount window surged during the financial crisis but returned to normal negligible levels afterward.

Source: FRED, Federal Reserve Economic Data, Federal Reserve Bank of St. Louis: Reserve Bank Credit, Loans to Depository Institutions, Primary Credit; Board of Governors of the Federal Reserve System. 2014 research.stlouisfed.org
Note: Shaded areas indicate U.S. recessions.

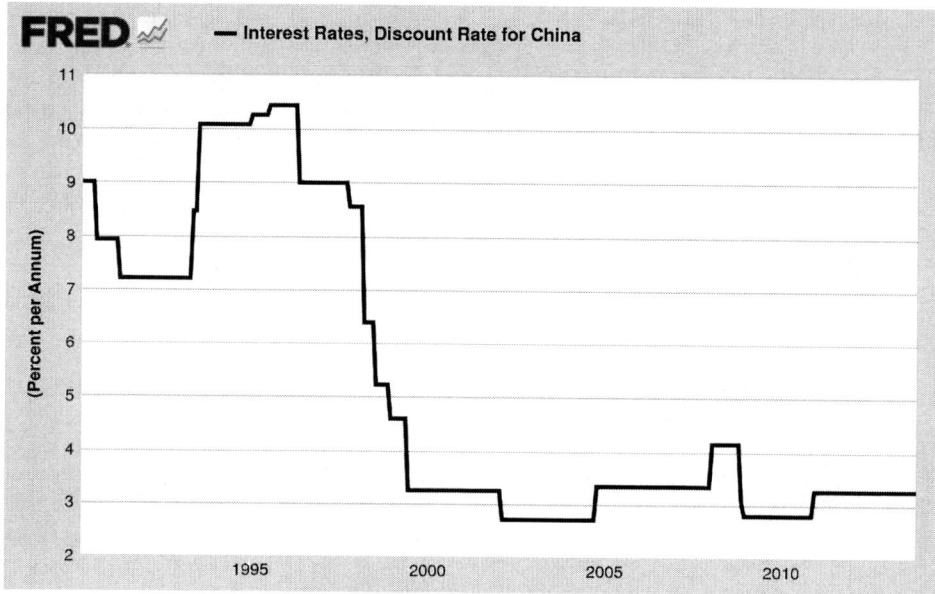

Figure 7.4 China's central bank actively uses the discount rate as a monetary tool with frequent adjustments.

Source: FRED, Federal Reserve Economic Data, Federal Reserve Bank of St. Louis: Interest Rates, Discount Rate for China; International Monetary Fund. 2014 research.stlouisfed.org

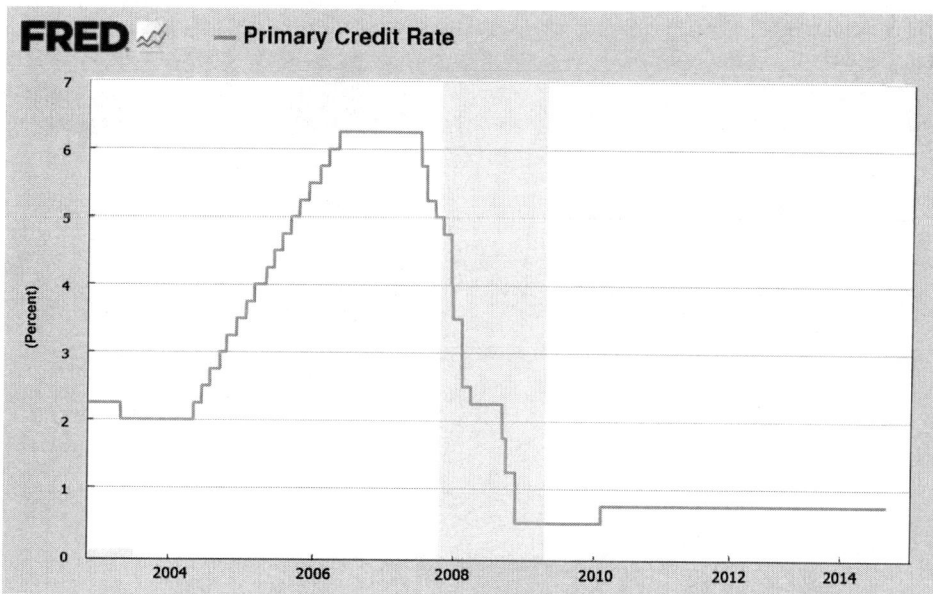

Figure 7.5 The Federal Reserve also makes frequent adjustments to its discount rate but actual borrowing at the discount window under normal circumstances is low.

Source: FRED, Federal Reserve Economic Data, Federal Reserve Bank of St. Louis: Primary Credit Rate; Board of Governors of the Federal Reserve System. 2014 research.stlouisfed.org
Note: Shaded areas indicate U.S. recessions

in the United States, and the pattern of discount rates in China and the United States. During the financial crisis, we see a peak, but then usage drops to negligible amounts both before and after the 2008–10 period in the United States. At the end of 2010, total credit to financial institutions by the PBC in China was around 11 percent of the monetary base—reflecting a significant role for discount window lending in China. In the United States, by 2011, the ratio had become negligible.

MACRO FINANCE INSIGHT 7.2: SEASONALITY AND AN ELASTIC CURRENCY

The Federal Reserve System was established in 1913 in response to a series of financial crises (known as "panics"), including the Panic of 1907. Beyond the broader goal of promoting financial stability, the Federal Reserve Act specified that the FED should supply an "elastic" currency. What this provided, in practice, was a method for meeting the seasonally determined needs of consumers and private businesses for money and credit (loans). These needs might be large in some months of the year but smaller in others. During times of high demand for credit, the Fed expands the monetary base to allow real economic activity to proceed smoothly. In times of low demand for credit, the Fed shrinks the monetary base to prevent rapid credit expansion and overheating. At the turn of the century, when the Fed was created, the United States was still an agrarian economy and seasonal patterns consistent with crop cycles were important.

Figures MF7.2a, MF7.2b, and MF7.2c show the pattern of an actual manufacturing firm in the United States whose production is quite constant year-round, but whose sales rise in the last half of the year in the run-up to Christmas. The firm builds up inventory in the first half of the year, drains down cash holdings, and borrows to finance its working capital. It is in the second and third quarters that financing is critical for this firm's survival. The company must pay for production in the abeyance of sales that will occur later in the year. The Fed plays a role here by providing an elastic currency which ensures that the financial system is not constrained when supporting the seasonal needs of this firm and others like it.*

Figures MF7.2d, MF7.3e, MF7.2f, and Table MF7.2a show the seasonal patterns for China and the United States for retail sales beginning in 1993. If the two countries had the same seasonal pattern, the line in the last chart would be flat. Clearly, it is not. In both countries, activity is highest in the last quarter

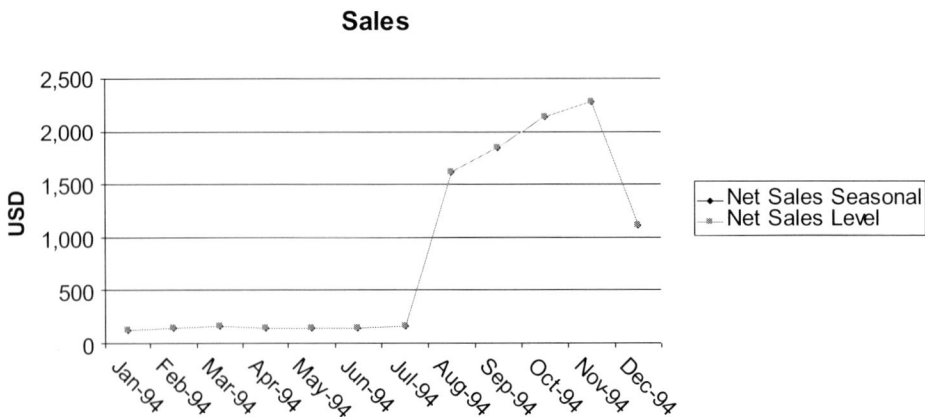

Figure MF7.2a The seasonal sales pattern of a typical manufacturing firm in the United States.

Source: Author created.

Notes Payable

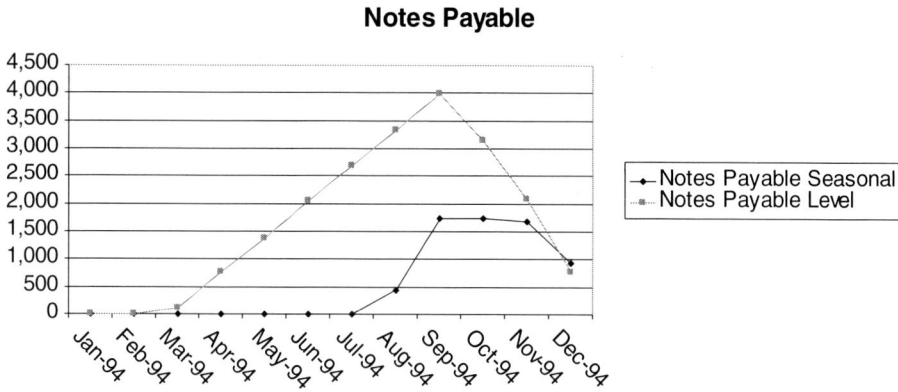

Figure MF7.2b The seasonal notes payable (cash payment of short-term debt) pattern of a typical manufacturing firm in the United States.

Source: Author created.

Inventory

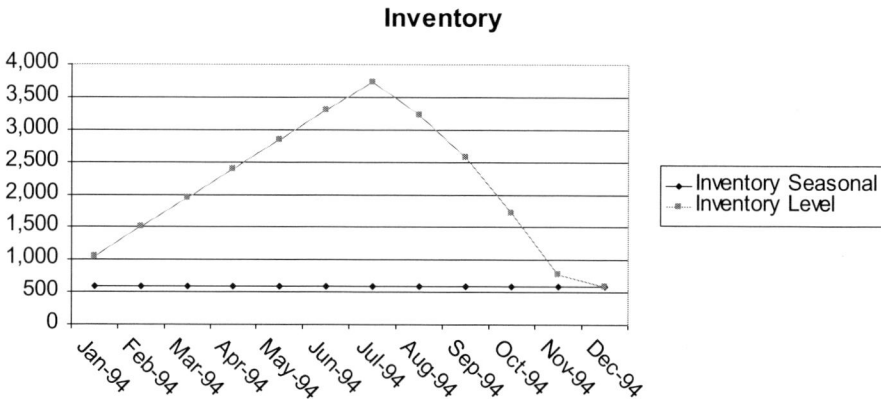

Figure MF7.2c The seasonal inventory pattern of a typical manufacturing firm in the United States.

Source: Author created.

of the year. China has relatively low activity in the second and third quarters of the year, while the United States has normal activity in those quarters. China's annual Spring Festival (Chinese New Year) boosts first quarter activity compared to the same period for the United States.† Assuming that production financing needs correspond to production patterns (as in the United States), we can assume that the PBC tends to increase the monetary base in the first quarter of the year, consistent with our notion of an elastic currency. On the consumption side, China experiences a burst of consumer activity in late January or February, during the run-up to Spring Festival. In fact, the BBC reported that China injected over RMB 255 billion into the financial system in January of 2014 to meet the increased liquidity needs of the vast traveling and *hongbao*-carrying Chinese population en route to their home villages for the Chinese New Year.‡ Apparently successful, interbank short-term rates which had surged to 6.5 percent, dropped abruptly to 5.25 percent (BBC, 2014).

In contrast, if we look at China's seasonal GDP (production rather than demand) we see a sharp decline in output in the first quarter. The surge in retail sales in the first quarter, matched by a drop in production, suggests declining inventories (built up in the last quarter) and, in turn, an increase in cash flow. A Spring Festival for companies, indeed! Given that China's economy still weighs production and investment more heavily than consumption, we can guess that the production seasonality effect rather than the consumer finance effect is more pronounced relative to the United States.

So why is an elastic currency needed at all? Certainly, if production costs are outpacing revenues for a period of the year, the other side of the coin must be that workers are saving their income. Shouldn't they be able to lend back to the production sector to make up the imbalance? The situation would be symmetric in the United States if, when consumer sales surged in December, firms were able to

CHINA SEASONAL PATTERN RETAIL SALES

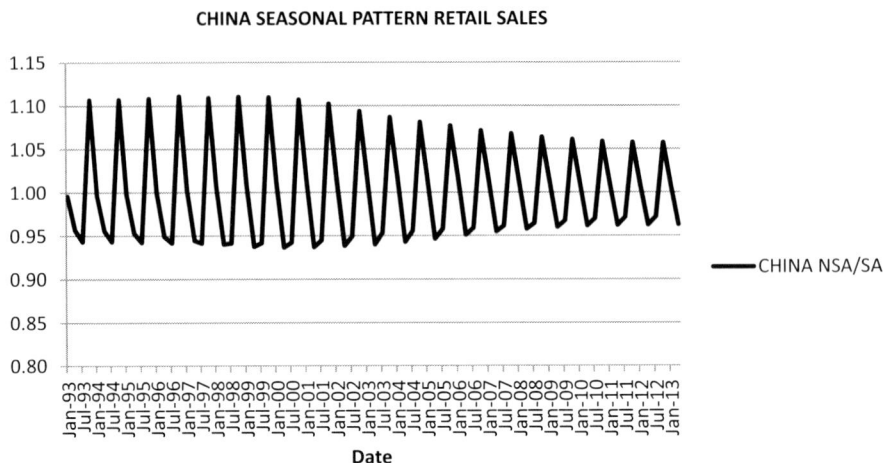

Figure MF7.2d China experiences a surge in sales in the last quarter of the year and in the first quarter with the arrival of the Spring Festival (or Chinese New Year) 新年快乐!

Source: Author created.

USA SEASONAL PATTERN RETAIL SALES

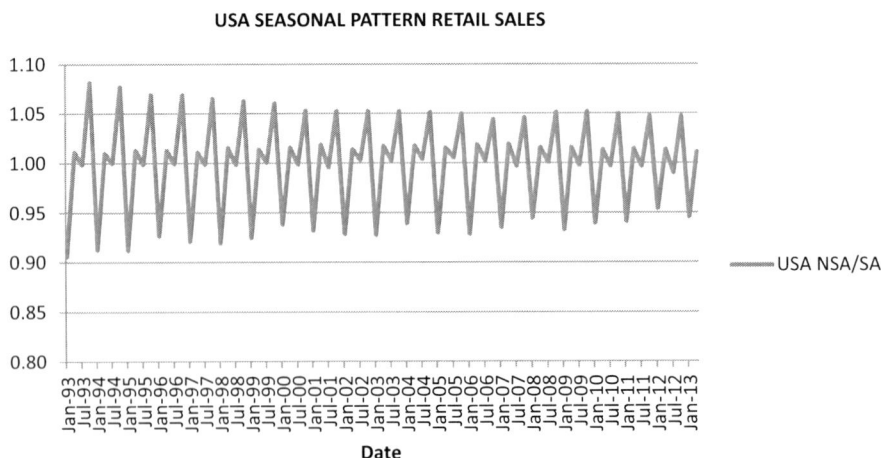

Figure MF7.2e The U.S. experiences a surge in retail sales in the last quarter (Christmas) but then the first and second quarters are relatively quiet periods.

Source: Author created.

US TO CHINA SEASONAL PATTERN

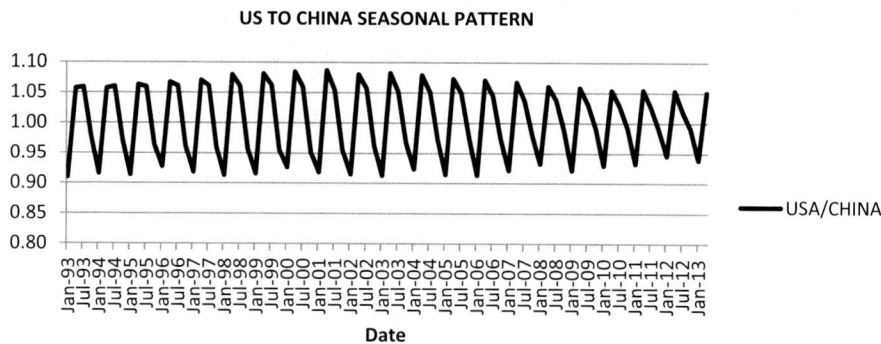

Figure MF7.2f The ratio of retail sales seasonal patterns of the U.S. to China. A flat line (which this is not) would suggest identical seasonal patterns. The ratio is lowest in the first quarter and highest in the fourth quarter.

Source: Author created.

Table MF7.2a Seasonal patterns for retail sales in China and the United States are different, especially in the first quarter of the year.

	Retail Sales Seasonal Pattern	
Quarter	*China*	*United States*
I	High	Low
II	Low	Normal
III	Low	Normal
IV	High	Very high

Source: Author created.

finance consumers. Or taking the question to an international level, if an entire economy has a seasonal imbalance, shouldn't it be able to borrow internationally? To some extent, this does happen, both domestically and internationally. However, the financial intermediation process can experience periods of uncertainty, lack of information, risk aversion, and irrationality (fear), and often does not provide a smooth and predictable intermediation from quarter to quarter. This can create severe working capital shortfalls for both firms and consumers in the short run and can even potentially trigger an economic crisis. Thus, the role of the Fed and PBC in providing an elastic currency remains critical. Eventually, no doubt, some clever financier will find a way to lend across the seasonal cycles between these two major economies, helping residents in each country smooth economic activity (and, of course, help him/herself financially).

*Prior to the creation of the Fed, most financial panics of the nineteenth century occurred in the Spring and Fall seasons, when farmers needed to support planting and harvesting production but lacked adequate cash. Investment and inventory accumulation required cash (working capital), but these activities typically occurred at different time periods from peaks in consumption and cash receipts.

†The Chinese New Year occurs at an irregular date in the first two months of the year based on the lunar cycle. Cash needs are further exacerbated by companies giving several months of salary in the form of a bonus right before the Chinese New Year begins.

‡A *hongbao* (红包) meaning red envelope, is an envelope containing cash that older relatives give as a gift to the younger generation on the Chinese New Year. Of course with the admonition that it should be saved.

Window Guidance

Window guidance is a broad term describing how the central bank can persuade financial institutions to follow stated monetary policies. It is an attempt to actually affect the operational aspect of financial decisions through communication, persuasion, and even regulatory threat. Specifically, a central bank would like to affect how much is lent by banks in the overall economy. The PBC, for example, stated in its

Fourth Quarter Report for 2006 (PBC Monetary Policy Analysis Group, 2007):

> By communicating with the commercial banks and other financial institutions on a regular basis, the central bank is in a better position to have the market anticipate its monetary policy and thus to make its policy more effective. China's experience in recent years indicates that improving transparency through window guidance is not only conducive to reducing costs of monetary policy operations, but also to helping the central bank realize its policy objectives and enhance the effectiveness of monetary policy.

The PBC actively engages the banking system (the principal shareholder of the largest banks remains the central government) to follow its directives. Specifically, the PBC announces regular targets for lending growth during the year, and it attempts to ensure that banks in the aggregate meet these targets. Furthermore, as we see in other PBC statements, the guidance regarding which industries need more credit and which need less goes even to the disaggregated industry level. This PBC guidance naturally flows from and is consistent with the central authorities' Five-Year Plan. The PBC's top policymakers meet with the banks on a monthly basis and provide more formal window guidance pronouncements on a quarterly basis.[11]

In the United States, the Fed has not provided anywhere near the level of window guidance found in China. On the contrary, some have argued that there has been an absence of transparency in Fed policy goals and targets over the years. That perception comes perhaps from the Fed's careful distance from financial markets, ensuring that traders cannot unfairly take advantage of imminent market movements resulting from Fed actions. Furthermore, central banks historically have been wary of establishing specific goals and targets which might tie their hands in certain exigencies.

The chairman of the Fed is, however, required to testify before Congress twice a year to set out monetary policy goals. Between 1978 and 2000, the Fed set growth targets for monetary growth, as a result of Congressional legislation known as the Humphrey–Hawkins bill. Since 1990, the Fed has published a target range for the interbank (federal funds) rate. In January 2012, the Fed announced a formal long-run inflation target of 2 percent as part of an effort at greater transparency.

In summary, the Fed provides broad general guidance regarding future policy targets. It then relies on market forces to summon an appropriate response. China's guidance includes this, to some extent, but also involves telling financial institutions what they must do operationally to help the PBC and the central government implement both broad and specific policy goals.

Reserve Requirements

Reserve requirements represent how much cash financial institutions are required to hold either in their own vaults or on deposit (typically as a credit) at the central bank. Reserve requirements serve two main purposes:

1. As a precautionary amount providing the bank with adequate liquidity should depositors withdraw an abnormal amount from the bank.
2. Even more importantly, as a tool for controlling the amount of money (e.g., M2) in circulation.

Regarding the latter role, recall that money is created by banks through receiving a deposit in, for example, a checking account, re-lending that amount, and then accepting further deposits from those who have borrowed from the banking system. Thus, a recycling of high-powered money sets off a "chain reaction" of new bank deposits. These new deposits are all captured, by definition, in M2 and thus become bank-created money.

When financial institutions have higher reserve requirements, they can lend out less. Reserve requirements, in effect, create "dead-in-the-water" money since this money is held either in bank vaults or on deposit at the central bank. In fact, while these amounts held as reserves are part of the monetary base, they are not part of either M1 or M2 and, by definition, are not part of the money supply. Technically, if r represents the fraction of deposits that are held in reserve (the reserve ratio), and c represents the fraction of deposits held in actual cash (not in banks or the currency-to-deposit ratio), we can say that the money multiplier mentioned above (the ratio of M2 to the monetary base) is:

$$\text{M2 / Monetary Base} = \text{Money Multiplier} = (1 + c) / (r + c)$$

There is a substantial difference in the way China and the United States use this tool for controlling the money supply. From January 2010 to June 2011, the PBC raised the reserve requirement twelve times and currently has one of the highest reserve requirement ratios in the world, at 21 percent. Both in terms of the reserve ratio and the degree to which this tool is used, China, among all large economies in recent years, relies on this tool more. Recent utilization involves tightening the money supply. In contrast, over the past fifty-four years, the FED has changed reserve requirements roughly twice per year. Most of these changes were minor and were part of longer-term structural considerations rather than part of a targeted monetary policy. In the United States, for example, banks must maintain a marginal reserve requirement of 10 percent on transaction-based accounts (e.g., checking accounts) over US$79.5 million—a much narrower base for reserves than China's.[12] Remarkably, as a share of GDP, China's required reserves are near 30 percent and, in the United States, less than 1 percent. Figure 7.6 shows an increasing pattern of reserve requirements as China has tried to rein in the inflationary effect of increased inflow of U.S. dollars on trade and capital accounts, as discussed in Chapters 3 and 8.

Interest is paid on required reserves both in the United States and China.[13] In the United States, the current rate on required and excess reserves is 0.25 percent, while in China, the corresponding

Reserve Requirement Ratio

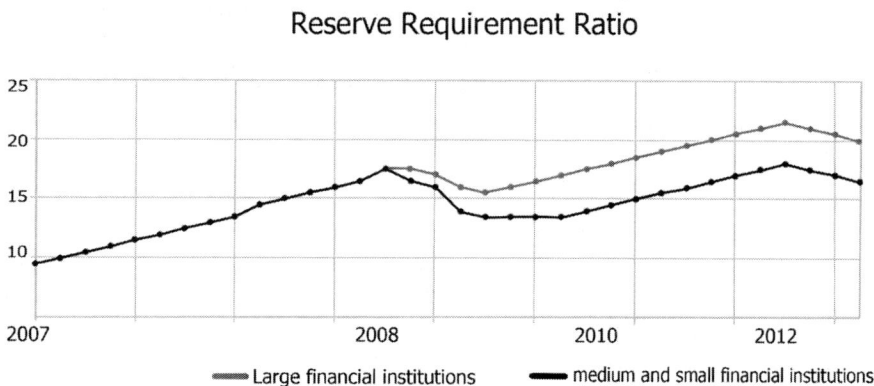

Figure 7.6 China's PBC has used the reserve requirement on banks far more often and aggressively than any of the major economies around the world (including the United States). It has been one way for the PBC to offset the impact on the Chinese money supply of massive purchases of foreign exchange.

Source: PBC China Monetary Policy Report.

rates are 1.62 and 0.72 percent. China's extensive use of reserve requirements is consistent with its efforts at controlling monetary growth instead of overnight interest rates (i.e., controlling the quantity rather than the price of money); this in turn is related to China's massive efforts to sterilize the foreign exchange inflows since 2007 in order to halt rapid monetary growth. Furthermore, it has been a less expensive alternative form of monetary control—the interest rate paid on required reserves in China is less than the amount needed to pay banks to hold additional central bank bills through open market operations.

In both countries, the holding of excess reserves is large by international norms. In the United States, this is a recent phenomenon reflecting asset purchase programs implemented by the Fed during the financial crisis which, in turn, increased cash holdings by the banks. In China, excess reserve holdings are chronic, reflecting longer-term monetary policies to control the amount of money circulating in the Chinese economy.

Prior to the rise in the use of reserve requirements as a tool in 2007, the sale and purchase of central bank bills was the primary tool. In the United States, open market operations remain the most significant tool however, the financial crisis created an unusual situation in which the Fed acquired troubled assets such as mortgage-backed securities and American International Group (AIG) obligations. This rare situation was different from the more traditional Fed open market sale and purchase of treasury securities.

MACRO FINANCE INSIGHT 7.3: RETURN ON EQUITY (ROE) AND THE MONEY MULTIPLIER

The money multiplier links the monetary base with the actual amount of money (M1 or M2) circulating in the economy. The ratio of currency held by the public to bank deposits (c) and reserves held against deposits by the financial institution (r) will combine with the amount of high-powered money created by the central bank (H) to magnify out to the money supply (M).

$$M = H \times (c / (c + r))$$

The money multiplier ratio in parentheses above also serves as a constraint in terms of how fast the money supply can grow. But another very important constraint is often overlooked in macroeconomic discussions on determining the size of the money supply: the capital adequacy ratio (CAR). CAR represents the required ratio of capital or investor funding beyond citizen deposits to the amount of loans granted by financial institutions. The Bank for International Settlements, based in Switzerland, has recommended ratios and relevant metrics for CAR, referred to as BASEL I, II, or III.

Let's simplify the complex set of guidelines by saying that financial institutions in a country are required to hold a minimum ratio of capital or equity (E) against loans or domestic credit (LC) or:

$$E / LC = e \text{ or } LC = 1 / e \times E$$

Furthermore, let's summarize an entire nation's financial system with the following balance sheet:

Assets	*Liabilities*
	Money (*M*)
Loans or Credits (*LC*)	Equity (*E*)

Here we include all financial institutions ranging from the country's central bank down to the lowest-level regulated small financial institution. Equity includes everything from paid-in-capital and retained earnings, to holdings of other acceptable forms of capital by the financial system. Loans or credits include both domestic and foreign loans, on a net basis. Thinking of money as "broad money" or M2, let's substitute our ratios into this balance sheet:

Assets	Liabilities
	$H \times c/(c + r)$
$1/e \times E$	E

Dividing by E, we have:

Assets	Liabilities
	$H/E \quad c/(c + r)$
$1/e$	1

Assuming that e, c, and r are constants and the balance sheet remains in balance, the above balance sheet says: if H grows (the monetary base grows) then E must grow at the same rate. But the growth rate of E, (meaning E/E) is the same as the return on equity (ROE) for banks. If H grows faster than ROE, banks will be constrained from making loans by their capital requirements; as a result, banks will hold excess reserves. If H grows slower than ROE, banks will lack adequate liquidity to offer loans.

During an economic recession, the economy-wide ROE declines (the companies' ROEs that banks have lent to) and so banks' ROE (profitability) may turn negative due to bad loans. Providing greater liquidity through H may not create greater lending in this situation since banks are constrained by their capital inadequacy. It is this situation that corresponds to shrinking collateral and credit rationing in times of financial crisis (Bernanke and Gertler 1995).

Interest Rate Ceilings and Floors

Interest rate ceilings and floors are a form of "financial repression"; an effort at bypassing market-determined interest rates with fixed ones. Ceilings and floors can appear on both deposits and loans, and are intended (at one level) to control interest rates in the economy. At another level, they are a means of either subsidizing banks (when deposit rates are ceilinged) or subsidizing borrowers (when lending rates are ceilinged).[14] In the case of controls, interest-rate ceilings can be viewed as another tool in the monetary policy toolkit. In the case of a subsidy, the goal is usually to enhance bank profitability or encourage certain types of investments. While possibly achieving certain short-term credit market goals, ceilings and floors tend to be distortionary at a microeconomic level and can lead to financial disintermediation, rationing, and black markets for borrowing in the long run.

Figure 7.7 shows the supply and demand of investable funds in an economy against the interest rate (or cost of capital) charged. If a ceiling is set below the equilibrium rate (where the two curves intersect), a shortage results and the potential for credit rationing and shortages exist.

The United States eliminated ceilings on interest rates for bank savings accounts in 1980 and by 2010, ceilings on rates for demand deposits were also fully eliminated.[15] China continues to have ceilings on deposit interest rates for bank deposits. Until July 2013, it had floors on lending rates (see Table 7.3) but these were completely eliminated as a further step toward liberalizing credit markets. Deposit ceilings remain both an instrument for short-run monetary policy in China and a long-run source of profits (subsidy) to the largely state-owned banks.[16] In the United States, deposit and lending rates serve as an intermediate target toward the final targets of inflation, real economic

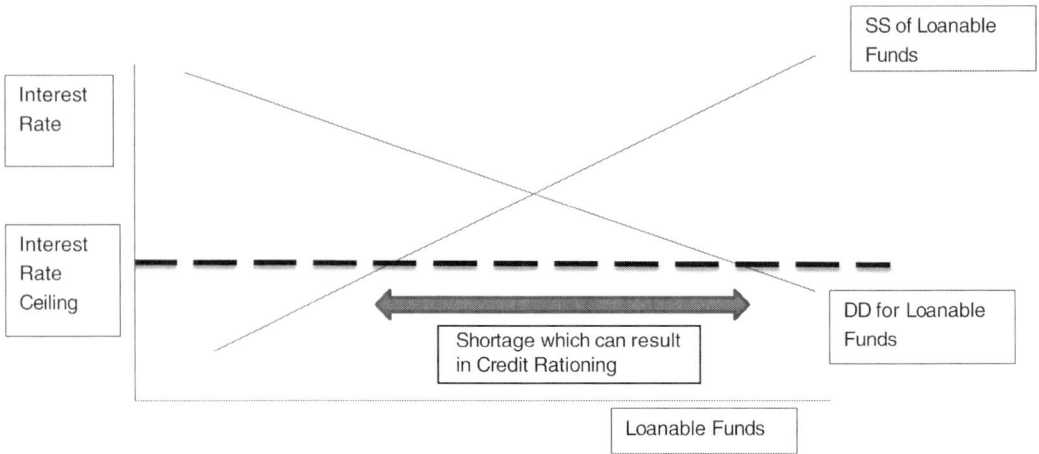

Figure 7.7 Interest rate ceilings can lead to shortages of available funds and credit rationing.

Source: Author created.

Table 7.3 One form of financial repression in China in recent years has been ceilings and floors on interest rates that financial institutions could charge.

Official Ceilings on Deposit and Loan Interest Rates China 2012*

Official Interest Rates on Deposits & Loans of Financial Institutions	January 1	June 8	July 6	December 31
Interest Rates on Deposits				
Demand deposits	0.50	0.40	0.35	0.35
Time deposits				
3 Months	3.10	2.85	2.60	2.60
6 Months	3.30	3.05	2.80	2.80
1 Year	3.50	3.25	3.00	3.00
2 Years	4.40	4.10	3.75	3.75
3 Years	5.00	4.65	4.25	4.25
5 Years	5.50	5.10	4.75	4.75
Interest Rates on Loans				
6 Months	6.10	5.85	5.60	5.60
6 Months ~ 1 year	6.56	6.31	6.00	6.00
1~3 Years	6.65	6.40	6.15	6.15
3~5 Years	6.90	6.65	6.40	6.40
Longer than 5 years	7.05	6.80	6.55	6.55

Source: PBC Monetary Survey.
*Note: Ceilings on bank loans were eliminated in 2013.

growth, and employment. In recent years, deposit rates have remained exceptionally low, also serving as a source of profits for the troubled financial sector.

Table 7.3 provides a list of interest rate ceilings and floors (recently removed) for deposits and loans in China. As suggested above, these ceilings provide, at one level, a mechanism for banks to tighten credit (lending) and to discourage or encourage deposits in different types of bank accounts. These intermediate targets then go on to affect some of the final targets mentioned above. At a different level, however, the large regulated gap between deposit and lending rates serves as a subsidy to banks. In the past, Chinese banks have needed this subsidy due to state-directed loans which could not be repaid. This solution, however, results in subsidizing banks for making even more loans, and that may be planting the seeds for another crisis.

Figure 7.8 shows various interest rates in China in recent years. The lines that appear as step functions representing ceilings and floors are non-market-based.[17] Deposit rates, lending rates, and remuneration for reserve holding are all set by the PBC and are used as part of a broader package of monetary policy tools. Figure 7.9 provides the market-based interbank borrowing/lending rate that generally falls between the regulated rates in Figure 7.8. These are still evolving as price-based tools for monetary policy.

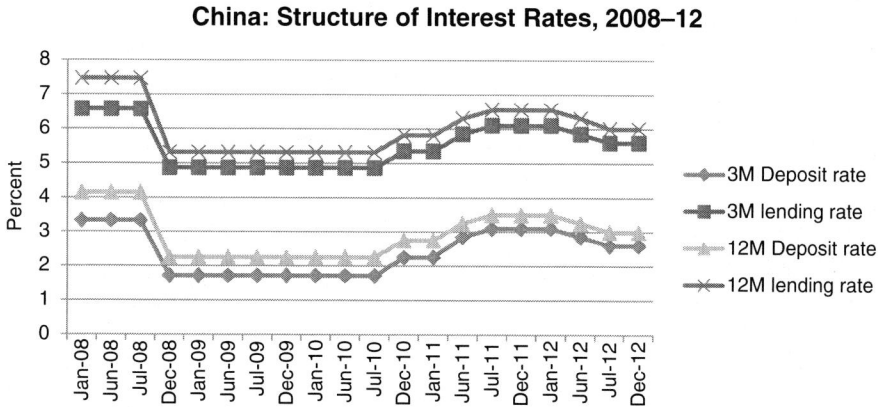

Figure 7.8 The gap (spread) between deposit and lending rates for banks has not been a market-determined one in China. Rather it reflects regulated borrowing/lending rates which have served as a subsidy to banks.

Source: PBC China Monetary Policy Report.

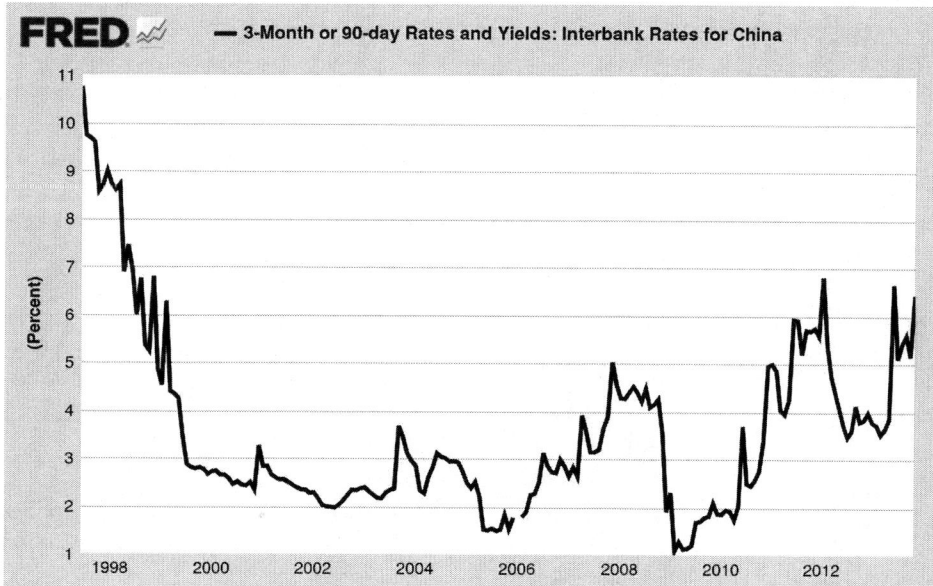

Figure 7.9 The interbank interest rate (the rate at which financial institutions borrow and lend from one another) provides a market-based measure of the interaction between monetary policy and the market's demand for credit.

Source: FRED, Federal Reserve Economic Data, Federal Reserve Bank of St. Louis: 3-month or 90-day Rates and Yields: Interbank Rates for China; Organisation for Economic Co-operation and Development. 2014 research.stlouisfed.org

Directed Credit

Directed credit involves a central bank targeting specific industries or companies to receive financing. This could take two main forms:

1. A central bank could instruct financial institutions to lend to these target industries.
2. The central bank could purchase directly a targeted company's financing instruments.

Figure 7.10 illustrates how a central bank interfaces with end user firms or industries. We typically think of central banks as making credit available to financial institutions through open market operations or discount window activity. These institutions in turn lend to the private economy (companies and consumers) based on their own assessment of risk, return, and opportunities. This is the generally accepted practice for central banks. Most countries prefer to see private financial institutions make decisions regarding creditworthiness and borrowing or lending opportunities. Central banks are charged with the task of broad macro aggregates (not corporate creditworthiness, valuation, or industry selection) including inflation, economic growth, unemployment, and setting the overall level of nominal interest rates and exchange rates.

When central banks require or encourage financial institutions to target industries or companies for lending, we have a form of directed credit. The central bank may also interface directly with companies, target industries, governments, or even local consumers by buying their securities or equivalently making loans.[18] This would be a direct form of directed credit. In both instances, the central bank typically acts on behalf of the government to establish industrial policy or to meet the more short-term goal of rescuing a company from bankruptcy or an industry from collapse.

Until the mid-1980s, the PBC was engaged in direct lending to companies and industries in China. Virtually all companies, at the time, were state-owned, and loans were considered to be part of the industrial policies set out in the government's Five-Year Plans. When China's Big Four commercial banks (see Case Study 7.5) were eventually carved out of the PBC and allowed greater independence, they undertook more and more lending. They still, however, made most of their loans at the behest of the PBC and central government—a very clear form of direct lending. A more decisive step was taken in 1994, with the creation of a separate category of policy lending banks (China Development Bank, Export Import Bank, Agricultural Development Bank of China). However, policy lending still continued, with encouragement from local governments. After China's major banking crisis in 2000–03 (a result of the prior policy loans turning into non-performing loans), policy lending was further curtailed and banks were permitted to make lending decisions on more market-based criteria. As evidenced by the 2010 annual PBC report (People's Bank of China, 2011); however, we still see a substantial role for directed credit in China:

> Following the requirement to make differentiated credit policies, the PBC guided financial institutions to enhance financial support to key industries, areas, and regions, including key industrial reinvigoration programs, energy-conservation and environmental protection, strategic emerging industries, service sector, weak links in the economy, employment, consumption, balanced regional economic development, and disaster response and reconstruction, improved agro-supporting financial services, as well as financial services to SMEs. While ensuring credit to key projects under construction, the PBC reduced lending to high energy consuming and polluting industries, as well as industries with excessive capacity, and restricted unauthorized lending to local government financing platforms.

Directed credit in the China context can also mean targeting major markets such as the real estate market and the stock market. Traditionally, in the United States, the Fed's policies have been directed at the broader notion of financial market stability and have specifically avoided policies directed at the stock market.

The Interface between the Central Bank and the Economy

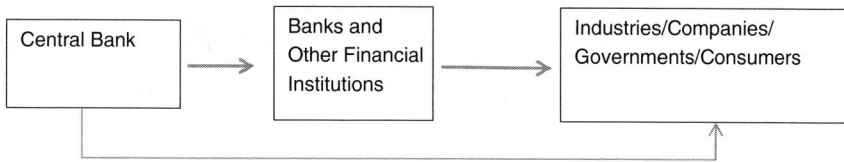

Figure 7.10 Normally we think of the central bank interfacing with the financial sector and the financial sector providing finance to the "real economy" based on profit-maximizing principles. Sometimes (as in the case of China; or the U.S. during the recent financial crisis) the central bank goes around the financial system and interfaces directly with the real economy.

Source: Author created.

The Fed was structured as an independent entity; not subject to day-to-day political pressures from the United States government. As such, it has viewed its mandate as applying to the broad macro targets mentioned earlier rather than directed credit. That being said, the financial crisis that began in 2007 has seen a more intrusive role for the Fed in specific industries—the acquisition of AIG securities, the purchase of mortgage-backed assets, and the broader purchase of government agency debt.[19] While the Fed balance sheet expanded tremendously after 2007, it is gradually returning to its pre-2007 level (total Fed assets were about US$900 billion at the end of 2006 but, by mid-2011, reached US$2.3 trillion). In the Fed's view, this expansion was consistent with maintaining stability in the financial system during the financial crisis and did not target specific industries for economic development. Rather, it prevented the broad financial system (with a focus on real estate finance) from collapse.

Case Study 7.4: Developments in China's Financial Markets

As mentioned above, China's financial sector and markets remain in the early stages of development. The PBC served, in effect, as the financial sector up until the early 1980s before the Big Four state-owned banks were reconstituted as deposit-taking institutions. In December 1990, the Shanghai Stock Exchange (SSE) was reopened, as was the Shenzen Stock Exchange (SZE). In October 2009, a Shenzen-affiliated NASDAQ-like exchange was established (CHINEXT). Notwithstanding the short history, China's combined equity markets, by the end of 2012, had the second-highest market capitalization in the world (US$3.6 trillion), after the United States. Virtually all of the approximately 2,000 companies traded still had the state as their majority shareholder.

If the 1980s was the decade for banking institutions, and the 1990s focused on equity institutional development, the first two decades of the new millennium were the period for bond market development. Today, China's bond market is the world's fourth largest, valued at around US$3.1 trillion. Most bond trading occurs in the interbank market. Central bank notes and bills are the most actively traded short-term instruments in the interbank market. In addition, government bonds for a wide range of maturities are also traded. Central bank bills and government bonds (central and local governments) are used primarily in PBC open market operations (with central bank bills used more often in recent years). The majority of transactions in the interbank market are repurchase agreements with virtually all the instruments mentioned here or below used as collateral.

Financial bonds are the most actively traded long-term instruments in China.* Other long-maturity bonds include enterprise bonds, which are either issued by SOEs or private corporations. The latter private issuances still are a relatively small share of the bond market and are traded on the Enterprise Bond Exchange rather than the interbank market. In summary, the bond market has grown from insignificant levels in the 1990s to an important tool for short-term liquidity management and long-term yield by 2013. That being said, the instruments which continue to dominate the market remain government-related instruments (PBC notes and bills, government bonds, policy bonds, and a majority of enterprise bonds). In China, only about 8 percent of bonds and commercial paper instruments are issued by private companies as compared to about 28 percent in the United States. The remainder in both countries is government related.†

*Financial bonds represent loans to financial institutions, especially the policy banks: China Development Bank, Export Import Bank of China, and Agricultural Development Bank. These loan projects, in turn, are used for large infrastructure projects. Financial bonds are also issued by commercial banks and other financial institutions such as large insurance companies.

†Estimates from Goldman Sachs Liquidity Management. FAQ: China's Bond Market, and Federal Reserve Board of Governors. Credit Market Debt Owed by Financial Sector. Report Z.1, Table L.2.

Regulatory Fiat

China's State Council, in conjunction with the PBC, has also used regulations targeted at specific markets such as the housing market or construction industry. For example, in late 2011, the down payment on second-home purchases was raised from 50 percent to 60 percent and the mandated interest rates on second-home purchases were raised. Furthermore, local governments were urged to increase the supply of land available for housing. All these measures were used to rein in steep rises in property prices in recent years. Traditionally, the FED has not targeted specific industries or asset classes—although steep changes in equity or real estate markets are part of the Fed's broader mandate toward "maintaining financial stability." In an oft-quoted speech, Ben Bernanke, the Fed's then-governor, made his views very clear on this matter: that it was beyond the Fed's mandate and ability to determine what constitutes an equity market bubble and then attempt to counter it (Bernanke, 2002). China's PBC, meanwhile, includes such policies in its toolkit to complement the more traditional monetary policy tools mentioned above.

Government Deposit Management

Government deposit management involves the way in which the central authorities manage their typically large bank accounts, with respect to their impact on bank reserves. Government funds held on account with the central bank reduce (tie-up) the amount of reserves, loans, and money supply in the general economy. The reverse happens when the government writes checks (makes payments) to the private sector from its central bank account, expanding, the money supply. Since central banks around the world act not only as the banker for the financial system but for the government as well, such movements from the central bank system to the private economy can have the same effect as an open market operation.

The U.S. government (the Treasury) maintains bank accounts both at the Fed and at private financial institutions (Treasury Tax and Loan Accounts). Because, in the United States, the responsibility for monetary control rests with the Fed, the Treasury is obligated not to move its funds back and forth from Fed accounts in ways that impact the money supply.[20] For this reason, the Treasury attempts to keep a fairly constant balance in its Fed account.

In China, by contrast, the PBC actually utilizes the central government's accounts as a tool for affecting the money supply in the same spirit of an open market operation. For example, should the PBC wish to constrain monetary growth, it will move the Chinese government's funds from the private banking system to its own accounts.

Price-Based vs. Quantity-Based; Market-Based vs. Non-Market-Based

One way of classifying the above monetary tools is to determine whether the quantity or price of an asset is being targeted, and whether the tool is market based or non-market based (i.e., implemented by government mandate). For example, a central bank could choose to sell a certain quantity of bills in order to affect the quantity of reserves that the banking system holds, or it could sell bills at a specific price (interest rate) in order to directly impact interbank interest rates. In a market-based system, the central bank can control either the quantity or the price, but not both. In the former case, it controls quantity by allowing the demand of banks to determine the interest rate. In the latter case, it controls the interest rate (the price) but allows banks to determine how many reserves (quantity) they wish to hold at that price.

Non-market tools (such as regulations on how much cash borrowers must provide as a share of a home mortgage) represent controls on ultimate lending by banks in ways they may not choose on their own. China tends to use tools in the upper-left quadrant, upper-right quadrant, and lower-right quadrant of Table 7.4. That is, China tends to use quantity-based tools (e.g., the growth of the money supply) and non-market-based tools. The United States traditionally has used price- and market-based tools, though once again the recent financial crisis and the Fed's quantitative easing have been an important exception. These differences have important implications for both the effectiveness of monetary policy and the sophistication of the downstream financial sector.

Summary of Differences

Both in terms of ultimate targets (output, employment, and inflation in the United States; economic growth, the value of the exchange rate, and inflation in China) and in terms of intermediate targets (the federal funds rate in the United States; monetary growth, and a kit of non-market tools in China), there is a wide range of differences in how and to what purpose monetary policy is conducted within each country.

The PBC utilizes a wider range of available tools for the conduct of monetary policy compared to the Fed. While the Fed relies primarily on open market operations to affect the federal funds rate, the PBC makes substantial use of other tools that we have described. By the end of 2012, however, the PBC had moved to a heavier reliance on open market operations.

Table 7.4 China's PBC utilizes a wide range of tools in conducting monetary policy. Some relate to targeting the cost of funds while others relate to the availability of funds (the two targets are intertwined). Some are market-based tools; others are dirigiste.

	Market Based	Non-Market Based
Quantity Based	Issuance size of PBC bills	Targeted PBC bills
	Size of repurchases and reverse repurchase arrangements	Special deposits from specific banks
	Reserve requirements	Controls on bank credit
		Controls on bank credit by sector
		Window guidance
Price Based	Issuance rate of PBC bills	Floors and ceilings on bank loans and deposits
	Rates paid on bank reserves at the PBC	Regulatory fiat (e.g., down payment on home mortgages)
	Repurchase arrangements rates	Restricted range on interest rates (e.g., corporate bonds or interbank market)

Source: Author created.

One important reason why China relies on a wider arsenal of monetary policy tools is related to the complexity of tasks undertaken. Keeping a fixed (or "crawling peg") regime in place while at the same time controlling the money supply to curb inflation and manage economic growth requires controlling the flow of international capital (as we discuss in Chapters 3 and 8). Notwithstanding a sophisticated set of capital controls, China cannot let its interest rates stray too far from international rates lest the wall of capital controls be breached. This basic paradox creates a need for intervention in the economy at a variety of levels. How long China can maintain its balance in trying to achieve so many goals remains to be seen.

Case Study 7.5: China's "Big Four" Banks

China's largest four banks now rival the largest U.S. banks and are among the largest banks in the world as measured by assets (see Tables CS7.5a and CS7.5b). At one level, this is unremarkable given China's enormous savings rate and limited alternative asset classes. It is remarkable because these banks were, until the late 1980s, not recognizable as independent entities but rather entities operating under the wing of either the Ministry of Finance or the PBC. All banks in China were among the first institutions to be nationalized after the founding of the PRC in 1949. Even today, the majority of shares in these institutions are owned by the government. For example, over 70 percent of Bank of China shares are state owned. Beginning in the 1980s, however, these banks gained increasing independence from direct

Table CS7.5a Top ten domestic banks in China ranked by assets at the end of September 2013.

Chinese Bank	Assets (US$ billions)	Share of Total Assets*
Industrial and Commercial Bank of China	3,062.06	15%
China Construction Bank	2,449.89	12%
Agricultural Bank of China	2,385.18	12%
Bank of China	2,225.95	11%
Bank of Communications	942.35	5%
Postal Savings Bank of China	788.35	4%
China Merchants Bank	634.77	3%
Industrial Bank Company	593.65	3%
Shanghai Pudong Development Bank	587.16	3%
China Citic Banking Corporation	555.70	3%
Total Assets of Depository Institutions*	**20,713.22**	

Source: Tor and Sarfraz, 2013.
*Author estimate.

Table CS7.5b Top ten insured U.S.-chartered commercial banks ranked by consolidated assets as of December 31, 2013.

Financial Institution	Assets (US$ billions)
JP Morgan Chase	1945.5
Bank of America	1433.7
Wells Fargo	1373.6
Citibank	1346.7
U.S. Bank NA	360.5
PNC Bank	310
BNY Mellon	296.6
State Street Bank	239
Capital One	238.4
TD Bank	217.6

Source: Data from the Federal Reserve Board,
http://www.federalreserve.gov/Releases/Lbr/current/lrg_bnk_lst.txt

Total assets of commercial banks, percent of GDP

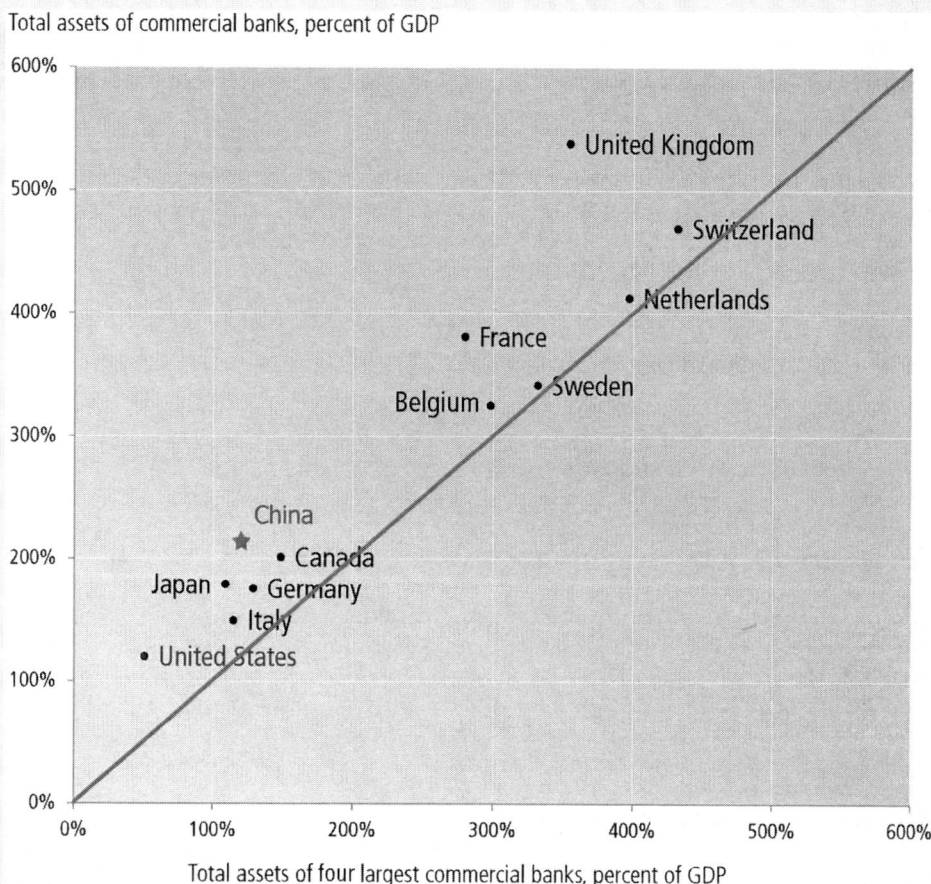

Figure CS7.5a China's largest banks have about the same level of concentration as in the United States.

Source: U.S. Treasury and author's estimates. United States Government Department of Treasury (2012).

government control, were allowed to accept individual deposits, and between 2000 and 2010 had each issued shares (IPOs) on domestic and international stock exchanges with small minority ownership.

Each bank's name gives a clear indication of its traditional source of deposits and loans, for example, the ABC has principally operated in rural areas, while the Bank of China has traditionally engaged in international operations, including foreign exchange activities.* These banks, however, are edging over time into each other's traditional lines of businesses.

Figure CS7.5a reveals two noteworthy features of China's banking system.

1. Banks in both the United States and China are not as large a share of GDP as in many other countries.
2. If we were to draw a line from the origin through China, the United States, and the United Kingdom, we could infer from the line's slope that all three countries have similarly top-heavy (China's Big Four banks) levels of concentration. But countries such as Germany and Canada fall below that line and have an even heavier Big Four concentration.

*In fact, the Bank of China (not to be confused with the People's Bank of China (PBC)) has SAFE—the State Administration for Foreign Exchange—as its majority shareholder.

State majority ownership of the five largest banks in China compared to privately owned banks in the United States is another difference which serves as a necessary condition for greater PBC intervention. China's banking system is relatively new and still evolving. Until 1979–80, the PBC was effectively China's only bank. But by 1994, the PBC had assigned the traditional banking role of deposit taking and lending to four major state-owned banks: Bank of China, Industrial and Commercial Bank of China, China Construction Bank, and Agricultural Bank of China. These four major banks still dominate the banking landscape in China in terms of both deposits and loans. A plethora of financial instruments for the private sector to invest in the United States compared to a paucity of instruments in China is another factor. In Chapter 8, we build on this institutional understanding to interpret actual monetary policy in recent years in each economy.

Case Study 7.6: Financial Innovation or Financial Disintermediation in China?

Taobao (Treasure Chest), the most popular online shopping site in China, has recently found plenty of treasure to fill its chest. By providing higher returns on money market-like assets (6–7 percent compared to the regulated 3.3 percent) than those delivered on deposits at the staid Big Four banks in China, Taobao has attracted over 80 million investors and US$40 billion in the span of eight months in 2013–14. Taobao is owned by Alibaba, another Chinese online giant which provides information on suppliers around the world of products and services (Barboza, 2013). The money market funds provide both a higher return and a transaction account on Taobao's site. Other Internet retailers also see an opportunity and are now offering their own money market funds. Current estimates for the size of the market are around US$50 billion compared to total bank deposits in China of US$7.6 trillion.

The PBC has also taken notice and is looking for ways to regulate but not stifle this emerging financial segment. For regulators and policymakers there are three key issues: First is the degree of risk to investors (depositors) and, in turn, implications for systematic risk throughout the financial system. After all, one critical juncture of the global financial crisis in the United States was when the Primary Reserve money market fund saw a decline in its net asset value from US$1 to 0.97 in September of 2008 (it "broke the buck"); an event that had been assumed close to impossible. A second concern relates to monetary control. The PBC has relied heavily on reserve requirements and guidance to the Big Four banks as monetary policy tools. It is unclear how the same mechanisms would work for the Internet-based money market funds. A final concern relates to the Big Four banks. In recent years, they have relied on a vast reliable source of virtually free funds (in real terms) and have become comfortable making loans under the operating assumption that this would continue. But now the situation is changing rapidly.

Ceilings on bank deposits have created an opportunity for Taobao and other companies like Tencent to siphon off bank deposits from the traditional banking sector. Taobao invests in both the short-term interbank money markets and also in some of the companies that provide products and services on the Alibaba site. It contends that it has pierced the veil of asymmetric information since it knows the credit history of these borrowing companies. Meanwhile, China's citizens perceive this as a long-awaited opportunity for the small depositor to finally get a positive real return on their money holdings.

What no doubt worries regulators is that this phenomenon might just be the "tip of the iceberg." After all, if a doubling of deposit returns as described above has led to a mere shift in funds of less than 1 percent (US$50 billion out of US$ 7.6 trillion) on all bank deposits, regulators may be closing the barn door a bit too late—possibly the horse has already bolted (to the shadow banking sector). Meanwhile, estimates for Taobao's profits on its Leftover Treasure money market fund are reported to be close to US$250 million.

MACRO FINANCE INSIGHT 7.4: DEMAND FOR MONEY AS AN OPTION—THE PRECAUTIONARY MOTIVE

What are some of the motivations for individuals to hold money, an asset whose return or yield is either zero or very low? Economists such as John Maynard Keynes and James Tobin offer several theories, namely the transactions-inventory motive and the speculative motive.

The transactions-inventory motive states that individuals manage money as a company would manage an inventory: based on the volume of transactions (sales) and the opportunity cost of holding working capital, as well as the interest rate on a money market investment. Transactions occur on an ongoing basis, but income occurs at intervals. Money serves as a buffer between income and transactions, and moving wealth from less liquid assets (such as equities) into money on a continuous basis results in transaction costs.

The speculative motive states that individuals move wealth into money when bond yields are low (to avoid capital losses on bonds) and out of money into bonds when yields are high (to "speculate" on potential gains and avoid capital losses on bonds). The portfolio motive states that since the return on money is constant and capital gains and losses do not occur, money provides an anchor to one's portfolio that stabilizes its performance. While holding money has the disadvantage of a zero or low yield, that same feature yields a distinct advantage in terms of no possibility for a capital loss.* This makes money a desirable method of holding wealth. A fourth motive is the precautionary motive for holding money, which states that money serves as a form of insurance against uncertain necessary transactions that might require payment with money—such as medical emergencies.†

Expanding on and combining the speculative motive, the portfolio motive, and the precautionary motive, we can think of holding money as having an optional value. Money gives the holder the right, but not the obligation, to acquire something without incurring the transaction cost of converting from a less liquid asset (such as an equity or real property). This could occur in unfavorable circumstances, such as during a medical emergency, or an opportunity such as a product or financial instrument that randomly dips below its true (average) market value. Consider the following example and variables related to this notion of money as an option, where S_{AVG} is the market (average) nominal price for a market basket of commodities or assets, constant over time, and K is the amount of money held that gives the holder the ability (the right) to acquire K's worth of a market basket of commodities or assets whose nominal value is K. Purchase can be made up to time (T). $K = S_{AVG}$, the nominal price level.

St = The actual price of a market basket of goods or assets at time t; a variable whose mean is S_{AVG}; assumed to follow Brownian motion:‡

- σ = A measure of the volatility or dispersion of $St / St-1$, either across time or geography.
- T = The period of time for which the distribution of prices is stable with mean, S_{AVG}.
- r = The excess return on the best alternative risk-free asset above the return, if any, paid on money holdings.

Under the above framework, individuals receive payments in amounts of money (K), which on average can be used to acquire one basket of assets or commodities whose average nominal price is S_{AVG}. At time 0, the value of receiving K is equivalent to receiving one market basket. These baskets, however, randomly vary in price (St) over time. Individuals use money to take advantage of this price variation, choosing to buy when the price is at or below the average, and not to buy when the price is above the average. Figure MF7.4a shows the payoff from holding money, which is very similar to the payoff from holding a put option.**

The model above, based on option pricing theory, suggests that holding money is more valuable and therefore demanded more when:

1. "σ" the measure of volatility of price changes (inflation) or price dispersion or pricing uncertainty is higher.
2. T (the period in which money's average purchasing power is constant) or maturity is longer.
3. K / S_{AVG} the real purchasing power of money is higher (assumed to be one in the above framework).
4. The net risk-free interest rate that could be earned on the best alternative asset to money is lower.

Figure MF7.4b shows the demand for money with respect to the interest rate (traditional) and how it shifts with changes in the above parameters. Because money can be used to buy anything (unlike the traditional financial option, which is tied to only one underlying asset or commodity), the multi-asset optional value of money should be higher than that of any option on a single asset. Table MF7.4a compares CPI volatility between China and the United States and equity market volatility (SSE and NYSE). In recent years, the former is about six times more volatile and the latter about three times more volatile

Payoff from
Holding
Money

S_{AVG}

S_i

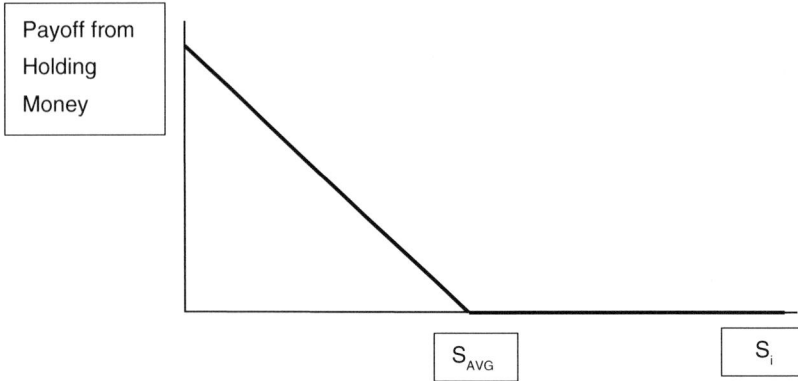

Figure MF7.4a As the random price of a market basket of goods, S_i falls below its average, S_{AVG}, the option value of money increases.

Source: Author created.

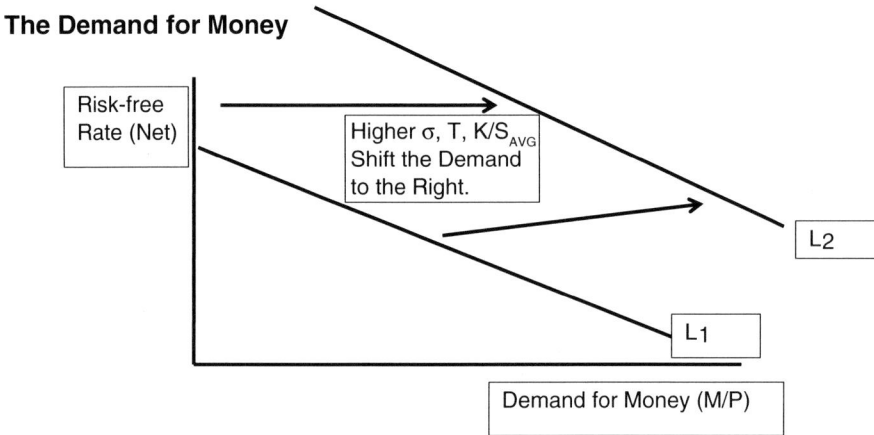

The Demand for Money

Risk-free
Rate (Net)

Higher σ, T, K/S_{AVG} Shift the Demand to the Right.

L2

L1

Demand for Money (M/P)

Figure MF7.4b Theory predicts that the higher the volatility of inflation or the return on other financial assets, the greater will be the demand for money.

Source: Author created.

Table MF7.4a Both the volatility of inflation and asset returns is higher in China than in the United States. The "option value of money" is one more reason to hold on to money in China.

	CPI Inflation and volatility 1985–2011		Equity market returns and volatility 2001–10 (Shanghai Stock Exchange and New York Stock Exchange)	
	China	*United States*	*China*	*United States*
Average percent change	6.0%	2.9%	21.8%	5.3%
Volatility or SD	6.9%	1.1%	64.9%	22.2%

Source: Author created.

in China compared to the United States. The greater volatility suggests a greater option value to holding onto money in China (when all other aspects are equal) and this is consistent with actual money holdings. Furthermore, in this light, money is not just an anchor (as in the portfolio motive), but an actual hedge in which the return varies inversely with a basket containing many assets and commodities.

*Of course, for foreigners holding U.S. currency, a capital gain or loss can take the form of an appreciation or depreciation. This is the exception that proves the point—most foreign currencies do not fully meet the threshold for being "money" in another country.

†In fact, the availability of medical insurance in China is still quite limited. Most doctors, hospitals, and clinics require payment in cash prior to treatment.

‡The index (T) could instead be measured at a point in time but be an index of geographic location where prices vary by location according to a mean, S_{AVG}. In this case, the holder of K dollars would have the option of purchasing at a particular location.

**As an alternative formulation, nominal prices (K) could be "sticky" for a time period (T), while the underlying equilibrium price (St) randomly moves above or below K. In this case, the variable of interest would be K/St. Since the purchase (sale) of money can be made at any time up to T, the option would be an American rather than European option.

Challenging Questions for China (and the Student): Chapter 7

1. Go to the Federal Reserve Economic Database (FRED) and provide three different charts depicting China's money supply, with at least one in terms of China's real money supply.
2. Explain China's relatively large holdings of M1 in terms of the transactions motive, precautionary motive, or holding of wealth motive. In terms of excess money holdings (relative to the United States), which factor appears more important?
3. Using the Walras relationship, explain the impact of an excess supply of money on other asset prices (the prices of other ways of holding wealth) in China. Be specific about which assets you are referring to.
4. Suppose new ways of holding wealth start to appear in China (as in the case of Taobao and other Internet bankers offering high-yielding money market funds).
   a. Explain the impact on bank deposits (sight deposits, for example) as Chinese citizens learn of these opportunities.
   b. Is the arrival of this alternative a good or bad thing? What might be the impact on the prices in equity or real estate markets?
   c. Why might China's Banking Regulatory Commission (CBRC) cast a wary (regulatory) eye toward such new asset classes?
5. Go the Federal Reserve Economic Database (FRED) and provide monthly seasonally adjusted and non-seasonally adjusted money supplies for China. Calculate (infer) the seasonal adjustment factor for China.
6. If China's capital markets were fully open (which they are not), explain as a hedge fund manager how you might arbitrage the seasonal difference in credit demands between China and the United States.
7. Explain the notion of "directed credit" and its relative importance in China compared to the United States as a tool of monetary policy.
8. Explain why in periods of normal economic growth, capital adequacy types of rules will allow for more rapid loan growth in China than in the United States. Explain why in times of financial turmoil, when companies are losing money, such rules may slow lending growth more dramatically in China compared to the United States.
9. In the first half of September 2014, it was estimated that China's PBC lent the five largest Chinese banks around RMB 100 billion to spur slowing economic growth.
   a. Using an economic model discussed in this chapter, explain how this policy is intended to have an impact on the real economy.
   b. Because the injection of high-powered money came not through open market operations, but through some of the other monetary policy tools discussed in this chapter (such as discount window lending), Western economists criticized the move as a step backward in terms of financial market liberalization in China. Discuss.

Notes

1. Gold has often served as money because it is difficult to counterfeit, does not corrode, is easily divisible, has a limited short-run supply and has the added advantage of easy conversion to uses in the real economy such as for specialized electronics (its malleability and conductivity are unique) and jewelry.
2. The flip-side of the liquidity definition is the impact on the price of what is being acquired. If purchases can be made of a good, service, or asset with virtually no impact on its price, we describe the associated market as being "liquid."
3. Money is generally considered "risk free" because it does not suffer from capital gains or losses like stocks and bonds. It can, however, experience a gradual loss of purchasing power through inflation. Furthermore, in an international context, whenever the exchange rate moves up or down, money experiences a capital gain or loss in global currency markets.
4. China is currently in the process of allowing for greater holdings of foreign assets by individuals.
5. This difference becomes even more dramatic if we consider that an estimated 60 percent of United States currency is held outside of the United States.
6. It is important to remember that an estimated 60 percent of the U.S. monetary base is held outside of the United States, suggesting a larger actual multiplier in the United States than in China.
7. A repurchase agreement is an agreement to sell a security now and buy it back at a fixed date at (typically) a higher price, which yields an implicit interest rate.
8. Since May 2012, China became the first foreign government allowed to acquire U.S. Treasury instruments directly from the U.S. government rather than going through one of the U.S.-based primary dealers. Given China's vast holdings of U.S. Treasuries (at least US$1 trillion), the United States agreed to allow purchases at a "wholesale" price.
9. Since the 2008 financial crisis, the Fed has transacted in a wide range of non-public financial assets of longer maturities in order to flatten the yield curve and to increase the "quantity" of money. This policy was known as quantitative easing.
10. In the United States, there are three types of discount window lending rates: the primary credit rate, secondary credit, and seasonal. The primary credit rate applies to sound financial institutions temporarily in need of funds to meet their reserve requirement. The secondary rate applies to banks which are encountering more serious liquidity needs. Seasonal borrowing applies to reserve imbalances which result from normal seasonal fluctuations, such as holiday demands. In early 2003, the Fed discontinued the use of the term discount rate in favor of these definitions.
11. Geiger (2008) notes that the governor of the PBC has a higher political ranking within the Communist Party than bank presidents in China; therefore such guidance is fully effective.
12. In the United States, reserve requirements only apply to "net transaction" accounts—liquid demand deposits. In China, reserve requirements apply to bank deposit accounts of all maturities.
13. The United States began paying interest on reserves in October 2008.
14. High reserve requirements are also a form of financial repression since reserves typically pay low interest rates. The government collects an implicit tax on these reserves, resulting from its ability to create and use money now while paying very little interest on it—a phenomenon known as "seignorage" or "the king's right to create money." Given China's high reserve requirements and relatively low interest paid on those reserves, it is likely to be a significant source of revenue to the central government.
15. The Depository Institution Deregulation and Monetary Control Act of 1980 disabled these features of Regulation Q; the Dodd–Frank Wall Street Reform Act of 2010 did the same for demand deposits.
16. China's four large state-owned banks were technically bankrupt by 2003, as a result of decades of bad policy-mandated loans. The ceilings and floors were a critical element in their return to profitability and recapitalization. Furthermore, asset management companies were created to take many of the bad loans off the books of these banks, and government assets were, in effect, substituted for the removed bad loans.
17. Conversely, lines showing a lot of random variation would reflect market forces.
18. As part of normal open market operations, central banks buy government securities. But when the central bank is independent from the central government, these purchases come typically from the general public, not directly from the government. When central banks do buy directly from the government and fully fund the central government's financing needs, we have an accommodative monetary policy. As we shall see, this can be inflationary and/or crowd out the private sector.
19. AIG, which went bankrupt in 2009, was a global insurance company based in the United States.
20. Such impacts have, on occasion, occurred, suggesting that controlling inflows and outflows is not easy.

References

Arora, Raksha. 2013. "Homeownership Soars in China." GPNS Commentary, Gallup Organization March 1.
Barboza, David. 2013. "Chinese Way of Doing Business: In Cash We Trust." *New York Times*, April 30.
———. 2014. "High-Interest Web Banks on the Rise in China." *New York Times*, March 2.

Bernanke, Ben. 2002. Speech before the National Association of Business Economists, New York, NY. October 15.

Bernanke, Ben S., and Mark Gertler. 1995. "Inside the Black Box: The Credit Channel of Monetary Policy Transmission." *Journal of Economic Perspectives* 9(4): 27–48.

British Broadcasting Corporation (BBC) World News Service. 2014. "China Injects Fresh Cash into Banks." January 20.

Chaudhury, K.N. 1990. *Asia Before Europe: Economy and Civilization of the Indian Ocean from the Rise of Islam to 1750*. Cambridge: Cambridge University Press.

Conway, Paul, Richard Herd, and Thomas Chalaux. 2010. "Reforming China's Monetary Policy Framework to Meet Domestic Objectives." OECD Economics Department Working Paper No. 822. Organisation for Economic Co-operation and Development Publishing.

Federal Reserve Bank of St. Louis (FRB of St. Louis). 2013. Home Ownership Rate for the United States. http://research.stlouisfed.org/fred2/series/USHOWN (accessed May 9, 2014).

Federal Reserve Board (FRB) of Governors and U.S. Commerce Department. 2014. Federal Reserve Statistical Release. Bureau of Economic Analysis. Flow of Funds Accounts. Table Z.1. www.federalreserve.gov/releases/z1/current/data.htm

———. 2012. *Federal Reserve Monthly Index of Industrial Production*. Washington, DC: Board of Governors of the Federal Reserve System.

Franses, Philip, and Heleen Mees. 2010. "Approximating the DGP of China's Quarterly GDP." Econometric Institute Research Papers from Erasmus University Rotterdam, Erasmus School of Economics (ESE), Econometric Institute No. EI-2010–04.

Fukumoto, Tomoyuki, Masato Yigashi, and Yasumari Inamura. 2010. "Effectiveness of Window Guidance and Financial Environment—in Light of Japan's Experience of Financial Liberalization and a Bubble Economy," Bank of Japan Review 2010-E-4.

Geiger, M. 2008. "Instruments of Monetary Policy in China and Their Effectiveness: 1994–2006." United Nations Conference on Trade and Development, Discussion Paper No. 187.

Glick, Reuven, and Michael Hutchison. 2009. "Navigating the Trilemma: Capital Flows and Monetary Policy in China." *Journal of Asian Economics* 20(3): 205–24.

Goodfriend, Marvin, and Eswar Prasad. 2006. "A Framework for Independent Monetary Policy in China." IMF Working Paper No. 06/111. Washington, DC: International Monetary Fund.

Ma, Guonan, Yan Xiandong, and Liu Xi. 2011. "China's Evolving Reserve Requirements." Bank for International Settlements (BIS) Working Paper No. 360. www.bis.org

Maurice, Jay, C. Shambaugh, and Alan M. Taylor. 2004. "The Trilemma in History: Tradeoffs among Exchange Rates, Monetary Policies, and Capital Mobility." NBER Working Paper No. 10396. Cambridge, MA: National Bureau of Economic Research.

Mehrotra, Aaron, and Jose R. Sanchez-Fung. 2010. "China's Monetary Policy and the Exchange Rate." Federal Reserve Bank of San Francisco, Working Paper Series No. 2010–19.

National Bureau of Statistics. 2012. *China Statistical Yearbook*. Beijing: China Statistics Press.

People's Bank of China. 2011. "Annual Report of the People's Bank of China Annual Report, 2010." www.pbc.gov.cn/image_public/UserFiles/english/upload/File/Annual%20Report%202010.pdf

People's Bank of China Monetary Policy Group. 2007. "China's Monetary Policy Report." February 9. http://www.pbc.gov.cn/history_file/files/att_19518_1.pdf

People's Bank of China (PBC). "China Monetary Policy Report. Various years and quarters." http://www.pbc.gov.cn/publish/english/955/2012/20120628153831855651031/20120628153831855651031

Porter, Nathan, and TengTeng Xu. 2009. *What Drives China's Interbank Market?* Washington, DC: International Monetary Fund.

Porter, Ruth D., and Judith A. Judson. 1996. "The Location of U.S. Currency: How Much Is Abroad?" *Federal Reserve Bulletin* (October): 883–903.

Shu, Chang, and Brian Ng. 2010. "Monetary Stance and Policy Objectives in China: A Narrative Approach." *China Economic Issues* 1(10): 1–40.

Tor, Maria, and Saad Sarfraz. 2013. "Largest 100 Banks in the World." *SNL Financial* (December 23).

United States Government Department of Treasury. 2012. "The Financial Crisis Response in Charts." April, 2012. Slide 15.http://www.treasury.gov/resource-center/data-chart-center/Pages/Financial-Crisis-Response-In-Charts.aspx.

Yang, Lien-Sheng. 1957. "Economic Justification for Spending—An Uncommon Idea in Traditional China." *Harvard Journal of Asiatic Studies* 20(1/2): 36–52.

8   Monetary Policy in Action

慈不掌兵，义不掌财
Neither Controlling an Army nor Controlling Finances is for the Timid

The tools mentioned in the last chapter are used to impact economic performance in a positive direction. Figure 8.1 provides the traditional mechanism by which monetary policy works—what is known as the *transmissions mechanism*. It also depicts the enhanced set of tools and goals included in China's monetary policy (note that enhancements are shaded). Clearly, the transmission mechanism in China is even more complex than the traditional one since it includes multiple tools and goals. In this chapter, we will explain why. The transmissions mechanism represents a chain of actions and outcomes, starting with the central bank trying to either stimulate or slow the economy using policy tools.

The initial policy action typically impacts bank reserves, which in turn impact the short-term interest rates that banks charge each other (the interbank market rate), as well as longer-term interest rates—and end users. China's transmission system also affects the availability of credit—influencing the size of the loan or even the possibility that a loan application is turned down. As these types of lending constraints are passed on to companies and consumers within the economy, their decisions to purchase investment goods or consumer goods are affected. This in turn impacts overall economic activity.

The transmission mechanism can be shown graphically by using the investment–savings/liquidity–money demand (IS/LM) framework found in Chapter 9 and described in Figure 8.2. The LM curve shifts to the right due to the increase in the monetary base, which creates an excess supply of money in the interbank market. Interbank rates fall as a result of the excess money supply. Investment and other interest-sensitive components of demand rise as economy-wide, long-term interest rates fall. The increased demand triggers rising output and employment on the part of firms.

Clearly, the domino-like chain of reactions triggered by monetary policy is complex, which explains why the great economist John Maynard Keynes doubted the effectiveness of monetary policy when used alone, especially during an economic downturn. As we discussed in Chapter 7, Chinese monetary authorities have added even more tools to their toolkit for conducting monetary policy. So why in China are these additional tools and interventions needed, beyond the standard ones?

Broad Goals of Monetary Policy

The People's Bank of China has, as its broad monetary policy, this goal:

> Maintain the stability of the value of the currency and thereby promote economic growth (The People's Bank of China).[1]

Meanwhile, the Federal Reserve System has the following broad goals, as set out in a 1977 amendment to the Federal Reserve Act:

> Maintain maximum sustainable output and employment and stable prices (FRB of San Francisco, 2004).

As we will discuss, this difference in goals helps to explain many of China's variations in operating policy. For example, one key difference in operating policy relates to key intermediate targets. In the United States, the emphasis on the interbank market interest rate has been much greater than in China. Or for example, a U.S. long-run target of 2-percent inflation is a stated goal; but in China, maintaining the exchange rate level has been the implicit key policy target. In the next section, we present a simple theory explaining how different end policy goals lead to divergent policy paths toward achieving those goals.

The Chinese Dilemma and the Policy Trilemma

The Basic Conflict

One simple way to think of China's reliance on a multiplicity of tools for managing monetary policy is in terms of the simple curves for the demand and supply of money. Figure 8.3, depicts a standard demand curve found in any introductory economics course with quantity on one axis and demand on the other. For any given price, P_1, there is a corresponding quantity, Q_1, determined by the shape of the demand curve (preferences). A combination of P_1 and Q_2 will simply not work unless we intervene in the market in some regulatory fashion. Even then, determining P_1 and Q_2 independently is usually only temporarily possible (in the short run). In Figure 8.4, the y-axis shows the opportunity cost of holding money—the interest rate on an asset which is less liquid than M2 (e.g., a government or corporate bond). The x-axis shows the amount of real money (defined as M2 / P, where P is a measure of the price level—e.g., the CPI index or a GDP deflator). This is a simple demand-and-supply figure, in which *Quantity,* M2/P, represents the amount of real balances supplied and demanded, while the *Price* of money is the interest rate (r) or opportunity cost of holding our wealth in a particular asset, namely, money. The higher the interest rates on alternative assets (such as treasury or corporate bonds) the lower the demand for money.

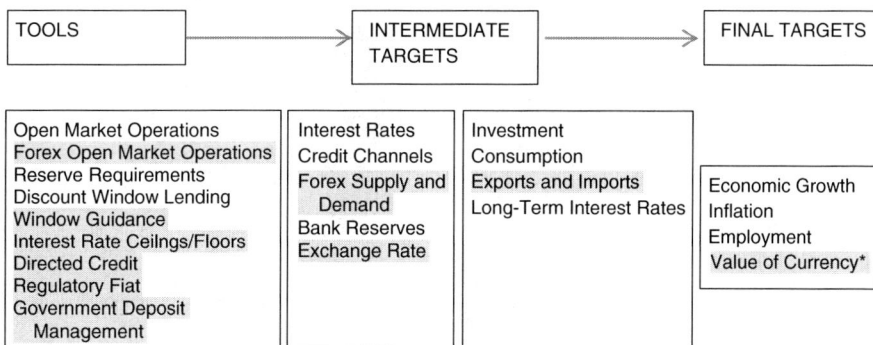

TOOLS	INTERMEDIATE TARGETS	FINAL TARGETS

Open Market Operations
Forex Open Market Operations
Reserve Requirements
Discount Window Lending
Window Guidance
Interest Rate Ceilngs/Floors
Directed Credit
Regulatory Fiat
Government Deposit
  Management
	Interest Rates
	Credit Channels
	Forex Supply and
	  Demand
	Bank Reserves
	Exchange Rate
		Investment
		Consumption
		Exports and Imports
		Long-Term Interest Rates

		Economic Growth Inflation Employment Value of Currency*

*Value of Currency is included in Final Target for China since that is included in PBC main policy mandate.

Figure 8.1 The traditional transmission mechanism in the United States and the more c
China (shaded text indicates additional tools/targets in China).

Source: Author created.

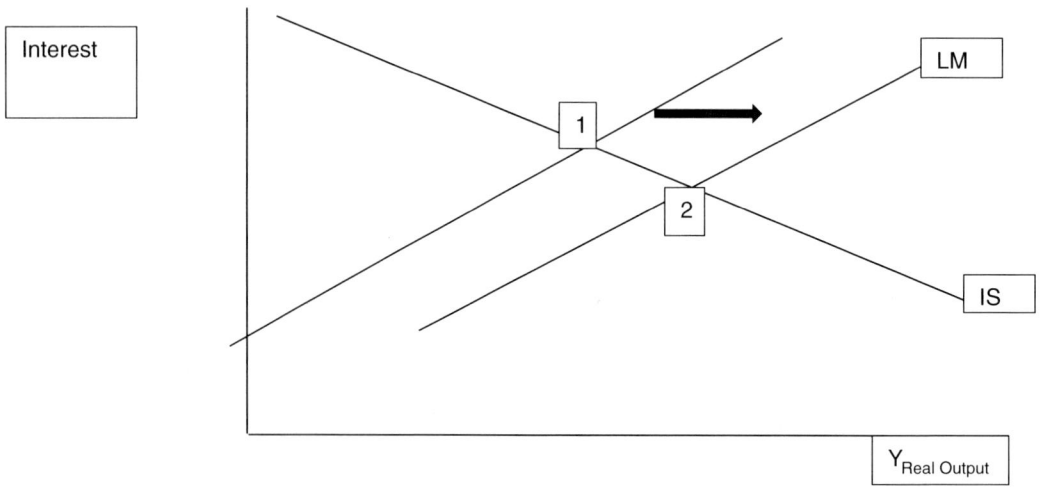

Figure 8.2 The transmissions mechanism can be represented in the standard IS/LM framework where the LM curve shifts to the right as a result of expansionary monetary policy and higher output and lower interest rates result.

Source: Author created.

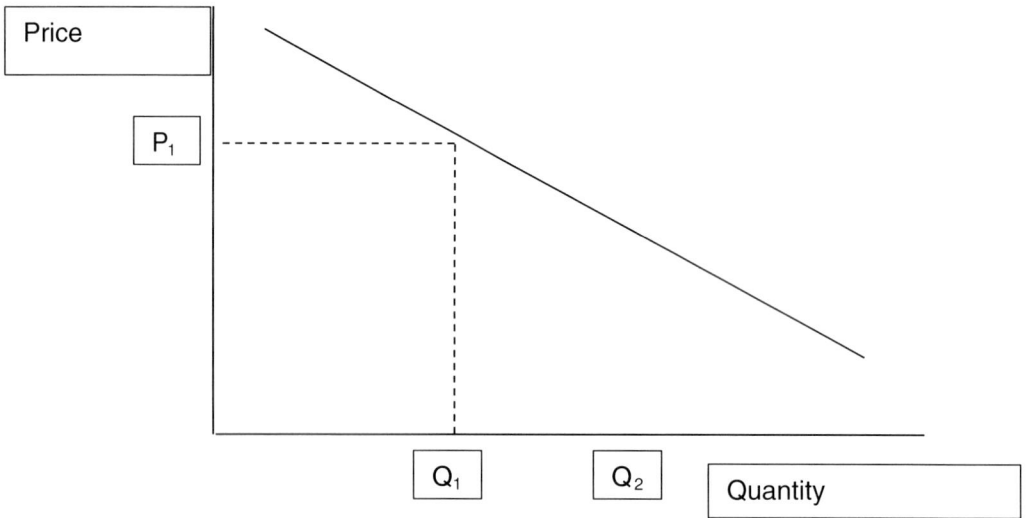

Figure 8.3 Given a demand curve and a competitive market, there is only one degree of freedom: given a price there is an implied quantity and vice versa.

Source: Author created.

The middle vertical line in the figure shows the supply of money as determined by the PBC (central bank). Since money supply is controlled by the central bank, we assume it is vertical—the supply is constant for any interest rate. If the PBC reduces the supply of money (using the tools mentioned above), the supply curve will shift to the left (as in *SS*1). On the other hand, if the PBC wishes to ease the money supply, it will shift the supply curve to the right (as in *SS*2). Each shift implies a higher or lower equilibrium interest rate, in which the demand for money equals the supply of money. The dilemma for the PBC, however, is that while it may want to move the supply of money to impact either output, exchange rates, or inflation, it may prefer a different interest rate than the implied equilibrium rate. The control of interest rates is triggered by China's desire, in recent decades, to control the exchange rate. The desire to control the amount of money and the interest rate (or, alternatively, *both* the quantity and the price) has led to the use of multiple monetary policy tools. Supplementary tools—such as interest rate ceilings, directed lending, or window guidance—are part of a package of efforts to control the two variables of money and interest. Attempting to control both can mean shortages and surpluses of money and credit; a situation in which more direct or dirigiste methods need to be employed. Most central banks only target the interbank interest rate; China targets both M2 and the interest rate (the latter in order to control exchange rates).

The PBC's efforts at controlling both the price and the quantity of money, for the sake of controlling the exchange rate, are part of broader phenomenon seen across many countries and over many centuries (Obstfeld et al., 2004). It is known in the field of international finance as the *policy trilemma*. The policy trilemma states that, while the following policy intermediate targets:

1. having a fixed exchange rate;
2. controlling monetary policy (controlling domestic interest rates);
3. allowing capital to flow in and out of the economy (capital mobility);

are often viewed as useful and desirable by policymakers, they are also in conflict with each other and are therefore inconsistent.

A fixed exchange rate means that a country's central bank can, in a sustainable way, act as a market maker in its own currency—buying and selling at a fixed (predetermined) rate. The opposite of a fixed exchange rate is an exchange rate that is determined by market forces and fluctuates continuously based on supply and demand. In normal circumstances, a floating exchange rate would not have a central bank intervening to achieve a particular exchange rate. Figure 8.5 shows that China's exchange rate roughly follows a "step" pattern, an indication that the RMB has been fixed to the U.S. dollar for prolonged periods of time. Contrast this with Figure 8.6, showing the U.S. dollar against the Swiss franc. Here, we see the erratic movements of that exchange rate—a clear indication of a floating or flexible rate moved by market forces.

Controlling monetary policy means achieving a target interest rate (such as the interbank rate) via the monetary policy tools discussed earlier. Allowing capital mobility means the regulatory permission of unfettered movement of funds into and out of the country for purposes of financial investment—also known as convertibility on the capital account. A related but different concept is current account convertibility or allowing unfettered access to foreign exchange for international trade in goods and services. While virtually all economists, especially those at international organizations such as the International Monetary Fund (IMF), have encouraged countries to adopt current account convertibility, they have been more cautious regarding capital account mobility.[2]

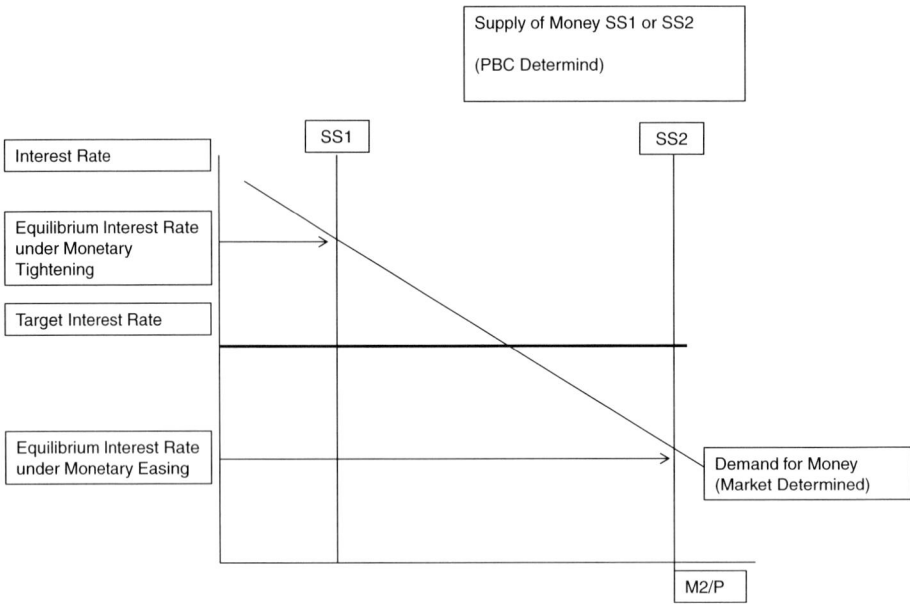

Figure 8.4 Under monetary targeting the equilibrium interest rate may not be the same as the target interest rate.
Source: Author created.

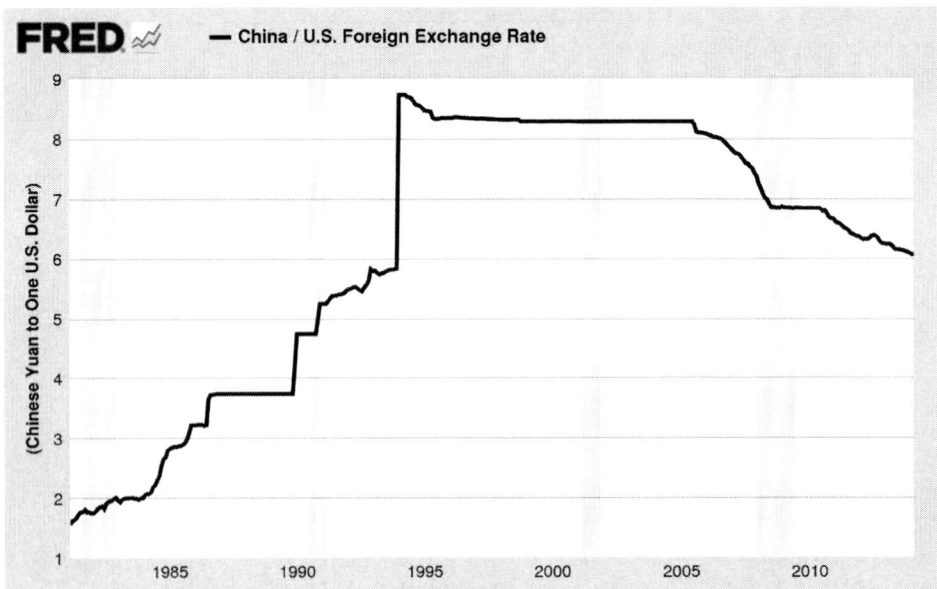

Figure 8.5 The step function profile of China's exchange rate is a clear indication that it has been fixed over prolonged periods of time.

Source: FRED, Federal Reserve Economic Data, Federal Reserve Bank of St. Louis: China/U.S. Foreign Exchange Rate; Board of Governors of the Federal Reserve System. 2014 research.stlouisfed.org
Note: Shaded areas indicate U.S. recessions.

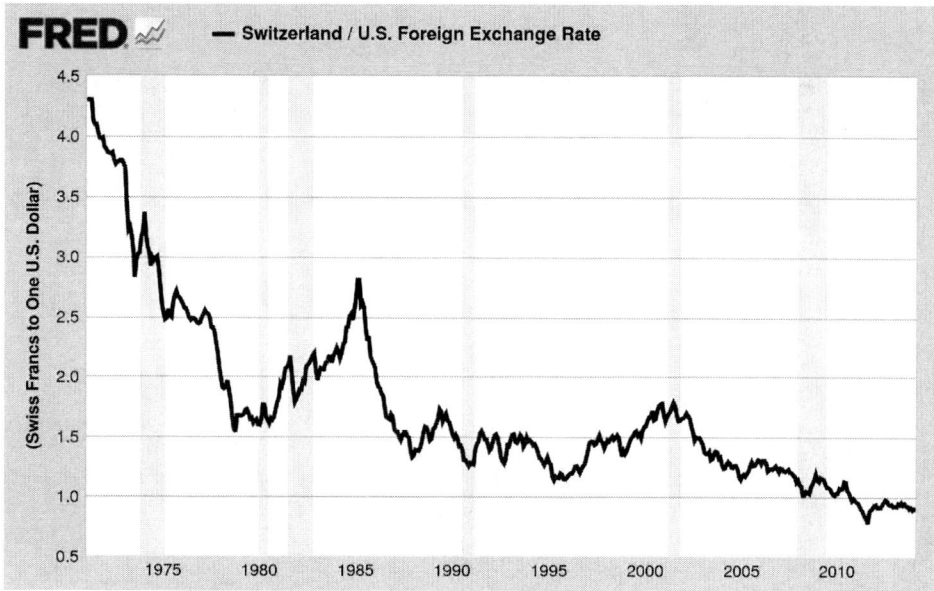

Figure 8.6 The "wiggly" random movements of the Swiss franc vs. the US dollar are a clear indication of a floating exchange rate.

Source: FRED, Federal Reserve Economic Data, Federal Reserve Bank of St. Louis: Switzerland/ U.S. Foreign Exchange Rate; Board of Governors of the Federal Reserve System. 2014 research.stlouisfed.org
Note: Shaded areas indicate U.S. recessions.

MACRO FINANCE INSIGHT 8.1: CURRENT ACCOUNT SURPLUSES AND THE POLICY TRILEMMA

Figures MF8.1a and MF8.1b show which factors have contributed to China's reserve accumulation. Non-FDI flows, representing capital mobility beyond foreign direct investment (FDI), have been mostly positive in recent years, but inbound equity flows declined post-financial crisis while external borrowing has surged.

What is obvious in Figure MF8.1a is the significance of current account items (rather than capital account items) in explaining China's foreign exchange reserve growth and, in turn, monetary growth. While the policy trilemma is expressed in the context of arbitrage opportunities and capital mobility, the reality for China is that since 2004, a controlled (fixed) exchange rate has presented a much simpler arbitrage opportunity: cheaper tradable goods for the rest of the world, particularly the United States. While China has largely controlled capital flows, the trade flow since 2001 (when China became a member of the World Trade Organization) has greatly impacted its money supply. In effect, China's example since 2004 is closer to the gold-specie mechanism.* This was arguably a self-correcting mechanism under the nineteenth-century gold standard, in which countries with trade imbalances could lose or gain gold, thereby shrinking or expanding domestic demand. This chain reaction would, either directly or via inflation, cause the country to restore balance on the current account. The gold-specie mechanism is essentially an earlier version of the policy trilemma, stating:

A country can only do two out of the following three:

1. Have a disequilibrium fixed exchange rate.
2. Control monetary policy (controlling the domestic level of interest rates).
3. Allow exports and imports to be a significant part of domestic demand.

It is the second item above in particular with which China's monetary authorities have increasingly struggled.

*For further reading on this, see: Krugman, Paul R., Maurice Obstfeld, and Marc Melitz. 2011. *International Economics (9th Edition)*. Chapters 19–20. Pearson Addison-Wesley.

China's Forex Reserves Increase and Current Account Balance

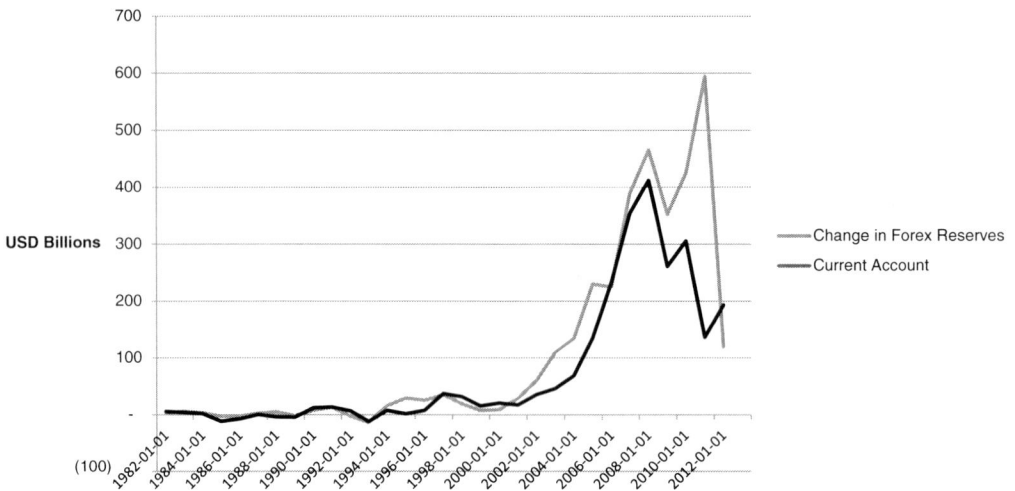

Figure MF8.1a In past decades most of China's gross foreign exchange accumulation has come from trade-related surpluses on the current account.

Sources: Author created based on data from IMF: International Financial Statistics.

China: Other Sources of Foreign Exchange*

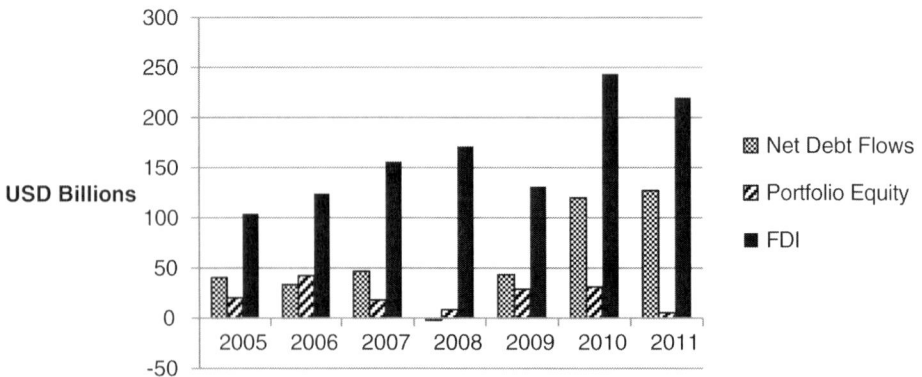

Figure MF8.1b On the capital account, non-FDI financial flows have been positive. But after the financial crisis external borrowing by China has surged while equity flows have fallen.

Source: Author created based on data from World Bank International Debt Statistics 2013.
http://data.worldbank.org/sites/default/files/ids-2013.pdf
*Some of FDI is not a source of foreign exchange; it may enter China as a physical import.

Capital Mobility and the Policy Trilemma

A benefit of greater capital mobility is either a lower cost of capital (for borrowing countries) or higher returns (for lending countries). Another benefit is global portfolio diversification. Capital account mobility may result, however, in destabilizing the real economy via disruptive capital inflows and outflows (hot money), thus countries have been encouraged to insure that their institutions and regulatory frameworks adequately support capital account convertibility. Obstfeld (1986) provides some excellent insights into the relaxation of capital controls in the post-World War II era worldwide, which has gained momentum in emerging economies over the past twenty-five years.

To understand why a country can only achieve two out of the three policy targets mentioned above, examine Figure 8.7. The y-axis measures real returns in China versus the United States, taking into account both risk-adjusted interest rates and expected appreciation or depreciation of the exchange rate. The x-axis measures the net financial capital (money) leaving or entering China. If real returns are the same, then there would be no net movement (i.e., at the intersection of the x-axis and y-axis).

If, however, real returns are higher in China (after taking into account anticipated changes in the exchange rate), then international capital would tend to flow into China. Consider this equation:

(RMB returns – US$ returns) – (Expected US$ Depreciation)

found on the y-axis of Figure 8.7—specifically, the last part of this expression "Expected US$ Depreciation." While any positive or negative number could be used, depending on a variety of

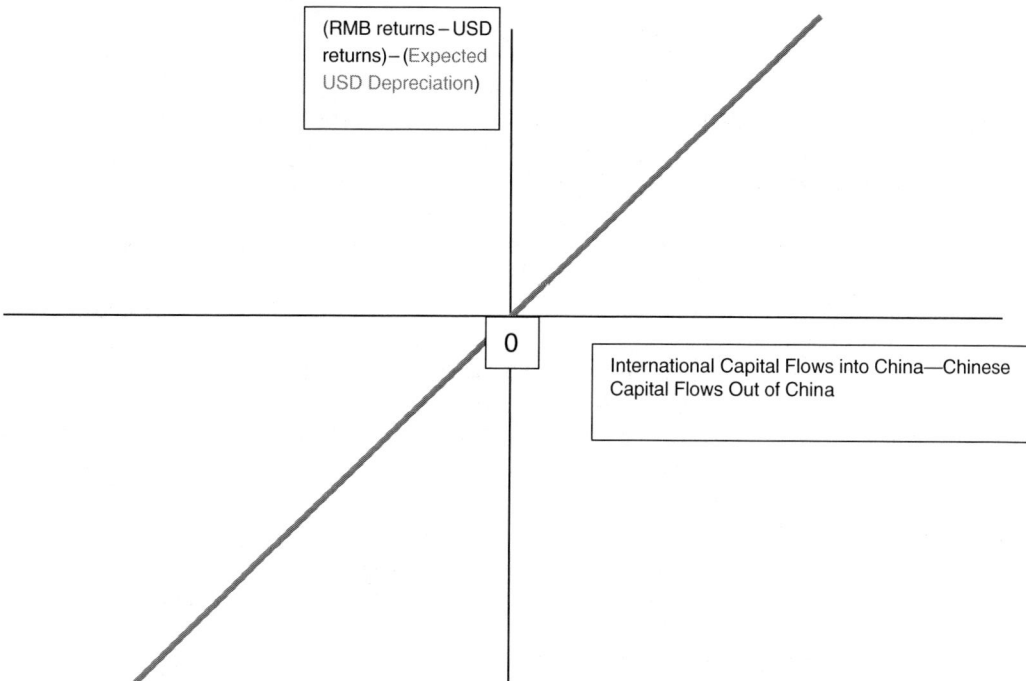

Figure 8.7 If international capital mobility were unfettered (which it is not) into and out of China, capital would flow into (out of) China if risk-adjusted returns were higher (lower) in China. Expected appreciation or depreciation of the currency determines all-in returns.

Source: Author created.

factors, let's consider two benchmark critical values. Under a stable *fixed* exchange rate regime, the value of this term would be 0 since the US$ / RMB exchange rate would not be expected to change.

Under a *floating* exchange rate regime in which there is no arbitrage possibility, we would have:

(RMB returns – US$ returns) = (Expected US$ Depreciation)

thus resulting in another benchmark value for the "Expected US$ Depreciation" term above.[3] When the interest differential equals the expected exchange rate depreciation or appreciation, this implies that (after taking into account the exchange rate) capital movements into or out of China could not yield a return exceeding the amount earned at home. Now that we understand the framework, let's consider the first benchmark case—in which the exchange rate is fixed and the expression equals 0. In this case, if the PBC raises interest rates (RMB returns) relative to US$ returns, there will be a capital inflow into China from abroad. This capital inflow will lead, in the short run, to more money circulating in China's economy (a phenomenon we will shortly explain explicitly). This, in turn, will place downward pressure on interest rates, thus reversing the initial efforts at raising them. Such pressure would persist until interest rates or returns in China were restored to their initial level. It is in this way that China could maintain a fixed exchange rate and international capital mobility but *not* maintain control over its interest rates. Other scenarios are possible but lead inevitably to the same conclusion. For example, a hike in interest rates that leads to a capital inflow could also be inflationary—making it difficult for China to remain competitive using a fixed exchange rate. In this scenario, China would have to stop fixing the exchange rate, allowing a weaker, more competitive RMB to obtain.

Now let's consider the second benchmark value: in which expected U.S. dollar depreciation equals the return differential between China- and U.S.-based assets. This would occur when the exchange rate is floating (not fixed), therefore allowing (under the trilemma) the two goals of capital mobility and control of the money supply (interest rates). In this case, if the PBC raises interest rates, any incipient capital inflow will cause the RMB to appreciate far above its fundamental long-run value, so that its eventual expected depreciation just matches the return differential initially established by the PBC. In this way, we will never stray too far (and, in fact, return very quickly) to our 0 point on the graph. Since any return difference is exactly offset by an anticipated depreciation of the RMB, the PBC can maintain that return difference (unlike in the case of fixed exchange rates) and will have benefitted from both capital mobility and ultimate control over its own interest rates. In the absence of capital mobility, a country's monetary policy can "follow the beat of its own drummer." That is to say, in the absence of the threat of capital flowing in or out of the country and "subverting" the goals of the central bank, a country can have a fixed exchange rate and also independently determine whether it wants a tight or expansionary (high interest rate or low interest rate) monetary policy. There are economies (such as those of Hong Kong or French-speaking West African countries) which choose not to have an independent monetary policy. Instead, they fix their exchange rate, remaining open to capital flows but surrendering their monetary policy to the partner country or region to which their currency is fixed (the United States, in the case of Hong Kong, the eurozone in the case of French-speaking West Africa).

China and the United States have adopted different policy goals based on the trilemma perspective. Clearly, as with all large and important economies, both countries choose to keep control over their monetary policies (independent interest rates). Over the years, however, China has maintained a fixed and then a pegged exchange rate while the U.S. currency has floated freely since 1974. The third leg of the trilemma must also be different in both countries. The United States remains one of the most open economies with respect to capital flows, while China has attempted to maintain strict control over capital flows. It is clear that, as China's government moves toward greater capital account liberalization (more capital mobility), it must simultaneously allow greater flexibility in its exchange rate.

How does the above discussion pertain to China's need to use a much wider range of monetary policy tools than does the rest of the world? China's efforts to control capital inflows and outflows have become increasingly difficult, due to a number of factors. The increasing attractiveness of investing in China, based on its comparative advantage in the production of labor-intensive goods and the broader range of assets presented by domestic financial market liberalization, makes outside investors increasingly eager to enter China's financial markets. Furthermore, the integration of Hong Kong into China since 1997 has opened additional avenues for funds to flow in and out of China. (Note that Hong Kong's capital markets are ranked among the most open in the world.) China faces increasing challenges in its efforts at working its way around the policy trilemma. In short, fixing interest rates and the exchange rate when capital mobility is ever-growing is becoming more and more difficult. Chinese authorities have as a result evolved a broader array of monetary policy tools to temporarily offset the gravity-like force of the policy trilemma.

Sterilization and the Monetary Authority's Balance Sheet

Sterilization refers to the efforts of central banks to offset the impact of foreign exchange inflows on the domestic money supply using monetary tools such as open market operations. For example, if China receives substantial inflows of foreign exchange via exports, the financial system will exchange domestic currency for the foreign exchange receipts deposited by exporters.[4] That exchange, in turn, will increase the supply of money. To offset that increase, the PBC could either sell central bank bills or raise the reserve requirement of banks, thus offsetting the initial increase. To better understand this process, let's examine basic balance sheets of the PBC and the Fed in recent years.

Tables 8.1 and 8.2 show recent balance sheets for each institution. Central bank assets typically comprise the government obligations held by the bank and the foreign exchange cash or securities held by the bank. The central bank's liabilities are domestic currency which it issues, and the deposits of financial institutions held at the central bank as either required or excess reserves. Between 2009 and 2010, China saw both a substantial increase in foreign assets (in absolute terms) and a substantial increase in financial institution deposits (reserves). These two phenomena are linked under the concept of sterilization. Because the banking system acquires substantial amounts of foreign exchange—which ultimately filter up to the central bank as an asset—the PBC has attempted to offset the monetary impact (the liability side of the PBC Balance Sheet or currency) by enlarging an alternative liability, financial institution deposits at the PBC (reserves). Notwithstanding that effort, we still see a substantial increase in currency (around 17 percent) between 2009 and 2010. Undoubtedly, this is related to China's concomitant higher inflation.

Table 8.1 Unlike the FED, the PBC holds substantial foreign exchange reserve assets as the basis for its money supply.

People's Bank of China (PBC) Balance Sheet	2011*	2012*	% Increase (year over year)	Absolute Change (year to year)
Total assets	280,978	294,537	4.83%	13,559
Foreign assets	232,389	236,670	1.84%	4,281
Loans to the government	15,400	15,314	−0.56%	−86
Other assets	33,189	42,553	28.21%	9,364
Total liabilities and owner's equity	280,978	294,537	4.83%	13,559
Currency	55,850	60,646	8.59%	4,796
Deposits of financial institutions	168,792	191,699	13.57%	22,907
Other liabilities and owner's equity	56,336	42,192	−25.11%	−14,144

Source: PBC China Monetary Policy Report.
*Unit = 100 million RMB.

Table 8.2 As a result of the financial crisis, by 2009 the Federal Reserve's "Other Assets" ballooned as the FED purchased various private bank assets to support the financial system.

Federal Reserve System (FED) Balance Sheet	2009*	2010*	% Increase (year over year)	Actual Increase (year to year)
Total assets	2,238,971	2,430,890	8.6%	191,919
Foreign assets	25,272	26,049	3.1%	777
Treasury securities	776,588	1,021,493	31.5%	244,905
Other assets	1,437,111	1,383,348	−3.7%	−53,763
Total liabilities and owner's equity	2,238,971	2,430,890	8.6%	191,919
Currency	887,846	941,561	6.1%	53,715
Deposits of financial institutions	976,988	968,052	−0.9%	−8,936
Other liabilities and owner's equity	374,137	521,277	39.3%	147,140

Source: Federal Reserve Annual Report.
*Unit = millions of US$.

Case Study 8.1: Walras's Law, the Flow of Funds, and Missing Assets and Wealth

As we have seen in the last chapter, Walras's Law establishes a correspondence (identity) between total wealth and the financial instruments that lay claim to that wealth. The relationship can be described as:

Wealth = Cash + Bank Deposits + Bonds + Equity + Real Estate + Other Assets

The right-hand side of the equation above includes a much more extensive list of financial instruments in the United States than in China, encompassing everything from mortgage-backed securities to shares in a hedge fund. The quantities of the assets supplied often depend not only on real underlying wealth creation (such as via a newly invented medicine) and the need to hedge against risk, but also on the legal and regulatory structures that promote their development. After all, it is quite easy to create a piece of paper and define it as a claim on wealth. The critical question usually relates to the demand for these assets—whether other investors are willing to trade a valuable financial asset (such as money or a Treasury bill) for that financial asset. The presence (or absence) of demand has a direct impact on whether the other asset actually has value.

Walras's Law also holds in terms of changes:

$$\Delta\text{Wealth} = \Delta\text{Cash} + \Delta\text{BankDeposits} + \Delta\text{Equity} + \Delta\text{RealEstate} + \Delta\text{Other Assets}$$

Where the left-hand side of the equation, i.e., ΔWealth, corresponds to Savings (broadly defined to include the private and public sectors). We then recall from Chapter 2:

Savings = Current Account Balance + Investment

Combining the two above, we can say:

Savings = Current Account Balance + Investment
= ΔCash + ΔBank Deposits + ΔEquity + ΔReal Estate + ΔOther Assets

The above is known as the "flow of funds" and is actually calculated by China and the United States as part of their measurements of output and the financial sector.

Lin and Schramm (2009) examine China's flow of funds in the fashion described above and find that up to one-third of China's vast national savings is unaccounted for by any financial instrument. That is, a

Total Financial Assets to GDP United States

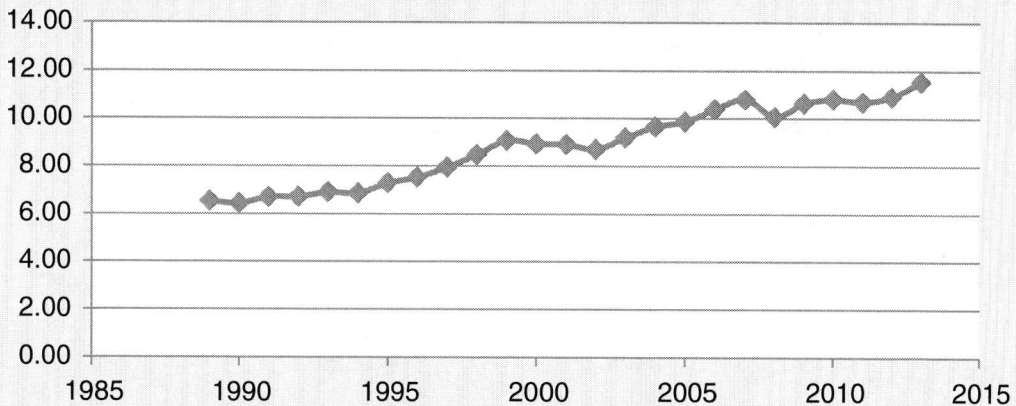

Figure CS8.1a Total Financial Assets have increased in value relative to GDP over the past several decades in the United States.

Source: Author Created based on data from Federal Reserve Board of Governors:
http://www.federalreserve.gov/datadownload/Download.aspx?rel=Z1&series=5ebbabcc600e8b3f55f4a3710f4 14aa2&lastObs =25&from=&to=&filetype=csv&label=include&layout=seriesrow&type=package; and Nominal GDP data from FRED.

large portion of China's savings is used to finance investments with no paper trail. This provides just one measure of the "gray market" or shadow banking sector which has become of even greater importance since the publication of their research. No doubt, much of this gray market reflects investment by small- and medium-sized enterprises as well as relationship or *guanxi* lending at the local level. Whether this is a good or bad thing for China's economic development is a question requiring further research. What is clear is that transparency and information are the "coin of the realm" in finance. The more Chinese authorities can work toward achieving financial transparency, the better.

Once again, the United States comes out at the other end of the spectrum. If the Chinese financial system seems "underidentified" with financial assets, the U.S. financial system appears "overidentified." Figure CS8.1a shows that the total nominal value of financial assets in the United States nearly doubled between 1989 and 2013 relative to GDP. Many of these securities were likely redundant in terms of hedging benefits, but, what is worse, were excessively valued in terms of the underlying real asset or income stream supporting their existence. Furthermore, the crisis revealed that the underlying asset itself (especially in real estate and individual income streams) was often overvalued, creating a false portrayal of total wealth.

We take this opportunity to examine other aspects of the two countries' balance sheets. The most dramatic difference is in the composition of assets; for China, approximately 80 percent of PBC assets represent foreign currency, while for the United States, the corresponding figure is 1 percent. Of course, this also reflects the PBC's past policy (created under a surrender requirement regime) of accumulating foreign exchange. In the United States, financial institutions, corporations, and individuals are allowed to hold onto foreign exchange—it becomes part of the private sector's assets.

In the United States, close to 42 percent of the Fed's assets are derived from its holdings of Treasury securities—a low figure by U.S. historical standards, due to the Fed's emergency increase in financial institution and other private sector assets following the financial crisis. Rather surprisingly, most of China's monetary base (the liabilities side) entered the economy via the acquisition of foreign currency holdings—most of which is still held in U.S. Treasury securities. In the United States, most currency has entered the economy via the Fed acquiring Treasury securities as well. In this peculiar way, the PBC and the Fed share something in common—a preference for holding U.S. Treasury securities as a way of injecting currency into their economies. But both countries have recently reduced their holdings of these securities on a relative basis—in China, as a portfolio preference; in the United States, in response to the improving economy. Interestingly, if we assume that 60 percent of the PBC's foreign reserves are held in U.S. treasuries; the PBC would actually hold more U.S. treasuries than the Fed (approximately US$1.3 trillion compared to US$1 trillion) as the asset base for each country's monetary base!

Case Study 8.2: Are China's Holdings of U.S. Dollars Profitable?

We estimate that China holds at least US$1.3 trillion in U.S. Treasury instruments. During 2011, those instruments paid negligible amounts for shorter maturities and up to 3.5 percent for a ten-year treasury bond. Let us assume an average US$ return of around 2 percent. During 2011, the US$ depreciated against the RMB by about 5 percent, suggesting a loss to China in RMB terms of around −3 percent (2 percent minus 5 percent). An alternative measure is calculated using the actual purchasing power in U.S. dollar terms. In 2011, U.S. inflation was around 3 percent. Weighing this against a return of 2 percent on treasury instruments, we still come up with a real loss in purchasing power from dollar holdings of about 1 percent. Measuring the return in euro terms presents a brighter picture because the US$ appreciated against the euro by about 1.5 percent. Combined with a return on treasuries of about 2 percent, the nominal yield for dollar holdings would be about 3.5 percent. European inflation for the year was 2.7 percent. Thus, in terms of real purchasing power in the eurozone, China's holdings of U.S. dollars yielded a return of close to 1 percent. Overall though, it appears that China's earnings on its U.S. dollar holdings have been disappointing. In terms of the PBC's stand-alone income statement (in which interest must be paid on bank reserves and discounted bills) the picture is even bleaker.

Recent Monetary Policy Developments

For both countries, the first decade of the millennium presented a number of unprecedented challenges regarding monetary policy. In China, the goal of maintaining a stable currency in the face of ever-growing capital mobility and large current account surpluses created tradeoffs for inflation and employment. In the United States, the 2008 financial crisis resulted in an epic expansion of the Fed's balance sheet in an effort to avert another Great Depression. Frequent changes in reserve requirements in China and quantitative easing in the United States became the "new normal" in any discussion of monetary policy.

Figures 8.8, 8.9, and 8.10 provide a quick snapshot of China's monetary policy over the past decade. Specifically, we see substantial loosening of monetary policy—either lower rates (market-based or regulatory), or increases in the money supply, or (as discussed above) changes in reserve requirements in response to exogenous economic events. In the post-Asian Financial Crisis of 1997–98, we saw a loosening of monetary policy. In the period building up to the 2008 financial crisis, in which China experienced a surge in prices and economic growth, we saw substantial increases in reserve requirements. Following that crisis, we see a surge in the money supply as the PBC moved to stimulate the economy.

Reserve requirement ratio in China

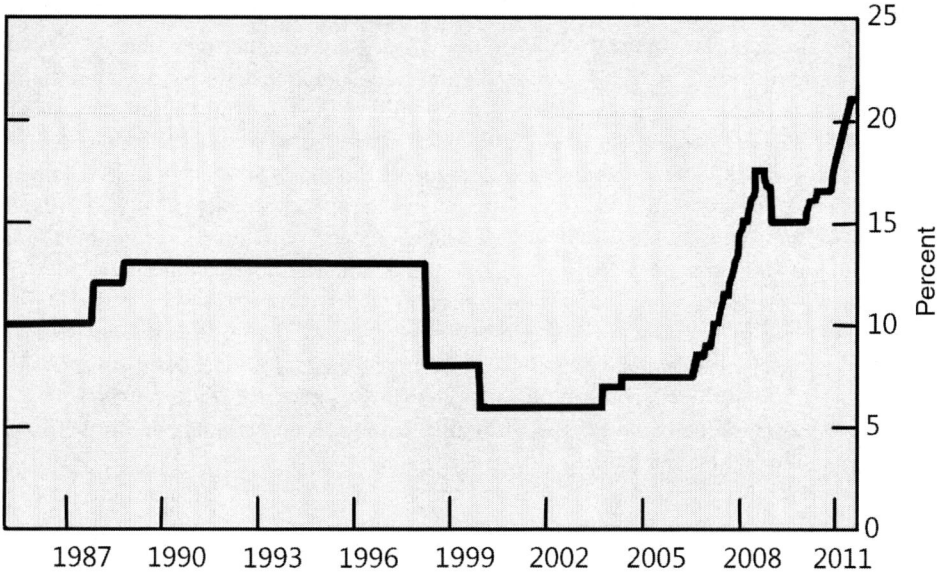

Figure 8.8 China (unlike the United States) has adjusted its reserve ratio frequently as a tool of monetary policy.

Source: PBC Annual Reports.

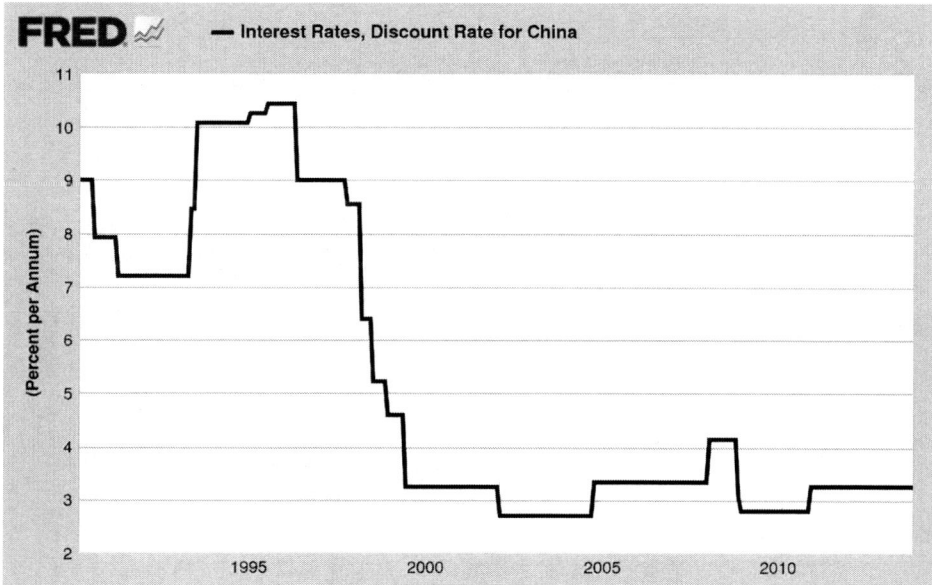

Figure 8.9 Unlike the United States, discount window borrowing occurs frequently in China. Rate changes (indicated below) are therefore an important tool.

Source: FRED, Federal Reserve Economic Data, Federal Reserve Bank of St. Louis: Interest Rates, Discount Rate for China; International Monetary Fund. 2014 research.stlouisfed.org

Figure 8.10 gives a measure of the dramatic increase in the growth of M2 during periods of slower industrial growth in China. The figure shows (in the shaded areas) both the 2001 U.S. recession and the 2008 financial crisis.[5] With high average growth rates, the figure suggests that, in the last decade, monetary policy in China was more a response to external shocks rather than internal ones. In the coming decades, as long-term growth slows and domestic consumption demand becomes a significant factor, we will no doubt see the internal business cycle influencing monetary policy more heavily.

To combat rising concerns over inflation in the second half of 2010, the PBC slowed monetary growth. The central bank then reversed its monetary policy in the second half of 2011, in response to concerns over the impact of an economic slowdown in Europe, especially in Italy, Greece, Spain, and Portugal. We gain an even clearer picture of China's monetary policy by examining the movements in reserve requirements in Figure 8.8. Given the policy trilemma, maintaining the exchange rate, economic growth, and controlling inflation present some serious policy tradeoffs. During the last decade, the order of importance for the trio of goals matches that of the previous sentence, in which control of inflation is decidedly the lowest priority, at least for now. Early estimates of a Taylor rule (Taylor, 1993) for China confirm this, though this research needs to be updated. The *Taylor rule* specifies how central banks respond to deviations from full employment and inflation targets via changes in interbank interest rates.

Given the myriad of tools used by the PBC to implement policy, it is often difficult to focus on one metric as a good measure of China's policy stance. Instead, Shu and Ng (2010) take a "narrative approach" by examining quarterly reports and press announcements from the PBC. They come up with a broad spectrum of measures ranging from "strong tightening" to "strong loosening." What is clear from this and other studies is that Chinese authorities do indeed respond (i.e., have a monetary "reaction") to innovations in real economic growth and prices. Most scholars find that monetary policy in China responds more, and in the expected direction, to economic growth rather than inflation targets. In other words, monetary policy is tightened when growth rises above long-term averages

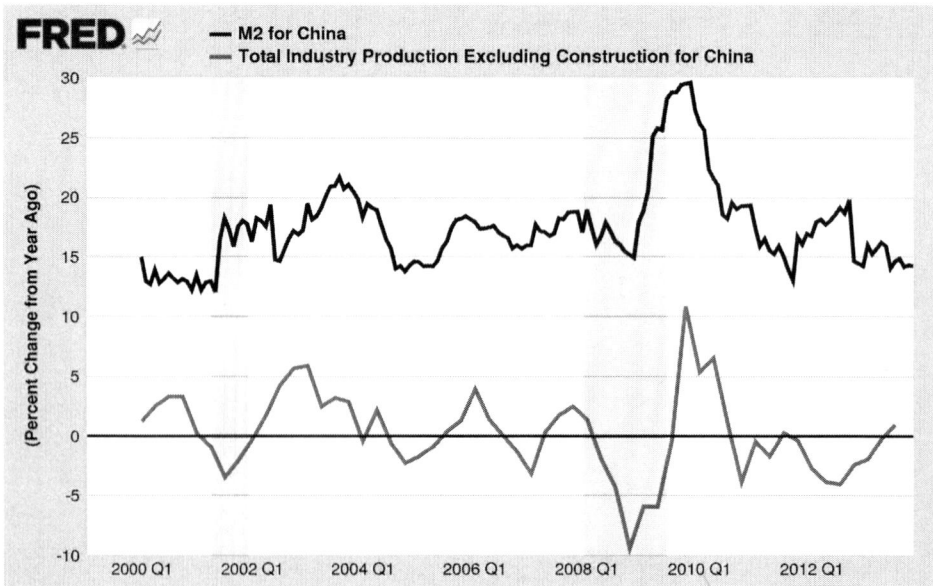

Figure 8.10 It appears that monetary growth and industrial production in China respond very much to recessions in the United States.

Source: FRED, Federal Reserve Economic Data, Federal Reserve Bank of St. Louis: M2 for China, Total Industry Production Excluding Construction for China. 2014 research.stlouisfed.org
Note: Shaded areas indicate U.S. recessions.

and loosened when it falls below the trend. The response to inflation is generally weaker; in fact, Mehrotra and Sánchez-Fung (2010) find that it may even be pro-cyclical, that is, expansionary in periods of high inflation or vice versa.[6]

Table 8.3 presents the extraordinary efforts of the Fed to expand money and credit during the financial crisis by launching eleven different programs beyond the standard methods of open market operations and discount window lending. Figure 8.11 shows the unprecedented nearly fivefold increase of the monetary base as the financial crisis unfolded in 2008–09. What the Fed and other central banks engaged in during this period was called "quantitative easing" (BBC, 2013). Unlike traditional monetary easing in normal times, in which the Fed attempts to simply lower the federal funds rate through open market operations, quantitative easing attempts to create a continuous excess supply of money in financial markets and a reduction in some financial assets (including troubled assets such as mortgage-backed securities). The Fed accomplishes this by creating large amounts of money in the form of the monetary base, then uses these funds to purchase excess financial assets. The hope is that the new money will be lent, boosting investment in property, plants and equipment, and housing and consumption.[7]

As we saw in Figure 8.1, the traditional transmission mechanism relies on a complex chain reaction of events to ultimately impact output and employment. If any link in the chain is broken, the transmission of monetary policy will be weakened. The 2008–09 financial crisis verified the existence of what Keynes called a "liquidity trap," or an important break in the link. In that situation, interest rates cannot be pushed any lower either because the demand for money was infinitely elastic or because nominal rates were at 0 (the "zero lower bound"). Individuals and corporations, out of fear caused by the risky environment, were more than eager to hold their wealth in money or Treasury bills at interest rates as low as 0, or even negative real rates. Since increasing the money supply was met by the eager demand for money, its price (the interest rate) could not fall and the transmission mechanism would be off to a bad start.

One simple way to represent the response to the failure of the transmission mechanism—quantitative easing—is via the quantity theory of money. Recall that velocity is the average number of times the money supply (M) circulates in the economy in a certain year. P and Q represent the price level and real output, respectively. If velocity is assumed to be constant, we have:

$$M \times V = P \times Q$$

where the right-hand side of the equation represents the overall price level times Q, real output. $P \times Q$ represents nominal GDP. To the extent that monetary policy affects the availability of credit, M shifts up or down, in turn impacting either prices or real output. The goal of "quantitative easing" is to bypass a faulty "transmission mechanism" by increasing the monetary base. The results is an increase in the overall money supply, which spills over directly into demand in the economy. In terms of the IS/LM framework, the role of money is no longer limited to the LM curve. Rather, in the "quantitative easing" variation of the IS/LM framework, consumption becomes a direct function of money as does investment. Formally:

$$C = f(M / P)$$
$$I = f(M / P)$$

An increase in the money supply not only shifts the LM curve to the right but influences the IS curve itself. Figure 8.12 illustrates a liquidity trap, in which the IS shifts to the right due to an increase in the money supply and the LM "shifts into itself" due to an infinitely elastic demand for money (liquidity trap).

In fact, the above IS/LM framework not only provides a more suitable description of the FED's activities during a financial crisis, but may also be a way of viewing how monetary policy works in China. Since interest rates in China still represent a mix of government intervention and market

Table 8.3 The FED also used an entirely new set of tools during the financial crisis of 2008.
Forms of Federal Reserve Lending

	Regular OMOs	Discount Window[1]	Term Discount Window Program (announced August 17, 2007)	Term Auction Facility (announced December 12, 2007)	Primary Dealer Credit Facility (announced March 16, 2008)[2]	Transitional Credit Extensions (announced September 21, 2008)
What are they borrowing?	Funds	Funds	Funds	Funds	Funds	Funds
What collateral can be pledged?	U.S. Treasuries, agencies, agency MBS	Full range of Discount Window collateral	Full range of Discount Window collateral	Full range of Discount Window collateral	Full range of tri-party repo system collateral	Full range of Discount Window collateral and tri-party repo system collateral
Is there a reserve impact?	Yes	Yes	Yes	Yes	Yes	Yes
What is the term of loan?	Typically, term is overnight-14 days	Typically overnight, but up to several weeks	Up to 90 days	28 days or 84 days	Overnight	Overnight
Is prepayment allowed if term is greater than overnight?	No	Yes	Yes	No	N/A	N/A
Which Reserve Banks conduct operations?	FRBNY	All	All	All	FRBNY	FRBNY
How frequently is the program accessed?	Typically once or more daily	As requested (standing facility)	As requested (standing facility)	Every other week, or as necessary	As requested (standing facility)	As requested (standing facility)
Where are statistics reported publicly?	Temporary OMO activity	H.4.1—Factors Affecting Reserve Balances	H.4.1—Factors Affecting Reserve Balances	TAF activity[1]	H.4.1—Factors Affecting Reserve Balances	H.4.1—Factors Affecting Reserve Balances

Source: Federal Reserve Bulletin.

Reciprocal Currency Arrangements (first announced December 12, 2007)[3]	Securities Lending	Term Securities Lending Facility (announced March 11, 2008)[2]	ABCP Money Market Fund Liquidity Facility (announced September 19, 2008)[2]	Commercial Paper Funding Facility (announced October 7, 2008)[2]	Money Market Investing Funding Facility (announced October 21, 2008)[4]	Term Asset-Backed Securities Loan Facility[5] (announced November 25, 2008)
U.S. Dollars	U.S. Treasuries	U.S. Treasuries	Funds	Funds	Funds and subordinated note	Funds
Central banks pledge foreign currency and lend against eligible collateral in their jurisdiction	U.S. Treasuries	U.S. Treasuries, agencies, agency MBS, and all investment grade debt securities	First-tier ABCP	Newly issued 3-month unsecured and asset-backed CP from eligible U.S. issuers	U.S. dollar-denominated certificates of deposit, bank notes and commercial paper issued by highly rated financial institutions	Recently originated U.S. dollar-denominated AAA, ABS, CMBS, and legacy CMBS
Yes	No (loans are bond-for-bond)	No (loans are bond-for-bond)	Yes	Yes	Yes	Yes
Overnight to 3 months	Overnight	28 days	ABCP maturity date (270-day maximum)	3 months	N/A	3 or 5 years
Yes	N/A	No	No	N/A	N/A	Yes
FRBNY	FRBNY	FRBNY	FRB Boston	FRBNY	FRBNY	FRBNY
Typcally on schedule with FRBNY TAF auctions or as requested by central banks	Daily	Every 4 weeks	As requested (standing facility)	As requested (standing facility)	As requested (standing facility)	Twice a month, alternation between non-mortgage-backed ABS and CMBS collateral type
H.4.1—Factors Affecting Reserve Balances	Securities lending activity	Term securities lending facility activity	H.4.1—Factors Affecting Reserve Balances	H.4.1—Factors Affecting Reserve Balances	H.4.1—Factors Affecting Reserve Balances	TALF activity

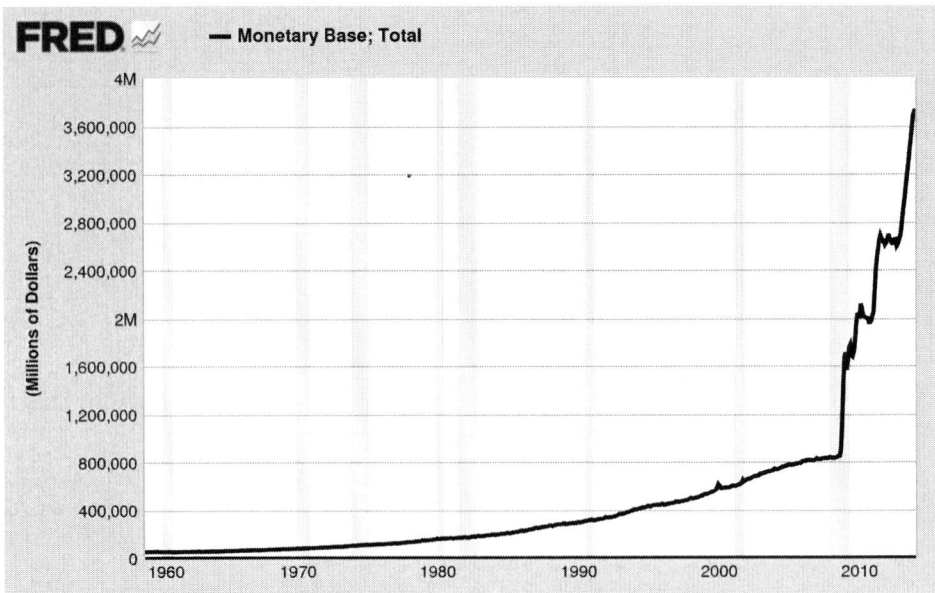

Figure 8.11 The Federal Reserve's response in the financial crisis included a dramatic increase in the monetary base—a "quantitative easing" policy.

Source: FRED, Federal Reserve Economic Data, Federal Reserve Bank of St. Louis: Monetary Base; Total; Board of Governors of the Federal Reserve System. 2014 research.stlouisfed.org
Note: Shaded areas indicate U.S. recessions.

determination, the direct impact of the availability of money and credit plays a more important role in China in terms of monetary policy. In this sense, monetary policy as undertaken in China—via window guidance, credit directives, and interest ceilings and floors—functions through direct shifts in the IS curve. In China, the complicated path of the LM curve shifting via the transmissions mechanism is still a "work in progress." Meanwhile, in the United States by 2011, credit markets were returning to the normal traditional IS/LM mode in which the transmissions mechanism could actually work.

Case Study 8.3: China's Capital Structure

Capital structure relates to how a company chooses to finance itself—particularly the choice made between debt and equity as sources of funds. Two competing theories on capital structure in corporate finance are the pecking order theory (Myers and Majluf, 1984) and the tradeoff theory (Kraus and Litzenberger, 1973). Pecking order posits that, in the presence of asymmetric information, firms rely on internal funds before external funds, and debt before equity. This order will be the least expensive since outside investors will charge a premium for funds when they have less information than inside shareholders. Furthermore, debt holders need less information about the binomial possibility of payment or default compared to equity investors' valuation concerns across an infinite spectrum of values. The tradeoff theory weighs the tax benefits of more debt versus the incremental cost of risking bankruptcy when more debt is incurred.

For traditional corporate finance then, the issues facing an individual company and its investors (in terms of capital structure) are information availability, costs of different types of capital, tax rates, and the costs and likelihood of bankruptcy. From a country's perspective, such as China's, we need to qualify

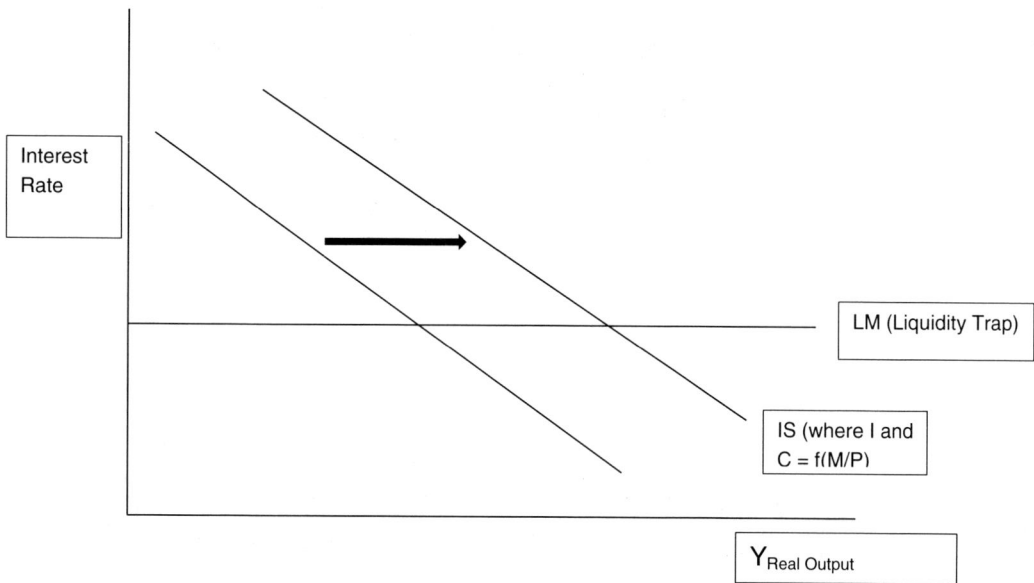

Figure 8.12 When the demand for liquidity (money) is infinitely elastic, expanding the money supply is ineffective—money holdings simply increase (a "money under the mattress" type story). This is also known as the "zero lower bound" since the nominal interest rate cannot fall below zero; monetary stimulus bumps up against a constraint. In such situations, shifting the IS curve to the right is the best hope—and the availability of additional liquidity and credit may help in this process.

Source: Author created.

or modify the significance of some of these factors. Certainly, while increased debt and bankruptcy are of concern, the effect may be reduced in the presence of state-owned enterprises where the government may readily step in to rescue the firm—a problem of moral hazard.* Conversely, while a company may prefer the deductibility of interest expenses on debt, countries tend to prefer more tax revenues (and in turn, less debt). If the state can receive corporate net income via interest paid to state-owned banks, that effect is neutralized.

China's production sector has lagged and continues to lag behind the developed world in terms of transparency, that is, the availability of symmetric information shared between the enterprise and investors. At both the national and corporate level, the goal is an efficient and low cost of capital. In the face of asymmetric information, achieving a low cost of capital can be difficult. China (as well as many emerging markets around the world) has found that internal finance along with bank finance are the most efficient ways of keeping capital costs low (and investment high). Sources of finance that better pierce the veil of asymmetric information include "arms around" finance (such as that found in family owned businesses), wholly owned foreign enterprises with retained earnings, and internal pension funds or banks. "Arm's length" investors (such as outside equity investors or bond holders in public markets) remain cautious about providing finance when they do not have as much information as do company insiders.

But beyond the variables for the corporation mentioned above, in China, there are other significant factors of concern at the national/government level: (1) Control of the enterprise, for example, tends to be easier to achieve via "arms around" financial structures. This becomes even more significant when the investors are local rather than foreign, that is, a domestic state-owned bank as compared to a wholly foreign-owned enterprise (WOFE); (2) Privatization (or outside equity participation) of enterprises is a relaxation of control and ideally a move to greater efficiency; and (3) Technology transfer becomes much more important when considering capital structure. For example, a foreign joint venture with equity participation is much more likely to inbound transfer new foreign technologies than is, say, a firm whose only source of finance is a state-owned bank.

China has moved in stages from state investment (thus the notion of an SOE) in the 1950–80s, to state-owned bank finance in the 1980s, to stock market finance in the 1990s, to bond finance after 2000. Clearly, these stages represent China's efforts to "triangulate" in an optimum way across the traditional corporate finance capital structure factors and the other macro-based factors such as control, privatization, and technology transfer.

*This occurred frequently in China, particularly in the 1990s.

Summary

China's monetary policy remains complex, but is evolving toward simpler, market-based mechanisms. Given China's size and its key trading and international financial relationships with the rest of the world, the path China takes in this regard is of global importance. China has, in recent decades, focused on controlling (targeting) the money supply as its key tool in targeting output, prices, and the exchange rate. China's recent historical focus on trade and the exchange rate and its ongoing focus on economic growth have made the nation reliant on a wider range of other tools and controls (both market and non-market based).

In recent years, however, open market operations involving the outright sale of central bank bills and government debt instruments (so as to impact overnight rates) have begun playing a more important role. In turn, China is relying more on the transmissions mechanism (as employed in advanced economies) for impacting final economic targets. Empirical evidence suggests that this more recent effort is impacting intermediate and long-term interest rates (Conway et al., 2010). Both the structure of the real economy and the still underdeveloped financial system, however, remain a hindrance to the new approach significantly impacting the real economy.

In terms of policy response, PBC tends to react more to output gaps than to contemporaneous inflation. It also appears that monetary policy responds more to shocks from outside of China (the United States in particular) than from inside of China. This situation is likely to change as investment becomes more susceptible to market forces within China. There is no evidence that monetary policy responds to changes in the exchange rate; the latter point is consistent with a fixed exchange rate system and, at least until recently, the ability of the Chinese authorities to control international capital flows.

Challenging Questions for China (and the Student): Chapter 8

1. Go the Federal Reserve Economic Database (FRED) and compare the Lending–Deposit spread with the ninety-day interbank interest rate (produce a graph to show the comparison). Explain why one is highly volatile and the other is relatively stable (period to period).
2. What is the main difference between the stated goals of the People's Bank of China (PBC) and the Federal Reserve Bank of the United States (the Fed).
3. Why does China's PBC use so many tools to control the financial system compared to the Fed?
4. Eventually if China is to have a high degree of international capital mobility, explain what it will have to give up in terms of a key policy variable. Explain why.
5. Go to the IMF's Annual Report on Exchange Arrangements and Exchange Restrictions (2013) (www.imf.org/external/pubs/nft/2013/areaers/ar2013.pdf) and identify how China's exchange rate regime is classified. Explain its regime classification with its monetary policy classification.
6. In terms of the traditional capital structure theories for companies, explain how China's government policies and special economic circumstance may modify the conventional approaches to capital structure.

7. Even though China does control international capital mobility, it still needs to undertake the increasingly difficult task of sterilization. Explain why China, in its efforts at controlling its exchange rate, has in effect lost a degree of control over its monetary policy. Discuss both the magnitude and volatility of exports as factors.
8. Explain the traditional "transmissions mechanism" and why it still a "work-in-progress" description of how monetary policy works in China.

Notes

1. There is some ambiguity here as to whether stability of the currency means maintenance of an exchange rate peg or maintenance of the RMB's domestic purchasing power. In practice, it appears to mean both!
2. Current account mobility allows citizens to acquire foreign exchange for current account activities such as importing, exporting, and the payment of interest and dividends on international obligations. Specifically, it excludes the use of foreign exchange for the acquisition or sale of real and financial assets. Most countries around the world, including China, allow for current account convertibility under the IMF charter (referred to as Article VIII convertibility).
3. In international finance, this is called *uncovered interest rate parity*. It occurs when the expected exchange rate movement exactly offsets interest rate differential between countries on a risk-adjusted basis. Covered interest rate parity is a close companion, no-arbitrage condition in which, instead of the expected exchange rate, we use the forward (contractual obligation) exchange rate.
4. China has historically had very large foreign exchange surrender requirements. These require recipients of foreign exchange, such as exporters, to turn these receipts over to the banking system in exchange for local currency. For countries around the world with such requirements an important question is whether the conversion rate (the exchange rate used) is too favorable to the central authorities and unfavorable to the exporter.
5. In step with the monetary stimulus, the State Council announced a series of measures which ultimately led to an additional fiscal stimulus of RMB 4 trillion in November 2008.
6. This, however, could be a spurious correlation related to the clear monetary response to economic growth.
7. Quantitative easing is a demonstration of Walras's Law. Creating excess demand in one financial market (the demand for bonds) is identical to increasing an excess supply in another financial market (the supply of money). The goal is that the excess money supply will spill directly into creating an actual demand for goods and services.

References

British Broadcasting Corporation (BBC) World News Service. 2013. "What is Quantitative Easing?" March 6.

Conway, Paul, Richard Herd, and Thomas Chalaux. 2010. "Reforming China's Monetary Policy Framework to Meet Domestic Objectives." OECD Economics Department Working Paper No. 822. Organisation for Economic Co-operation and Development Publishing.

Federal Reserve Bank (FRB) of San Francisco. 2004. "What are the Goals of U.S. Monetary Policy?" www.frbsf.org/us-monetary-policy-introduction/goals/ (accessed May 9, 2014).

Kraus, A., and R.H. Litzenberger. 1973. "A state-preference model of optimal financial leverage." *Journal of Finance* 28(4): 911–22.

Krugman, Paul R., Maurice Obtfeld, and Marc Melitz. 2011. *International Economics (9th Edition)*. Chapters 19–20. Pearson Addison-Wesley.

Lin, G., and R.M. Schramm. 2009. "A Decade of Flow of Funds in China (1995–2006)." In *China and Asia: Economic and Financial Interactions*, eds. Y.W. Cheung and K.Y. Wong. London: Routledge.

Mehrotra, Aaron, and Jose R. Sánchez-Fung, 2010. "China's Monetary Policy and the Exchange Rate." BOFIT Discussion Papers No. 10/2010, Bank of Finland, Institute for Economies in Transition.

Myers, Stewart C., and Nicholas Majluf. 1984. "Corporate Financing and Investment Decisions When Firms Have Information That Investors Do Not Have." *Journal of Financial Economics* 13(2): 187–221.

Obstfeld, Maurice. 1986. "Capital Controls, the Dual Exchange Rate, and Devaluation." *Journal of International Economics* 20(1): 1–20.

Obstfeld, Maurice, Jay C. Shambaugh, and Alan M. Taylor. 2004. *The Trilemma in History: Tradeoffs among Exchange Rates, Monetary Policies, and Capital Mobility*. DNB Staff Reports (discontinued) No. 94, Netherlands Central Bank.

The People's Bank of China (PBC) website. "Objective of the Monetary Policy." www.pbc.gov.cn/publish/english/970/index.html (accessed August 19, 2014).

———. Annual Report (various years). Beijing. www.pbc.gov.cn/publish/english/960/index.html (accessed May 8, 2014).

———. China Monetary Policy Report (various years). http://www.pbc.gov.cn/publish/english/955/2012/2012 0628153831855651031/20120628153831855651031

Shu, Chang, and Brian Ng. 2010. "Monetary Stance and Policy Objectives in China: A Narrative Approach." *China Economic Issues* 1(10): 1–40.

Taylor, John B. 1993. "Discretion Versus Policy Rules in Practice." *Carnegie-Rochester Conference Series on Public Policy* 39: 195–214.

9   The Keynesian Model: Extensions to China and Beyond

能者多劳
The Capable are Fully Employed

There is very little research attempting to apply the Keynesian framework (new or old Keynesian models) to China's economic policies. The next chapter, however, shows that in times of economic downturn, China has decisively turned to Keynesian solutions (as has the United States). In addition, we suggest that, during periods of greater stability, China has viewed fiscal policy as mainly investment policy and a tool for economic growth (i.e., supply-side management). Although published in 1936, Keynes's *General Theory of Employment, Interest, and Money* was not translated into Chinese until 1957; it was initially banned in China for being too pro-capitalist (Cox, 2011). In this chapter, we will examine the special case of China using the investment–savings/liquidity–money demand (IS/LM) framework and aggregate demand and supply framework. This is a very useful heuristic device for understanding the constraints and opportunities of an emerging economy (such as China's). Later examples, more complex versions of the IS/LM framework, are more appropriate for advanced economies (such as that of the United States) and the China of the future.

Traditional Keynesian Framework: Investment, Savings, Liquidity Preference, and Money Supply

IS/LM: A Review[1]

It is said that all of economics is about supply and demand and whether or not markets are in or out of equilibrium. This certainly holds true in macroeconomics. While a variety of macro models are now part of the economist's toolkit for analysis, the Keynesian model remains the workhorse for analyzing short-term economic fluctuations in output and employment. As we will see in the section below, both fiscal and monetary policy responses to the recent financial crisis and earlier shocks closely followed Keynesian policy prescriptions, but with characteristics unique to China. In the Keynesian IS/LM framework, we examine supply and demand in two separate markets: (1) supply and demand for GDP, and (2) supply and demand for money. The first describes equilibrium in flows, the second equilibrium in stocks—just as an income statement describes a flow during an accounting period and a balance sheet equates stocks of assets with outstanding equity and liabilities at a certain point in time.

Equilibrium in the Market for Goods and Services (the Market for GDP or the IS Curve)

Reviewing the IS/LM model, we recall that to achieve equilibrium in the market for goods and services (the IS relationship):

Supply

- Y = GDP = Income = Supply of Output

Demand Components

- C = Consumer demand for goods and services
- I = Investor demand for plant, property, and equipment; other interest-sensitive forms of demand such as auto and home purchases; and inventory (stock-building) accumulation.
- G = Government demand for goods and services
- NX = Exports – imports or net exports of goods and services
- t = tax rate – transfer rate on all of income[2]
- i = the interest rate or rate of return on the best alternative to holding money and this is assumed to be equal to cost of borrowing funds for the sake of investment (I).

Setting Supply = Demand, we have:

$$Y = C((1 - t) \times Y) + I(i) + G + NX(Y)$$

in which the expressions in parentheses represent independent variables that influence (+/−) the components of demand or dependent variables. Assuming linear relationships throughout, we have:

$$Y = C + I + [c \times (1 - t) \times Y] - [d \times I] + G + X - [m \times Y]$$

In which c, d, and m are sensitivities of consumption, investment, and imports to net income, the interest rate, and income. Autonomous changes in consumption, investment, government spending, or exports would change the constants, C, I, G, and X respectively. In Figure 9.1, we show a standard IS curve which would shift to the right if any of the constants just described changed for some exogenous reason (such as a shift in consumer or investor behavior). **The IS curve represents combinations of Y and i, in which the supply of the economy's goods and services just equals the demand for those goods and services**. Above the curve, for any given Y, there is too little demand (implying inventory accumulation); below the curve there is excess demand (implying inventory reduction). In the former case, companies would cut back on production and decrease output, Y, over time; in the latter case, companies would increase production. Either way, output would gravitate toward the IS curve. This is another way of looking at that curve as a set of equilibrium levels of output and interest rates.

In this framework, there are two key variables at work and one not at work: At work are investment and inventory accumulation; not at work is the overall level of prices. Let's discuss prices first. Prices are assumed to be sticky (fixed) and for purposes of simplification, constant. As such, we don't see prices at all in our demand framework. This may seem strange—how can we discuss supply and demand without including prices?—but Keynes argued that prices at the aggregate level tend to be fixed or sticky, and this is a critical assumption in the Keynesian framework. Economists have suggested menu costs, meaning that it takes time for any firm to change its menu of prices in response to short-run fluctuations in demand. Eventually, firms do change their prices (in the long run), but in the Keynesian world (the short run), prices are not flexible but sticky. Other economists have also suggested that changing prices (particularly reducing them) changes revenues—and this may, in turn, trigger cost-cutting or wage reductions to keep a firm profitable. Employees will resist real wage reductions despite the possibility of losing their jobs. While economists have long debated downward wage rigidity, research utilizing a behavioral economics approach—in which workers have a wage benchmark or "anchor"—is useful in explaining the phenomenon (Bewley, 1999).

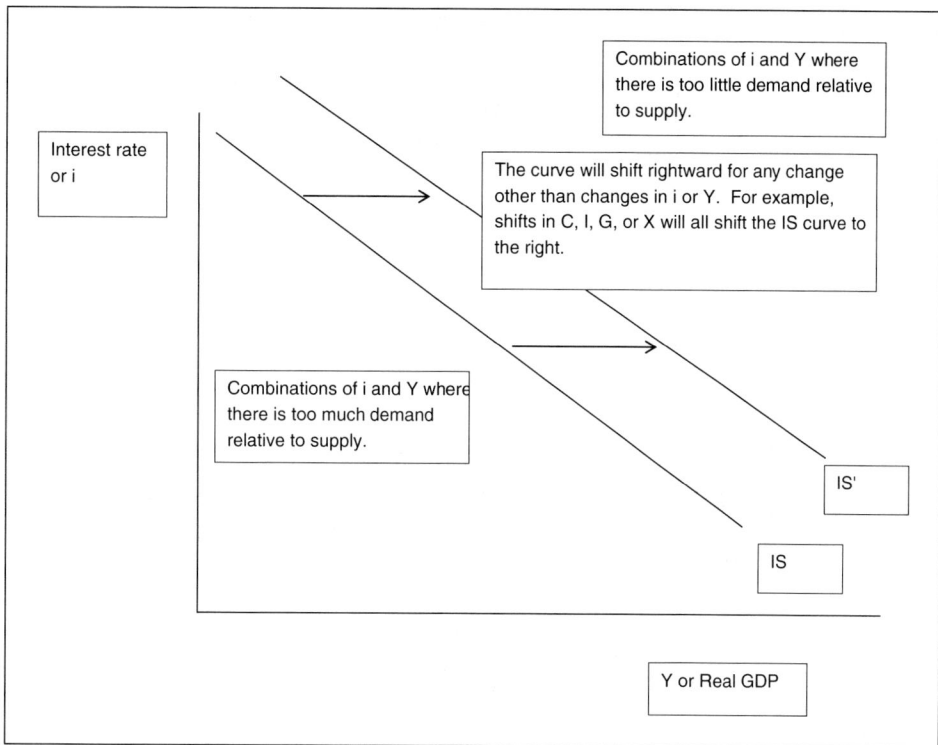

Figure 9.1 The IS curve represents combination of output and interest rates where the goods market is in equilibrium. If we are off the IS curve, then there is an excess supply or demand for goods. Any exogenous increase in C, I, G, or NX would cause a shift in the curve rightward.

Source: Author created.

Since prices cannot (under the model's assumption) relieve much of the pressure typically resulting from demand or supply shocks, another variable must relieve the pressure in the system. This is where inventory accumulation or reduction comes into play. When demand drops, for example, instead of prices changing, inventory accumulates. In response to unwanted inventory, firms cut output. Inventory represents both planned and unplanned (unintended, unwanted) inventory accumulation. In the latter case, firms alter production in response to the unwanted and unanticipated changes in inventory.[3] Figure 9.2 shows these two critical aspects of the Keynesian system in a simple demand and supply framework.

Equilibrium in the Money Market (the LM Curve)

As we discussed in the chapter on monetary policy, the LM curve describes equilibrium in the money market, but just as easily (via Walras's Law) extends to equilibrium in all financial markets—whether they be equities, bonds, or currencies.[4] If the money market is not in equilibrium, then by the requirements of Walras's consistency, at least one other market is not in equilibrium. We start with the supply of money (*M*), assumed to be exogenously determined by the monetary authorities and the banking system. The overall price level is represented by *P*, and *i* represents the interest rate on the opportunity cost of money. The expression *L*(*Y*, *i*) represents the demand for the real stock of

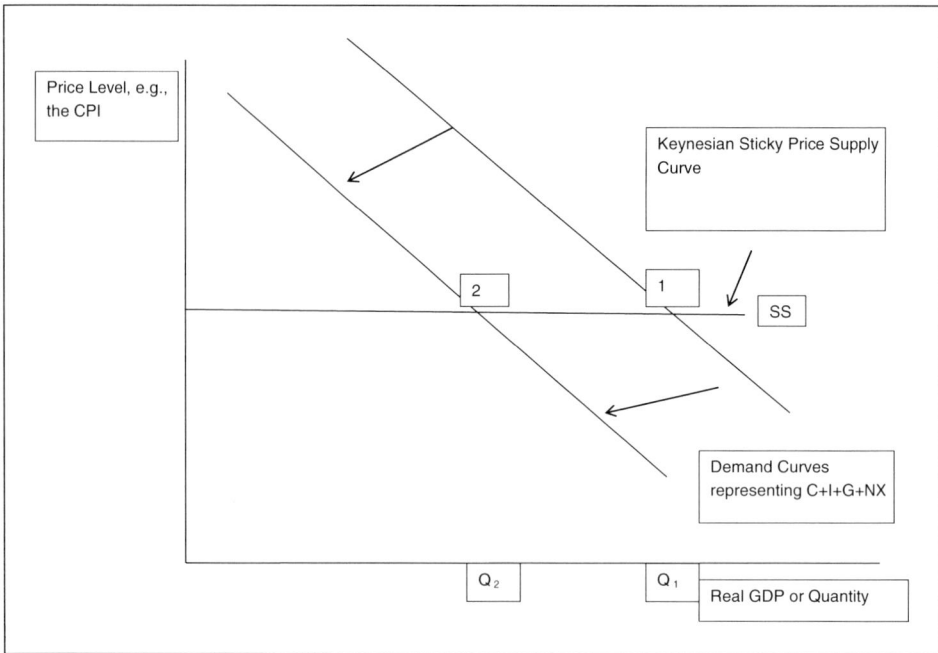

Figure 9.2 In a Keynesian framework we represent sticky prices by a perfectly elastic supply curve—any shift in demand (either an increase or a decrease) results in GDP fluctuating rather than prices.

Source: Author created.

outstanding money, in which demand is positively related to real income and negatively related to the nominal interest rate. We then have:

Supply or Stock of Real Money

$$M/P \equiv m$$

Demand for Real Money

$$L(Y, i)$$

Setting Supply = Demand, we have:

$$M/P = L(Y, i)$$

Assuming linear relationships throughout, we have:

$$M/P = e \times Y - f \times i$$

in which e and f are the sensitivities of money demand to the level of real income and the nominal interest rate.[5] For now, we assume **M/P** is constant. In Figure 9.3 we see the **LM curve which shows all combinations of Y and i in which the money market is in equilibrium.** An increase in the money supply will shift the LM to the right. Any point above the LM curve corresponds to

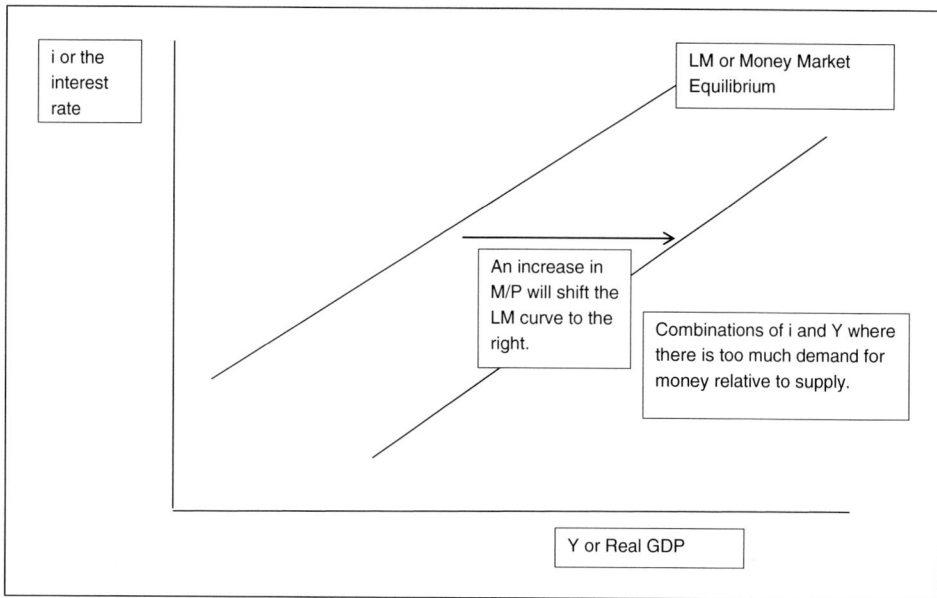

Figure 9.3 The LM curve represents combinations of interest rates and output where the money market is in equilibrium. An increase in the real money supply (from either nominal money increasing or the price level dropping) will shift the LM curve to the right.

Source: Author created.

Note: IS/LM: An increase in Real Money, MP, causes the LM to shift rightward.

an excess supply of real balances relative to demand; any point below, an excess demand relative to supply.

Equilibrium in Both Markets

In the IS/LM framework, there is only one combination of levels of real income, Y, and interest rates, i, in which both the market for goods and services, and financial assets, are in equilibrium. That point is "A" as indicated in Figure 9.4. If the economy enters quadrants 1, 2, 3, or 4, we have excess supply or demands for goods and services and money. Imbalances in inventories, output, and interest rates will force a move to the equilibrium level of output and interest rates. In the China context, being off these curves is an important and relevant concept. We suggest below that because of a multiplicity of policy goals, China employs a multiplicity of tools which allows the economy to linger for prolonged periods off both IS and LM curves, that is, a sustainably long period out of equilibrium.

Any autonomous increase in the demand for goods (such as an increase in government spending, G, or an increase in consumption, C) will shift the IS curve to the right. This will cause Y to increase and i to increase as well.[6] An increase in the real money supply, M/P, shifts the LM curve to the right and downward. This also causes output to rise, but, in this case, triggers interest rates to fall. As shown in Figures 9.5 and 9.6, both expansionary monetary policy and fiscal policy result in output increasing in the standard Keynesian framework, but will impact interest rates in opposite directions. Case Study 9.1 elaborates on the LM curve shift and what it means for China in terms of the "transmission mechanism."

There is a natural (psychological) tendency to think of "equilibrium" as a good situation.[7] However, that presumption is definitely false in the Keynesian framework. In that framework, equilibrium

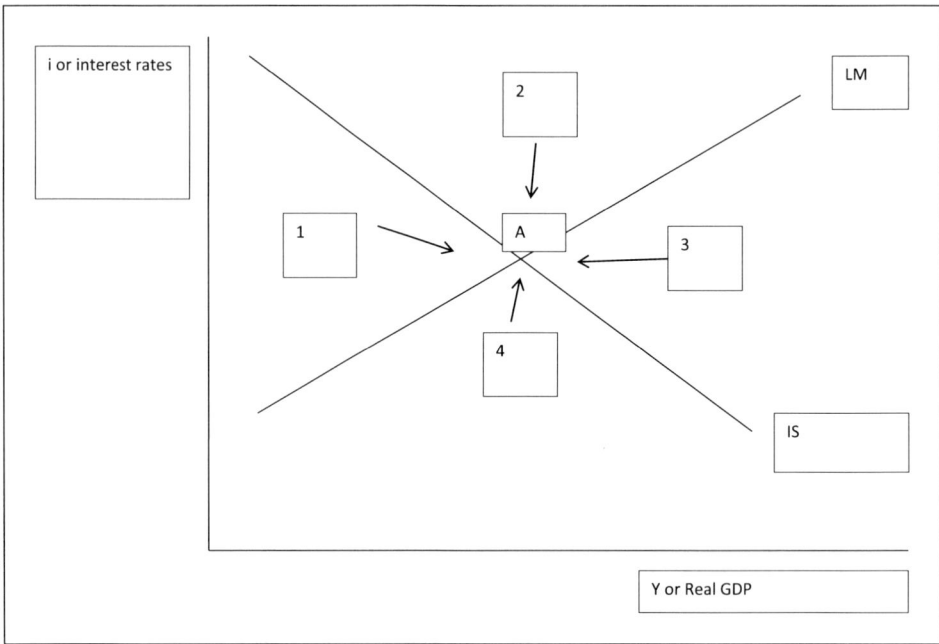

Figure 9.4 At A both the goods market and financial markets are in equilibrium. In quadrants 1, 2, 3, or 4 we have either inventory accumulation/decumulation or an excess supply of money or excess demand for other financial assets.

Source: Author created.

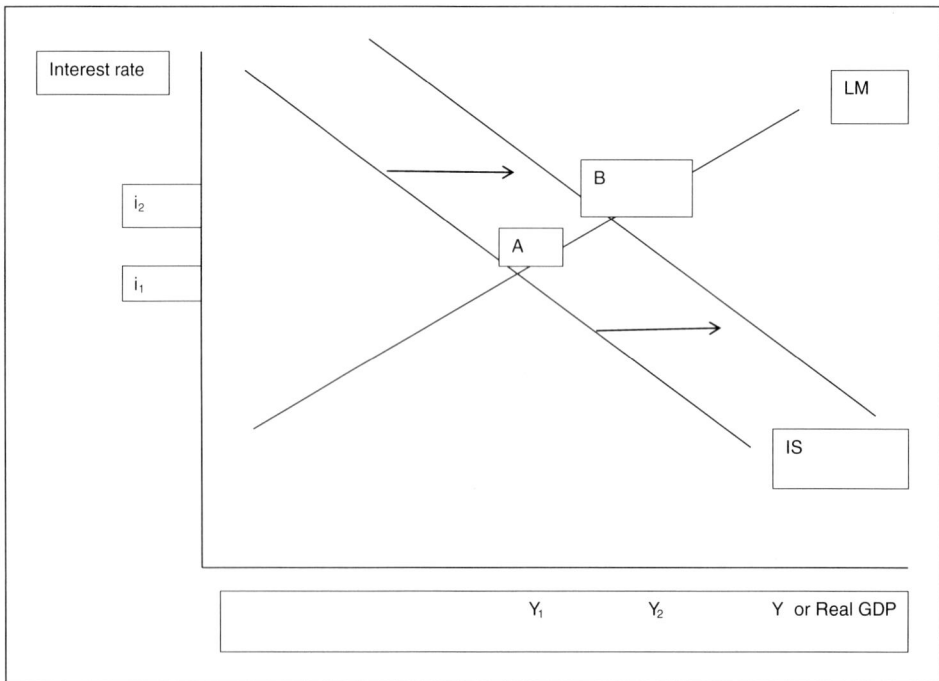

Figure 9.5 An increase in C, I, G, or NX will shift the IS to the right and cause output to rise as well as interest rates.

Source: Author created.

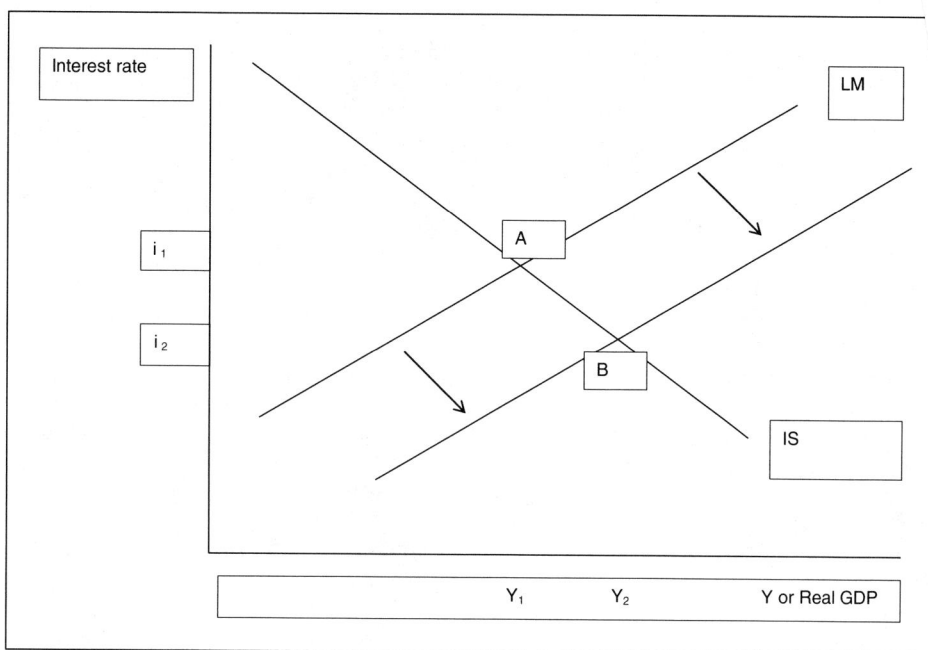

Figure 9.6 An increase in the real money supply shifts the LM downward increasing output and decreasing interest rates.

Source: Author created.

simply means the situation where the economy stabilizes—a situation which could be good but could also be very bad, corresponding to high rates of unemployment and low levels of output. This is Keynes's main point: the economy could stabilize (reach equilibrium) in a situation which is very undesirable. It would then be up to policymakers to move the economy to a better equilibrium.

Case Study 9.1: The Chopstick Economy

We have suggested, in Chapters 7 and 8, that the "transmission mechanism" for monetary policy is not yet fully operational in China. The *transmission mechanism* is the mechanism found in advanced economies whereby central banks intervene (use open market operations involving repurchase agreements) in overnight interbank lending markets (i.e., the U.S. federal funds market). This intervention, in turn, impacts overnight interbank interest rates. Overnight rates then spill over into longer-term borrowing or lending rates, which impact interest-sensitive components of demand (such as housing or new company investments). Next, these changes in demand impact output and employment—possibly with a multiplier effect. In other words, in order for monetary policy to be effective, it must pass through a number of institutional gateways—any of which might not be open. China still faces some institutional impediments to a fully functioning transmissions mechanism. The bottom line is that the pricing of the money mechanism (the interest rate) is still "under construction." As a result, China relies heavily on quantity of money effects, in which the availability of money operating through the lending channels of the financial system is quite important. Interestingly, this is very similar to the U.S. Fed's quantitative easing policy in the post-financial crisis era (which also occurred as a result of the breakdown of the transmissions mechanism). Macro Finance Insight 7.3 sheds some light on this important issue.

In terms of deriving an LM relationship, the lack of interest sensitivity implies a steep demand-for-money curve (as seen in Figure CS9.1a). This suggests a money market that is in equilibrium over a range of interest rates, as long as the amount of money supplied is consistent with the level of economic output. The box represents a range of possible interest rates and money supplies in which market disequilibrium is possible given imperfect capital markets in China. The People's Bank of China (PBC) can pick and choose interest rates and the money supply independently (both a price and a quantity) because the demand for money is inelastic and financial markets are still imperfect. (We allude to this in our discussion of disequilibrium scenarios in Figure 9.4.)

We suggest a monetary policy closer in spirit to the quantity theory of money (QTOM) presented earlier—along with the notion of "channels of credit" or credit rationing suggested by Laurens and Maino (2007). Rather than a neat LM line showing equilibrium points for money demand and supply, we have a box showing a range of combinations of output (Y) and interest rates (i) from which the PBC chooses (a "toolkit," as shown in Figure CS9.1a). The upper and lower boundaries of the box represent constraints—interest rates above or below the box would not be consistent with a sticky exchange rate regime; setting interest rates outside the box would create too tempting an arbitrage opportunity, inviting capital inflows or flight. However, if we move beyond the borders of the box to the right or left, we risk creating shortages or surpluses in financial markets.

China's IS curve, meanwhile, is also somewhat steep. Its slope is determined by the sensitivity of investment demand to interest rates. There is some evidence that investment in China is still not very sensitive to interest rate changes (e.g., Geng and N'Diaye, 2012). This can be represented as a steep IS curve. Figure CS9.1b suggests that China has a range of interest rates—not just a single one—which are all stable in the short run. A steep IS curve allows for many possible interest rates, as does a steep LM curve. In turn, there is a range of interest rates that the PBC can pursue without either impacting

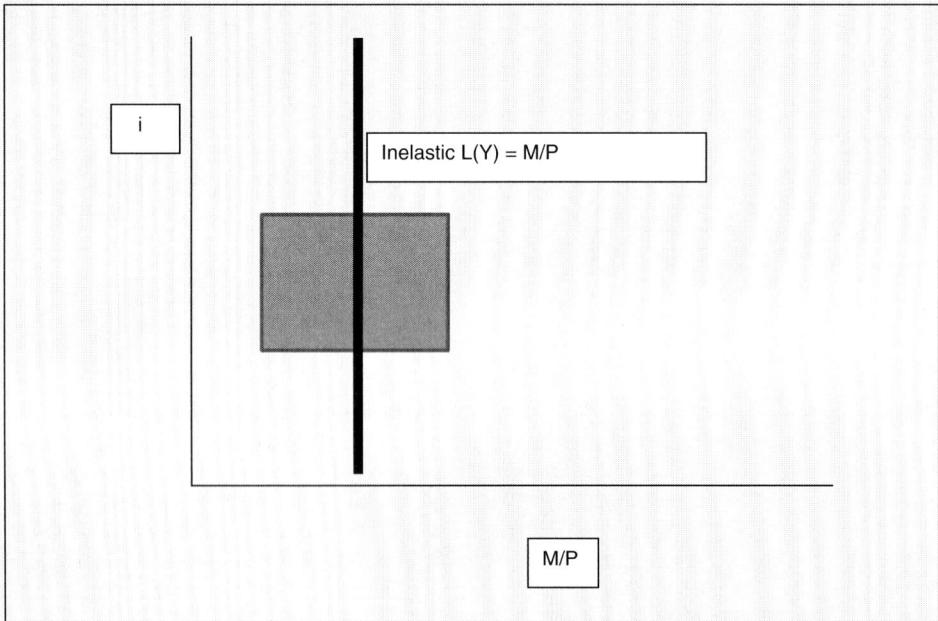

Figure CS9.1a With inelastic money demand in China and imperfect capital markets, there are many possible interest rates, consistent with a level of output. The gray box shows a range of combinations of disequilibrium interest rates and money supplies that the PBC can attempt to manage before severe imbalances in money markets occur.

Source: Author created.

demand for goods or the demand for money very much. Furthermore, it is possible in China to be off our equilibrium IS and LM curves for prolonged periods. (For a related concept, see the discussion below on interest rate overshooting.)

The above discussion suggests that the PBC has greater flexibility in terms of fiscal and monetary policy. In fact, the boxes we have drawn represent policy boundaries. The upper and lower sides of the rectangle represent the constraints on how high or low interest rates can go, given China's regime of capital controls and a sticky exchange rate. The right and left borders represent the constraints that China (and all economies) have: economic output (to the right) cannot exceed a nation's limited resources (supply). On the left, economic output is politically constrained to avoid falling too far, given the high costs of unemployment and expectations about improved prosperity. China's constraint to the right is relatively soft compared to that of the United States, given China's still vast growth potential. Its constraint to the left is relatively hard, given the lack of a social safety net and high expectations for economic growth.

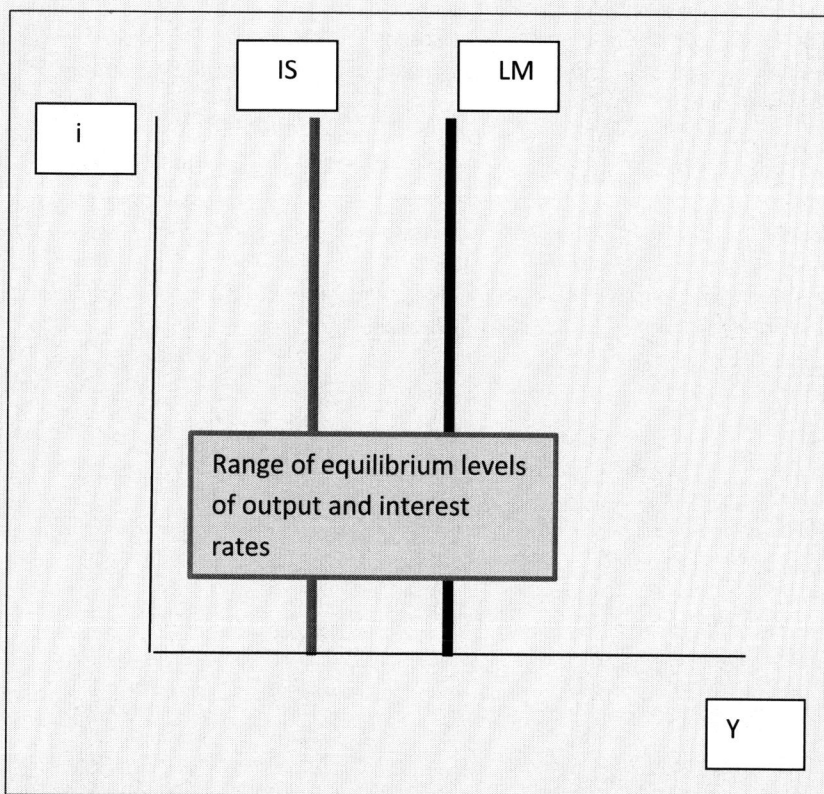

Figure CS9.1b The Chopstick Economy. Rather than a single equilibrium point, China has a range of combinations of interest rates and levels of output that are possible. Authorities can choose to be on or off an IS or an LM curve for prolonged periods as long as they operate within a range permitted by capital mobility and employment constraints (the shaded box).

Source: Author created.

Aggregate Demand and Supply

The absence of explicit roles for prices (since they are sticky), and the supply of goods are clear shortcomings of the traditional IS/LM framework. A broader framework of supply and demand

(AS and AD) has proven a useful step forward (in reality, a step back to earlier macroeconomic roots). We first introduce the new element, aggregate supply. Both a short-run supply curve and long-run, full-employment supply curve are presented. Figure 9.7 shows both curves in which (as always) *P* represents an index of average prices, and *Y* represents real GDP. On the long-run or Y_{FULL} curve, we have a classical supply curve—a constraint or boundary representing full employment of the economy's labor force and other key factors of production. This curve is shaped by long-run fundamental factors (described in Chapter 4). Factors of production, such as capital stock, labor force, and technology all determine this boundary. While these can change over time, in the short run, they act as constraints. Obviously, it is difficult to quickly change the labor force or capital stock at full employment. As they do increase over time (as we saw in Chapter 4 with the Solow framework), the long-run supply curve moves to the right.

The short-run supply curve represents temporary possibilities to be either below full employment (to be on the short-run curve to the left of the vertical long-run supply curve) or above full employment (to the right of full employment on the short-run supply). If we are above full employment, the short-run curve gradually drifts upward representing economy-wide price increases. If we are below full employment, the short-run curve gradually shifts downward, representing price declines caused by falling demand.[8]

The aggregate demand curve comprises all of the demand-creating components of the IS/LM framework: *C, I, G, t, NX,* and *M*. We can consider it as a "reduced-form" (or summary) of the IS/LM framework. Anything that increases any of these components of demand will shift the AD curve to the right and move us along a short-run supply curve initially, then eventually to a new position on the long-run supply curve (AS).

A second, simpler and more intuitive way to derive the AD curve is to view it from the perspective of the quantity theory of money (discussed in Chapters 7 and 8):

$$M \times V = P \times Y^{\text{Real}}$$

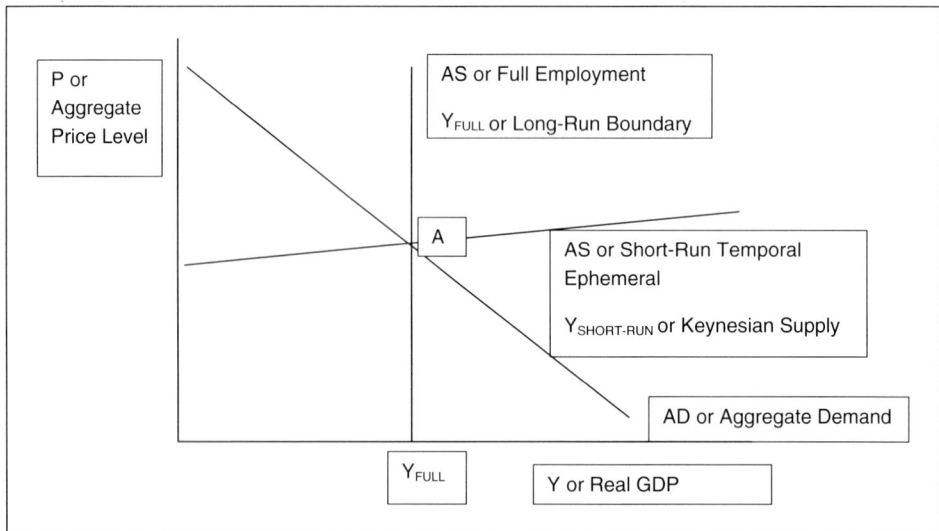

Figure 9.7 The aggregate demand and supply framework (AD and AS) is more comprehensive in that it allows for prices to play a role in the long run while allowing for sticky prices in the short run.

Source: Author created.

Recall that M is the nominal money supply. Velocity (V) is the average number of times the money supply circulates to acquire GDP, and P and Y are as defined earlier. Rearranging, we have:

$$Y^{Real} = (M \times V) / P$$

Assuming that $M \times V$ is constant, the above represents a rectangular hyperbola (or, graphically, a demand curve relating the price level with demand for real GDP). If either M or V increases, the demand curve shifts to the right. In the IS/LM framework, V will increase if C, I, or G rise, or if t declines; an expansionary monetary policy, for example, would increase M and shift the curve to the right; expansionary fiscal policy increases V if we are below full employment. Therefore, this approach is fully consistent with the IS/LM approach in terms of explaining how the AD curve shifts to the right.

Figure 9.8 shows the effect of a policy causing the AD curve to shift to the right (due to changes in C, I, G, t, or M). If we begin at A (full employment) and try to move the economy above full employment, we first succeed in moving to point B. However, eventually, the ephemeral (temporary, unstable) AS short-run curve would float upward until intersecting with the AS long-run curve at C. Our expansionary policy would have only accomplished either increasing prices or crowding out some other component of demand—and we would be right back at full employment. In other words, our expansionary policy would have been completely ineffective. If on the other hand, we had initially started at point Z, our expansionary policy might have prevented economic stagnation below full employment.[9]

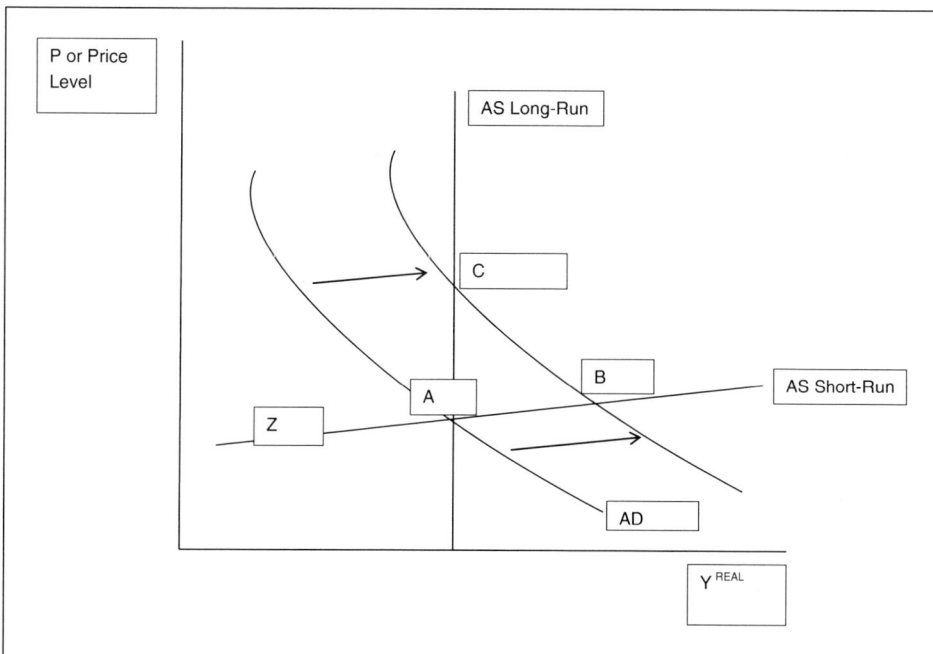

Figure 9.8 If we assume we start at full employment (A), an increase in the money supply would cause the aggregate demand curve, AD, to shift rightward increasing output in the short run to B, but in the long run only causing higher prices (C).

Source: Author created.

Keynesian Model Extensions

Goods Market Equilibrium and Interest Rate Overshooting

One extension of the standard Keynesian model presented above is to assume that the market for financial assets is always in equilibrium, while the goods market could be out of equilibrium for a period of time. Money markets, equity markets, and other financial markets usually have extremely flexible prices—responding instantaneously to news (the efficient markets assumption from finance). Because prices can be adjusted instantaneously to equilibrate demand and supply for financial assets, those markets are always in equilibrium. In contrast, prices in the goods and services markets adjust slowly (if at all), causing excess demand or supply, inventory decumulation or accumulation, and markets temporarily out of equilibrium. In our IS/LM framework, the implication of these assumptions about the speed of price adjustment in each market suggests that we are always on an LM curve (the original LM or a new LM, after a change in the money supply), but we can fall off of an IS curve (above or below it). In other words, unplanned inventories might be accumulating or decumulating.

Figure 9.9 shows an example of a contractionary monetary policy (i.e., in which the money supply is decreased). In this case, the LM curve shifts upward as does the interest rate—a vertical jump from i_1 to $i_{1.5}$ in which interest rates "hop" to the new LM curve. We are temporarily stuck at Y_1 but gradually move along this LM curve to a new, lower economic equilibrium, Y_2 and i_2. Note that, during the transition from Y_1 to Y_2, we are in goods market disequilibrium (off and above the IS curve); that curve is the equilibrium locale. While off the IS curve, we have an excess supply of

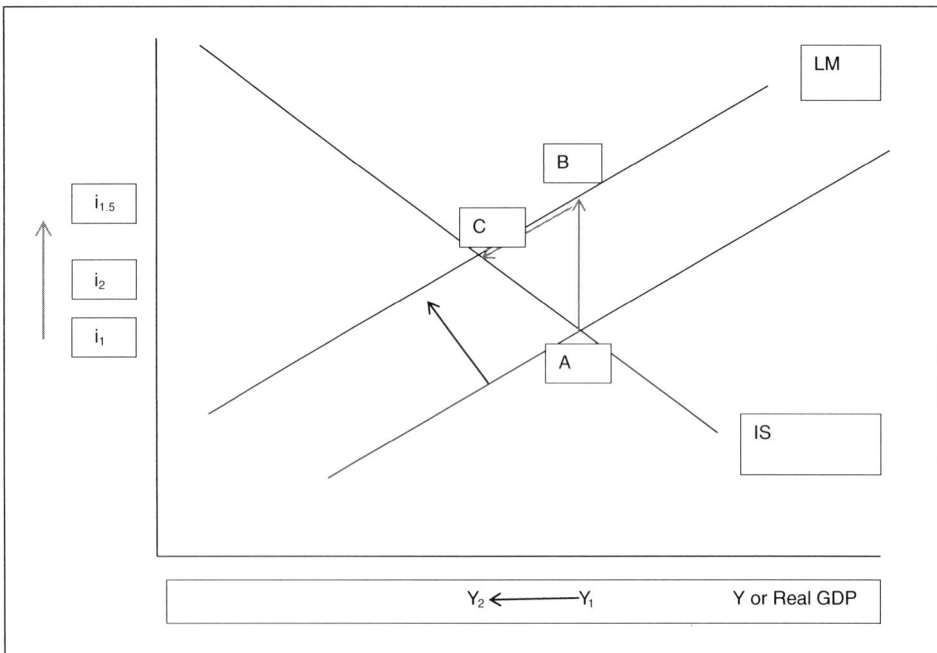

Figure 9.9 In the case of efficient financial markets which clear immediately but a goods market that does not clear in the short run, there can be overshooting. Here a decrease in the money supply causes interest rates to first jump to point B from A, but then output eventually falls consistent with the decrease in the money supply and we end up at C. The vertical gap between B and C is referred to as overshooting.

Source: Author created.

goods and inventory accumulation. In response, companies will cut back production, causing output, Y, to decrease over time. In summary, interest rates adjust instantaneously and we "overshoot" the long-run equilibrium interest rate (i_2), causing output to decline in a prolonged transition of disequilibrium in which the supply of goods and services exceeds their demand.

The disequilibrium situation of being off the IS curve is fully caused by the sticky price assumption. In a more classical model, only one interest rate equates savings with investment—and the IS curve would be flat at that interest rate. If the IS curve is flat at an interest rate consistent with savings equaling investment, then monetary policy (shifts in the LM) would have no impact on the equilibrium interest rate. If prices adjust in tandem with the money supply, such that M/P is constant, then changes in nominal money would not matter (i.e., would not shift the LM curve). With such assumptions, the economy would always operate at long-run equilibrium and there would not be much room for policy action. However, we must question how reasonable it is to assume market clearing prices in goods markets when, even in financial markets (contrary to our assumption above), prices of financial assets do not always clear markets. The existence of circuit breakers in equity markets, or the collapse of auction rate securities markets in February 2008, are examples of financial markets not operating with complete smoothness—and these are markets with sophisticated participants in a normally liquid environment. If even these markets sometimes fail to clear and encounter frictions, it is reasonable that the market for goods, services, and labor (which are much less transparent and less liquid) could regularly fail to clear.

Overshooting in Currency Markets

In the scenario above, we saw that the overshooting of interest rates occurs when prices are sticky and the goods market does not equilibrate. In the following scenario, we examine a situation in which exchange rates can overshoot, prices are sticky, and the exchange rate is in disequilibrium for the short run. Disequilibrium occurs when the exchange rate does not immediately adjust to its purchasing power parity (PPP) or long-run value. Recall that PPP states that the price of a homogeneous product expressed in the same currency should have the same price—otherwise, an arbitrage opportunity exists. Both domestic prices and the exchange rate should adjust, to prevent arbitrage opportunities. For example, the price of an apple in Detroit, Michigan, expressed in US$ should be the same as the price of an apple in Windsor, Ontario, also expressed in US$. Otherwise, consumers and wholesalers would buy all their apples from the cheaper location.[10]

In the overshooting model for exchange rates, as developed by Dornbusch (1976), we utilize the following relationships:

Purchasing Power Parity

$$P^Z_{US\$} = US\$ / RMB \times P^Z_{RMB}$$

That is, the price of product Z expressed in US$ will be the same in the United States and China after factoring in the exchange rate. We assume this holds true in the long run but not the short run.

Uncovered Interest Rate Parity and Capital Mobility

$$r^{United\ States} - r^{China} = \text{Depreciation (+) of the US\$ / RMB exchange rate}$$

The second relationship above assumes that capital flows freely across borders between two countries, so as to seek the highest return. As such, it is an arbitrage condition for financial assets. If the risk-free return on U.S. assets is higher than the risk-free returns on Chinese assets, then the dollar must be expected to depreciate over time so as to make the returns expressed in US\$ the same. This is another arbitrage condition (in which there is no risk premium) on asset returns. We assume that this always holds true except during the initial period after an unexpected policy change.

Quantity Theory of Money

As described above, here we assume the following relationship where V, is the assumed constant velocity of money, P is the price level, M is the nominal money supply, and Y^{Real} is real GDP:

$$(M \times V) / Y^{REAL} = P$$

In other words, large increases in M relative to Y^{REAL} will yield increases in prices or inflation.

Short-Run Keynesian Economics with Capital Mobility

We use the same standard Keynesian model assumptions discussed in the prior chapter but with the additional assumption that capital can flow into or out of an economy when domestic interest rates go above or below world interest rates (Mundell 1963; Fleming 1962). With these assumptions and conditions, we can examine the impact on the exchange rate of an increase in the money supply in one country. Since capital is still not freely mobile into and out of China, we will use an example for the United States and Europe instead. Suppose our initial exchange rate in Figure 9.10 at time 0 is 1, and that interest rates in each country are initially equal. For expansionary policy purposes, the United States decides to increase monetary growth above trend. This is our initial assumed shock to the system.

We solve this problem at the end, or out toward the infinity benchmark in Figure 9.10. Following PPP and the quantity theory of money, the long-run impact of more money in the U.S. economy would be greater inflation and a weaker U.S. dollar (at point 1.2)

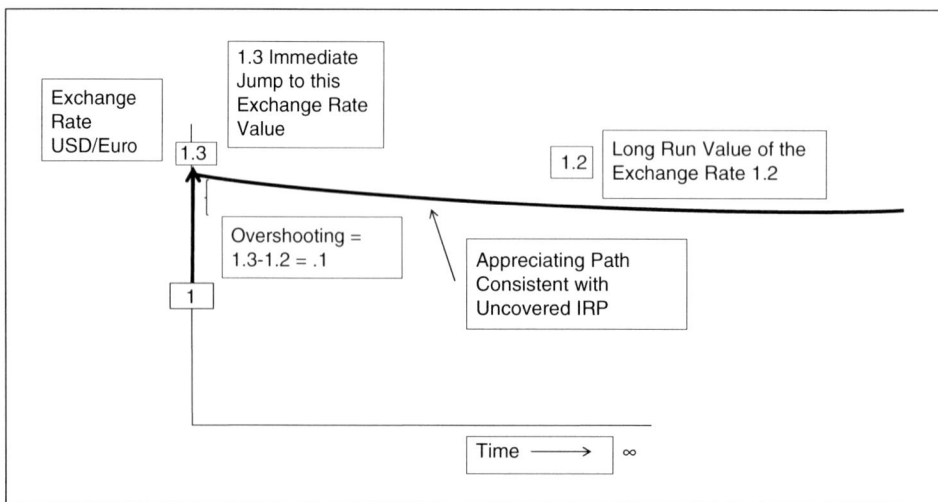

Figure 9.10 In the case of exchange rate overshooting, an increase in the money supply in the United States leads to an "overshooting" of the exchange rate. In this case, the dollar first weakens by a substantial amount but then strengthens over time. It never fully recovers, however.

Source: Author created.

Moving now to the first instant after the monetary expansion is known (the very short r turn to the expanded IS/LM model. In this model of capital mobility (Mundell, 1963; F 1962), capital flows out of the United States and into Europe due to the initial drop in U.S. interest rates—a shift that would weaken the value of the U.S. dollar. How far would it weaken the dollar? Far enough from its fundamental PPP long-run value that it would be expected, over time, to actually appreciate. That appreciation would be just sufficient (à la uncovered interest rate parity) to offset the initial lower interest rate differential caused by U.S. monetary expansion. That path of appreciation is represented by the curved line in the center of Figure 9.10. In summary, we start off with an exchange rate of 1, immediately jump to 1.3 (after the announcement), then gradually appreciate to 1.2 over time.

The notion of "overshooting" assumes that we depreciate beyond what is "necessary" in a PPP sense by 1.3–1.2 or 0.1. But then the exchange rate gradually works its way back from 1.3 to 1.2. Once again, overshooting occurs when a key variable (such as price) is sticky, causing other variables to adjust more than they otherwise would in order to absorb the monetary shock.

MACRO FINANCE INSIGHT 9.1: IS A NATION'S EXCHANGE RATE ITS "STOCK PRICE"?

The notion of efficient markets in finance states that stock prices reflect all publicly available information on the value of a company to shareholders, and that non-random movements in the share price reflect new fundamental information.* Does the value of a country's currency (the exchange rate) similarly capture fundamental information regarding the strength or weakness of an economy? In some ways, the exchange rate provides a clearer signal since it is relative prices (against another country's currency) while the movement of a stock price must always be gauged against the overall market, a comparable industry, or another asset class.

For the special case surrounding financial crises in countries (corresponding to situations of corporate financial distress), the exchange rate plays the same role as stock prices—showing a sharp depreciation. Based on a survey of more than eighty academic studies on financial crises, Frankel and Saravelos (2012) state that the "vast majority of studies include some measure of changes in the exchange rate"—specifically, a depreciation of 25 percent or more. In fact, financial crises are often defined in terms of sharp depreciations (relative to trend) in the exchange rate. But the story does not stop here. The authors also find that the real exchange rate (the exchange rate adjusted for inflation in each country) tends to appreciate in the months before a financial crisis. That appreciation corresponds, in some cases, to a speculative bubble found in overvalued stocks. As in the case of equities, a surge in capital inflows (or investor interest) pushes up either the exchange rate or stock price. The surge in inflows corresponds to either "irrational exuberance" or, in other cases, as the counterpart to current account deficits. We see an overshooting of the exchange rate, devastation on the trade balance, and, ultimately, a violation of the intertemporal budget constraint. Unsustainable, the path of the economy leads to a crisis.†

A more normal, secular, and non-crisis relationship between exchange rates was explained in Chapter 3. There, we identified $S - I$, or the adjusted current account balance as a measure of a nation's cash flow. The larger the cash flow (corresponding to net external lending), the higher the valuation, or in our case, the stronger the exchange rate.‡ Broadly speaking, current account deficits (negative cash flows) imply a currency depreciation (see Obstfeld, 2012) or earlier arguments dating back to the gold standard, to find the basis for this conclusion. In effect, depreciation of the currency rebalances current account imbalances. In the context of stock prices, bad news must result in a stock price low enough to ultimately yield a competitive return. The latter effect is, in fact, identical to the exchange rate overshooting model (see our earlier discussion), in which the exchange rate must adjust sufficiently far from its long-run equilibrium to attract foreign investors to continue holding assets denominated in that currency.

The above discussion expands on the valuable work of Calvo and Mishkin (2003) and others who examine the costs and benefits of different exchange rate regimes. They conclude that what really matters is the institutional framework including independence of the monetary authorities and the soundness of the financial system underlying the exchange rate system. We are suggesting here that a critical benefit of a floating exchange rate regime is that it provides a clear signal regarding government policies and economic performance, by providing greater transparency than fixed exchange rates. We could argue that the fixed exchange rate regime found under the euro system since 1999 hid many fundamental problems that would have been seen earlier and more clearly under a floating exchange rate regime for countries such as Greece and Spain. This is one critical advantage of a floating exchange rate over a fixed exchange rate regime.

Figure MF9.1a and Figure MF9.1b show China's nominal and real exchange rate. The nominal exchange rate begins appreciating substantially in 2005, while a secular and significant real appreciation of the RMB began in 1994 (rising by nearly 40 percent in that period). How should we interpret this? In this scenario, we could interpret the pressure on the RMB to appreciate either as: (1) a reflection of its artificial undervaluation compared to very upbeat valuations of the Chinese economy by the international community; or (2) a leading indicator of an imminent financial crisis, as discussed above.

In the first case, the causes stem from international investors' appetite to hold RMB as an investment. In the second case, the causes stem from an overvalued RMB leading to current account deficits and a precipitous depletion of foreign exchange. Frankel and Saravelos (2012) shed light on this question by pointing out that another significant leading indicator for financial collapse in conjunction with an appreciating real exchange rate is a secular loss of foreign exchange reserves. Figure MF9.1c shows that this is clearly not the story in China; rather, China has seen an enormous gain in foreign exchange reserves (i.e., its cash flow has been positive and very large) in recent years. Together, this suggests that the strengthening of the RMB reflects the international community's fundamental assessment of the Chinese economy as growing in value. (We also observe, in Figure MF9.1b, a flat real exchange rate

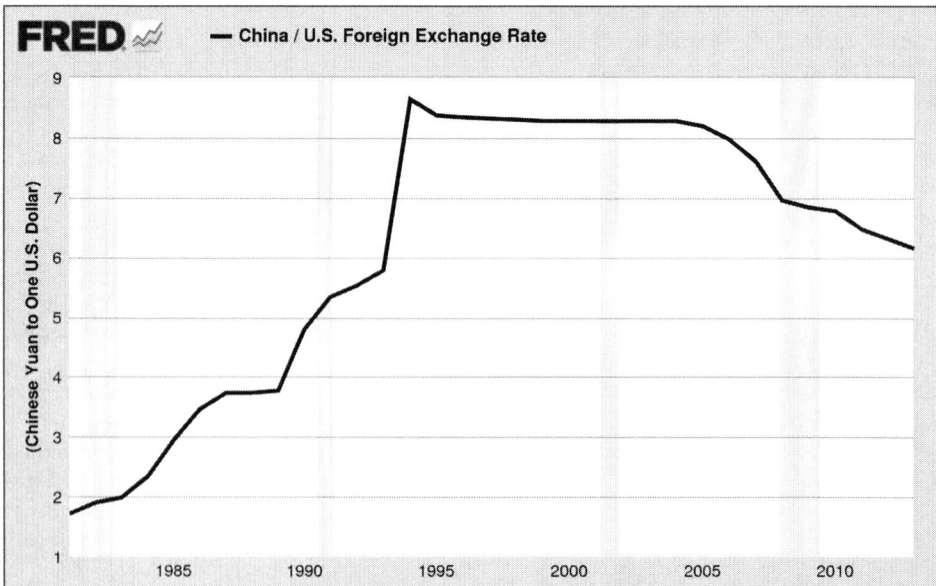

Figure MF9.1a

Source: FRED, Federal Reserve Economic Data, Federal Reserve Bank of St. Louis: China/U.S. Foreign Exchange Rate; Board of Governors of the Federal Reserve System. 2014 research.stlouisfed.org
Note: Shaded areas indicate U.S. recessions.

Real Effective Exchange Rate: BIS

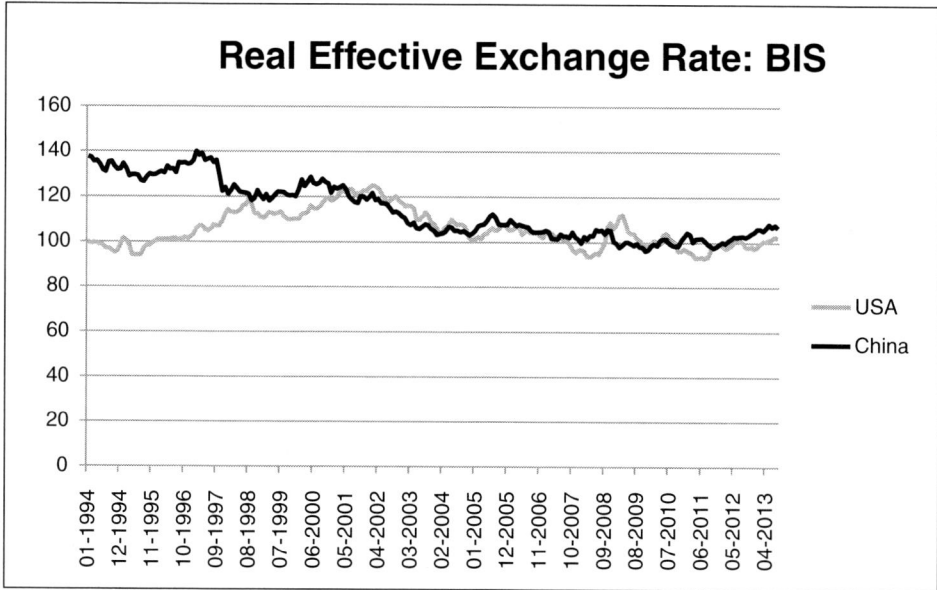

Figure MF9.1b China's real exchange rate has been appreciating since 1994.

Source: Author created based on data from Bank for International Settlements. *BIS Effective Exchange Rate Indices*, http://www.bis.org/statistics/eer/

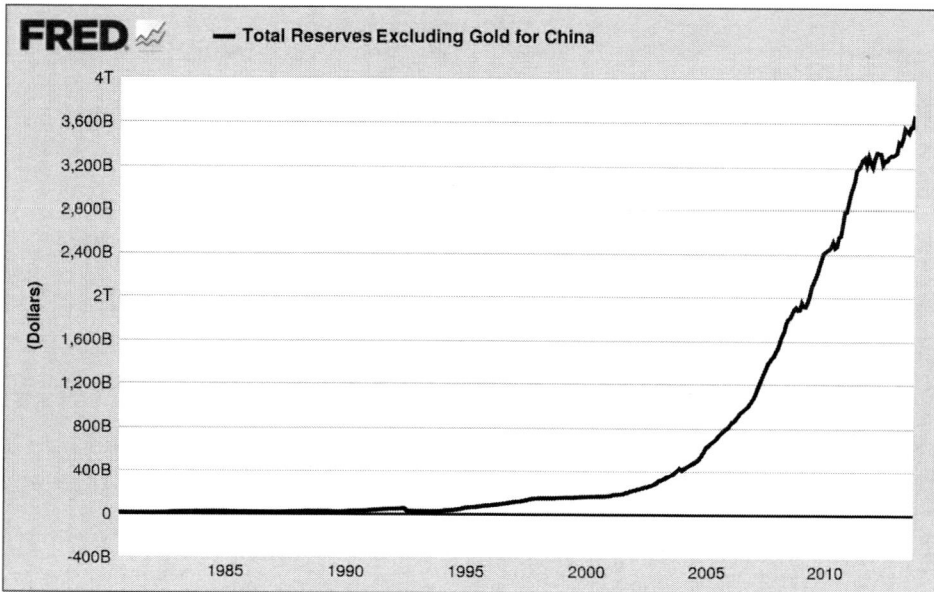

Figure MF9.1c China's forex reserves have grown explosively over the past two decades suggesting a more optimistic view with respect to its appreciating currency.

Source: FRED, Federal Reserve Economic Data, Federal Reserve Bank of St. Louis: Reserve Bank; Board of Governors of the Federal Reserve System. 2014 research.stlouisfed.org

over most of the period for the United States.) Nevertheless, the longer China maintains a quasi-fixed exchange rate with its concomitant lack of transparency, the greater the opportunity for fundamental problems to accumulate. The current arrangement also confounds efforts at financial liberalization.

*This is the semi-strong form of the efficient markets hypothesis. The strong form asserts that even non-public "insider" information is reflected in the stock price.

†Sometimes, overvaluation results from a fixed exchange rate regime combined with rapidly rising domestic prices (inflation). The outcome remains the same as described above.

‡Recall that, for valuation purposes, we exclude cash flows related to financing activities—specifically, borrowing and investing activities. From a pure accounting perspective, the cash flow statement does include financing flows.

MACRO FINANCE INSIGHT 9.2: STICKY CAPITAL STOCK: OVERSHOOTING IN EQUITY MARKETS

By now, we should be fairly familiar with the notion of overshooting and how it can occur. In this case, we consider the role of equity markets regarding international capital mobility. Consider a country such as China which has restricted international capital flows for many years. By this, we mean that, the financial flows in and out of the country have been strictly controlled.* Furthermore, we reasonably assume that the capital stock (plant, property, equipment, infrastructure, and even broadly defined to include human capital) is a very sticky variable. In other words, we cannot increase the capital stock overnight; in most countries, it takes decades to make substantial capital stock enhancements.

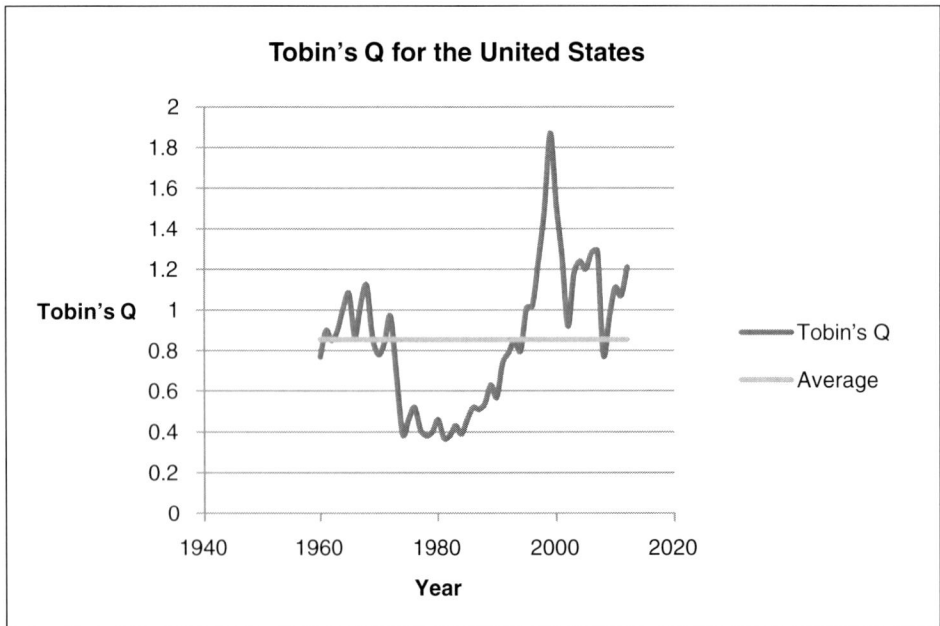

Figure MF9.2a Tobin's Q represents the ratio of market value to the book value of a company.

Source: Author created based on data from the United States Commerce Department *Survey of Current Business* (Hodge et al., 2013).

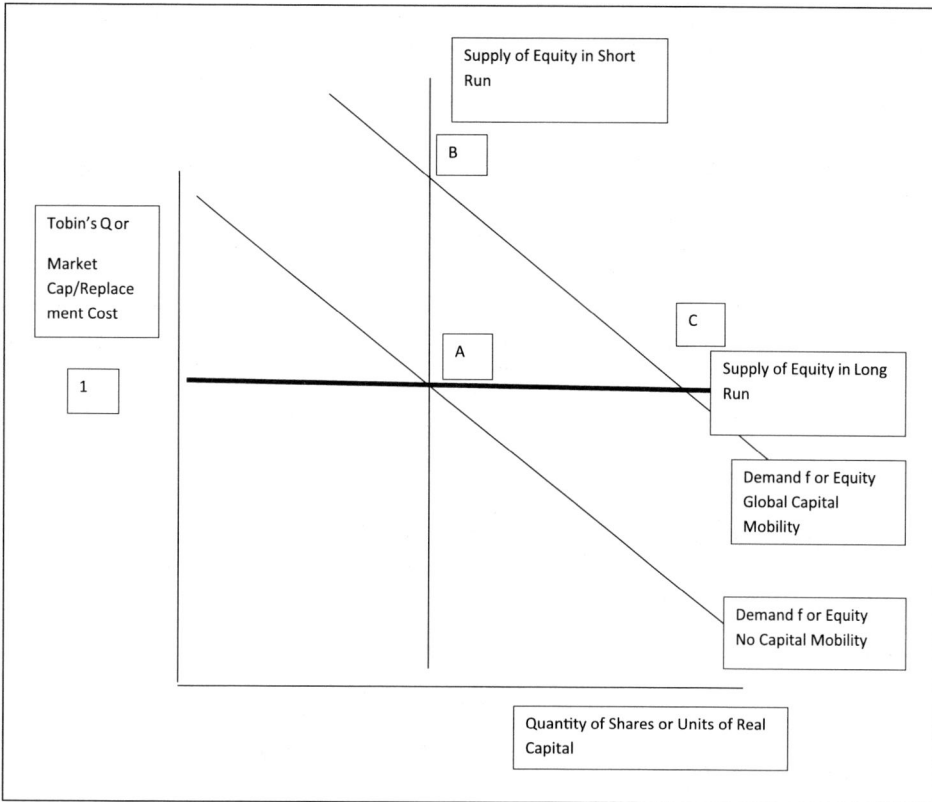

Figure MF9.2b For a country that opens up its markets to foreign financial capital inflows, demand for assets could surge, causing the price to jump from A to B. In that initial overshooting, the stream of excess future returns (capital gains) are captured by the initial owners of the assets (local owners). It is therefore critical that the process of capital account liberalization and sale of assets be "fair" to all citizens, particularly to those locals who are not owners of the sold assets.

Source: Author created.

Finally, we introduce Tobin's Q, as defined above:

Q = Market Capitalization of the Capital Stock / Replacement Cost of the Capital Stock†

In normal equilibrium circumstances, we expect Q to be close to 1. If it is greater than 1, there would be an incentive to raise funds in capital markets and acquire additional units of the cheaper capital. If Q is less than 1, firms would sell off some of their capital and use the cash proceeds to enhance value. In fact, Q can deviate from 1. In periods of optimism regarding growth prospects and options for the firm, investors may place a premium in equity markets over the underlying cost of capital assets. Figure MF9.2a shows Tobin's Q for the United States.

Figure MF9.2b shows the effects of a country such as China opening its capital markets fully to foreign capital. Initially, we start with a closed economy at point A, where Q equals 1 and is at equilibrium. The demand for equity (or an even broader range of local assets) is purely local and the supply of equity in the short run is relatively inelastic (vertical). Once we open capital markets to foreign investors, the demand for equity shifts to the right.‡ Since the physical supply of capital cannot shift instantaneously (i.e., it is sticky, but does increase over a much longer timeframe), we adjust to point B in the short run.

That is, the price of equity adjusts instantaneously (overshoots). The price will move sufficiently high so as to restore a return to equilibrium in the equity market from the combined domestic and international investor base. The high Q will result in a compelling incentive for firms to add new capital until long-run equilibrium is restored at C. Thus, in this case, the amount of overshooting is the vertical gap between B and C.

The above model demonstrates why countries must be very careful in their efforts to open capital markets. The movement from A to B creates an enormous capital gain for the pre-existing owners of capital in-country. In fact, they capture all future excess returns instantaneously. This raises serious questions of wealth distribution and fairness. How were those initial shares acquired and then sold? If the initial wealth holders acquired their wealth in an unsavory fashion, the enormous returns generated from the opening of capital markets may very well lead to social, political, and economic problems. The cases of privatization of capital markets, foreign involvement, and transfer of state assets in Eastern Europe and Russia in the 1990s are instructive in this context. And as China moves toward greater capital account liberalization, lessons learned there are of great use.

*If it were possible to increase the capital stock quickly, emerging economies could more easily converge rapidly to the same level of development as the developed economies.

†Sometimes the book value of capital is used as a surrogate for replacement cost.

‡In finance, this may sound odd. The value of companies is simply the net present value of their cash flows—so how can changes in the investor base affect that value? A change in the investor base can change value since foreigners will have different costs of capital based on different macro policies (interest rates) and different needs for diversification.

Challenges to Fiscal Policy for Economic Management

The effectiveness of fiscal policy, as we have described it above, has been questioned on a number of fronts—both economic and political. This represents a generally conservative "free market" approach regarding the role and size of government in an economy. That role is viewed as a zero-sum game with the private sector at the short end (losing) when the government intervenes. We now discuss economic arguments against using fiscal policies to manage an economy.

Crowding Out: The Case Against More Government Spending

The crowding out argument states that fiscal policy, particularly increased government spending, serves only to squeeze out private-sector spending. In other words, while government spending may move the economy one step forward, reduced private spending moves the economy one step back. How does this work? In the basic IS/LM framework (as we saw in Figure 9.5), an increase in government spending shifts the IS curve to the right. That shift causes interest rates to rise (assuming that the demand for money is not completely sensitive to changes in interest rates—all cases except for a flat LM curve). The resulting increase in interest rates leads to reduced investment and other interest-sensitive sources of demand (such as auto purchases). The more sensitive investment demand is to interest rates, the flatter the IS curve, and the greater the investment reduction. This process is known as "crowding out," since private-sector spending and the private sector's share of the economy shrinks as a result of increased government spending or fiscal policy. The financial market counterpart to this is increased government spending that is financed with debt. This, in turn, collides with private-sector financing needs, driving up borrowing costs and crowding out the private sector's investment plans.

Alternatively, we could see crowding out in the AS/AD framework (see Figure 9.8), in which the aggregate demand (AD) curve shifts to the right due to increased government spending and the

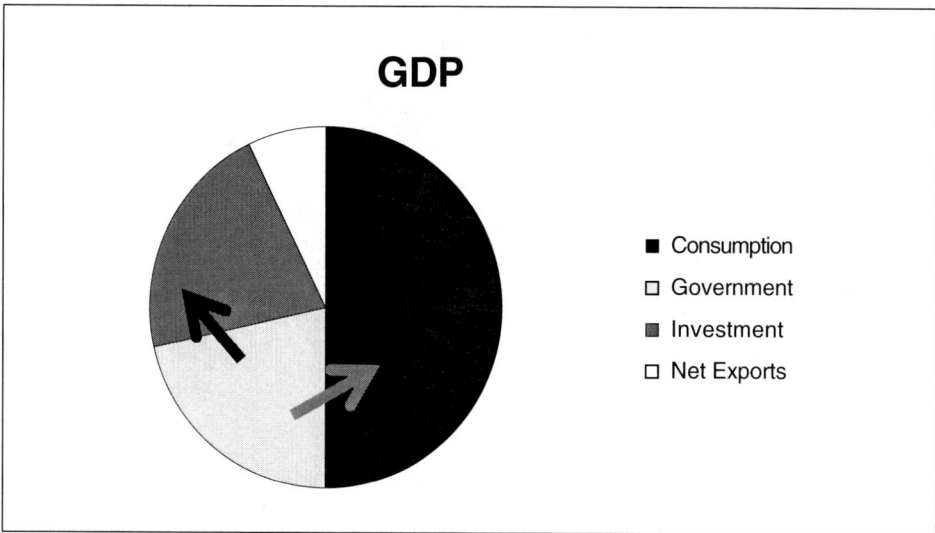

Figure 9.11 Crowding out occurs when the government sector expands but the GDP pie remains the same size. The implication is that other sectors' share of the pie must be reduced.

Source: Author created.

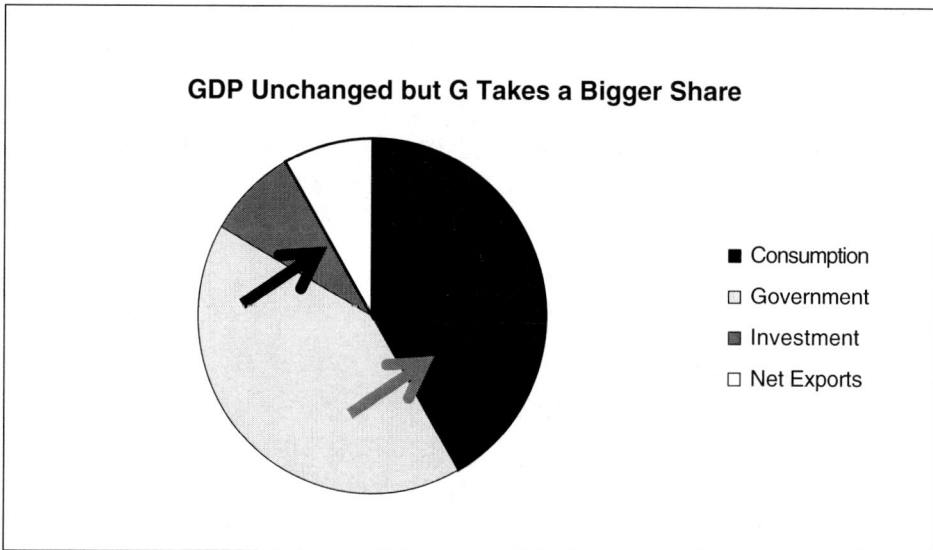

Figure 9.12 The government sector is larger but investment, consumption, and exports are all smaller.

Source: Author created.

aggregate supply (AS) curve is vertical. The vertical AS curve corresponds to an economy operating at full employment. Thus, any shift rightward of AD leads to higher prices (from 1 to 2, or P_1 to P_2)—and these higher prices correspond either to a reduction in the real money supply and higher interest rates or the same chain of events described in the earlier paragraph. If government spending

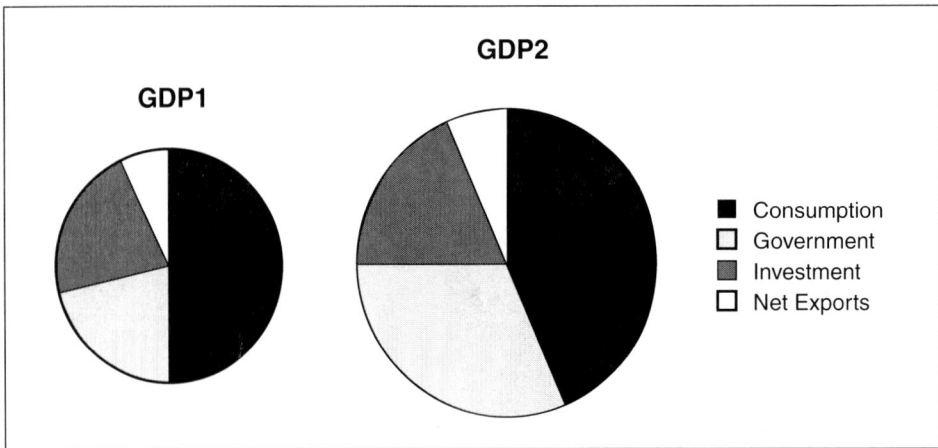

Figure 9.13 In the Keynesian case of unemployment and recession: an increase in government demand increases the size of the pie and everyone benefits from a bigger share.

Source: Author created.

is paid for with increases in the money supply, we simply get inflation, and private consumption is crowded out due to the higher prices—with no corresponding increase in overall output.

The Keynesian response to the above critique is "of course, this is obvious." Attempting to increase output beyond full employment is indeed pointless. The Keynesian world corresponds to Figure 9.2, in which the aggregate supply curve is perfectly elastic or flat because workers and suppliers of goods and services have such a high rate of unemployment that they are willing to supply output without constraint and without a tendency toward price increases. Instead of prices rising, real output rises from Y_1 to Y_2. Fiscal policy is fully effective in this case, with no crowding out.

An alternative way to view crowding out is shown in Figure 9.11 and Figure 9.12. Here, the expansion of the government sector squeezes into the investment and consumer shares of GDP; meanwhile, overall GDP (the whole size of the pie) does not change at all. Figure 9.13 corresponds to the Keynesian view of the effectiveness of fiscal policy. Here, increased government spending expands the pie so that all the sectors actually expand—from recession to recovery mode.

Case Study 9.2: Crowding Out in China

The notion of crowding out takes on a very special meaning in the Chinese context for four separate reasons: First, China is in a stage of continued rapid growth (as we have discussed), in which the risk is not traditional recessions but rather growth recessions. In China, crowding out depends on whether the government is capturing a larger share of fresh economic growth rather than a larger share of an economy that is fixed in size. Second, the role of China's state-owned enterprises (SOEs) in producing private-sector goods remains significant, albeit diminishing.* For China, the question of crowding out relates more to SOEs producing private goods rather than private firms producing them. In contrast, traditional crowding out relates to the production of public goods and services at the expense of private goods and services.† Third, China's Big Four (the four largest banks) still have the government as their principal shareholder, and these banks (on a secular basis) channel funds to the state-owned sector as opposed to the private sector. Fourth, government policies related to crowding out fall just as heavily on the production side as the expenditure side. In the past, government policies biased the economy toward the production of investment goods over consumption goods, and exchange rate policies pushed the economy to export production over consumption production (as we discuss elsewhere). These outcomes turn the Western notion of crowding out upside down; in the West, crowding out is often viewed as government expenditures squeezing out investment.

*As an indication of that, by 2010, about half of China's workforce was still employed in state-owned units; in 2001, approximately three-fourths worked in the state sector.

†Public goods are often defined by the characteristics of non-excludability and non-rival; the former represents goods or services which, once provided, are inevitably "open-access" (such as national defense). The latter represents goods in which one person's use does not preclude another person's use (such as the benefit of a lighthouse in a harbor).

Ricardian Equivalence: Linking Government Spending to Future Taxation

Ricardian equivalence is a budget constraint applied to a government's ability to borrow, spend, and tax over time. It states that governments cannot persistently borrow to finance current budget deficits if they cannot afford to service the resulting obligations through tax collections and/or reduced expenditures in the future. Alternatively, budget deficits must ultimately stabilize as a share of GDP. In this chapter's appendix, we present a form of this type of argument, but adjusted for an entire country and its financial relationship with the rest of the world. There, we show that countries would be constrained by international capital markets from borrowing more internationally than they could afford to pay back via trade and non-factor service balance surpluses in the future. Recall that:

$$S - I = (G + Tr - \text{Taxes}) + (X - M + NFP)$$

In other words, the intertemporal budget constraint in the international sphere corresponds to the $(X - M + NFP)$ term, while $(G + Tr - \text{Taxes})$ corresponds to the budget deficit (+) and Ricardian equivalence. The two constraints are linked and coexist; the domestic private sector $(S - I)$ and foreign lenders $(X - M + NFP)$ will not finance an unsustainable budget deficit (Ricardian equivalence), while international lenders will not finance an unsustainable current account deficit.

As the key corollary to Ricardian equivalence, any expansion of government spending or reduction of taxes today will require raising taxes or reducing government spending in the future in order to be sustainable. Ricardian equivalence therefore implies that fiscal policy is neutralized once taxpayers/citizens realize that today's expansion only implies a future reduction in government benefits and services, or increased taxes. Today's government spending increases (fiscal policy) are offset by concurrent reductions in private-sector consumption or investment, in a rational anticipation of either reduced benefits to consumers or a heavier tax burden.

These conclusions, although algebraically correct (if we assume a full employment economy), are controversial. Whether such rational calculations can be assumed to take place in an economy such as China's is an open question. In recent years, both the senior leadership and the common man (the *lao bai xing*) in China have questioned the sustainability of current policies described throughout this text. The question of sustainability has led the Chinese to seek ways to either build wealth or diversify their wealth internationally, and to increase consumption. While in some ways this is following the spirit of Ricardian equivalence, it is unlikely to hold much weight in discounting the effectiveness of short-run fiscal policy in China.

Flexible Wages, Prices, and Efficient Labor Markets

Another argument casting doubt on the stabilizing effects of fiscal policy is that, in the long run, it is unnecessary because the markets for labor and other factors of production and goods and services will move toward equilibrium through price adjustment. If there is unemployment, real wages will fall in the long run. To this argument, Keynes is said to have responded: "In the long run, we are all dead." As we have shown above, the economy normally operates on a short-run supply curve, which can correspond to either underemployment or overemployment. Clearly, the greater the flexibility of wages and prices, and the less rigid are the labor markets (e.g., rules restricting hiring, firing, wages, and benefits), the more likely the economy will operate at full employment. That is, the less time the economy will spend on a "disequilibrium" short-run curve and the more time it will spend on the long-run full employment curve.

In this context, it has been suggested that approximately half of all U.S. recessions have been caused by supply rather than demand shocks (i.e., the long-run supply curve shifting to the left due to adverse events such as oil price increases, natural disasters, or technological shifts resulting in parts of the labor force becoming obsolete). If this is true, demand-shifting policies such as increases in government spending can only generate price increases without improving the long-run equilibrium level of output. Whether the source of the business cycle is a demand or supply shock, the return to full employment will be hastened when the economy is more flexible (has fewer structural rigidities). In the case study below, we examine one of the great sources of strength for the Chinese economy—the flexibility of its labor force and adaptability of its citizens.

Case Study 9.3: The Chinese Citizen as a Great Economic Shock Absorber

Flexibility and adaptability are two key assets of the Chinese citizen, as worker, saver, and consumer. These two qualities allow the citizenry to act as a "shock absorber" for economic changes occurring to either the supply or demand curve. The United States' "automatic stabilizers" consist mainly of unemployment benefits and automatic tax receipt declines, which help cushion the economy in economic downturns. But China is unique in that its key resource—its labor force—is critical in absorbing a wide array of economic shocks. A good example of this flexibility is the willingness of many citizens to relocate rapidly and at long distances in order to seek employment. The migration of rural workers to urban areas in China is now at a historical magnitude. One indicator is that an estimated 46 percent of China's urban laborers in 2007 were migrant workers (Cai et al., 2005). In 1978, about 76 percent of the workforce was located in rural areas; by 2010 that number had declined to 54 percent. Today, an estimated 150–200 million Chinese workers are "floating" within China, seeking employment opportunities. The coming years should see an acceleration of this trend, given that an expected 15 million rural residents will be moving to urban areas every year! This willingness to relocate in search of employment is a sign of a very dynamic and flexible workforce—and will likely lead to better matching of positions with job applicants, resulting in a more efficient use of the labor force.

One feature peculiar to the Chinese economy, which at first seems to add rigidity to the labor market—the *hukou* system—may paradoxically make the market more flexible and competitive. The *hukou* is a system of national identification in which residents are given an ID card based on their official legal residence. Established in the 1950s, the system restricts local government benefits (such as healthcare and employment protection including minimum wage laws and education) to local residents.* In the past, the *hukou* system restricted the movement of labor around the country. Today, it no longer serves that purpose; instead, its main impact relates to the non-provision of local government benefits and protections for those living in an area (typically a large city) with no *hukou* status. As such, various laws including local minimum wage laws—which might otherwise create a wedge between workers' offer price and the bid price of employers—are absent. It is estimated that migrant workers in the informal sector in urban areas earn about 70 percent less than local residents, and most of this difference cannot be attributed to skill differences. Employers, for better or worse, can hire non-*hukou* (migrant) workers at a lower overall cost (including non-payment of social welfare benefits) than is stipulated by local laws. We have already discussed the role of government monopsony power in hiring. Recent government efforts geared toward increased urbanization have opened up limited channels for changing one's *hukou* to become official urban residents (such as through the purchase of a residence).†

Another way in which Chinese citizens act as shock absorbers is in their role as savers. Chinese families have continued to deposit savings within the state-owned banking system despite the negative real return earned on typical deposits. This has helped the banks remain quite profitable as they lend to both the government and the private sector. The same phenomenon occurred in the 2000–03 period, when the large state-owned banks had a sufficiently large number of bad assets (loans) on their books to effectively make them bankrupt. In such situations elsewhere in the world, a distinctly negative outcome usually occurs; typically, when depositors lose confidence in banks' ability to protect depositor savings, a bank run occurs. Given China's lack of explicit bank insurance at the time, the willingness of citizens to continue depositing may portray their faith in the government's obligation to protect citizens' assets.‡

A central tenet of the Keynesian framework is that sticky prices serve as a form of economic sclerosis. In China, labor force flexibility acts as a shock absorber and an antidote—allowing economic growth even in times of exogenous harmful shocks. Even shock absorbers, however, wear out over time and the most recent Five-Year Plans emphasize improving income distribution and expanding the social safety net. In the coming years, China must find alternate means to manage its vast and valuable human resource and, simultaneously, maintain flexibility.

*Minimum wage limits do exist in China, but differ by province. The median minimum wage in China is about US$200 per month.

†For the very largest cities—Shanghai, Beijing, and Chongqing—acquiring a *hukou* is still very difficult.

‡An alternative interpretation might be that the absence of financial transparency at the time prevented most depositors from truly understanding the dire situation of their banks.

MACRO FINANCE INSIGHT 9.3: ADJUSTED TOBIN'S Q AS A MEASURE OF ECONOMIC PERFORMANCE

We suggest in Macro Finance Insight 9.1 above that one gauge of economic performance is exchange rate performance. But lacking a freely floating exchange rate, we need a different approach. Another method is to examine a variation of Tobin's Q. Recall that great economist and Nobel Laureate James Tobin suggested in 1969 that a good way to gauge stock valuations is to compare the ratio of the market price of the stock to the replacement cost of its capital net of liabilities.* This approach closely matches the thinking of value investors, including Warren Buffett.

Using macro data, Tobin's approach can be generalized to entire stock market valuations in the United States and other industrialized economies.† For our purposes, it is also consistent with a well-known relationship between stock market performance and economic activity; stock prices lead economic activity by six to twelve months, and are one of the United States' leading indicators.

Although stock market capitalization data is readily available in China, replacement cost data are not.‡ A good variation, however, which appears to track Tobin's Q very well is the "equitization ratio"— the ratio of overall stock market capitalization to nominal GDP. This ratio has been used by a number of economists. Figure MF9.3a shows the equitization ratio for both the United States and China. We see both countries experiencing substantial overvaluations at the pre-financial crisis peak, then a sharp drop, followed by a recovery in the United States and a leveling off in China. Thus, the equitization ratio serves as another useful indicator of economic performance. Whether the ratio itself leads or coincides with economic activity is an area for further research.

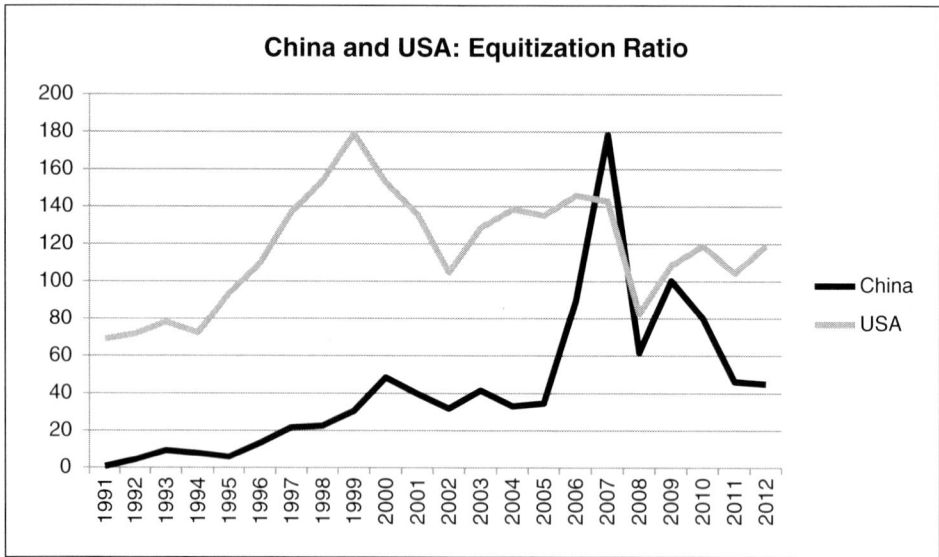

Figure MF9.3a The equitization ratio is a variation on Tobin's Q. It has recovered in the United States
            after the financial crisis but not in China.

Source: Author created.

*The former is readily available from stock market data published in each country and the latter from the company's
balance sheet.

† In the United States, replacement cost data are available both from the Federal Reserve Flow of Funds Z.1 report and the
U.S. Commerce Department.

‡See, for example, the Hong Kong Stock Exchange website: http://www.hkex.com.hk/eng

Appendix: National Budget Constraint in International Financial Markets

In this Appendix, we cover two key concepts: Ricardian equivalence (discussed in this chapter) and
the measurement of a country's cash flows (covered in Chapter 3). Ricardian equivalence argues
that current government consumption and deficits are constrained, over time, by available resources.
Here, we suggest that a country's international deficits and its access to external finance are constrained by its ability to produce and service its debt. Meanwhile, in Chapter 3, we presented a definition of a country's cash flow (an important metric for providers of external finance to a country)
which was equivalent to its current account balance. Any outside investor (whether issuing equity or
debt) will ask a very basic set of questions: when and how much will I get paid back? An investor provides money to a company and wants to be assured of the timing and amount of payment. Of course,
the more "risky" or uncertain the cash flows, the higher the required return. This approach can readily
be applied to a country which is seeking finance from world financial markets. The critical question
is the feasibility of repayment—and this is directly related to the country's cash flows and valuation.

Intertemporal Budget Constraint (ITBC)11

A country that seeks resources (finance) from the rest of the world must be able to provide resources
(cash flow) over time to pay back its loans. What resources will a country have over time? Its GDP.
Specifically its sources of payment will be:

$$Y_0 + \frac{Y_0}{(1+r)} + \frac{Y_2}{(1+r)^2} + \frac{Y_3}{(1+r)^3} \ldots$$

In which (Y) represents real GDP and (r) represents the country's discount factor or weighted cost of capital. We look at the country's potential for output over an infinite horizon and discount it to its present value.

We can consider the uses of GDP as either consumption, investment, or service over time of debt to foreign creditors. This can be written as $r \times D_i$. We assume that (for both the private and public sectors) all uses can be collapsed into two categories, C and I:

$$(C+I)_0 + \frac{(C+I)_1}{(1+r)} + \frac{(C+I)_2}{(1+r)^2} + \frac{(C+I)_3}{(1+r)^3} \ldots$$

$$+$$

$$r \times D_0 + \frac{r \times D_1}{(1+r)} + \frac{r \times D_2}{(1+r)^2} + \frac{r \times D_3}{(1+r)^3} \ldots$$

We can first subtract uses of GDP from sources $(Y - C - I)$, then use the fact that $Y - C - I$ is the same as the trade balance (TB). For the second term involving external debt, we can sum the infinite series to yield $(1 + r) \times D_0$:

This yields:

$$(TB_0) + \frac{(TB_1)}{(1+r)} + \frac{(TB_2)}{(1+r)^2} + \frac{(TB_3)}{(1+r)^3} \ldots - (1+r) \times D_0 \geq 0$$

The above inequality states that, in order for a country to offer value to external investors, its trade balances (in present value terms) must be greater than its external debt (D_0). Alternatively, if a country has no foreign equity holders, its present value of trade balances must be at least as great as its external debt—otherwise its creditors will consider the country insolvent. Once again (as noted earlier), the role of trade balances is similar to the role of cash flow at the macroeconomic level— an exact analogy to the corporate context. While our earlier discussion covered the gap between $S - I$, here we derive the resulting comparison of sources and uses of output—but the results are the same. Each provides a unique insight into policy prescriptions—similar to the discussion of current account balance perspectives.

An interesting scenario is when trade balances average zero over the infinite horizon. Even if the country has no external debt, its value to internal investors and external shareholders is zero at a macroeconomic aggregate level. If it has external debt, its value is less than zero. Does this seem reasonable? In the corporate context, such a situation is equivalent to a company having zero projected cash flows over the future horizon. While the company is able to pay its employees, suppliers, and taxes, it is unable to service its investors; thus, the situation is not sustainable. Ultimately, investors will withdraw their capital by refusing to reinvest and the company will go out of business.

We note that, when a country has a stock of either foreign debt or equity obligations, a perennial trade balance of zero is still inadequate to satisfy foreign investors. It would still need to service its obligations, implying a negative current account balance and further accumulation of external debt. Assuming that the cost of external finance (the cost of capital) is greater than the country's long-term growth rate, a perennial current account deficit and concomitant rise in external debt would lead to an ever-rising ratio of external obligations to GDP. In this scenario, 100 percent of GDP would be needed to service external obligations (interest and dividends). Once a hint of such a scenario appears, international financiers will step back, halt any further finance, and even attempt to withdraw their existing investments.

In the country context, when $S - I$ is perennially zero or negative, or equivalently when the equation above showing trade balances (TB) less than or equal to 0, we see international investors halting their investing (lending or equity investment) in the country for lack of returns. If in fact the economy is closed to external finance, and the cash flow remains 0, we see self-financing of investment at the domestic level. Formally, we can decompose domestic savings, $S^D - I^D$, as follows:

$$S^D - I^D = (S^P - I^P) + (S^C - I^C) + (S^G - I^G)$$

In which P, C, and G represent the private savings investment gap by individuals, C by corporations (net income), and G by the government (the budget surplus or deficit). In the special case in which $S^D - I^D = 0$ (given no international financing), a surplus in one of the sectors implies at least one deficit in the other sectors. Typically, the corporate sector would have a negative $S^C - I^C$ balance which must be financed either by the excess savings of either private individuals or the government. Similar reasoning applies in the international case. If private individuals do not ultimately see a surplus of cash in the corporate sector in coming years, they will stop providing their excess savings. This would cause a financing shortfall for the corporate sector. If policymakers view this situation as untenable (since employment may be impacted, for example), the government may choose to channel funds to the corporate sector. In the past, this has been China's response to funding shortfalls in the production sector. Of course, this is much easier for the government to do if it has a surplus (of savings). The real question, though, relates to whether corporations should be supported by the government if their long-run viability is in doubt.

Challenging Questions for China (and the Student): Chapter 9

1. Go the Federal Reserve Economic Database (FRED) and graph government consumption as a share of GDP in China.
2. Suppose that China's economy in Figure CS9.1b is located right between the two chopsticks in the shaded area. Using Figure 9.4, show what natural economic forces will tend to build up and move the economy in one direction or the other?
3. Explain why "crowding out" in China has a very different meaning compared to the notion in the United States. Be specific about where crowding out is occurring—on the production side or the uses side, and which sectors (C, I, G, or NX) are crowding out which other sectors.
4. Explain why flexible pricing (or its absence) is a linchpin (a critical assumption) in the Keynesian framework. Now explain the analogous role that the "great economic shock absorber" plays.
5. Explain why it would be important for any emerging economy (including China) to clarify, in a legal sense, the ownership of domestically owned assets before opening its assets markets to international capital mobility. In this context, explain the advantages and disadvantages of an emerging economy delaying the opening up of its financial markets to international investment.
6. Explain what warning signs are and are not contained in China's appreciating exchange rate in recent years.
7. If in fact, China comes to rely less on exports and less on investment as a source of demand in the coming years, how will fiscal policy need to be different from its current situation?
8. Discuss: In the coming years, China's labor force will come to show increasing inflexibility and this will present new challenges for fiscal policy.

9. In Macro Finance Insight 9.2, what assumption must we be making in the background regarding the fixity or flexibility of the exchange rate? How would Macro Finance Insight 9.2 be altered if we changed that assumption?

Notes

1. The convention of labeling IS as the point at which supply = demand for goods and services relates to the fact that when supply = demand, savings will also equal investment in a closed economy. Savings is the "absence" of consumer and government demand; investment is the activity whose "presence" fills in a needed demand to rebalance supply and demand. We will discuss this point more fully when we introduce the role of inventories as a part of investment demand. The LM label represents the demand for money or a liquid asset (L) and the supply of money (M).

2. The tax rate is an index of corporate, personal, and all other tax rates. The transfer rate represents what share of income derives from transfer payments that include social security, unemployment and welfare, and veterans' benefits.

3. Investment is clearly a critical component of demand that can trigger short-run fluctuations in output (recessions and recoveries). PP&E and residential investment are interest-sensitive components of demand. Unplanned inventory accumulation or decumulation are also part of investment (by definition) and have an important impact on the output decisions of firms.

4. Recall that Walras's Law states that demand for assets cannot exceed the underlying basis for demand—the supply of wealth. In turn, excess demand for any asset must be offset by an excess supply of some other asset or set of assets.

5. In alternative financial markets, such as the bond market, there would be an excess demand for bonds (consistent with Walras's Law).

6. Recall that the rise in interest rates results from an unchanged money supply meeting an increased demand for money which is caused by the rise in economic activity (output) and results in greater demand for money.

7. Being dead, for example, is a bad kind of equilibrium.

8. In reality we rarely see outright deflation or declines in prices. Rather, we see a deceleration of the inflation rate.

9. One would reasonably ask why we would try to stimulate the economy if we are already at full employment (A). One explanation might be that policymakers are not sure exactly what the full employment level of output is in the economy.

10. There are many caveats to PPP (the law of one price). It is assumed that trade barriers and transportation costs are insignificant and that information about price differences is widely available. Empirically, relative PPP seems to hold much better than absolute PPP. Relative PPP states that percent price changes and percent exchange rate changes tend to move in a way that prevents large price discrepancies from appearing.

11. Also known as the *transversality condition* in dynamic programming or optimal control.

References

Bernanke, Ben, and Mark Gertler. 1995. "Inside the Black Box: The Credit Channel of Monetary Policy Transmission." NBER Working Paper No. 5146. Cambridge: National Bureau of Economic Research.

Bewley, Truman F. 1999. *Why Wages Don't Fall During Recession*. Cambridge and London: Harvard University Press.

Cai, Fang, Meiyan Wang, and Yang Du. 2005. "China's Labor Market on Crossroad." *China and World Economy* 13(1): 32–46.

Calvo, Guillermo, and Frederic S. Mishkin, 2003. "The Mirage of Exchange Rate Regimes for Emerging Market Countries." NBER Working Papers No. 9808. Cambridge, MA: National Bureau of Economic Research.

Cox, Simon. 2011. "Keynes v. Hayek in China." *The Economist*, November 17.

Dornbusch, Rudiger, 1976. "Expectations and Exchange Rate Dynamics." *Journal of Political Economy* 84(6):1161–76.

Fleming, J. Marcus. 1962. "Domestic Financial Policies Under Fixed and Floating Exchange Rates." *International Monetary Fund Staff Papers* 9: 369–79.

Frankel, Jeffrey, and George Saravelos. 2012. "Can Leading Indicators Assess Country Vulnerability? Evidence from the 2008–09 Global Financial Crisis." *Journal of International Economics* 87(2): 216–31.

Geng, N., and P. N'Diaye. 2012. "Determinants of Corporate Investment in China: Evidence from Cross-Country Firm Level Data." IMF Working Paper No. 12/80. Washington, DC: International Monetary Fund.

Keynes, John Maynard. 1936. *The General Theory of Employment, Interest and Money*. London: Macmillan.

Laurens, Bernard J., and Rodolfo Maino. 2007. "China: Strengthening Monetary Policy Implementation." IMF Working Paper No. 07/14. Washington, DC: International Monetary Fund.

Mundell, Robert A. 1963. "Capital Mobility and Stabilization Policy Under Fixed and Flexible Exchange Rates." *Canadian Journal of Economic and Political Science* 29(4): 475–85.

Obstfeld, Maurice. 2012. "Financial Flows, Financial Crises and Global Imbalances." *Journal of International Money and Finance* 31(3): 469–80.

10 Public Finances and Fiscal Policy in Action

天不生无用之人，地不长无名之草
Heaven Does Not Create Useless People—Earth Does Not Grow Nameless Plants

Fiscal policy relates to the government's taxing, spending, investing, lending, and social welfare, as well as redistribution activities, and how these activities affect a country's economic performance. In China, the Ministry of Finance (MOF), the National Development and Reform Commission (NDRC), and, of course, the State Council all play important but different roles in managing fiscal policy.[1] In the United States, the U.S. Treasury is primarily responsible for fiscal policy. In both economies, local governments have a significant role in how fiscal policy is implemented. In any economy, investors (capitalists), suppliers of labor, and the institution that we know as "the government" are the three critical stakeholders in the production process. There are substantial differences between China and the United States in terms of the government stakeholder's role in production, investment, and claims on income (taxation), as we shall see.

In the United States, the president submits an annual national budget to Congress each February, and Congress adjusts the proposed budget in the following months. Congress sets limits on tax revenues, spending through various appropriation bills, and the national debt. After extensive negotiations over priorities, spending and tax levels, and the ultimate deficit, the budget in its final form is presented to the President for his approval and signature. The U.S. fiscal year runs from October 1 through September 30. China's fiscal year corresponds to the normal calendar year. Local spending (provinces-states, prefectures, counties, towns, and villages) is also an important part of fiscal policy—particularly if it is tied to national priorities (discussed below). In the United States, the President's Council of Economic Advisors submits its Annual Report (also known as the Economic Report of the President) in early March of each year. This extensive document surveys the U.S. economy and international linkages, and sets out policy priorities for the coming years.

Case Study 10.1: Administrative Levels in China

Similar to the governmental divisions of national, state, county, township, and city found in the United States, China's different levels of government can be seen in Table CS10.1a. Below the Chinese central government are thirty-one provinces (*sheng* 省) which include twenty-six entities on the geographic scale of a state (Guangdong, for example) and five autonomous regions (Tibet, Inner Mongolia, Guanxi, Ningxia, Xinjiang), as well as four mega-cities (Beijing, Tianjin, Shanghai, and Chongqing). Within these provinces are prefectures (*diqu* 地区—large cities or powerful clusters of smaller cities). Counties (*xian* 县) are either the urban part of a prefectural city or a rural area with no large city. Townships (*zhengqu* 镇区) are rural areas in a county and villages, and (*cun* 村) are small communities with only an indirect administrative role.

Table CS10.1a Description and number of China's different administrative levels.

Provincial level	Prefectural Level	County Level	Township Level	Village Level (estimate)
31	332	2,852	40,466	900,000
Provinces 22	Cities 285	Districts 860	Towns 19,881	
Autonomous	Prefectures 48	Cities 368	Townships 13,281	
Regions 5		Counties 1,453	Street Communities	
Municipalities 4		Other 171	7,282	
			Other 22	

Source: China Statistical Yearbook 2012; Ministry of Civil Administration; CECD WP 1030 (2013).
Note: Following the practice of the China Statistical Yearbook, these statistics cover mainland China only.

If the mix of administrative levels described above seems complex and overlapping, that's because it is. China's long history and large population centers make it difficult to divide administrative regions in a tidy way. The current structure of provinces was formed over the last three dynasties: the Yuan, Ming, and Qing. In part, the many governmental divisions reflect a "divide and rule" policy by various emperors. By splitting powerful groups into separate entities within China's long-standing borders, emperors could prevent cohesive challenges to their power. In fact, large multinational companies do very similar things. For example, companies organized around geographic lines find that foreign subsidiary managers see only their own local interests at the expense of the goals of the entire company. The CEO of a multinational company may then choose to split the company up along functional lines (e.g., finance or marketing) so as to have managers thinking more broadly about corporate goals rather than their own geographical turf.

These same issues arise in the United States with large towns located in otherwise rural counties or suburban communities located in townships. Large population centers feel that they deserve a closer link to the central government even though the actual geographic area that they cover may be small. Ultimately over time, these efforts at greater representation get reconciled at the cost of greater complexity.

China's budget policy is rooted in its Five-Year Plans. The 35-member State Council in Beijing representing the major components of the Chinese government establishes policy goals for the long, medium, and short term. The most recent 2011–15 Plan, for example, establishes targets ranging from urbanization, to the state of the environment, and the size of the service sector. The Five-Year Plan is updated on an annual basis in response to the economic environment and provides the framework for short-term fiscal and monetary policy in its traditional role. Every October, the People's Congress and top leadership meet to establish short-run macroeconomic goals. At this time the budget is also presented to establish priorities for the coming year and the general stance of monetary policy is set. For example, in the 2013 budget, goals for inflation, monetary growth, and real economic growth of 3.5, 13, and 7.5 percent, respectively, were established. Given the uncertainties found in any economy, the targets set in the annual budget are often missed.

Case Study 10.2: China's Five-Year Plans

The strategic planning function is an important activity for most large companies around the world. Among governments, arguably no country in the world has achieved the same level of sophistication as China in terms of planning via its Five-Year Plans. China is now following its twelfth Five-Year Plan for National Economic and Social Development. The first plan was issued in 1953, with new major plans issued every five years subsequently—the most recent one was deliberated and approved in 2011. These plans establish priorities for the Chinese government starting at the macro level and moving downward to impact sectors, industries, companies, and even individual townships and villages. Based on the national Five-Year Plan, sub-levels of government establish their own strategies that, in turn, are used by local level institutions (such as banks and universities) establishing their own five-year plans.

China's budget policy is rooted in its Five-Year Plans. The 35-member State Council representing the major components of the Chinese government establishes policy goals for the long, medium, and short term. The most recent 2011–15 plan, for example, establishes targets ranging from urbanization and the state of the environment, to the size of the service sector. The current Five-Year Plan is updated annually in response to the economic environment and provides the framework for short-term fiscal and monetary policy in its traditional role. Every October, the People's Congress and top leadership meet to establish short-run macroeconomic goals. At that time, the budget is also presented, establishing priorities for the coming year and setting the general stance of monetary policy.

More broadly, the goals of the most recent Five-Year Plan include: reducing social inequality, enhancing the social safety net, shifting the economy from an investment and export focus to greater domestic consumption, and, finally, protecting the environment. We should not dismiss these targets as mere blandishments; the Chinese government uses its powerful fiscal and financial (lending) tools to achieve these goals. Furthermore, the Five-Year Plans can be quite specific about precise targets to be met. For example, the current plan sets an explicit target of 7 percent real GDP growth; proposes an annual minimum wage increase of 13 percent through 2015; states specific fuel efficiency targets; and names specific industries/sectors to be supported, including healthcare, education, technology, and energy. Promotions of local officials are often based on how well they meet Five-Year Plan targets. Given the uncertainties found in any economy, these targets are sometimes missed. And some targets are not mandatory but serve as recommended guidelines. However, the Chinese government's impressive track record in achieving its goals makes it essential for investors and businesses to carefully assess the Five-Year Plan when setting their strategy in China.

China's short-term fiscal and monetary policies are more formally linked to a longer-term strategy—the Five-Year Plan—than what we find in the United States (see Case Study 10.2).[2] As we shall see, fiscal policy in China has historically focused more on long-term investment strategies than has that of the United States. In contrast, U.S. fiscal policy places more weight on short-term macroeconomic issues including demand management related to unemployment and inflation. Furthermore, since China's central bank is not independent of the central government (as in the United States), fiscal and monetary policy are highly coordinated. The PBC's role in allocating credit to specific sectors and industries is critically different from that of the U.S. Federal Reserve. China's annual meetings in October also differ in that a key policy variable (the exchange rate) is an important discussion point. Also different is the focus on key sectors and industries in the economy; in recent years, China's property market has been an important part of the policy, while in earlier years, cement production (for example) was targeted.

Although China's State Council establishes long- to short-term policies, implementation is accomplished by various institutions and government agencies. The PBC (monetary policy), SAFE (exchange rate policy), and the National Development Resource Council (NDRC—responsible for investment in infrastructure) all play a role in implementation. As we will discuss, the local governments are of equal—if not even greater importance—in terms of implementation. Finally, state-owned enterprises play a significant role in implementing policy, particularly as it pertains to investment.

Key Goals of Fiscal Policy

At one level, fiscal policy is similar to the activities of a company in that it involves the provision of goods and services, the collection of revenue, investment in plant and equipment, the raising of capital, and maintaining the quality of its balance sheet. At another level, the corporate goal of value creation is more complex and ambiguous in the case of governments where maximizing social welfare or operating at full employment are important objectives. Perhaps the European corporate model, which considers all stakeholders (not just shareholders), is relevant in this context. Fiscal policy activities include:

- Providing goods and services that are needed but which the private economy does not provide as efficiently, or at all (public goods production).
- Maintaining economic output at levels consistent with full employment (counter-cyclical policy).
- Investing in physical capital or infrastructure and human capital so as to sustain value-creating economic growth over the long term (economic development).
- Promoting a fair distribution of income, resources, and opportunities across different regions and citizens (income distribution).
- Creating incentives for the private sector to engage in value-creating activities (tax and spending policies, or taxes and subsidies).

Table 10.1 provides counterparts to the above-mentioned government activities with corporate activities. Many of the corporate sector's activities are consistent with government activities. For example, both seek full and efficient employment of their labor force.

We could think of the role of government as "filling in the gaps" caused by targets that are unmet or out-of-synch with the corporate sector. For example, corporate governance tries to strike a workable balance between various stakeholders—workers, management, investors, and the government. For a variety of reasons, including principle–agent problems, corporate governance may fail to provide a fair or even efficient distribution of the value added to each stakeholder. The government may want to step in and "tidy up" the distribution of income. Governments use their tax and spending power to encourage or discourage certain activities. For example, the U.S. government encourages home ownership (a tax incentive) by allowing the deductibility of interest payments on first- and second-home mortgages. It is generally agreed, however, that U.S. tax rules have become too complex. As a result, the rules and regulations related to federal taxes are contained in twenty volumes, or about 17,000 pages. China's tax laws are considerably shorter, but perhaps less transparent.

Some policy goals are long term and some are short term. In this chapter, we will examine the role of policy in both timeframes. First, we assess the broad outlines of taxing and spending in both countries. We will then employ the workhorse for understanding fiscal (and monetary policy): the Keynesian model in the context of the recent financial crisis. Next, we will examine fiscal policy in the long run as an engine for economic growth—something relatively important in China. Finally,

Table 10.1 The goals of governments and the corporate sector can align across a range of areas, but there are a number of areas in society where governments need to "fill in the gaps."

Government Activities	Corporate Activities
Public goods and services including national defense and education	Private goods and services
Counter-cyclical policy	Full and efficient use of all resources including employees, capital stock, and inventories
Economic development	New investment in capital stock, inventories, and research and development
Income distribution	Corporate governance; satisfying stakeholders
Taxes, subsidies, or incentives	Compensation and human resources management

Source: Author created.

in the context of decentralization and federalism, we discuss the links between central government fiscal activities and local government activities. This latter discussion allows for some interesting comparisons between China and the United States.

Overall Budgets

Fiscal budgets are significant at both the central and local levels, in terms of their real economic impact. Recent defaults at the central government level (in Europe) and at the local level (in Detroit) are cases in point.[3] Furthermore, central government revenues are often shared with local governments through grants and loans. We will first compare and contrast revenues and expenditures in China in detail at the central and local levels, then see how this breakdown corresponds to patterns found in the United States. Tables 10.2 and 10.3 provide an overview of each country's overall revenues, expenditures and deficits, and surpluses at both the national and local level (province, state, and local).

China runs a surplus at the central level, and a deficit locally; the United States runs a deficit at all levels. As a share of GDP, China's overall deficit is around 1 percent while the deficit in the United States is close to 9 percent (more than doubling since the 2008 financial crisis). In China, the large positive savings balance found in the private sector can easily fund the relatively small budget deficit. In the United States, savings deficits occur across both the government and private sectors, and therefore have been funded by foreign savings (international borrowing).[4] In both countries, there are constraints on local governments running deficits. As we will see, this implies substantial grants (revenue sharing) from the national to local levels in both countries.

Table 10.2 China's central and local budget revenues and expenses.

	China 2011 Distribution of Revenues and Expenses (100 million RMB) and % of GDP					
	Central Government	Share of GDP	Local Government	Share of GDP	Total	Share
Revenues	51,327.32	11%	52,547.11	11%	103,874.43	22%
Expenses	16,514.11	3%	92,733.68	20%	109,247.79	23%
Surplus or deficit(−)	34,813.21	7%	−40,186.57	−8%	−5,373.36	−1%

Source: China Statistical Yearbook Tables 8–4 and 8–5.

Table 10.3 U.S. government revenues and expenses at the national and local level.

	U.S. 2011 Distribution of Revenues and Expenses (US$ billions) and % of GDP					
	Federal Government	Share	Local Government	Share	Total	Share
Revenues*	2,519.6	17%	1,566.6	10%	4,086.2	27%
Expenses*	3,259.2	22%	2,166.3	14%	5,425.5	36%
Surplus or deficit(−)†	−739.6	−5%	−599.7	−4%	−1,339.3	−9%

Source: Economic Report of the President.
*State-local revenues adjusted downward by US$497.8 billion and federal expenditures reduced by same amount to net out federal revenue sharing.
†Does not include off-budget items (social security and postal service balances) that reduce the 2011 deficit by US$67 billion.

MACRO FINANCE INSIGHT 10.1: THE ODD ACCOUNTING FOR BUDGET DEFICITS

In financial accounting, we learn to exclude certain expenditures from the income statement. Specifically, capital expenditures are excluded since they do not reflect a cost of production but rather an increase in a firm's assets. The corresponding cost included in the income statement is depreciation. In contrast, GDP accounting often includes capital expenditures as an expense in the "headline" calculation of budget deficits. This undoubtedly reflects the desire to reveal the critical borrowing that governments must undertake to finance both current and capital expenditures. Meanwhile, given that the "G" in GDP stands for gross, depreciation is usually not included in budget deficit numbers.

Governments usually do provide a breakdown, however, between activities related to government consumption and those related to government investment. Government consumption represents expenditures for providing current services, including the acquisition of goods and services from the private sector and employment of the civil service. Table 10.4 provides a comparison of the Chinese and United States' governments in terms of consumption and investment. We can see once again the heavy bias of investment, even at the government level in China compared to the United States.* In China, over 40 percent of government expenditures represent investment, while in the United States, this figure is only 15 percent. In the United States, most government spending is consumption related—mainly transfer payments and defense spending. This very much mirrors the balance between investment and consumption in the broader macroeconomy. A corollary is that much of the government investment in China appears to be financed through borrowing—specifically bank borrowing, since state funding appears to cover only about one-third of government investment spending.

To our main accounting point: Even if we exclude investment spending from the U.S. fiscal accounts, the budget deficit would still be very large; however, excluding investment in the case of China would turn the already small deficit into a surplus. Viewed from a cash flow (rather than income statement) perspective, both governments need to borrow.

*In fact, these figures probably understate true Chinese government investment since they do not include SOE investment at the behest of central and local governments. These investments, while often not funded directly from the government, are funded by the state-owned banks.

Table 10.4 Mirroring the broader economy in each country, China's government spends a substantially larger share of its budget on investment compared to the United States.

	China		United States	
	RMB 100 Million	*%*	*Billions US$*	*%*
Government investment	45,631.7	42%	472.6	15%
Government consumption	63,616.1	58%	2,590.3	85%
Total government spending	109,247.8	100%	3,062.9	100%
Note for China:				
State budget for investment	14,677.8			
All domestic lending for investment	47,258			
Implied domestic lending for government investment	30,953.9			

Source: China Statistical Yearbook Table 2–18, 5–1, and 8–5; Economic Report of the President of the U.S.: Table B-20.

Tax Revenues

China's current tax system is based on the tax reform laws of 1994, in which the explicit goal of reform was to recentralize tax collection away from indirect taxes levied locally (e.g., sales- or transactions-based taxes) to national taxes based on both income and value added. The end result was that provinces and localities have virtually no taxing power in China today, either in terms of how much they receive in taxes or in terms of their control over tax structure. This contrasts sharply with most advanced countries worldwide. In the United States, state and local governments are free to establish sales taxes, taxes on individuals and corporations (income taxes), and property tax.[5] In the United States, taxes that are autonomously set locally amount to about 8 percent of GDP compared to zero percent in China.

Meanwhile in China, as Figure 10.1 shows, expenditures (the provision of services) have increasingly become the mandate of local governments. Revenues for localities have risen too, but not as fast as expenditures (Figure 10.2). Particularly acute is the shortfall of revenues compared

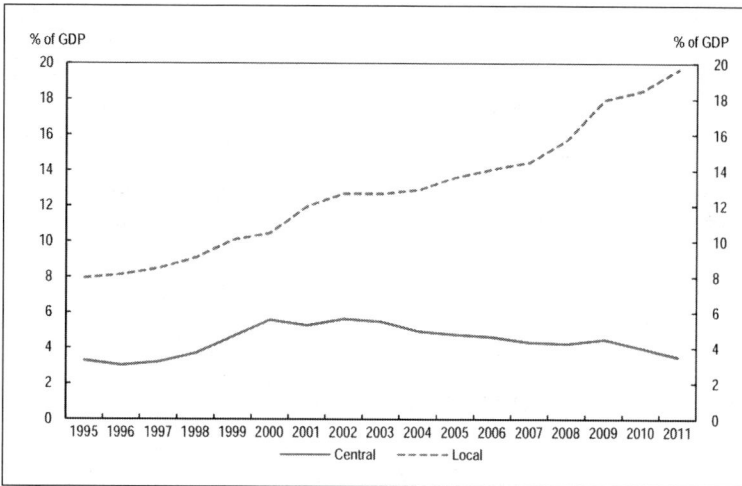

Figure 10.1 Local governments have an increasing burden in providing services to Chinese citizens. China's central and local governments, expenditures as share of GDP (excluding Social Security).

Source: China Statistical Yearbook, Tables 2–1 and 8–3; and Wang and Herd, 2013.

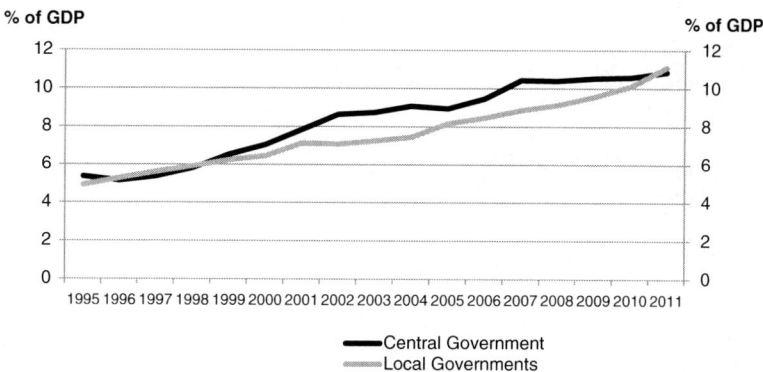

Figure 10.2 Local government revenue as a share of GDP has risen over the years in tandem with central government revenue since there is a specific formula for how most tax revenues are to be shared.

Source: Author created.

to required expenditures at the rural and urban district levels. If provincial and local governments have no taxation ability, what are their sources of revenue? Case Study 10.3 delves into this question.

Case Study 10.3: Revenue Sharing

China's 1994 Budget Law provides a specific formula illustrating how central government tax revenues are to be shared with localities. Table CS10.3a provides a breakdown based on the most recent revision of the formula (2003). On average, the central government retains around 54 percent of collected taxes while transferring the remaining 46 percent to provincial and local governments. The three main types of taxes shared in this way are the VAT, corporate income tax, and personal income tax. But this shared tax revenue in 2011 represented only about 40 percent of provincial and local expenditures. As we will see, over time these regions have come to rely on even less stable and less transparent sources of revenue.

  The bottom line, for purposes of comparison, is that, in the United States, localities collect about 40 percent of government revenues and make up about 40 percent of government spending.* In China, while localities collect less than half of all revenues, they are responsible for over 85 percent of expenditures. Both in China and in the United States, substantial revenue sharing is required. Insufficient revenue sharing in China causes substantial budgetary pressure at the local level. Shortfalls are particularly felt in Chinese villages, which come at the bottom of the governmental "food chain"—a system in which bilateral transfers start with the central government and move down to the provinces.†

Table CS10.3a There is a specific formula for revenue sharing between the central and provincial governments in China.

	Legal Sharing Rate		Receipts as % of		CNY Billion	
	Central	Provincial	Central	Provincial	Central	Provincial
Central Taxes			32.7	0.0	1,593	
Consumption tax	100	0	14.3	0.0	694	0
Tariffs	100	0	5.3	0.0	256	0
International trade-related consumption tax and VAT	100	0	27.9	0.0	1,356	0
Refunds of VAT and consumption tax	100	0	−18.9	0.0	−920	0
Vehicle purchase tax	100	0	4.2	0.0	204	0
Cargo tax	100	0	0.1	0.0	3	0
Shared Taxes			66.5	36.9	3,236	1,517
VAT	75	25	37.6	14.6	1,828	599
Corporate income tax	60	40	20.6	16.4	1,002	675
Personal income tax	60	40	7.5	5.9	363	242
Stamp tax on securities	97	3	0.9	0.0	43	1
Sub-national Taxes			0.7	63.1	34	2,594
Business tax	1	99	0.4	32.9	17	1,350
Resource tax	0	100	0.0	1.4	0	60
Urban maintenance and development tax	0	100	0.3	6.3	17	261
House property tax	0	100	0.0	2.7	0	110

(*Continued*)

	Legal Sharing Rate		Receipts as % of		CNY Billion	
	Central	*Provincial*	*Central*	*Provincial*	*Central*	*Provincial*
Real estate tax	0	100	0.0	3.0	0	122
Urban land use tax	0	100	0.0	5.0	0	206
Land appreciation tax	0	100	0.0	0.7	0	30
Tax on vehicles and boat operation	0	100	0.0	2.6	0	108
Tax on the use of arable land	0	100	0.0	1.5	0	60
Tobacco tax	0	100	0.0	0.2	0	9
Tax on deeds	0	100	0.0	6.7	0	277
All Taxes	54.2	45.8	100.0	100.0	4,863	4,111

Source: Wang and Herd, 2013.

*Since overall expenditures are greater than revenues, localities still have a shortfall in revenues which must come from the federal government.

†In China, approximately 46 percent of expenditures from localities must be funded by transfers from the central government. In the United States, an estimated one-third of local level expenditures require federal funding.

Tables 10.5 and 10.6, and Figures 10.3 and 10.4 identify the main sources of revenues at both the central and local government levels in China. For the central government, about half of revenues are derived from a form of sales tax—the value-added tax or the domestic consumption tax. The corporate income tax follows, in order of importance, at about 20 percent of central government revenues. For localities, the principal source of revenue is a business tax (26 percent). China's business tax is closer in spirit to a retail sales tax on services (e.g., banking or restaurants). All of this tax is returned to localities; while the value-added tax is levied solely on goods in which value is added at intermediate stages of production, and the increased value is then shared nationally and locally. Interestingly, the second-largest source of revenues at the local level is related to real estate (21 percent). About two-thirds of this revenue source is based on real estate transactions, the remaining one-third on the value of the underlying land or property value.

Shared tax revenues alone cover less than half of expenditures as seen in Table CS10.3a. Various other non-tax revenues are also implemented including user fees at the local level, penalties and fines, and income from local state-owned enterprises (covering about 21 percent of expenditure). Local governments also sell land use rights (another 11 percent). Still facing a financing shortfall, local governments rely on government transfers or grants to fill the remaining gap in expenditures. About 23 percent of revenues for localities in China are the result of grants from the central government whereas in the United States the comparable figure is 25 percent. Localities in China rely not only on grants, but also on shared tax revenues collected by the central government (an estimated 50 percent of local revenues). In Figure 10.5 we see that China earmarks (restricts for a specific use) about 15 percent of national tax revenue when it transfers funds to localities. The U.S. earmarks relatively more funds to localities than China (25–30 percent). But this is mainly because of one area of earmarking in the United States—healthcare (or, more specifically, support of Medicaid—a program for the poor, designed and administered at the local level that receives about 60 percent of funding from the federal government). In China, the

Sources of Tax Revenue at the National Level
in 2011

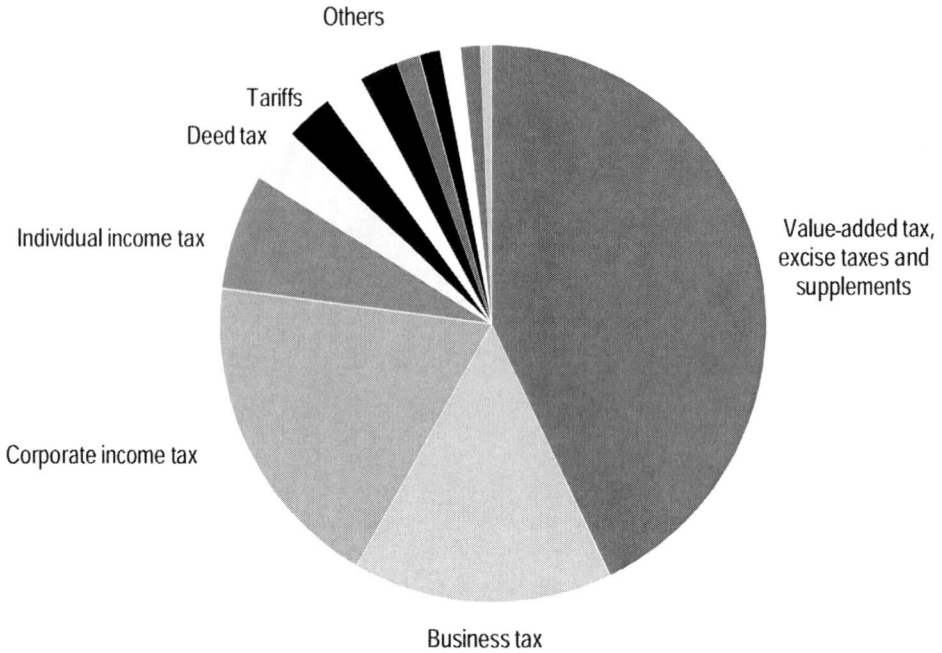

Figure 10.3 At the national level in China, the Value Added Tax (VAT) remains the largest source of revenue.
Source: Wang and Herd, 2013.

Percentage of Total Locally Assigned Tax Revenue in 2011

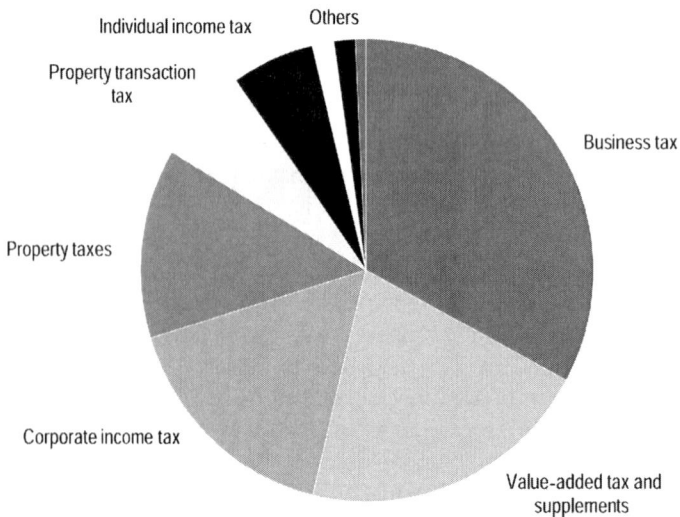

Figure 10.4 The sharing formula for collected taxes gives localities a significant share of business and VAT revenues.
Source: China Statistical Yearbook and Wang and Herd, 2013.

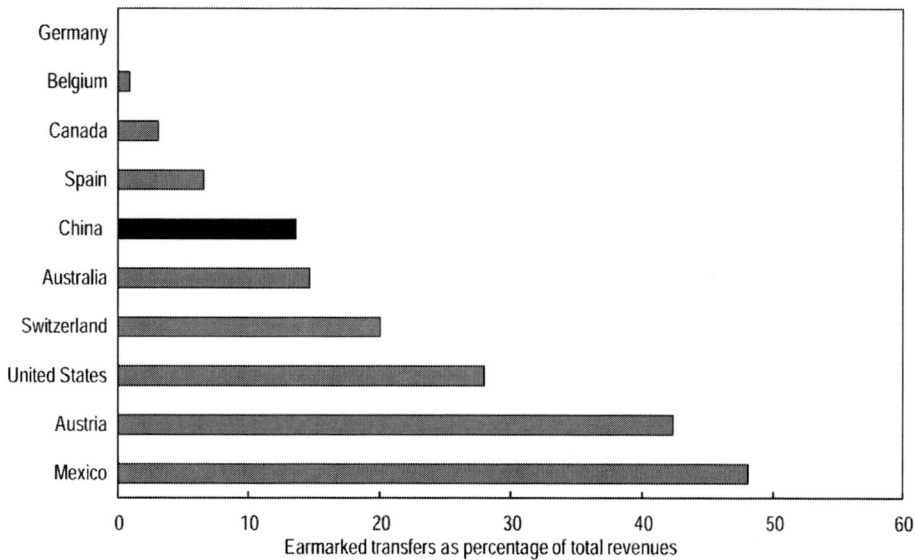

Figure 10.5 China has relatively fewer funds earmarked as part of its revenue sharing scheme than does the United States in large part due to earmarking under the U.S. Medicare program.

Source: Wang and Herd, 2013.
Note: 2006 data are used for OECD countries and 2011 data for China.

Table 10.5 The sources of revenue for the central and local governments in China.

	China 2011 Distribution of Revenues and Expenses (100 million RMB)				
	Central	*%*	*Local*	*%*	*Total*
Domestic value-added tax	18,277.38	36%	5,989.25	11%	24,266.63
Domestic consumption tax	6,936.21	14%		0%	6,936.21
Business tax	174.56	0%	13,504.44	26%	13,679
Corporate income tax	10,023.35	20%	6,746.29	13%	16,769.64
Individual income tax	3,633.07	7%	2,421.04	5%	6,054.11
Trade-related taxes*	6,914.79	13%		0%	6,914.79
Real estate-related taxes†	169.37	0%	10,838.37	21%	11,007.74
Other‡	2502.9	5%	1,607.3	3%	4,110.27
Total tax-based revenues	48,631.7	95%	41,106.7	78%	89,738.4
Total non-tax revenues	2,695.67	5%	11,440.4	22%	14,136
Total government revenues	51,327.3	100%	52,547.1	100%	103,874

Source: Ministry of Finance.
*Includes tariffs and net value-added taxes.
†Includes city maintenance and constructon, house property, urban land use, land appreciation, farm land use, and deed taxes.
‡Includes user charges and fines.

Table 10.6 Local government revenues and other finance as a share of expenditures in 2011.

	RMB 100 Million	%
Taxes (revenue sharing)	41,107	44%
Non-tax revenues*	19,388	21%
Land sales	9,931	11%
Grants from central government	23,097	25%
Statistical discrepancy	−789	−1%
Total†	92,734	100%

Source: Author's estimates.
*Includes penalties, user-based fees, and income from locally owned SOEs.
†Assumes total revenues match total expenditures.

non-earmarked grants are available for general local government uses; this type of transfer (the equalization transfer) is allocated to each province, based on a formula measuring the shortfall between expenditures and revenues. General grants also aim to reduce income inequality across provinces.

MACRO FINANCE INSIGHT 10.2: RISK POOLING, TAX SHARING, AND CONGLOMERATES

China's central government shares its tax revenues with the provinces based on a strict formula. This limits the amount of risk sharing that is possible across provinces. The financial notion of risk pooling states that individual (provinces) can benefit by sharing in a national pool of collected taxes rather than relying (as under the current system) solely on a share of what is collected in their own province. To see how this works, suppose that each province (i) receives a random tax rebate (TR_i) from the central government. (Note that the rebate is random because income (or output) in that province is random. Also tax rebates to the province are proportional to provincial income.) For the sake of simplicity, we assume that all provinces are alike.

Under the current system, each province will receive, in any given year, an expected rebate in an amount and variance

$$\text{Expected Value} = E(TR_i) = \mu \text{ and Variance}(TR_i) = \sigma^2$$

Suppose now that, instead, each province receives an equal share of the entire pool, or

$$1/N \times \sum_1^N (TR)_i$$

In the case of China, $N = 31$. Thus, when pooling for each province:

$$E(TR)_i = \mu \text{ and Variance } (TR)_i = \frac{1}{N}\sigma^2$$

In the latter pooling case, there is no reduction in average tax rebates (TR) and the variance of the rebate has been reduced by a factor of N. Or, in the case of China, the variance is close to 3 percent of what it would be without risk sharing.*

Because we have simplified, some caveats are needed. First, income is assumed to be independent across provinces, for example, impacted locally by an area flood or crop failure. If this is not the case and incomes are highly correlated (e.g., if PBC monetary policies cause trans-province economic losses) then the reduction in risk through pooling is diminished. Second, provinces differ in size and volatility of income. Large provinces or those with higher incomes receive less benefit from pooling.† Third, if residents of one province already have the opportunity to invest and earn across all provinces, then pooling tax rebates will be less beneficial.

The above discussion parallels another topic in management and finance: Are conglomerates (for example, *chaebol* in South Korea or *keiretsu* in Japan) good corporate structures? Because by definition they may contain many different kinds of businesses, they may offer significant risk-sharing benefits as a form of self-insurance. When one subsidiary encounters trouble, it can be cross-subsidized by another subsidiary experiencing better times. The counter-arguments include those made in the paragraph above. But even more germane to our discussion is the question of moral hazard. Insurance comes at a price—subsidiaries, states, and provinces can become too comfortable with the notion that a rescue plan is always available, losing valuable incentives for efficiency. Furthermore, they may take undue risks. It appears that China has taken a path of letting provinces bear individual risk as a way of promoting greater provincial efficiency. In the United States, a variety of "automatic stabilizers" such as unemployment, welfare, and tax code benefits suggest a more nuanced approach to risk pooling.

*We normally measure variability by the standard deviation, not the variance, which implies that volatility is now less than 20 percent of the current system.

†Such provinces, in fact, may feel that risk pooling is harmful. Central government involvement then becomes necessary to force participation in a risk-pooling scheme.

Revenues in the United States

In the United States, personal income tax and various other withholding taxes (including Social Security) are the main source of revenue for the federal government (about 83 percent combined) as indicated in Figure 10.6. A much smaller share comes from corporate taxes (8 percent).[6] At the state and local levels in the United States (Figure 10.7), we see that governments rely on a mix of revenue sources: The largest (in 2010) being property taxes (35 percent), sales taxes (34 percent), and individual income taxes (20 percent).[7] Expenditures typically outstrip own-source revenues across states and localities necessitating grants from the federal government. The amount is comparable to the amount raised locally via property taxes.

Summary on Revenues

At the national level, we note that while the U.S. government relies mostly on personal income tax as a source of revenue, the Chinese government relies mainly on value-added taxes and sales taxes for the bulk of its revenue. No doubt, this is tied to the administrative ease with which China's government can collect taxes at the company level, as compared to the difficulty in collecting taxes from individual citizens—many of whom work in the informal economy or in the agricultural sector, where subsistence farming is still important.[8] China relies more heavily on tax collection at the corporate level through a value-added tax (VAT)—a tax whose incidence may, in the end, fall heavily on consumers since it is, in effect, a sales tax. The VAT system is not used in the United States.[9] This may help to explain, in part, China's low level of consumption compared to the United States.

The United States relies largely on individual income taxes at the federal level, and property and sales taxes at the state and local levels. Given the hierarchy of funding based on local income

United States: Sources of Federal Tax Revenues: Fiscal Year 2011

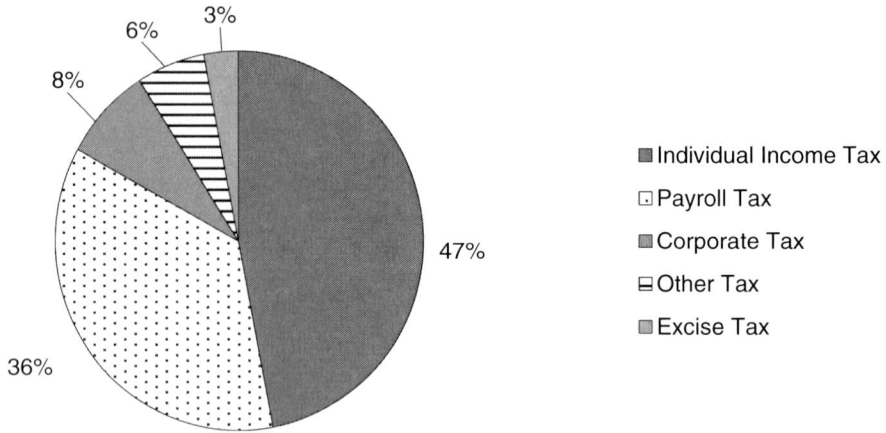

Figure 10.6 Unlike China, the personal income tax (not the VAT) is the major source of government revenue at the federal level.

Source: Budget of the United States Government, Fiscal Year 2012, Historical Tables: Table 2.1.

United States: State and Local Government: General Revenues by Source

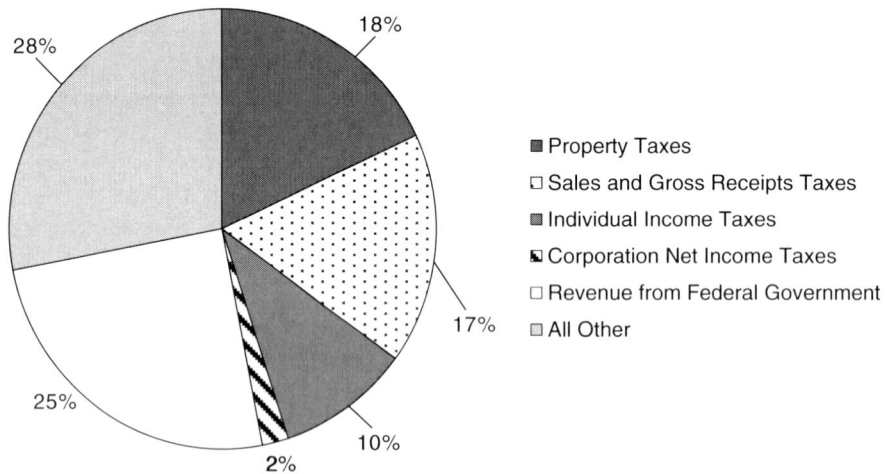

Figure 10.7 Property taxes and revenue from the federal government are major sources of revenue for localities in the United States.

Source: Budget of the United States Government, Fiscal Year 2012, Historical Tables: Table 2.1.

(starting from the central government in China, and moving down to the villages), we can also see why, beginning with provincial level officials, political leaders are so eager to attract industries with high value-added production to their areas. Increasing production provides additional sources of steady revenue.

While property taxes in China have not become as widespread a source of income as in the United States, the various fees related to the use of property in China are an important revenue source for local governments. Furthermore, personal income as a share of national income is substantially higher in the United States than in China. Simply put, tax revenues are relatively higher where the tax base is higher. U.S. property taxes are used to fund local public services, particularly education. Chinese localities, where the land is not owned by private citizens or corporate entities but leased from the government, rely heavily on revenue sharing via shared taxes and grants, and a sales tax on service and fees related to the use of land.[10]

The lack of reliance on property taxes in China no doubt reflects the fact that private land ownership does not exist in China, and that private property ownership of land improvements (such as a building) is a fairly recent phenomenon. The fact that localities in China lack an assured source of revenues (such as via property taxes) has led many localities to rely on various user fees and the sale of land rights to the private sector.[11] This, in turn, has triggered a number of conflicts related to excessive burdens on the local population, as well as issues of corruption and fairness related to land use rights. In recent years, even after tapping into the sale of land rights, local governments have still encountered funding shortfalls. The creation of special purpose vehicles (SPVs) for borrowing from the public or the China Development Bank (see Chapter 6) in order to avoid rules restricting local governments from borrowing has become another source of finance. This, of course, presents its own challenges as seen in the recent financial crisis in the United States, in which SPVs were part of a shadow banking sector tied to mortgages. Recognizing the funding problems that localities and provinces face, the central government in 2014 initiated a pilot program in which ten local governments could issue bonds.

Central government grants support up to 25 percent of local expenditures in China, and 23 percent in the United States—not a striking difference. In recent decades in China, four important factors have together placed tremendous financial stress on localities:

1. Inability to raise taxes locally
2. Central government mandates that local governments cover many expenditure categories
3. Reward system from the central government for local officials who achieve their growth targets (which requires local investment expenditures)
4. Assumption that central government tax and revenue sharing efficiently and fairly trickles down to the lowest levels of government: the townships and villages.

China's system of a heavy reliance on hierarchical funding (from central government to provinces, and down to localities) leads to a great deal of intra-governmental negotiation. It also results in an ongoing effort to show evidence that one's own province or district is more deserving of funding than another. In past decades in China, raw economic growth has been the "coin of the realm" in this context. In the United States, much of the negotiation for funding takes place within and between Congress and the Executive Branch, and has come to be known as "pork barrel."[12]

Government Expenditures in the United States vs. China

Table 10.7 provides a breakdown of expenditures for China by the eight largest central and local categories. China classifies its government expenditures across twenty-one different ministries.[13] In the United States, government expenditures are also aligned with fifteen Cabinet positions, albeit more loosely. In the aggregate, expenditures by China's local governments are larger than expenditures by the central government by almost a factor of six. In the United States, states and localities spend about one-third as much as the federal government. The largest share of China's expenditures are for education (15 percent of total), mostly undertaken at the provincial/local level. This is followed by general administration (10 percent), social safety net (10 percent), healthcare (6 percent), public

U.S. Federal Spending—Fiscal Year 2012 ($ Billions)

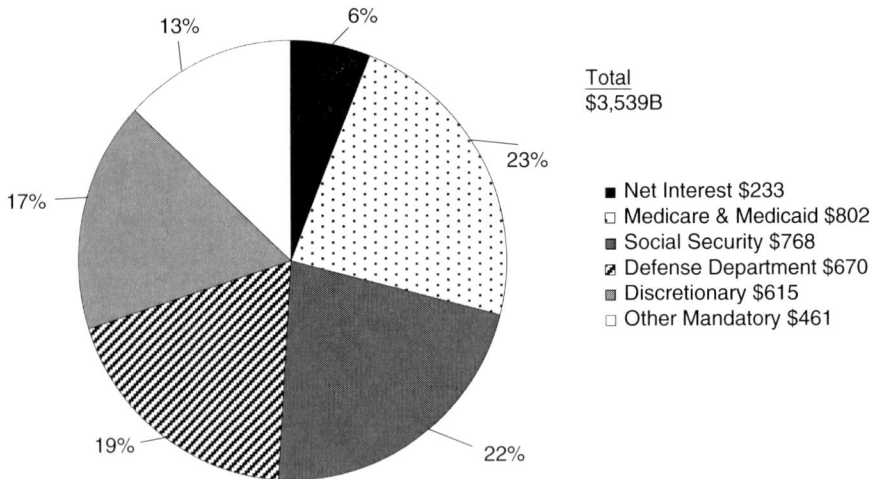

Total
$3,539B

■ Net Interest $233
□ Medicare & Medicaid $802
■ Social Security $768
▨ Defense Department $670
▧ Discretionary $615
□ Other Mandatory $461

Figure 10.8 Social welfare programs and defense take up a large part of federal spending in the United States.

Source: Budget of the United States Government, Fiscal Year 2012, Historical Tables: Table 3.1.

Table 10.7 Shares of expenditures by central and local governments in China.

	China 2011 Distribution of Revenues and Expenses (RMB 100 million)					
	Central Government		Local Government		Total	
Expenditures						
Education	999	6%	15,498	17%	16,497	15%
Social safety net and employment	502	3%	10,607	11%	11,109	10%
General administration	903	5%	10,085	11%	10,988	10%
Health and medical	71	0%	6,358	7%	6,430	6%
Public security	1,037	6%	5,267	6%	6,304	6%
National defense	5,830	35%	198	0%	6,028	6%
Other*	1,3001	79%	44,918	48%	57,920	53%
Total	16,514	100%	92,734	100%	10,9248	100%

Source: Author created based on CSA Table 8–5.
*Includes expenditures from about sixteen other ministries including: foreign affairs; culture, sport, and media; environmental protection, etc.

security (6 percent), and national defense (6 percent). Of the twenty-two separate categories of expenditures, seventeen are larger at the local level, often by a wide margin. The two key exceptions are for national defense and interest on the public debt.

Figure 10.8 reveals that, for the United States, Medicare and Medicaid, Social Security, and national defense represent about two-thirds of the federal budget. Most education expenditure is spent at the local level and represents about one-third of local budgets. America's substantial human services component is largely implemented locally but financed from the national budget. Figure 10.9 shows the high share of local expenditures on education in the United States. In Figure 10.10 we see that the federal government in the U.S. transfers substantial sums to localities for these same items.

**United States: State and Local Goverments:
General Expenditure by Function**

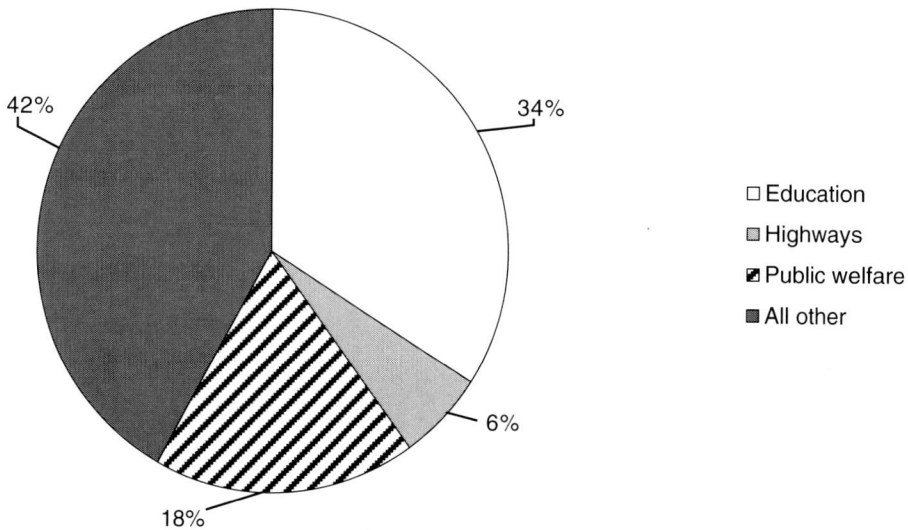

Figure 10.9   United States localities spend substantial sums on education and social welfare.

Source: Congressional Budget Office Historical Tables.

Both countries must grant substantial funds from the central government to localities, but China transfers relatively more as a share of central government revenues if we take tax revenue sharing into account. The purposes of these grants appear to be different. It seems that, in China, most transfers are conducted for the actual provision of services at the local level by local governments (about 80 percent of all grants), while in the United States, the transfers represent cash payments (transfer payments) either in the form of income support, unemployment benefits, or provision of funds to healthcare providers (Medicaid or Medicare) for services rendered (about 80 percent of all grants).[14] In the United States, transfer payments from all levels of government to individuals, including Social Security payments, amounted to US$2.4 trillion or one-third of all expenditures in 2012 programs.

As we have seen, most grants from the national government to local governments and citizens in the United States are mandated; that is, by law they must be transferred and for specific purposes. In China, there is more flexibility in how much and for what purposes the funds are to be used—a question of negotiation among the various layers of government. The tradeoffs involve using intermediaries to manage these resources on behalf of citizens (the agency problem) versus giving greater control to government authorities in determining specific benefits to accrue to citizens.[15] The Chinese system allows for greater flexibility and adaptability, while the U.S. system is more predictable. The Chinese system also offers an incentive system to implement goals mandated under the Five-Year Plan.

Summary on Public Finance

An important tenet of public finance is that, to the extent possible, the devolution of public services to localities is a desirable goal (Tiebout, 1956; Oates, 1972). This idea stems from the notion that localities are better able to understand and meet the needs of citizens at the ground level. However,

Outlays for Federal Grants to State and Local Governments, by Budget Function and Type of Spending, 2011

(Billions of dollars)

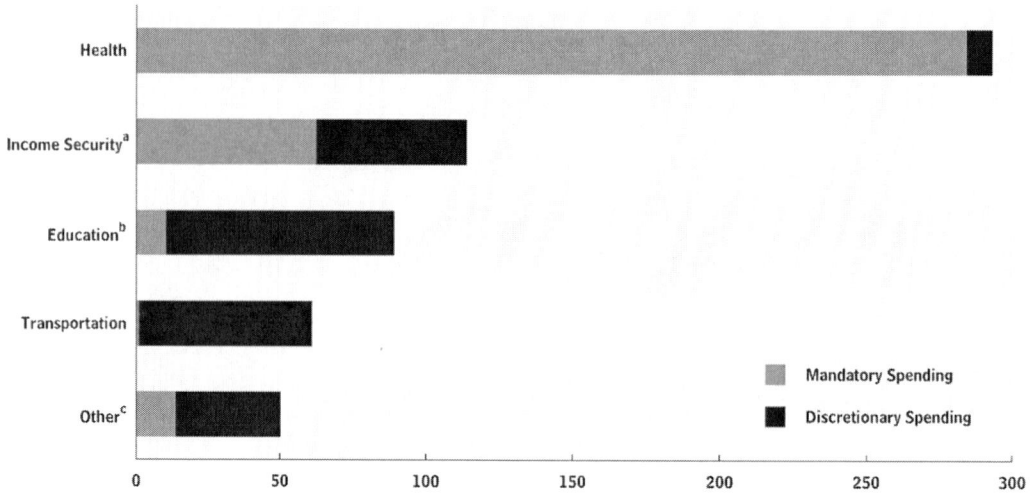

Figure 10.10 A large share of federal grants to localities in the United states relate to federally mandated spending on health.

Source: Congressional Budget Office based on *Budget of the United States Government, Fiscal Year 2013: Analytical Perspectives,* Table 18.1

Note: For the purposes of organizing the budget, federal resources are grouped in twenty general subject categories—referred to as a budget functions—so that all budget authority and outlays can be presented according to the national interests being addressed.

a. Includes programs that provide cash and other benefits (for assistance with housing, the purchase of food, and energy costs, for example to people of low income and to certain retirees, people with disabilities, and unemployed people.

b. Includes for education, social service programs, and employment and training programs.

c. Includes the following budget functions: national defense, international affairs, energy, natural resources and environment, agriculture, commerce and housing credit, community and regional development, Social Security, veteran's benefits and services, administration of justice, and general government.

it is also recognized that empowering local governments to fund local public services will result in unequal distribution of funding, simply because some localities are richer than others. It is here that revenue sharing and redistribution (mandated from the central government) can play a role. It would appear that China has devolved a great deal of responsibility to localities in terms of the provision of public services; the tradeoff here may be greater inequality across regions.

Case Study 10.4: Global, Multinational, or Transnational Structure

Large corporations with worldwide operations must decide how to structure the management of their often complex global operations. Similarly, countries must develop different methods of economic governance for national versus provincial or local control.

Companies with a global (centralized) structure tend to conduct most decision making at headquarters, across all functions (e.g., finance or marketing), allowing subsidiaries to carry out mandates from the center. Companies with a multinational (decentralized) structure tend to allow subsidiaries a great deal of autonomy in decision making, with profits and losses (for example) deemed a local responsibility and a measure of local performance. For "transnational" companies (which fall somewhere in between), certain decisions are made at headquarters (e.g., strategic financial decisions) while other local deci-sions are made by subsidiaries (e.g., marketing). There is no single correct structure for all companies. For example, a company such as Shell would be categorized as "global" while a large international accounting firm may be considered "multinational," and Nestle, "transnational." Relevant factors which determine an optimal structure include:

- Need for localization or local customization
- Need for coordination of activities
- Need for technology transfer between subsidiaries
- Level of international competition
- Homogeneous or non-homogeneous product
- Brand recognition
- Foreign operations based on market access or local cost structure
- Economies of scale
- Establishing a brand, standardization of production
- Cross-subsidization
- Diversification across subsidiaries (which is a form of self-insurance).

In a comprehensive discussion of China's institutions and internal governance structure, Xu (2011) states that China's governance structure is unique particularly in the relationship between the central, provincial, and local governments. Neither a centralized Soviet system nor an American-style federal system, Xu suggests that China falls somewhere in between and goes well beyond mere fiscal revenue sharing. Instead, China's system is regionally decentralized yet authoritarian, and relies on a great deal of local provision of government services and collection of local revenues, while encouraging local experimentation, innovation, and competition among provinces. Key personnel decisions (appointments of provincial and local leaders), however, are made at the central or national level in Beijing. Senior officials are regularly rotated around the country for new positions, and promotions rely on prior perfor-mance at the local level. Furthermore, strategic decisions are made via the Five-Year Plan at the central level.

Xu suggests that this hybrid structure between national strategy and local autonomy has played a criti-cal role in China's phenomenal economic growth. Local initiatives such as the household responsibility system (introduced in the 1970s to promote market-based practices in the agricultural sector in provinces such as Anhui and Guangdong) or the town and village enterprise structure (launched in the 1980s to introduce collective privatization of small- and medium-size enterprises in place such as Wenzhou or Xiamen) percolated upward to the national level. But while the unambiguous goal of numerical eco-nomic growth has been achieved, the system has tradeoffs in terms of inequality in income distribution and the provision of social services. On balance, it appears that China has both inherited and adopted a "global" structure for fiscal budgets, incorporating elements of a "multinational" structure for policy implementation or an overall "transnational" structure. This has a number of consequential outcomes—both good and bad.

At face value, China appears to use one of the world's most decentralized systems in terms of the provision of public services. However, a more nuanced story emerges when we consider that many local expenditures in China are mandated by the central government and that localities have virtually no control over tax rates and revenues. Close to 85 percent of all public budgets (compris-ing local and central expenditures) are the responsibility of provinces and localities (Table 10.2). Meanwhile, less than 50 percent of revenues are collected by localities through shared taxes and other user fees and the implication here is that there is a need for revenue sharing (i.e., from central government to localities). Further, if that shared revenue is insufficient, great budgetary pressure would (and does) exist at the local level. In recent years, this has led to pressure on land rights sales and bond issuance at the local level.

Case Study 10.5: China's *Fapiao* (发票)

Foreign travelers in China are often confused by the small piece of paper they receive when they purchase goods or services. The paper typically contains an official stamp; Chinese characters, a serial number, and a small gray scratch-off box (see Figure CS10.5a). First introduced in mainland China in the 1980s, and even earlier in Taiwan, a *fapiao* (发票) is an official invoice, receipt, tax document, and lottery ticket all rolled into one. Presented to a company or the tax authorities, it provides evidence of an expense. As recorded by the tax authorities, it provides a basis for the value-added, sales tax, and "business" tax or tax on services (e.g., a meal at a restaurant—which explains why it is often given with hesitation). The lottery element (included on some types of *fapiao*) is a clever tax authority effort at incentivizing the customer to ask for a *fapiao*—who wouldn't want to win a lottery—and incidentally trigger a tax liability for the seller?

In recent years, a huge market in counterfeit *fapiao* has developed. These are used to defraud employers and tax authorities—notwithstanding the risk of the death penalty for defrauding the government. Sellers charge a commission (2 percent or more depending on quality of face value) for the counterfeit item. In recent years, thousands of individuals, enterprises, gangs, and even government officials have been arrested for promoting or participating in the counterfeit *fapiao* market. In 2012, a businessman in Zhejiang Province was arrested for helping 315 companies evade millions of dollars in taxes with fake *fapiaos*.

Low civil service salaries and the continued predominance of cash transactions are some of the reasons why fake *fapiaos* exist. Of course, one cannot dismiss outright greed and the entrepreneurial spirit as further causes (Barboza, 2013).

Furthermore, though mandated by the central government, the collection of personal and income taxes are the responsibility of local governments. Much public expenditure—especially expenses related to health, education, welfare, and, importantly, agricultural support—is the responsibility of local governments even though it is mandated by the central government. Central government responsibilities include the traditional roles of national defense, foreign affairs and diplomacy, key infrastructure and construction projects, and overhead expenditures.

China's unique fiscal accounting for expenditures does not give a complete picture of full central and local government spending on current (consumption) vs. investment-related activities. Especially murky is the role of SOEs, which conduct investment activity on behalf of the government. We do know that China's government, at all levels, devotes substantially more of its revenues to investment (hard assets), while the United States devotes a significantly larger proportion to individuals, social services, and national defense. Both countries, out of necessity, seem to be incrementally moving toward some average of these two extremes.

Finally, we note that in the United States, total government spending as a share of GDP is about 20 percent, while in China the figure is only slightly higher, at 22 percent. This, however, ignores the output of SOEs that produce a range of goods and services for the private sector, ranging from consumer to export categories.

Fiscal and Monetary Policy in Action

Three fundamental factors distinguish China and the United States in terms of the causes of business cycles and the resulting counter-cyclical policies on the demand side. First, China remains well below its steady-state growth rate (as we saw in Chapter 4) compared to the United States, which is arguably at its long-run steady state. Second, China's sources of demand are weighted more toward exports and investment, of which FDI is still significant. This contrasts with the United States, where consumption is a principal source of demand. Third, as we have discussed, China's government has

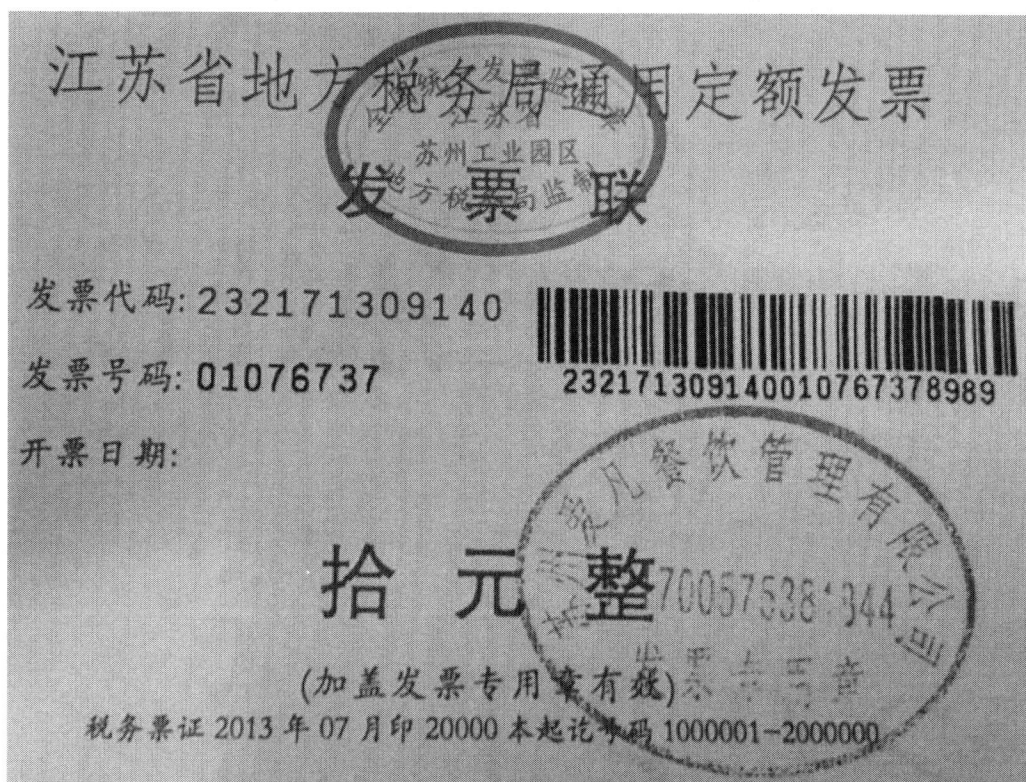

Figure CS10.5a A *Fapiao* a receipt used for reporting sales revenue to the tax authorities in China (and also a lottery ticket). Source: Author's collection.

greater direct control over economic activity than does the U.S. government. Let's discuss the first two factors now (the role of government is discussed throughout this chapter, and Chapters 7 and 8).

MACRO FINANCE INSIGHT 10.3: GROWTH CYCLES VS. BUSINESS CYCLES

Economies such as China, which are still building up their capital stock via high savings rates, tend to experience growth rates in output that far exceed those of developed economies in the OECD (such as the United States). The possibility of those growth rates dipping below zero (becoming negative) are remote for countries such as China, but quite possible for those with rates hovering around 3 percent, such as the United States. However, we normally define a recession in terms of prolonged and widely dispersed negative growth (a negative first derivative) for such key economic variables as GDP, industrial production, retail sales, and a corresponding increase in unemployment. In this sense, it is unlikely that China will experience an outright recession (or business cycle fluctuation, as it is commonly defined). Instead, China has experienced and will experience growth recessions (periods in which economic growth dips below trend growth) causing a persistent and widespread negative second derivative in economic performance. Table MF10.3a provides a record of U.S. recessions as measured by the National Bureau of Economic Research (a non-governmental research institute located in Cambridge, MA). Table MF10.3b provides a record of growth cycles based on a set of algorithms employed by the OECD. Although roughly similar in their intent, the former is a measure of fluctuations in absolute output (the traditional measure of business cycles), while the latter is based on fluctuations in growth rates. Some stylized facts about business cycles and growth cycles do emerge from both tables. First, recoveries are longer than contractions.* Second, growth cycles occur more frequently than more traditional business cycles. Specific to China, we see in Figure MF10.3a two prominent growth contractions: one occurring as part

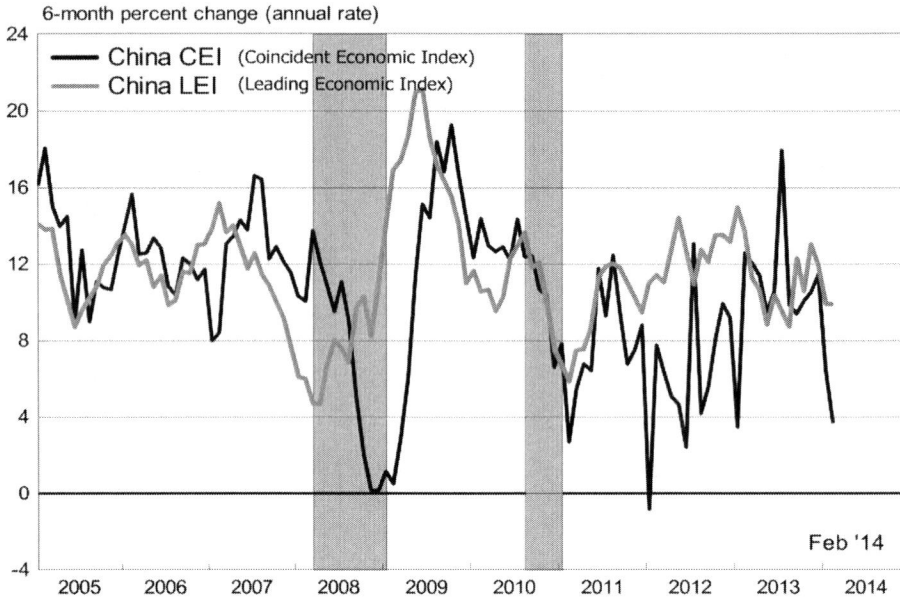

Figure MF10.3a China tends to experience only growth cycles (slower positive growth) as indicated by the shaded areas.

Source: Conference Board.

Table MF10.3a The United States has outright recessions (a fall in the level of GDP); China, an emerging economy, has growth recessions (below trend growth).

U.S. Business Cycle Expansions and Contractions

Contractions (recessions) start at the peak of a business cycle and end at the trough.

Also see the latest announcement from the NBER's Business Cycle Dating Committee (www.NBER.org).

Peak Month	Trough Month	Duration, Peak to Trough	Duration, Previous Trough to Peak	Duration, Peak from Previous Peak	Duration, Trough from Previous Peak
	December 1854				
June 1857	December 1858	18	30		48
October 1860	June 1861	8	22	40	30
April 1865	December 1867	32	46	54	78
June 1869	December 1870	18	18	50	36
October 1873	March 1879	65	34	52	99
March 1882	May 1885	38	36	101	74
March 1887	April 1888	13	22	60	35
July 1890	May 1891	10	27	40	37
January 1893	June 1894	17	20	30	37
December 1895	June 1897	18	18	35	36
June 1899	December 1900	18	24	42	42
September 1902	August 1904	23	21	39	44
May 1907	June 1908	13	33	56	46

January 1910	January 1912	24	19	32	43
January 1913	December 1914	23	12	36	35
August 1918	March 1919	7	44	67	51
January 1920	July 1921	18	10	17	28
May 1923	July 1924	14	22	40	36
October 1926	November 1927	13	27	41	40
August 1929	March 1933	43	21	34	64
May 1937	June 1938	13	50	93	63
February 1945	October 1945	8	80	93	88
November 1948	October 1949	11	37	45	48
July 1953	May 1954	10	45	56	55
August 1957	April 1958	8	39	49	47
April 1960	February 1961	10	24	32	34
December 1969	November 1970	11	106	116	117
November 1973	March 1975	16	36	47	52
January 1980	July 1980	6	58	74	64
July 1981	November 1982	16	12	18	28
July 1990	March 1991	8	92	108	100
March 2001	November 2001	8	120	128	128
December 2007	June 2009	18	73	81	91
1854–2009 (33 cycles)		17.5	38.7	56.4	56.2*
1854–1919 (16 cycles)		21.6	26.6	48.9	48.2**
1919–1945 (6 cycles)		18.2	35.0	53.0	53.2
1945–2009 (11 cycles)		11.1	58.4	68.5	69.5

Source: The National Bureau of Economic Research.
*32 cycles
**15 cycles

Table MF10.3b China has only experienced slowdowns in its growth rate below trend (growth recessions) with the exception of 1988–89 where it had an outright business cycle recession.

China Growth Cycles Based on Industrial Production

	Cycle	Expansion: Trough to Peak (in months)	Contraction: Peak to Trough (in months)
January 1979	Trough		
February 1980	Peak	13	
October 1982	Trough		32
April 1985	Peak	30	
March 1986	Trough		11
September 1988	Peak	30	
July 1990	Trough		22
September 1994	Peak	50	
March 1996	Trough		18
December 1996	Peak	9	
June 1999	Trough		30
August 2000	Peak	14	
February 2002	Trough		18
March 2004	Peak	25	
March 2005	Trough		12
January 2008	Peak	34	
January 2009	Trough		12
January 2010	Peak	12	
Median duration (months)		25	18
Average duration (months)		24	19

Source: Author created based on data from OECD,
http://www.oecd.org/std/leading-indicators/CLI-components-and-turning-points.pdf

*A common feature of time-series data is that growth rates fluctuate substantially more than levels of data.

of the Asian Financial Crisis (1996–99), the other occurring in 2008. In between those two were several other growth contractions, including one corresponding to the dot-com bubble of 2000–02 and compounded by China's own banking crisis. All told, since 1979, China has experienced nine growth cycles. In the same period, the United States has had five traditional business cycles.

Policy Responses

The Asian Financial Crisis that began in Thailand in 1996 moved rapidly through the Philippines, Indonesia, Taiwan, and South Korea, and inevitably impacted China. Chinese policymakers were proactive in their response, raising budget expenditures 12 percent over programmed expenditures. The central government issued construction bonds to raise funds that were transferred to local governments for capital improvement projects (investments). Because tax revenues remained close to budgeted amounts, the expansionary impact was substantial (increasing GDP by at least 1.4 percent). From late 1998 through 1999, the PBC also had a very accommodative monetary policy (with monetary growth rates of over 35 percent in 1997) and a surge in the money supply as discussed in Chapter 8. Taken together, these are clear indications of both expansionary fiscal and monetary policies by the Chinese authorities in response to the Asian Financial Crisis. These effects, recalling both the IS/LM framework and the AS/AD framework of Chapter 9, show a substantial Keynesian style stimulus.

The global financial crisis provided another opportunity for policymakers both in China and the United States to respond aggressively. China's central government announced a series of fiscal measures that cumulatively added RMB 4 trillion (US$585 billion) in spending from 2009 to 2010. This amounted to 3.1 percent and 2.7 percent of GDP for 2009 and 2010 respectively, and is estimated to have increased real GDP by 3.1 percent and 2.7 percent for those years (Cova et al., 2010). Of this amount, 90 percent was used for investment at all levels of government and 10 percent was used in various transfer payments. As also seen in Chapter 9, there was a substantial growth in the real money supply (over 25 percent in this period). These policies triggered similar responses as were seen during the Asian Financial Crisis.

In response to the financial crisis unfolding in the United States, the Obama administration introduced the American Economic Recovery and Investment Act in February 2009. A set of tax relief and spending measures were announced, amounting to US$787 billion or about 5.6 percent of that year's GDP.[16] By early 2012, approximately US$750 billion had been disbursed. Of this latter amount, about 40 percent was tax benefits, and the remaining 60 percent was evenly divided between government spending and transfer payments (entitlements). As discussed in Chapter 8, the FED increased the monetary base by almost a factor of five through the acquisition of troubled assets and substantially broadening the range of assets acquired beyond Treasury instruments. Monetary growth surged in the United States during the recent financial crisis. In both countries, there was nearly a doubling of the M2 growth rate as the crisis unfolded in 2009–10. Meanwhile, no dramatic increase occurred in the United States during the 1997–99 financial crisis, while China's M2 growth rate surged. Of course, China was much more proximate to that crisis.

Similarities and Differences in the Policy Response to the Global Financial Crisis

What is most remarkable about the responses of China and the United States to the 2008–09 financial crisis is how similar they were, not just qualitatively but quantitatively. In both cases, fiscal stimulus as a share of GDP reached roughly 6 percent and, in both cases, M2 growth rates nearly doubled. However, while the end product looked very similar, beneath the surface were fundamental differences based on the underlying economies.

In China, most fiscal stimulus was in the form of investment, with only 10 percent representing transfer payments. In the United States, close to 70 percent of the stimulus came in the form of tax relief or unemployment benefits and other transfer payments. Only a small share of the U.S. stimulus package came in the form of investment. In other words, while China's fiscal stimulus consisted mostly of government-sponsored investments, most of the U.S. package likely resulted in greater consumption. At one level, these differences simply reflect the disparity in sources of demand between the two economies. Looking deeper, we see that it would be very difficult to stimulate demand in China through tax policies. In China, personal taxes are an insignificant part of personal income, and personal income represents a very small share of national income (by international standards). Thus, stimulating the economy through lower taxes would have a muted effect. Establishing a system for transfer payments related to retirement, health, or unemployment benefits are structural reforms requiring time to implement. As a nation of savers, the fiscal multiplier from tax cuts in China is likely small. In the United States, however, consumption represents a large component of aggregate demand. Changes in tax rates that impact consumption can have a substantial impact on demand. Given the simple multiplier, M, with a propensity to consume of c and a tax rate of t we have:

$$M = 1 / (1 - (c(1 - t)))$$

Then the change in the multiplier, with respect to tax rate changes, is:

$$-c / (1 - (c(1 - t)))$$

Thus, the smaller the propensity to consume factor, c, the smaller the impact of lowering tax rates. Because corporations already devote a sizeable share of their income to investment, tax credit policies would also be relatively ineffective in China.

At a political level, there is a pronounced bias toward consumer-driven fiscal policy as opposed to "big government" in the United States. China's already large government involvement in the economy makes such concerns more or less moot.

While the short-run economics of such stimulus approaches make sense for each country, they do present problems in terms of long-run policy goals. In the United States, key long-run policy goals include: reducing the deficit and government debt, increasing savings, and increasing investment. In China, the most recent Five-Year Plan calls for increasing consumption, reducing the share of GDP devoted to investment, and enhancing the social safety net. Clearly, the short-run responses we have just described run counter to these long-run goals. In other words, the recent financial crisis was a setback from the perspective of longer-term policy goals for both countries.

Regarding monetary policy, while both packages stimulated the domestic economy, the relative focus in each country was quite different. In the United States, the expansion of the FED's balance sheet and the increase in the money supply was a response to the collapse of liquidity related directly or indirectly to mortgage-backed securities, the breakdown of the "transmissions mechanism" (described in Chapters 7 and 8), and a dramatic shrinkage of the money multiplier. The combined effects of the above exceptional phenomena nearly collapsed the U.S. financial system, potentially leading to a repeat of the Great Depression. China's response reflected an effort to directly stimulate lending by financial institutions; the transmissions mechanism itself has not matured sufficiently to provide a reliable mode of operation in China. In the United States, troubled or illiquid assets filled the FED's balance sheet as the central bank added liquidity to the financial system; in China, foreign exchange reserves continued to pile up as the PBC's counterpart to increased liquidity. In both countries, building construction and home purchases rose to center stage. China boosted its real estate market with monetary stimulus; the United States saw the collapse of the "transmissions mechanism" greatly diminish the effectiveness of monetary policy in the housing market.

Both fiscal and monetary policies appear to be more direct and to have a greater impact in China than in the United States. On the fiscal side, government spending does not suffer from the "leakages" that tax incentives and transfer payments create; these are partly saved (the propensity to save, *s*) especially in a weak economy. On the monetary side, directing credit for targeted purposes or industries, then channeling money through state-owned banks, is more likely to lead to spending than would the complex transmissions system. In the latter case, represented by the IS/LM framework, monetary policy must clear several hurdles before impacting demand. China's use of monetary policy is closer in spirit to the quantity theory of money, in which money is channeled directly into demand (specifically government and investment demand).

Challenging Questions for China (and the Student): Chapter 10

1. Go the Federal Reserve Economic Database (FRED) and update the chart, "General Government Gross Debt for China."
2. Decentralization of government spending and taxing has always been a central tenet (a basic principle) for guiding public finances (government spending and taxation). Describe what issues arise with decentralization in China's system of public finances.
3. Consider fiscal policy responses to the great financial crisis of 2008–09.
   a. Explain the different fiscal policy responses in the United States and China to the Great Recession of 2008–09.
   b. Explain whether the short-run policies in (a) are consistent with the longer-run goals of each country.
4. Compare and contrast monetary policy responses to the Great Recession of 2008–09 in China and the United States.
5. Based on estimates of China's Taylor rule response function (as described in Chapter 9), compare and contrast the likely Chinese and U.S. policy responses to future inflation and output shocks.
6. It is argued in this chapter that both fiscal and monetary policy are more likely to have an immediate impact in China than in the United States. Explain.
7. With respect to the relationship between provinces (states) and the central government, compare and contrast China and the United States in terms of a global, multinational, or transnational structure.
8. Discuss: Revenue sharing in the United States mainly involves federal revenue sharing with individual citizens at the local level. In China, revenue sharing mainly involves intra-governmental transfers.
   a. Explain why there is a difference.
   b. Explain the different implications for consumption and investment.
9. Based on what you have learned in this chapter, explain why there are such great tensions over land rights at the local level in China.
10. What are the major challenges for the Chinese economy in the coming years? Compare and contrast with those of the United States.

Notes

1. We can think of the MOF as responsible for short-term taxing and revenue functions, the NDRC (formerly the State Planning Commission) for long-term policies including economic reform, and the State Council as setting out even longer-term fiscal strategies, as described in the Five-Year Plan.
2. However, one could argue that, with the election of each U.S. President to a four-year term, a set of long-term policies are implicitly established, as a Four- (possibly Eight-) Year Plan.

3. As in the case of New York City's bankruptcy in 1975, both levels of government may play a role.
4. We are taking a net savings approach here. Net savings is the difference between sources of funds (domestic savings) and uses of funds (domestic investment).
5. This is true as long as these taxes do not interfere with commerce (trade) between individual states (i.e., do not inhibit intra-state imports and exports); see Commerce Clause of the United States Constitution.
6. Corporations do pay half of the Social Security tax included in the payroll tax, but this would still be considered a tax on individual income.
7. We note that at local (city and town) level property taxes make up over 90 percent of total revenues.
8. Though the number of SOEs is declining, the output of these state-controlled firms still represents a large share of China's national income.
9. The U.S. retail sales tax is on final, not intermediate, sales and is a local, not federal, tax.
10. Land lease terms typically run forty years for offices, fifty years for industrial use, and seventy years for residential use. These terms can vary considerably depending on the region within China.
11. As of this writing, China was experimenting with property taxes in Shanghai and Chongqing, suggesting that a more widespread "rollout" of this policy is likely in the coming years.
12. *Pork barrel* is a derogatory term dating back to the American Civil War, describing excessive government largesse on behalf of citizens.
13. These Ministries operate under the State Council as do four other key entities: the National Development and Reform Commission, the National Health and Family Planning Commission, the PBC, and the National Audit Office.
14. Medicare is a federal social insurance health program for the old and disabled; Medicaid provides health coverage for the poor through direct payments to healthcare providers.
15. The "agency problem" refers to the conflicting incentives of managers and owners in using the resources of a company—or, in this context, local governments versus the central government (which is assumed to represent citizens). For example, local governments may seek to use funds for their own interests (a better office or more impressive automobile) at the expense of end user citizens, whom the central government represents.
16. In fact, the figure was adjusted upward to US$840 billion, reflecting accounting adjustments.

References

Barboza, David. 2013. "Coin of Realm in China Graft: Phony Receipts." *New York Times,* August 4.
Bartlett, Christopher, and Sumantra Ghoshal. 1997. "Evolution of the Transnational." In *Current Issues in International Business*, eds Iyanatul Islam and William Shepherd, 113–36. Cheltenham: Edward Elgar.
Cova, Pietro, Massimiliano Pisani, and Alessandro Rebucci. 2010. "Macroeconomic Effects of China's Fiscal Stimulus." IDB Working Paper No. 72. Washington, DC: Inter-American Development Bank.
Dunaway, Stephen, and Annalisa Feddelino. 2006. "Fiscal Policy in China." In *China and India: Learning From Each Other. Reforms and Policies for Sustained Growth*, eds. Jahangir Aziz, Steven Dunaway, and Eswar Prasad. Washington, DC: International Monetary Fund.
Fock, Achim, and Christine Wong. 2008. *Financing Rural Development for a Harmonious Society in China: Recent Reforms in Public Finance and Their Prospects.* Washington, DC: World Bank.
Hodge, Andrew W., Robert J. Corea, Benjamin J. Hobbs, and Bonnie A. Retus. 2013. "Returns for Domestic Nonfinancial Business," *Survey of Current Business* 93(6): 14–18.
Kujis, Louis, and Gao Xu. 2008. *China's Fiscal Policy—Moving to Center Stage.* Beijing:World Bank Office.
Ministry of Civil Administration. 2013. *China Statistical Yearbook 2012.* CECD WP 1030. Beijing: Ministry of Civil Administration.
Ministry of Finance. N.d. *Fiscal Statistics of Prefectures, Cities and Counties.* Beijing: MOF.
———.N.d. *Local Fiscal Statistical Yearbook.* Beijing: MOF.
———.N.d. *Fiscal Statistical Yearbook of China.* Beijing: MOF.
Oates, Wallace E. 1972. *Fiscal Federalism.* New York: Harcourt Brace Jovanovich.
Tax Policy Center. 2012. "Tax Policy Briefing Book: A Citizens' Guide for the 2012 Election and Beyond." www.taxpolicycenter.org/briefing-book/
Tiebout, C. 1956. "A Pure Theory of Local Expenditures." *Journal of Political Economy* 64 (5): 416–24.
Wang, X., and R. Herd. 2013. "The System of Revenue Sharing and Fiscal Transfers in China." OECD Economics Department Working Papers, No. 1030, OECD Publishing. http://dx.doi.org/10.1787/5k4bwnwtmx0r-en
Xu, Chenggang. 2011. "The Fundamental Institutions of China's Reforms and Development." *Journal of Economic Literature* 49(4): 1076–115.

Appendix A

Gross Domestic Product for China in Nominal RMB

Data in this table are calculated at current prices.

Year	Gross National Income	Gross Domestic Product	Primary Industry	Secondary Industry	Industry	Construction	Tertiary Industry	Per Capita GDP (yuan)
1978	3645.2	3645.2	1027.5	1745.2	1607.0	138.2	872.5	381
1979	4062.6	4062.6	1270.2	1913.5	1769.7	143.8	878.9	419
1980	4545.6	4545.6	1371.6	2192.0	1996.5	195.5	982.0	463
1981	4889.5	4891.6	1559.5	2255.5	2048.4	207.1	1076.6	492
1982	5330.5	5323.4	1777.4	2383.0	2162.3	220.7	1163.0	528
1983	5985.6	5962.7	1978.4	2646.2	2375.6	270.6	1338.1	583
1984	7243.8	7208.1	2316.1	3105.7	2789.0	316.7	1786.3	695
1985	9040.7	9016.0	2564.4	3866.6	3448.7	417.9	2585.0	858
1986	10274.4	10275.2	2788.7	4492.7	3967.0	525.7	2993.8	963
1987	12050.6	12058.6	3233.0	5251.6	4585.8	665.8	3574.0	1112
1988	15036.8	15042.8	3865.4	6587.2	5777.2	810.0	4590.3	1366
1989	17000.9	16992.3	4265.9	7278.0	6484.0	794.0	5448.4	1519
1990	18718.3	18667.8	5062.0	7717.4	6858.0	859.4	5888.4	1644
1991	21826.2	21781.5	5342.2	9102.2	8087.1	1015.1	7337.1	1893
1992	26937.3	26923.5	5866.6	11699.5	10284.5	1415.0	9357.4	2311
1993	35260.0	35333.9	6963.8	16454.4	14188.0	2266.5	11915.7	2998
1994	48108.5	48197.9	9572.7	22445.4	19480.7	2964.7	16179.8	4044
1995	59810.5	60793.7	12135.8	28679.5	24950.6	3728.8	19978.5	5046
1996	70142.5	71176.6	14015.4	33835.0	29447.6	4387.4	23326.2	5846
1997	78060.9	78973.0	14441.9	37543.0	32921.4	4621.6	26988.1	6420
1998	83024.3	84402.3	14817.6	39004.2	34018.4	4985.8	30580.5	6796
1999	88479.2	89677.1	14770.0	41033.6	35861.5	5172.1	33873.4	7159
2000	98000.5	99214.6	14944.7	45555.9	40033.6	5522.3	38714.0	7858
2001	108068.2	109655.2	15781.3	49512.3	43580.6	5931.7	44361.6	8622
2002	119095.7	120332.7	16537.0	53896.8	47431.3	6465.5	49898.9	9398
2003	134977.0	135822.8	17381.7	62436.3	54945.5	7490.8	56004.7	10542
2004	159453.6	159878.3	21412.7	73904.3	65210.0	8694.3	64561.3	12336
2005	183617.4	184937.4	22420.0	87598.1	77230.8	10367.3	74919.3	14185
2006	215904.4	216314.4	24040.0	103719.5	91310.9	12408.6	88554.9	16500
2007	266422.0	265810.3	28627.0	125831.4	110534.9	15296.5	111351.9	20169
2008	316030.3	314045.4	33702.0	149003.4	130260.2	18743.2	131340.0	23708
2009	340320.0	340902.8	35226.0	157638.8	135239.9	22398.8	148038.0	25608
2010	399759.5	401512.8	40533.6	187383.2	160722.2	26661.0	173596.0	30015
2011	472115.0	473104.0	47486.0	220413.0	188470.0	31943.0	205205.0	35181.2
2012 (prelim.)		518942.0	52374.0	235162.0	199671.0	35491.0	231406.0	

Source: National Bureau of Statistics, China.

Note: Since 1980, the difference between the Gross Domestic Product and the Gross National Income (formerly, the Gross National Product) is the net factor income from the rest of the world.

Appendix B

Gross Domestic Product at Constant Prices for China

(100 million yuan)

Year	Gross Domestic Product	Primary Industry	Secondary Industry	Industry	Construction	Tertiary Industry
	Price Base Year=1970					
1978	3548.2	936.0	1766.2	1644.8	121.4	846.0
1979	3816.9	993.5	1911.0	1787.2	123.8	912.4
1980	4116.2	978.7	2170.3	2013.4	156.9	967.2
	Price Base Year=1980					
1980	4567.9	1371.6	2213.4	2017.9	195.5	982.9
1981	4807.4	1467.4	2254.7	2053.0	201.7	1085.3
1982	5242.8	1636.5	2380.1	2171.5	208.6	1226.2
1983	5811.8	1772.8	2626.8	2382.6	244.2	1412.2
1984	6693.8	2001.1	3007.2	2736.5	270.7	1685.5
1985	7595.2	2038.0	3565.6	3234.8	330.8	1991.6
1986	8267.1	2105.7	3930.0	3546.7	383.3	2231.4
1987	9224.7	2204.7	4468.2	4016.4	451.8	2551.8
1988	10265.3	2260.8	5116.9	4629.0	487.9	2887.6
1989	10682.4	2330.3	5309.7	4863.0	446.7	3042.4
1990	11092.5	2501.1	5478.0	5026.0	452.0	3113.4
	Price Base Year=1990					
1990	18547.9	5062.0	7717.4	6858.0	859.4	5768.5
1991	20250.4	5183.5	8786.6	7845.0	941.6	6280.3
1992	23134.2	5427.1	10645.3	9505.7	1139.6	7061.8
1993	26364.7	5682.3	12760.1	11415.4	1344.7	7922.3
1994	29813.4	5909.6	15102.8	13574.2	1528.6	8801.0
1995	33070.5	6205.2	17198.4	15480.3	1718.1	9667.0
1996	36380.4	6521.7	19280.5	17416.2	1864.3	10578.2
1997	39762.7	6749.9	21300.9	19387.8	1913.1	11711.9
1998	42877.4	6986.1	23198.9	21113.3	2085.6	12692.4
1999	46144.6	7181.7	25086.3	22911.4	2174.9	13876.6
2000	50035.2	7354.1	27451.7	25153.5	2298.2	15229.4
	Price Base Year=2000					
2000	99214.6	14944.7	45555.9	40033.6	5522.3	38714.0
2001	107449.7	15363.2	49401.5	43504.6	5896.9	42685.0
2002	117208.3	15808.7	54257.3	47842.2	6415.1	47142.3
2003	128958.9	16203.9	61132.7	53942.5	7190.2	51622.2
2004	141964.5	17224.8	67926.1	60151.3	7774.8	56813.6
2005	158020.7	18125.8	76133.1	67114.7	9018.4	63761.8

(Continued)

Year	Gross Domestic Product	Primary Industry	Secondary Industry	Industry	Construction	Tertiary Industry
	Price Base Year=2005					
2005	184937.4	22420.0	87598.1	77230.8	10367.3	74919.3
2006	208381.0	23541.0	99328.5	87175.1	12153.4	85511.6
2007	237892.8	24422.4	114290.6	100170.1	14120.5	99179.7
2008	260812.9	25735.9	125579.7	110117.4	15462.2	109497.4
2009	284844.8	26812.6	138062.7	119731.4	18331.3	119969.4
2010	314602.5	27957.8	154975.8	134175.5	20800.3	131668.9

Source: National Bureau of Statistics.

Appendix C

Gross Domestic Product by Expenditure Approach for China

Data in value terms in this table are calculated at current prices.

Year	Gross Domestic Product by Expenditure Approach (100 million yuan)	Final Consumption Expenditures	Gross Capital Formation	Net Exports of Goods and Services	Final Consumption Rate (%)	Capital Formation Rate (%)
1978	3605.6	2239.1	1377.9	−11.4	62.1	38.2
1979	4092.6	2633.7	1478.9	20.0	64.4	36.1
1980	4592.9	3007.9	1599.7	14.7	65.5	34.8
1981	5008.8	3361.5	1630.2	17.1	67.1	32.5
1982	5590.0	3714.8	1784.2	91.0	66.5	31.9
1983	6216.2	4126.4	2039.0	50.8	66.4	32.8
1984	7362.7	4846.3	2515.1	1.3	65.8	34.2
1985	9076.7	5986.3	3457.5	367.1	66.0	38.1
1986	10508.5	6821.8	3941.9	255.2	64.9	37.5
1987	12277.4	7804.6	4462.0	10.8	63.6	36.3
1988	15388.6	9839.5	5700.2	151.1	63.9	37.0
1989	17311.3	11164.2	6332.7	185.6	64.5	36.6
1990	19347.8	12090.5	6747.0	510.3	62.5	34.9
1991	22577.4	14091.9	7868.0	617.5	62.4	34.8
1992	27565.2	17203.3	10086.3	275.6	62.4	36.6
1993	36938.1	21899.9	15717.7	679.5	59.3	42.6
1994	50217.4	29242.2	20341.1	634.1	58.2	40.5
1995	63216.9	36748.2	25470.1	998.6	58.1	40.3
1996	74163.6	43919.5	28784.9	1459.2	59.2	38.8
1997	81658.5	48140.6	29968.0	3549.9	59.0	36.7
1998	86531.6	51588.2	31314.2	3629.2	59.6	36.2
1999	91125.0	55636.9	32951.5	2536.6	61.1	36.2
2000	98749.0	61516.0	34842.8	2390.2	62.3	35.3
2001	109028.0	66933.9	39769.4	2324.7	61.4	36.5
2002	120475.6	71816.5	45565.0	3094.1	59.6	37.8
2003	136613.4	77685.5	55963.0	2964.9	56.9	41.0
2004	160956.6	87552.6	69168.4	4235.6	54.4	43.0
2005	187423.5	99357.5	77856.8	10209.1	53.0	41.5
2006	222712.5	113103.8	92954.1	16654.6	50.8	41.7
2007	266599.2	132232.9	110943.2	23423.1	49.6	41.6
2008	315974.6	153422.5	138325.3	24226.8	48.6	43.8

(*Continued*)

Year	Gross Domestic Product by Expenditure Approach (100 million yuan)	Final Consumption Expenditures	Gross Capital Formation	Net Exports of Goods and Services	Final Consumption Rate (%)	Capital Formation Rate (%)
2009	348775.1	169274.8	164463.2	15037.1	48.5	47.2
2010	402816.5	194115.0	193603.9	15097.6	48.2	48.1
2011 (prelim.)	465731.3	228561.3	225006.7	12163.3	49.1	48.3

Source: National Bureau of Statistics.

Appendix D

Fixed-Base Price Indexes for China

Year	Consumer Price Index (1978=100)	Urban Household (1978=100)	Rural Household (1985=100)	Retail Price Index (1978=100)	Producer Price Index for Industrial Products (1985=100)	Purchasing Price Index for Industrial Producers (1990=100)	Price Index for Investment in Fixed Assets (1990=100)
1978	100.0	100.0		100.0			
1980	109.5	109.5		108.1			
1985	131.1	134.2	100.0	128.1	100.0		
1990	216.4	222.0	165.1	207.7	159.0	100.0	100.0
1995	396.9	429.6	291.4	356.1	307.1	222.9	186.9
1996	429.9	467.4	314.4	377.8	316.0	231.6	194.3
1997	441.9	481.9	322.3	380.8	315.0	234.6	197.6
1998	438.4	479.0	319.1	370.9	302.1	224.7	197.3
1999	432.2	472.8	314.3	359.8	294.8	217.3	196.5
2000	434.0	476.6	314.0	354.4	303.1	228.4	198.6
2001	437.0	479.9	316.5	351.6	299.2	227.9	199.4
2002	433.5	475.1	315.2	347.0	292.6	222.7	199.8
2003	438.7	479.4	320.2	346.7	299.3	233.4	204.2
2004	455.8	495.2	335.6	356.4	317.6	260.0	215.7
2005	464.0	503.1	343.0	359.3	333.2	281.6	219.1
2006	471.0	510.6	348.1	362.9	343.2	298.5	222.4
2007	493.6	533.6	366.9	376.7	353.8	311.6	231.1
2008	522.7	563.5	390.7	398.9	378.2	344.3	251.8
2009	519.0	558.4	389.5	394.1	357.8	317.2	245.8
2010	536.1	576.3	403.5	406.3	377.5	347.7	254.6
2011	565.0	606.8	426.9	426.2	400.2	379.3	271.4
2012 prelim.	580.1						

Source: National Bureau of Statistics.

Appendix E

Some Useful Websites Related to China's Economy and Financial Sector

Language	Name	Acronym	Website	Type of Data
English	Ministry of Commerce of the People's Republic of China	MOFCOM	english.mofcom.gov.cn/	Economy
Chinese/ English	National Bureau of Statistics	NBS	http://www.stats.gov.cn/ english/index.html	Economy
Chinese/ English	Market Supervision and NDRC National Development Resource Council	SAIC	http://www.saic.gov.cn/ english/index.html	Economy
Chinese/ English	Ministry of Land and Natural Resources of the People's Republic of China	MLR	http://www.mlr.gov.cn/ mlrenglish/	Economy
Chinese/ English	Ministry of Environmental Protection of the People's Republic of China	MEP	http://english.mep.gov.cn/	Environment
Chinese/ English	Ministry of Water Resources of the People's Republic of China	MWR	http://www.mwr.gov.cn/ english/	Resource
Chinese/ English	Ministry of Agriculture of the People's Republic of China	AGRI	http://english.agri.gov.cn/	Agriculture
Chinese/ English	The People's Bank of China	PBC	http://www.pbc.gov.cn/ publish/english/963/index. html	Finance
Chinese/ English	State-Owned Assets Supervision and Administration Commission of the State Council	SASAC	http://www.sasac.gov.cn/ n2963340/index.html	Economy
Chinese/ English	State Administration of Taxation of the People's Republic of China	SAT	http://www.chinatax.gov.cn/ n6669073/index.html	Economy
Chinese/ English	China Society and Science Net	CSSN	http://www.cssn.cn	Economy
Chinese/ English	Chinese Banking Regulatory Commission	CBRC	http://www.cbrc.gov.cn/ english/home/jsp//index.jsp	Finance
Chinese/ English	Chinese Securities Regulatory Commission	CSRC	http://www.csrc.gov.cn/pub/ csrc en/	Finance
Chinese/ English	China Economy	CE	http://www.ce.cn	Economy
Chinese	SINA Finance	SINAF	http://finance.sina.com.cn/	Finance
Chinese	HEXUN	HEXUN	http://www.hexun.com/	Economy
Chinese	EAST MONEY	EM	http://www.eastmoney.com/	Finance
Chinese	China Financial Circle	JRJ	http://www.jrj.com.cn/	Finance
Chinese	Ifeng Finance	IFENGF	http://finance.ifeng.com/	Finance
Chinese	China Finance Online	CNFOL	http://www.cnfol.com/	Finance

(*Continued*)

Language	Name	Acronym	Website	Type of Data
Chinese	Tencent Finance	TF	http://finance.qq.com/	Finance
Chinese/ English	Wind information	WIND	http://www.wind.com.cn/	Economy
Chinese	Stock Star	SS	http://www.stockstar.com/	Finance
Chinese	NetEase Finance	NF	http://money.163.com/	Finance
Chinese	Bosi Data R&D	BD	http://www.bosidata.com/	Economy
English	the US-CHINA business council	USCHINA	https://www.uschina.org/	Economy
English	China Economics Summer Institute	CESI	http://www. chinasummerinstitute.org/ cesi-working-papers/	Economy
English	USC US-China Institute	USCI	http://www.china.usc.edu/ default.aspx?AspxAutoDete ctCookieSupport=1	Economy
English	UTS China Research Centre	UTSCRC	http://www.china.uts.edu.au/	Economy
English	China Research Center	CRC	http://www.chinacenter.net/	Economy
English	Stockholm China Economic Research Institute	SCERI	http://www.hhs.se/SCERI/ Pages/default.aspx	Economy
English	U Research Center for Chinese Politics and Business	RCCPB	http://www.indiana. edu/~rccpb/Publications. html	Economy
English	New Zealand Contemporary China Research Centre	NZCCRC	http://www.victoria.ac.nz/ chinaresearchcentre/	Economy
English	U.S Department of Commerce	USDC	http://www.census.gov/	Economy
English	Centre for China Economy and Politics	CCEP	http://www.uni-sofia.bg/index. php/eng/the_university/ centres/centre_for_china_ economy_and_politics	Economy
English	China's Economy News— Bloomberg	CENB	http://topics.bloomberg.com/ china's-economy/	Economy
English	China Economic Review	CER	http://www. chinaeconomicreview.com/	Economy
English	Chinese economy	Economist	CEE	http://www.economist.com/ topics/chinese-economy	Economy
English	Chinese economy the world bank	CEWB	http://www.worldbank.org/en/ country/china/overview	Economy
English	OECD China	OECDC	http://www.oecd.org/china/	Economy
English	National Bureau of Economic Research	NBER	http://www.nber.org/	Economy
English	Research Papers in Economics	REPEC	http://www.repec.org/	Economy
English	UN data of china	UNDC	http://data.un.org/ CountryProfile. aspx?crName=CHINA	Economy
English	Social Science Research Network	SSRN	http://www.ssrn.com/	Economy
English	U.S Department of Commerce	USDC	http://www.census.gov/	Economy
English	World Bank Database	WB	http://data.worldbank.org/ indicator/	Economy/ Finance

Source: Author created.

Index

Where figures or tables fall outside of the relevant textual discussion, they are indicated by the page number followed by 'f' for figure or 't' for table e.g. 43f or 54t.

About the Author

Professor Ron Schramm has been conducting research related to China since the early 1990s and has recently joined the faculty of the International Business School of Suzhou (IBSS) at Xian Jiao Tong Liverpool University (XJTLU). He is the PhD Program Director there and is also on XJTLU's Research Steering Committee. He is currently the Area Editor in Finance for the *International Journal of Emerging Markets*. He had been on the faculty of Columbia Business School for over twenty-seven years. He holds a Bachelor's Degree from Harvard University (with honors) and Master of Arts, Master of Philosophy, and PhD in Economics from Columbia University. He was a Fulbright Scholar at the University of International Business and Economics in Beijing (where he taught the first course ever in corporate valuation in 2003); a Visiting Scholar at Shanghai Jiao Tong University (2000); and a Visiting Scholar at Hong Kong University of Science and Technology (1997). He was a Visiting Professor at Chinese-European International Business School (CEIBS) in Shanghai in 2008–13. In 2010, Professor Schramm taught the inaugural course in a new Kenyan EMBA program jointly sponsored by Columbia Business School, Goldman Sachs, and USIU. The course in corporate finance was offered in Nairobi, Kenya. He founded and led the China Business and Economy Group of the Harvard Club of New York City.

Professor Schramm has taught the widest range of courses of any faculty member at Columbia—having taught the PhD course in econometrics, forecasting, managerial economics, macroeconomics, international business, international financial management, international valuation, and corporate finance. He was the first recipient of the prestigious Chazen Institute Award for case writing on an international topic. He has led Columbia's MBA and EMBA course in China for over thirteen years. In addition to his research related to China, Professor Schramm specializes in international financial management. As an economist at the International Monetary Fund (IMF) in the early 1990s, Professor Schramm worked on debt workouts for heavily indebted countries and was instrumental in the reform of the foreign exchange system of Uganda. He has also done consulting work for the World Bank. He recently supervised the writing of over forty business school cases at Kenyatta University in Kenya. He was Associate Director of Columbia's Center for International Business Cycle Research where he wrote and edited numerous publications related to the international economic outlook. He is also CEO and founder of China Macro Finance in New York City. Professor Schramm speaks Chinese.